AF352467

RUSSIA'S TURKISH WARS

Russia's Turkish Wars

The Tsarist Army and the Balkan Peoples in the Nineteenth Century

VICTOR TAKI

UNIVERSITY OF TORONTO PRESS
Toronto Buffalo London

© University of Toronto Press 2024
Toronto Buffalo London
utorontopress.com
Printed in the USA

ISBN 978-1-4875-0163-1 (cloth)   ISBN 978-1-4875-1365-8 (EPUB)
                                   ISBN 978-1-4875-1364-1 (PDF)

Library and Archives Canada Cataloguing in Publication

Title: Russia's Turkish wars : the tsarist army and the Balkan peoples in the
    nineteenth century / Victor Taki.
Names: Taki, Viktor, author.
Description: Includes bibliographical references and index.
Identifiers: Canadiana (print) 20230552560 | Canadiana (ebook) 20230552625 |
    ISBN 9781487501631 (hardcover) | ISBN 9781487513658 (EPUB) |
    ISBN 9781487513641 (PDF)
Subjects: LCSH: Russo-Turkish Wars, 1676–1878. | LCSH: Russia. Armiia – Public
    relations – History – 19th century. | LCSH: Civil-military relations – Balkan
    Peninsula – History – 19th century. | LCSH: Balkan Peninsula – Population –
    History – 19th century. | LCSH: Russia – Military policy – 19th century.
Classification: LCC DK135 .T35 2024 | DDC 949.6/0387 – dc23

Cover design: Alexa Love
Cover image: Vasily Vereshchagin, *Two Hawks (Bashi-bazouks)*, 1878, oil on canvas,
78.5 × 110 cm, Kyiv Picture Gallery National Museum, Kyiv, Ukraine. Artefacft / Alamy
Stock Photo.

We wish to acknowledge the land on which the University of Toronto Press
operates. This land is the traditional territory of the Wendat, the Anishnaabeg, the
Haudenosaunee, the Métis, and the Mississaugas of the Credit First Nation.

This book has been published with the help of a grant from the Federation for the
Humanities and Social Sciences, through the Awards to Scholarly Publications Program,
using funds provided by the Social Sciences and Humanities Research Council of Canada.

University of Toronto Press acknowledges the financial support of the Government of
Canada, the Canada Council for the Arts, and the Ontario Arts Council, an agency of
the Government of Ontario, for its publishing activities.

For Alyosha

Contents

List of Maps and Illustrations   ix

Acknowledgments   xi

Note on Transliteration and Spelling of Geographical Terms   xiii

Introduction   3

1 The Eastern Balkan Christians and Muslims in the Early Russian-Ottoman Wars   17
Balkan Auxiliaries and the Politics of Resettlement in the Early Russian-Ottoman Wars   19
The Intellectual Impact of the War of 1812   25
Early Russian Theorization of Small War and Partisan Action   29
The Russian Military and the Ottoman Empire during the Greek Crisis of the 1820s   34

2 The Russian Army and the Eastern Balkan Population during the War of 1828–1829   42
The Russians and the Population of Danubian Bulgaria during the Campaign of 1828   45
Policies towards Muslims and Christians after the Crossing of the Balkans   51
The Management of Inter-confessional Relations after the War   59

3 Partisan Warfare and the Statistics of European Turkey: The Case of I.P. Liprandi   68
Liprandi's Partisan Detachment in 1829   70
Liprandi's Writings on Partisan Warfare   74
Between Orientalism and Occidentalism   80
Liprandi and the Crimean War   85

4 Russia and the Balkan Peoples during the Crimean War   93
  The Reports of Russian Military Agents in Constantinople on the Eve of the War   97
  Nicholas I and the Idea of Raising Russia's Orthodox Co-religionists   100
  Small War and the Planning of the Danubian Campaign of 1854   106
  Military Operations in Danubian Bulgaria and the Local Population   113

5 The Russian Army and the Ottoman Empire, 1856–1877   118
  The Development of Military Statistics in the Post-Crimean Period   119
  Criticism of Reform and Pan-Slavism   128
  The Eastern Crisis, Russian Perspectives on Islam, and Plans for the Mobilization of Balkan Christians   133
  Russian War Planning in 1876–1877   140

6 Russian Population Policies during the War of 1877–1878   149
  The Formation of the Russian Provisional Administration in Bulgaria   152
  Inter-confessional Violence and Population Dislocations in the Summer and Fall of 1877   158
  Inter-confessional and Inter-ethnic Violence in the Concluding Stages of the War   168
  San Stefano and the Outline of a New Political Order   174

7 Population Policies after the War   180
  The Rhodope Uprising and Muslim Resistance in Other Parts of the Eastern Balkans   185
  The Management of Muslim and Christian Migrations after the War   194
  Muslim Service in the Militia and Bulgarian Gymnastic Societies in Eastern Rumelia   200

Conclusion   210

Notes   217

Bibliography   269

Index   293

Maps and Illustrations

Maps

1.1 *Turkey in Europe before the War with Russia* by Henry Martyn Field, 1885 5
4.1 *Outline Map of Turkey from the Time of the Crimean War* by J.M. Adye, 1860 101
5.1 *Sketch Map to Illustrate Russo-Turkish War 1877–8* by Lucius Hudson Holt, 1918 143
6.1 French ethnographic map of the Balkans by Guillaume Lejean, 1861 176
7.1 *Changes in Turkey in Europe 1856 to 1878* by J.G. Bartholomew, 1914 182

Illustrations

1.1 Portrait of Denis Vasilievich Davydov by George Dawe 30
2.1 Engraving depicting the storming of Brăila by Karl Beggrov, 1829 44
2.2 Engraving showing the passage of Russian troops through the Balkan Mountains on 20 July 1829, by August Friedrich Andreas Campe, 1830 54
2.3 Russian troops enter Adrianople, 8 August 1829 60
4.1 Portrait of Nicholas I by Georg von Bothmann, 1850s 95
4.2 Russian crossing of the Danube, March 1854 114
5.1 Portrait of Dmitrii Alekseevich Miliutin, 1860s 121
5.2 Photograph of Nikolai Nikolaevich Obruchev 126
6.1 Portrait of Prince Vladimir Aleksandrovich Cherkasskii by I.N. Kramskoi, 1879 153
6.2 *Two Hawks (Bashi-bazouks)* by V.V. Vereshchagin, 1878 161
6.3 *The Road of the War Prisoners* by V.V. Vereshchagin, 1878–9 169
7.1 Photograph of Prince Aleksandr Mikhailovich Dondukov-Korsakov 184

Acknowledgments

The idea of this book came to me after I participated in two conferences hosted by the University of Pennsylvania and New York State University to mark the bicentennial anniversary of Napoleon's dramatic defeat in Russia. Both events challenged me to relate the story of the "peripheral" Russian-Ottoman wars that have always fascinated me to the main line of Russian military history, defined by confrontation with the Western powers. I would like to express my gratitude to Alexander Martin, Peter Holquist, Paul Werth, and Yanni Kotsonis, who organized these conferences and/or supported my early attempts to write on the subject of war and society.

Research for this book was funded by the Gerda Henkel Foundation (Germany), whose generous two-year grant (ref. no. AZ 14/F/13) made possible my extended stay in Moscow and St. Petersburg in 2014. I would like to thank the staff of the Russian State Military Historical Archive and the Russian State Historical Archive, as well as those of the manuscript divisions of the Russian State Library and the National Library of Russia. While in Russia, I benefited from both logistical and emotional support from my colleagues Alexey Miller, Vladimir Ryzhkov, and Tatiana Khripachenko. Aleksandr Semenov and Alexey Volvenko invited me to present my work in progress at the Higher School of Economics (St. Petersburg campus) and the Rostov State Economic University (Taganrog campus), which greatly helped me refine the main thesis of this book.

As was the case with my previous monographs, portions of the manuscript were discussed at the East Europeanist Circle of the Department of History and Classics, University of Alberta. I am sincerely grateful to the EEC participants – John-Paul Himka, Elena Krevsky, Mariya Melentyeva, Aileen Friesen, and Eugene Miakinkov, among others – for their criticisms and suggestions. My special thanks go to the organizer of the EEC, Heather J. Coleman, for her unfailing support of both this book project and my overall professional development. Heather kindly put me in touch with Richard Ratzlaff and Stephen

Shapiro, the acquisition editors at the University of Toronto Press, whose interest in this project was crucial, as was their tolerant attitude towards delays on my side.

Candan Badem and Lucien Frary helped me write this book by inviting me to contribute early versions of some of its chapters and sub-chapters to their edited volumes. My indefatigable friend Denis Vovchenko offered valuable observations on a more developed version of the manuscript. I am also grateful to the three anonymous reviewers at the University of Toronto Press, as well as the members of its Manuscript Review Committee, for their suggestions on how to make the book more accessible to non-specialist readers. Finally, the support and patience of my mother, my wife, and my children have been indispensable throughout. I dedicate this book to my son with the hope that he will one day read it and find it meaningful.

Chapter 1 includes portions of Victor Taki, "Russian Military Perspectives on the Ottoman Empire during the Greek War of Independence," *Open Military Studies* 2, no. 1 (2022): 165–78, https://doi.org/10.1515/openms-2022-0135, published by De Gruyter and licensed under the Creative Commons Attribution 4.0 International licence. Chapter 3 includes a major portion of Victor Taki, "From Partisan War to the Ethnography of European Turkey: The Balkan Career of Ivan Liprandi, 1790–1880," *Canadian Slavonic Papers* 58, no. 3 (2016): 257–85, https://doi.org/10.1080/00085006.2016.1202428, reprinted by permission of the publisher (Taylor & Francis Ltd.). Chapter 4 includes parts of Victor Taki, "Russian Occupation of Moldavia and Wallachia and the Plans for a 'People's War' in the Balkans," in *The Routledge Handbook of the Crimean War*, ed. Candan Badem (London: Routledge, 2021), 85–102, reprinted by permission of the publisher. Finally, chapter 5 is an expanded and modified version of Victor Taki, "Russian Army and the Ottoman Empire: Military Reform and Eastern Crisis," in *Imperial Designs, Postimperial Extremes: Studies in Interdisciplinary and Comparative History of Russia and Eastern Europe*, ed. Andrei Cuşco and Victor Taki (Budapest: Central European University Press, 2023), 76–111.

Note on Transliteration and Spelling of Geographical Terms

A modified Library of Congress system is used in the transliteration of Russian terms throughout this book. To facilitate smoother reading for anglophone readers, I have omitted the single prime representing the soft sign in Russian geographical and personal names (e.g., Дюгамель is rendered as "Diugamel" rather than "Diugamel'"). A number of Russian generals discussed here were of French or German origin, but I have chosen to use the Russian forms of their names (e.g., Dibich and Lanzheron rather than Diebitsch and Langeron). After all, even those who were born outside the Russian Empire spent most of their lives in Russian service, and thus assimilated to a considerable degree.

Balkan geographical terms represent a particular problem, not only on account of the differences between the historical Ottoman and contemporary Bulgarian or Romanian names of particular towns, but also because of the lack of uniformity in their nineteenth-century spellings in Russian, French, or English. Any attempt to impose a system on this onomastic diversity would therefore be arbitrary. Since this book is almost exclusively based on Russian- and French-language sources and deals with the Russian army's perspectives on and policies in the Balkans, I have opted to use the Russian versions of most Balkan geographical terms (transliterated in accordance with the Library of Congress system), while also providing Turkish and contemporary Bulgarian variants in parentheses at first mention. However, the most important and frequently mentioned towns are given in their nineteenth-century English rather than Russian forms (e.g., Adrianople and Philippopolis rather than Adrianopol and Filippopol).

RUSSIA'S TURKISH WARS

Introduction

On 10 June 1877, as the Russian army crossed the Danube, Alexander II issued a manifesto addressing different groups of the Balkan population. In this document, the tsar evoked the wars that his predecessors had waged to "relieve the woeful plight" of Balkan Christians, as a result of which they had managed to "consistently safeguard the lot of Serbs and Romanians." The time had now come "to protect forever" the Bulgarian nationality (*narodnost'*) and give Bulgarians "those sacred rights that are indispensable to the peaceful and regular development of [their] civic life." In the words of the manifesto, Russia's role was "to bring into accord and pacify all nationalities and all confessions in those parts of Bulgaria that are populated by the inhabitants of different origin and faith." From the point onwards, the Russian army pledged to protect "life, freedom, honour, and property of every Christian, whatever church he belongs to."[1]

Despite "recent atrocities and crimes that many Muslims committed against the helpless Christian population of the Balkans" – a reference to the abortive Bulgarian uprising of April 1876 – Alexander II promised to abstain from vengeance and to bring under "just, right and impartial trial only those few villains that were known to the Ottoman government and yet so far escaped the due retribution." Otherwise, Muslims were called upon to "submit to the lawful demands of the administration" that Russia was about to create in Bulgaria and "become peaceful citizens of the society that is ready to give [them] all the fruits of a well-ordered civic life." The tsar pledged to "leave intact the Muslim religion" and "sacredly protect Muslim lives and property, as well as the life and honour of [their] families."[2]

The seven or eight months that followed these announcements proved to be some of the most devastating in Balkan history. Thousands of Muslims fled from the central part of Danubian Bulgaria and from those trans-Balkan territories that were occupied in June and early July 1877 by the main Russian army and its vanguard detachment commanded by Lieutenant General I.V. Gurko. The subsequent reversal that the main Russian force suffered near Plevna

(Pleven) necessitated Gurko's retreat to the north of the Balkans, in which he was accompanied by scores of thousands of trans-Balkan Bulgarian refugees. The Ottoman surrender at Plevna in late November 1877 and the final advance of the Russian army on Adrianople (Edirne) and Constantinople the following January entailed an even greater dislocation of the trans-Balkan Muslim population. The overall number of Muslim refugees and civilian casualties in the territories that after the war became the Principality of Bulgaria and the autonomous province of Eastern Rumelia must have been in the order of half a million.[3] This turned the war of 1877–8, or '93 *Harbi*, as it is known in Turkish historiography, into a symbol of catastrophe. The war constituted an important stage in the process of contraction of the Muslim population in European Turkey that began with the Greek War of Independence in 1821 and ended with the collapse of the Ottoman Empire in the early 1920s.[4]

The scale of population dislocation during and after the war of 1877–8 is especially striking in view of the fact that it was not the first time that the eastern Balkans were occupied by Russian troops. The Russian-Ottoman war of 1828–9 led to the Russian occupation of the same territory, and yet one finds in this period nothing remotely comparable to the plight of the Muslims half a century later.[5] Although smaller than in 1877–9, the zone of military operations and of the post-war Russian occupation in 1828–30 included the most "Muslim" of the eastern Balkan territories, which makes the contrast with the events of 1877–9 all the more remarkable.[6] Comparison between the two Russian occupations of the region is a natural, though surprisingly unexplored, strategy for anyone seeking to explain what happened in the eastern Balkans in the late 1870s. Clearly, the unprecedented dislocation of the eastern Balkan Muslims in 1877–8 had something to do with the choices and decisions of the Russian military planners and commanders, which must have contrasted with those of their predecessors in 1828–9.

An examination of these choices and decisions, as well as of the intellectual context in which they were taken, will also produce a more complete picture of Imperial Russia's Balkan entanglements.[7] While there is no shortage of studies of Russia's role in the transformation of European Turkey into the South-Eastern Europe of small nation states, little attention has been given to the contribution of Russian military men *as military men* to this process. Both Russian and Western historians have focused on the role of tsarist diplomats in the elaboration of major international treaties that stipulated the autonomy or independence of Greece, Serbia, Romania, and Bulgaria.[8] Although Russian provisional administrations in the Danubian principalities in 1828–34 and in Bulgaria in 1877–9 were both headed by military men, their activities have so far been examined only as aspects of Imperial Russia's foreign policy.[9] Without denying the importance of the Foreign Ministry in the formulation of Imperial Russia's Balkan policies, the present study highlights the no less significant

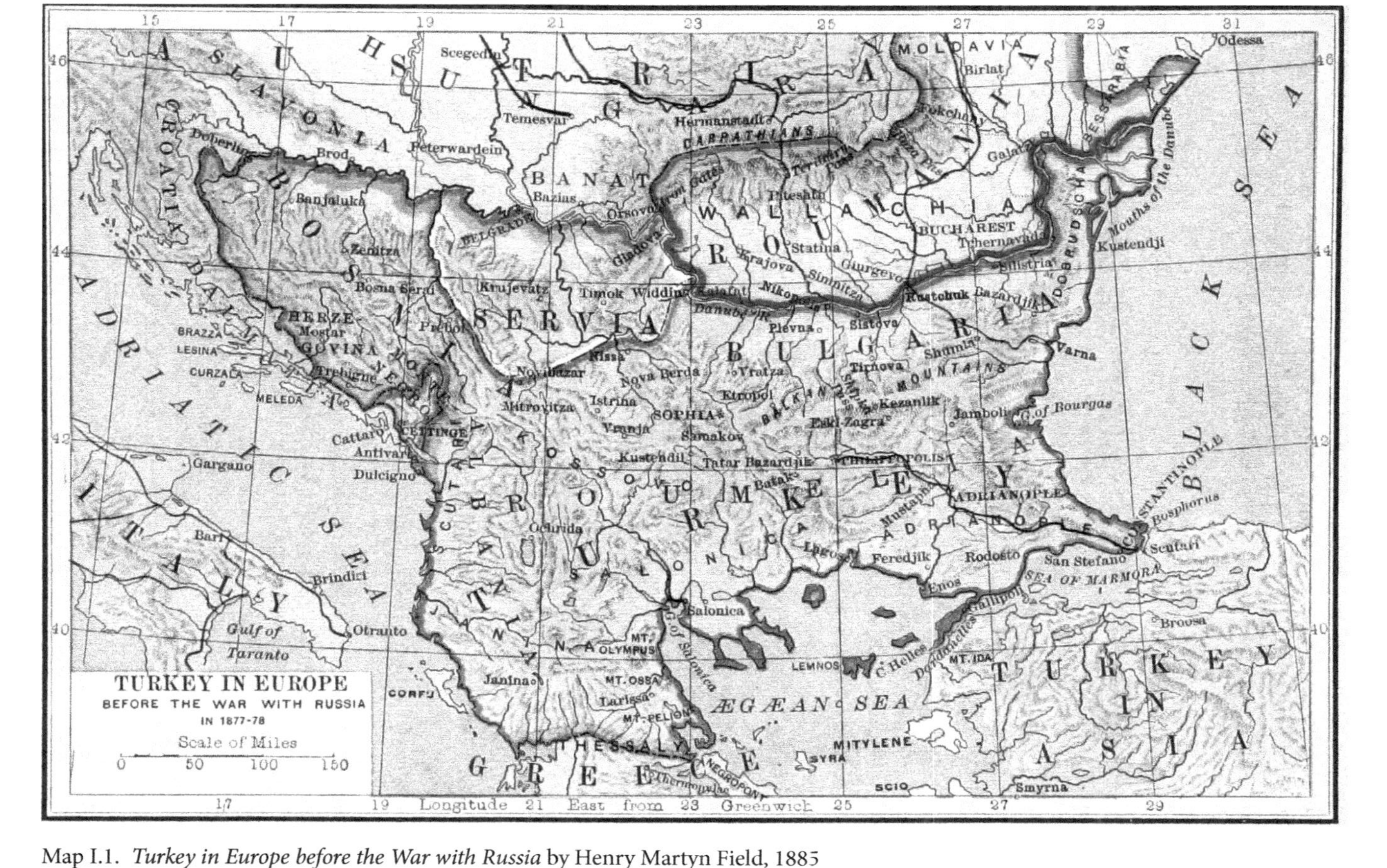

Map I.1. *Turkey in Europe before the War with Russia* by Henry Martyn Field, 1885
Source: Henry M. Field, *The Greek Islands and Turkey after the War* (New York: Charles Scribner's Sons, 1885), 195. British Library, Digital Store 10126.bb.12. Original held and digitized by the British Library. Via Wikimedia Commons/Flickr.

role of the Russian army. Taking Clausewitz's famous definition of war as a continuation of politics by other means, this book views the nineteenth-century Russian army as a major policymaker in the eastern Balkans. In addition to discussing the military operations that are the focus of earlier writings on these wars,[10] I seek to reconstruct the intellectual and cultural factors that informed the policies of the tsarist command with regard to different groups of the Balkan population.

I argue that the contrasting choices and decisions of the Russian commanders and strategists in 1828–9 and 1877–8 reflected a reconceptualization of the role of the people in war that took place in the long nineteenth century. This reconceptualization was part of a broader military transformation that redefined military-civilian relations in the wake of the French Revolution. The experience of the Revolutionary and Napoleonic Wars led European and Russian military men to focus increasingly on the people as both the foundation of the army's strength and a potential source of resistance to it. As a result, the efforts to implement the concept of the nation-at-arms in the post-Napoleonic period came to be supplemented with schemes for neutralizing potentially hostile population groups in the areas comprising the actual or prospective war theatre. Although this approach to population revealed its full destructive potential only after 1914, elements of it were increasingly visible in the choices and policies of the tsarist war planners and commanders in the Balkans during the 1800s. Russia's "Turkish" wars therefore constitute an important, yet hitherto underappreciated, aspect of military change in the nineteenth century.

The hundred years between the defeat of Napoleon and the outbreak of the First World War were unprecedentedly peaceful in European history, at least if one compares the amount of war between 1815 and 1914 to that of the sixteenth, the seventeenth, or the eighteenth century.[11] After the nearly continuous warfare of the early modern, Revolutionary, and Napoleonic periods, the European continent finally experienced a prolonged cessation of hostilities. Admittedly, this period witnessed internal political upheavals in many European countries, the wars that accompanied Italian and German unification, and the Russian-Ottoman wars of 1828–9, 1853–6, and 1877–8. Nevertheless, all these military conflicts proved to be quite short in duration, and as a result, by the turn of the twentieth century, Europeans were often unaware of both the scale of the military change and its implications for relations between the army and the population. As the First World War soon demonstrated, this transformation was nevertheless quite real, and Russia's nineteenth-century "Turkish" wars, by virtue of their repetitive character, offer the best means of assessing its gradual development. However, a general discussion of the nineteenth-century changes in relations between the army and the population through the prism of these wars first requires an overview of the eastern

Balkan region that constituted the main theatre of Russian-Ottoman confrontation during this period.

Unless one counts the failed 1569 Astrakhan expedition of Selim II, the Russian-Ottoman confrontation began in the late seventeenth century in the territories to the north of the Black Sea. Later, the front line moved southwest, turning the Lower Danube and, eventually, the broader region of the eastern Balkans into the main theatre of war.[12] The Turkic term *Balkan* entered European geographical literature in the early years of the nineteenth century as a value-neutral alternative to *Turkey-in-Europe*, yet it soon acquired negative connotations.[13] Accordingly, debates on what did and what did not constitute the Balkans became a major preoccupation for historians, as well as intellectuals more broadly.[14] While the Danube and its tributary – the Sava – provided a "natural" northern limit to the region, this purely geographical definition squared poorly with the historical and cultural realities, which were shaped by centuries of Ottoman dominance not only to the south of the river, but also to the north of it, namely, in the principalities of Moldavia and Wallachia.[15]

These Orthodox Christian countries entered the Ottoman orbit between the late fourteenth and the early sixteenth century and remained there until the late 1800s. The tribute that Moldavia and Wallachia paid to the sultan grew steadily over the early modern period, and eventually the native princes were replaced with the Phanariote Greeks.[16] The Porte tightened its control over the principalities in response to Habsburg and Russian challenges, particularly the latter. Indeed, from the unfortunate Pruth Campaign of Peter the Great of 1711 onwards, each Russian-Ottoman war resulted in the Russian occupation of either Moldavia or both principalities. Although on each occasion a peace treaty restored the Porte's suzerainty, Russia gradually asserted a formalized protectorate over the principalities, which it soon used to minimize Ottoman influence.[17]

Its repeated occupations of Moldavia and Wallachia and its establishment of the protectorate regime did nothing for Russia's popularity in the principalities, and eventually contributed to the development of a modern Romanian nationalism with a distinctly anti-Russian bent.[18] However, this anti-Russian sentiment was held primarily by the elites and was not immediately absorbed by the mass of the population. As a result, for much of the nineteenth century Russia benefited from the residual co-religionist sympathy of the local peasantry, who continued to view the Orthodox tsar as their champion.[19] The relative homogeneity of the Moldavian and Wallachian population from a religious and ethnic point of view was likewise an asset. After the Russian annexation of Bessarabia in 1812 and the reintegration of the Ottoman fortresses on the left bank of the Danube into Wallachia in 1829, the Russian army no longer encountered Muslim minorities in this region.

To the south of the river, the situation was quite different. Here, the Ottoman conquest of the late fourteenth and fifteenth centuries destroyed the Bulgarian and Serbian kingdoms and resulted in the conversion to Islam or emigration of their Christian Orthodox elites.[20] Transformed into *pashalyks*, the territories of present-day Bulgaria and Romanian Dobrogea had a mixed Christian and Muslim population. Alongside the Bulgarian majority, the eastern Balkan Christians included significant minorities of Greeks and Romance-speaking Vlachs (Aromanians). The Greeks were particularly numerous in the Black Sea ports and the coastal areas, as well as major cities such as Philippopolis (Filibe, Plovdiv) and Adrianople. They also controlled the Orthodox Church hierarchy in Bulgarian-majority areas, and this control ultimately provoked a Bulgarian nationalist reaction and the Greek-Bulgarian church schism of 1870.[21] The Christian population of Dobrogea was even more patchy: alongside ethnic Bulgarians, it also included Romanians, Ukrainian Cossacks, and Russian Old Believers.[22] Finally, not all eastern Balkan Christians were Orthodox, since some Bulgarians in the region of Philippopolis had converted to Catholicism in the seventeenth century.

The Muslims of the eastern Balkans were as diverse as the Christians. The largest group were the Ottoman Turks, who were usually urban dwellers, although in the region of Deliorman in the north-east they also predominated in the countryside.[23] The ethno-confessional mosaic of the region was further enriched by Muslim émigrés from the Russian Empire, who became particularly numerous after the Crimean War, when significant numbers of Crimean Tatars resettled in Dobrogea. The Crimean Tatars were accompanied by Circassians from the western part of the North Caucasus, although the latter would not stay in the eastern Balkans for long. In the south, the region of the Rhodope Mountains was populated by considerable numbers of Pomaks, or Bulgarian-speaking Muslims, whose origins are the subject of some controversy.[24]

The political structure of the Ottoman Empire reflected the confessional and ethnic complexity of its population. Ever since the Ottoman conquest of Constantinople in 1453, the empire had been organized as a cluster of confessional communities (called *millets* in the nineteenth century) that enjoyed considerable non-territorial autonomy.[25] Although recent historiography sometimes presents the Ottoman Empire as a prototype of modern diversity and multiculturalism, it needs to be stressed that the members of these communities were anything but equal in their status. For centuries, the Christians were not legally allowed to bear arms, had to dismount in the presence of a

Muslim, and could not build churches higher than mosques or ring church bells, among a host of other legal disabilities. They also bore heavier taxes, the most important of which – *jizya*, or protection tax – had its roots in the Prophet Mohammed's early legislation with regard to the tolerated "peoples of the book" (*dhimmis*): the Jews and the Christians. At the same time, by the early 1800s the controversial Ottoman practice of *devşirme*, or "child levy," exacted to replenish the sultan's famous janissary corps, had long been discontinued, while the westernizing reforms of the mid-nineteenth century (known as the Tanzimat, or Reorganization) affirmed the equality of Muslims and non-Muslims at least in principle.[26]

The physical geography of the region matched the complexity of the ethno-confessional landscape (see map 1.1). In contrast to the low and marshy area north of the Danube, the southern bank of the river was quite steep, constituting a natural defence line, which was further strengthened by several Ottoman fortresses. Of these, Vidin, Nikopol, Rushchuk (Ruse), and Silistria were the most significant. The Dobrogea region, formed by the northern bend of the Danube, its estuary, and the Black Sea coast, was fortified by several minor fortresses: Tulcha (Tulcea), Isakcha (Isaccea), Machin (Măcin), and Girsov (Hârsova). The fortress of Varna was the most important Ottoman stronghold on the western coast of the Black Sea. Together with Silistria, Rushchuk, and the fortified town of Shumla (Shumen) on the steep slope of the Balkan Mountains, Varna formed the so-called quadrilateral – the centrepiece of the Ottoman defence system on the Lower Danube.

The Balkan Mountains formed the second natural line of defence, extending from west to east 100 miles south of the Danube. Their forest-covered northern slopes made the Turkic toponym *Balkan* (literally, a mountain covered by forest) quite appropriate. To the south of the mountains was the valley of the Maritsa River, which ran diagonally from the north-west to the south-east before turning south at Adrianople and eventually feeding its waters into the Aegean Sea. The southern slope of the Maritsa valley was formed by the Rhodope Mountains, which extended along the northern littoral of the Aegean. To the south-west of the Rhodopes was the region of Macedonia, which would be hotly contested by Greek and Bulgarian nationalists from the late nineteenth century onwards.[27] To the south-east of Adrianople, a mixed population of Bulgarians, Greeks, and Ottoman Muslims extended to the walls of the capital city of Constantinople, which was even more multi-confessional and multi-ethnic.

Such was the ethno-confessional landscape in which the Russian army would engage the Ottoman forces in the wars of the nineteenth century. The changing perspectives of the Russian military on the eastern Balkan population should, however, be placed in an altogether different context, that of the gradual emergence of the people as a factor in modern warfare, which itself was closely related to political democratization in the wake of the American and French revolutions.

As soon as political sovereignty was claimed in the name of the people, the way one defined the people in question assumed critical importance, since it led either to the political management of tensions or their eruption in violent conflict. According to the historical sociologist Michael Mann, the "dark side of democracy" reveals itself when the people as the source of sovereignty is identified with a majority ethnic group. This conflation of the sovereign "demos" and the predominant "ethnos" leads to the exclusion of ethnic minorities and creates a basic precondition for their expulsion, or even destruction. Radicalized by a military defeat, an economic crisis, or both, the leaders of the ethnic majority can adopt murderous policies towards an ethnic minority group when they feel both threatened by this minority (or its external protectors) and, at the same time, confident enough of being able to pre-emptively destroy it. This, according to Mann, is what happened in virtually all cases of ethnic cleansing and genocide in the twentieth century.[28]

Mann's analysis helps us understand the implications and consequences of "democratization" of European warfare in the wake of the French Revolution. Revolutionary *levée en masse* turned all able-bodied males of the nation into an army, at least in theory, and demonstrated the unsettling potential of a war of the people, for the people, and by the people.[29] Confronted with this potential, the great powers of Europe were eventually forced to adopt reforms that ultimately produced mass armies of citizen-soldiers based on a combination of short-term universal military service and a system of national reserves.[30] These reforms constituted a concrete institutional framework for the identification of the army with a given people. At the same time, they raised the question of what to do with all those population groups on one's own or the enemy's territory that for various reasons did not constitute part of the "people" in question, and thus were not part of the army it was identified with.

Once "the people" was reconceptualized as a military force, the civilian population in the war theatre could no longer be considered neutral and thus had to enter the calculations of military strategists. The experience of the Napoleonic Wars, particularly in Spain, parts of Italy and Germany, and Russia, which witnessed significant grass-roots resistance, forced commanders and military planners to consider how to neutralize potentially hostile groups of civilians.[31] It also encouraged them to look for ways to capitalize on the support of potentially friendly and sympathetic groups. As a result, the civilian population of the prospective theatres of war became the potential victims of repressive military policies through which each of the potential belligerents hoped to secure a friendly demographic environment for its army. The actual implementation of the new approach towards population became possible through the development of military statistics in the post-Napoleonic decades, which was part of the broader phenomenon of "statistical enthusiasm" that characterized this period.[32]

The military men were certainly not the only group interested in population statistics. Over the nineteenth century, the governments of European states used statistics in order to assess the religious, ethnic, and linguistic diversity of their subjects or citizens and then fuse these diverse categories into a single national community. This goal, however, proved easier to accomplish in Western Europe.[33] In the east of the continent, the failure of civilian bureaucracies to assimilate diverse populations gave greater weight to the defensive preoccupations of the military. Like their French or German counterparts, the armies of the Habsburg, the Romanov, and the Ottoman empires eventually came to view universal military service as a way of strengthening the loyalty of their diverse populations, and even as means of forging a common imperial identity. However, the uncertainty of the success of such efforts necessarily led the military establishments of these empires to consider in advance which population groups had to be neutralized before their real or alleged hostility towards the empire and its army could play a fatal role in the conditions of a future war.[34]

The actual methods of handling potentially or actually hostile sections of the population were first tested in settings where the military-civilian distinction had never really applied. In French Algeria, in the Russian North Caucasus, and in British India and South Africa, European military men encountered forms of resistance that defied the distinction between combatants and non-combatants. Challenged by irregular warfare, the European colonizers responded with policies of scorched earth, hostage taking, resettlement of troublesome inhabitants, and colonization.[35] The most notorious (although by no means the most brutal) method associated with twentieth-century population politics – concentration camps – was likewise first practised overseas: by the Spanish during the Cuban War of Independence in 1895–8 and by the British during the Anglo-Boer War of 1899–1902.[36]

It must be stressed that "colonial" methods of warfare were the consequence of the emergence of the people as a factor in modern warfare in the wake of the French Revolution, and not just products of the blurred distinction between combatants and non-combatants that characterized indigenous forms of resistance to European conquest. Bearing this in mind helps resolve the disagreement between those historians who interpret the atrocities of the First and Second World Wars as the product of application of "colonial" methods on European soil, and those who challenge the colonial origins of the Holocaust while also highlighting the importance of the Eurasian borderlands in its genesis.[37] The colonies and the peripheries of Europe were really the laboratories for evolving

European forms and methods of war that compromised the military-civilian distinction at the very moment when proponents of the modern laws of war were trying to reinforce it.[38] Such humanitarian efforts ran counter to two fundamental assumptions that increasingly informed European military thought in the nineteenth century: (1) that the population was inherently non-neutral, and (2) that its attitudes and conduct were of major importance for the final outcome of any given war. Crystallized by 1914, both assumptions informed the policies of the military authorities along the continuous yet shifting eastern front lines of the First World War.[39]

In order to understand Imperial Russia's role in this process, it is necessary to take into account both the greater initial resistance of Russian military men to the concept of the "people's war" and their eventual embrace of it. Since the reign of Peter the Great, Russian officers had adopted the principles of regular, Old Regime–style warfare, which saw the non-military population as playing only a minor role in war.[40] Although the French Revolutionary and Napoleonic Wars challenged the military-civilian distinction, one should not underestimate the conservative resistance of the aristocratic officers to the idea of a mass army of citizen-soldiers or guerilla warfare.[41] Inasmuch as Imperial Russia was more successful in its confrontation with Napoleonic France than any other Continental European power, it lacked the incentive to embark on the military reform of the Prussian type that would result in the establishment of national reserves and the introduction of universal military service.[42] Instead, the ultimate victory over Napoleon validated the Petrine, Old Regime military organization, with its stark separation between the army and the rest of the population.[43]

The War of 1812 did include an element of irregular warfare and occasioned the blurring of the distinction between combatants and non-combatants. However, this aspect of the confrontation with Napoleon impressed contemporary military men rather negatively. It is important to understand that, unlike Leo Tolstoy, most veterans of 1812 among the Russian officers took a rather dim view of the "clout of the people's war," because it contradicted the principles of regular warfare.[44] The decades after 1812 were a period when the aristocratic officers became even more committed to these principles. Among the generation of 1812, enthusiasts of partisan action à la Denis Davydov were few, and one does not find any Russian advocates of the "people's war" as such before the second half of the nineteenth century. The Imperial Russian officer corps thus proved particularly reluctant to embrace "the people" as a new factor in warfare and initiate the transition to the modern mass army of citizen-soldiers or endorse the methods of guerilla warfare. However, once this mental and institutional transformation of the Russian military took place in the wake of the Crimean defeat, its implications proved to be much more far-reaching and dramatic than anywhere else in Europe.[45]

The Russian-Ottoman wars of 1828–9, 1853–6, and 1877–8 demonstrate this gradual change of attitude of the Russian military towards the "people's war." The first of these conflicts was characterized by the conscious efforts of Russian commanders to avoid such a war altogether. Although the conflict witnessed some partisan action on the part of the Russians, this was aimed at controlling the local Muslim population rather than mobilizing the masses of Orthodox Bulgarians for an all-out uprising against Ottoman rule. The overall Russian policy adopted in 1828–9 consisted in dissuading the Muslim population from leaving their places of residence. Instead of chasing out the Muslims, the Russian command in fact organized a mass resettlement of the Christian Bulgarian population in southern Russia in order to secure the latter against possible Ottoman reprisals following the conclusion of peace and the withdrawal of Russian troops from the eastern Balkans.

The outbreak of the Crimean War some twenty-five years later already revealed a greater openness towards the idea of a "people's war" in the Balkans, as is clear from the correspondence between Nicholas I and his commanders. Eager to compensate for the shortage of Russian troops on the Danube, the tsar and his advisers considered the possibility of mass mobilization of co-religionists, although they remained very uneasy about the politically subversive character of such a measure, and failed to implement it in any event. The development of pan-Slavic attitudes among members of the Russian officer corps during the 1860s and 1870s further contributed to a reinterpretation of partisan warfare as a means of unleashing an anti-Ottoman uprising among Russia's Slavic co-religionists. The ascendancy of the "people's war" manifested in the plans for the mobilization of Bulgarians proposed by a number of Russian generals in the context of the Eastern Crisis of 1875–8, as well as in the actual formation and use of Bulgarian militia during the Russian-Ottoman war of 1877–8. The concept of the "people's war" also exercised a certain influence on the Russian plans for the campaign, as well as on the actual policies of the Russian command and of the provisional administration in Bulgaria with regard to the different groups within the local population.

The two Russian-Ottoman wars of 1828–9 and 1877–8 that occasioned Russian occupations of the eastern Balkans define the chronological framework of this study. The baggage with which the Russian army approached the first of these conflicts is examined in chapter 1. In this chapter, I use published sources on the earlier Russian-Ottoman confrontations to explore the use of Christian irregulars by the Russian commanders, as well as their policy of resettlement of Christian inhabitants from the south to the north bank of the Danube. I then turn to early Russian theorization of partisan warfare in the wake of the Napoleonic Wars and demonstrate the generally cautious attitude of tsarist officers of this period towards the idea of a "people's war" in the Balkans. The chapter concludes with an examination of the place of the local Christian and Muslim population in the memoranda and reports (both published and unpublished) composed by the military advisers and agents of Alexander I and Nicholas I in the seven years that separated the outbreak of the Greek uprising in the spring of 1821 and the Russian declaration of war on the Porte in April 1828.

The materials of the Russian State Military Historical Archive in Moscow serve as the basis of the reconstruction of Russian population policies during the war of 1828–9. The second chapter begins with a review of the policies that Russian commanders pursued towards the inhabitants of Danubian Bulgaria during the first campaign of the war, in the course of which the tsarist army found itself harassed by Muslim irregulars. The chapter then examines the approach adopted by the Russian commander I.I. Dibich with regard to the Muslim and Christian inhabitants after his troops crossed the Balkan Mountains in July 1829. The chapter concludes with an overview of the impact of the war upon the local Muslims and Christians, based on a number of military-statistical descriptions of the eastern Balkans composed by Russian officers in the wake of the Treaty of Adrianople.

Chapter 3 relates the growing interest of Russian officers in the military statistics of the Ottoman Empire to the problem of partisan warfare in the region. The chapter represents a case study of the Balkan career of I.P. Liprandi, a colonel of the Russian General Staff, whose correspondence and writings are preserved in the Russian State Historical Archive in St. Petersburg. Liprandi was involved in intelligence gathering in the 1820s and fought against armed Muslim inhabitants at the head of a volunteer detachment in the summer and fall of 1829. This experience is reflected in Liprandi's voluminous writings on partisan warfare and the ethnography of European Turkey, which he brought to the attention of Russian commanders during the 1830s and the 1840s, as well as at the time of the Crimean War.

Various plans for the mobilization of the Ottoman Christian population considered by Nicholas I and his commanders in 1853–4 constitute the subject of chapter 4. This chapter begins with an overview of the pre-war reports of Russian military agents in Constantinople (preserved in the Russian State Military Historical Archive), which paid special attention to the attitudes of particular groups within the Ottoman population towards the Porte and the westernizing reforms that it was pursuing. The published correspondence of Nicholas I with his commanders and advisers in 1853–4 is then used to reconstruct his evolving attitude to the idea of mobilizing Russia's Orthodox co-religionists in the Balkans. The chapter concludes by relating these mobilization plans to Russian military operations on the Danube in the spring and early summer of 1854, which reveal the exaggerated hopes that the tsar and his commanders pinned upon Russia's co-religionists.

Despite a false start during the Crimean War, the idea of mass mobilization of the Balkan Christians increasingly interested Russian military men, as is demonstrated in chapter 5. Based for the most part on published sources, this chapter begins with an overview of the military aspect of the Great Reforms that followed Russia's defeat in Crimea. It then addresses the place of population within the discipline of military statistics, which became a major instrument of both military reform and Russian empire building during this period. The chapter shows how the "pacification" of the Northern Caucusus in the late 1850s and early 1860s made the confessional and ethnic composition of the eastern Balkan population an integral part of Russian thinking about future confrontations with the Ottoman Empire. This thesis is illustrated by an analysis of the plans for mass mobilization of the Balkan Christians that were proposed by several Russian generals following the outbreak of the Eastern Crisis in 1875. Although the Russian War Ministry and the General Staff did not subscribe to such plans, their own preparations for the war of 1877–8 reveal their readiness to consider the confessional and ethnic composition of the population in the prospective theatre of military operations.

The Russian-Ottoman war of 1877–8 and Russian policies towards different groups of the eastern Balkan population are examined in chapter 6. Based on multi-volume collections of published primary sources supplemented with occasional archival materials, the chapter describes the formation and activity of the Russian provisional administration in Bulgaria during the ten months of the war, with a special focus on its approach to the Muslims and Christians of the region. The chapter then discusses the dislocation of both the Muslim and the Christian population occasioned by the shifting front line. It also examines the outbreaks of inter-confessional violence involving the Russian and allied Romanian troops, as well as the Bulgarian militia, in the light of Russian sources. The chapter concludes with a discussion of the atrocities suffered by the eastern Balkan Muslims in the context of the final advance of the Russian army towards Adrianople in the winter of 1877–8.

Chapter 7 is devoted to the population policies of the post-war Russian provisional administration in the eastern Balkans, which oversaw the foundation of the Principality of Bulgaria and of the autonomous Ottoman province of Eastern Rumelia. Drawing once again on extensive collections of published documents, this chapter demonstrates that control over the local Muslim population and management of inter-confessional relations dominated the agenda of the Russian authorities. The chapter examines Russian efforts to suppress the Rhodope Uprising in the spring of 1878 and the attempts of the imperial commissioner A.M. Dondukov-Koraskov to prevent the return of Muslim refugees to the Principality of Bulgaria. The chapter concludes with a discussion of the decision of the Russian provisional authorities to arm the Bulgarians of Eastern Rumelia in order to secure them against reprisals after the withdrawal of Russian troops.

The conclusion summarizes the similarities and the differences in the population policies pursued by the Russian occupation authorities in the eastern Balkans in 1828–30 and 1877–9, and isolates the factors that explain these differences. It also discusses the impact of these policy changes upon the Muslim and Christian populations of the region in the context of the Eastern Crisis of the late 1870s.

1 The Eastern Balkan Christians and Muslims in the Early Russian-Ottoman Wars

Changing relations between armies and population constituted one of the most significant aspects of the early modern military revolution.[1] In the wake of the particularly destructive Thirty Years' War (1618–48), European rulers tried to establish firmer control over their armies in order to render them less harmful to the civilian population, whose economic well-being the mercantilist and cameralist royal advisers recognized as indispensable for the overall increase of taxable wealth.[2] As a result, the mercenary formations of the previous period, which frequently lived off the land, gave way to more uniform (and uniformed) permanent forces subjected to a notably higher level of drill and discipline. Given the costliness of such armies, statesmen and commanders soon realized that military power was directly proportionate to the amount of taxes collected, which would not grow unless direct plunder of the population by the troops was reduced through regular logistical systems.[3]

One can debate the extent to which these efforts actually succeeded in rendering war less destructive than in the preceding period.[4] It is undeniable, however, that they changed the general understanding of how war should be waged.[5] Led by aristocratic commanders, regular armies were now supposed to engage in a war of manoeuvre interspersed with relatively bloody, although increasingly rare, grand battles, in the course of which formations of well-drilled commoner soldiers were expected to execute the orders of noble officers with the unfailing obedience of human automata.[6] In parallel, the military-civilian distinction emerged as an element of European military culture, not least because eighteenth-century soldiers looked and behaved quite differently from the rest of the population. They wore uniforms, were increasingly accommodated in barracks, and were subjected to collective drilling.[7] By contrast, civilians were often disarmed and subject to policing, through which territorial states claimed a monopoly on legitimate violence.[8] Even if the military-civilian distinction did not greatly improve the lot of the eighteenth-century population in war, there was a shared assumption among European commanders and officers that civilians offering no resistance were not legitimate objects of military violence.[9]

Despite the obvious difference of Russia's serfdom-based social structure, post-Petrine Russian military organization generally fitted the European Old Regime pattern. More than a century of sporadic and largely unsuccessful borrowing of Western military technology by the Muscovite tsars and the two decades of Peter's own much more intensive (although still erratic) efforts had to elapse before a regular European-style army finally emerged in Russia towards the end of the tsar-reformer's reign and under his immediate successors.[10] Composed of lifelong soldiers conscripted from the serf population, this army was commanded by noble officers for whom state service (primarily in the military) was a formal requirement until 1762 and an informal, but still quite real, social injunction for a long time thereafter.[11] Although the quality of Russian noble officers remained inferior overall to that of their European counterparts, by the end of the eighteenth century they were well on their way to adopting and interiorizing the principles of regular European warfare.[12]

Inasmuch as the Russian soldier was the most underpaid and undersupplied of the soldiers of all the European great powers, he had little choice but to take what he lacked from the civilian population. As a result, tensions between the troops and civilians remained a persistent problem. These tensions were further exacerbated by the tax-collecting and policing functions that the regular Russian regiments fulfilled in both Russia's core provinces and the ethnically non-Russian borderlands.[13] At the same time, these peculiarities of the Russian army's relationship with the rest of the population should not be exaggerated, since in practice most eighteenth-century European armies often failed to show restraint in their treatment of civilians. "Restraint" was above all the *normative* aspect of the Old Regime culture of war. Inasmuch as the post-Petrine Russian military elite increasingly absorbed elements of this culture, the differences between Russian and Western or Central European armies were quantitative rather than qualitative.

Russia's Eurasian geography provided a much more serious constraint on the spread of the European Old Regime culture of war. In conditions of continued contact and conflict between the (semi-)nomadic and sedentary populations along Russia's southern steppe frontier, the principles of restrained warfare in the Old Regime mould were never really practicable. In their raids into Poland-Lithuania and Muscovy, the Crimean and Nogai Tatars sought to capture civilians rather than destroy the armed forces. The early response of the sedentary population to the challenge of these raids took the form of the Cossack communities, in which the military-civilian distinction was largely meaningless in both theory and practice.[14] The long-term solution to the problem of the open steppe frontier ultimately took the form of the colonization policy actively pursued by Russian rulers from the middle decades of the eighteenth century onwards.[15] Within this approach, the colonist population itself became the principal means of defeating the enemy – the Crimean Khanate as well as its North Pontic and Northern Caucasian allies and clients. The resulting transformation of the human ecology of the steppe region cast in doubt the future of these nomadic and semi-nomadic groups, as is demonstrated by the plight of the Volga Kalmyks in the 1770s.[16]

There was thus a significant difference between the actual conditions of warfare along the southern frontiers of Russia and the notions of "regular" war that the tsarist commanders and officer corps absorbed over the eighteenth century. This tension is examined in what follows under two headings: (1) the use of Christian volunteers by the tsarist commanders during the Russian-Ottoman wars of 1768–74 and 1806–12, and (2) their policy of resettlement of Balkan Christians. The chapter will then turn to the intellectual context of the post-Napoleonic period, in which the first attempts were made to summarize the experiences of the earlier Russian-Ottoman wars. I will demonstrate that Russian military men of the 1820s recognized the great potential of partisan action in European Turkey and, at the same time, feared the dangers of a "national war" in the region. These considerations conditioned the efforts of the Russian generals to put forward the best strategy against the Ottomans after the Greek uprising of 1821 made another Russian-Ottoman war imminent.

Balkan Auxiliaries and the Politics of Resettlement in the Early Russian-Ottoman Wars

In May 1773, as the main Russian army prepared to cross the Danube for the first time, its commander, P.A. Rumiantsev, released a manifesto aimed at the local population.[17] According to this declaration, farmers, traders, or soldiers, "whether Christian or Turkish," could each live according to his or her social status, under the protection of the Russian army, provided that they "did not take part in the fighting on the side of the enemy."[18] To prove that "ferocity and plunder have never been and will never be characteristic" of his troops, Rumiantsev pointed to the example of the "many Turkish families" of present-day Romanian Dobrogea who had asked for permission to resettle on the Russian-controlled left bank of the Danube following a recent victory of the advance Russian detachment over the Ottomans.[19]

Despite these declarations, the manifesto did not have the desired effect upon the population of Danubian Bulgaria. At the end of the campaign of 1773, the Russian commander complained that even the Christian inhabitants of the right bank "had not shown any sympathy towards the Russian troops." Rumiantsev attributed this to their "prolonged socialization with the Turks," which apparently constituted a "habit" that was more powerful than co-religionist sentiment.[20] As for the Muslim inhabitants, those living in the vicinity of the

Ottoman fortresses of Rushchuk (Ruse), Nikopol, Vidin, and Belgrade were, according to Rumiantsev, ready to "take up arms when necessary and had every capacity for war" (*k voennomu delu vse svoistva imeiut*)."[21]

Rumiantsev's proclamation to the Balkan inhabitants and his subsequent reports reflect the new predicament that Russian commanders would face whenever they crossed the Danube. The demographic landscape of the eastern Balkans was considerably different from that of the North Pontic steppe and the principalities of Moldavia and Wallachia, which had constituted the principal theatre of Russian-Ottoman confrontation prior to the early 1770s. Whatever policy the Russian commanders chose to pursue with regard to the Nogai vassals of the Crimean Khans, they had no need to think about how this policy would affect the local Christians, since the latter were few in the territories populated by the Nogai hordes. Similarly, Russian efforts to mobilize the Christian auxiliaries in Moldavia in 1711 and 1739 had minimal impact on the Ottoman Muslims, who were prohibited from settling in this Ottoman vassal principality. The situation changed with the transfer of military operations to the right bank of the Danube, where settled Muslim urban and rural dwellers lived side by side with their Christian counterparts. While the Muslims were armed and often hostile, the Christians were not always spontaneously cooperative and supportive. Moreover, any policy concerning one group of the religiously and ethnically diverse eastern Balkan population had to consider the possible repercussions of this policy for other groups of local inhabitants.

Irregular forces of Christian volunteers played a significant role in military operations in Moldavia and Wallachia at the beginning of the war of 1768–74, as well as at the concluding stages of this conflict, when Russian troops crossed the Danube. These irregulars (*arnauts*) represented an ethnically mixed force of Albanian, Serbian, Bulgarian, Wallachian, and Moldavian origin, who constituted the traditional mercenary class in the Danubian principalities during the early modern period.[22] Although the *arnaut* detachments did include considerable numbers of Moldavians and Wallachians, their leading elements were often foreign to the principalities and belonged to an ethnically and religiously diverse group of "professionals of violence" that went under a variety of names (*hajduks, kirdzhali, klephts*). Present in virtually every province of the Ottoman Empire, these "bandits" were distinct from both the local non-military population (both Christian or Muslim) and the Ottoman elites (both central and local), with which they often engaged in complex relations of resistance and cooperation.[23]

For this reason, the auxiliaries used by Rumiantsev and subsequent Russian commanders did not represent a form of mass mobilization of the local Christian population. The equivalent Ottoman practice – their use of *kirdzhali* for reprisals against rebellious Christian subjects during the war of 1787–92 – likewise cannot be considered a form of mobilization of the Muslim population, but was rather a form of governance in a context of imperial crisis.[24]

The confessional diversity of the "professionals of violence" likewise renders problematic attempts to present the Russian and Ottoman use of auxiliaries as a form of religious mobilization. Although Rumiantsev's auxiliaries were probably all Christian, the *kirdzhali* bands employed by the Ottomans were not exclusively Muslim and included some notable Bulgarian and Serb *hajduks*.[25]

The tsarist commanders of the late eighteenth and the early nineteenth century were well aware that neither the *arnauts* nor the Balkan Christian population more broadly were unambiguous supporters and collaborators of Russia. Instead, the Russians perceived them as wavering elements who could easily end up supporting the Ottomans unless they were attracted to Russia's side. Thus, several months before the outbreak of the war of 1806–12, the commander of the Russian army in Podolia, I.L. Mikhelson, wrote that "all the wavering Balkan peoples are presently in such a state that they are going to join whoever is closer and more likely to render them help and they can become harmful to the opposite side."[26] Unable to assign more than 30,000 soldiers for the occupation of Moldavia and Wallachia in November 1806, Alexander I sanctioned "the invitation of Bulgarians and the Arnauts and others" to join the Russian troops.[27]

At the same time, the attitude of the Russian command towards the volunteers remained ambiguous. Mikhelson's enthusiasm about them is undoubtedly explained by the scarcity of the regular troops under his command. As a result, in 1806, as in 1769, the Wallachian, Serbian, and Bulgarian *arnauts* played an important role in the Russian capture of Bucharest.[28] Later, some of their units joined the Russian Cossack detachment of Major General I.I. Isaev, which crossed the Danube in order to help the Serbian insurgents led by George Petrović.[29] By contrast, the conclusion of an armistice at Slobodzeia (Slobozia) in August 1807 and the growing peasant unrest in the southern Russian *gubernias* and the principalities meant that Mikhelson's successor, A.A. Prozorovskii, was only too happy to get rid of the potentially troublesome *arnaut* elements.[30] Later still, the Russian commanders P.I. Bagration and N.M. Kamenskii again came to appreciate the importance of the auxiliaries soon after the reopening of hostilities in 1809 and the beginning of the military operations to the south of the Danube.

Characterized by the already familiar employment of the *arnauts*, the war of 1806–12 also witnessed the first attempts by Russian commanders to mobilize the broader Christian population. In doing so, they were influenced by Ottoman practices. According to P.I. Bagration, who briefly commanded the Russian army in 1809–10, the Ottomans drew many of their effectives and virtually all of their provisions from the Turkish population of Danubian Bulgaria, "who have become quite fit for war." Unless they were "threatened and attacked," he argued, these "warlike inhabitants … were sure to run to aid" their co-religionists in those territories through which the Russian army advanced. For this reason, in his plan for the campaign of 1810 Bagration proposed to divide the army into three corps that would operate simultaneously in eastern, central, and western parts of Danubian Bulgaria and thereby deny the Ottoman army the option of recruiting the local Muslim population.[31]

At the same time, Bagration insisted on "strict implementation of the rules of friendly treatment of the Christian inhabitants" for the purpose of securing their active involvement in the struggle with the Ottomans. To that end, on the eve of the campaign of 1810, Bagration enquired with the most important Russian intelligence agent, Manuk-bey Mirzoian, about the possibility of raising the Bulgarian population of Tyrnovo (Tarnovo). He also asked the Bulgarian archbishop Sofronii Vrachanskii about the prospect of a similar rising in the Vidin region.[32] Bagration was not the first Russian commander to explore this possibility. As early as April 1807, Mikhelson reported that in Tyrnovo, "all the Christians are armed and are ready to rise up for us." Mikhelson was also aware of the possible consequences of such an uprising for the Muslims and the Bulgarian Christians. According to him, there was "talk between the Bulgarians to kill all the Turks in Tyrnovo," which was counterbalanced by the fear that the Russian troops "will not come to help them or else will abandon them later."[33]

A similar fear explained the evasive attitude of Archbishop Sofronii towards the idea of an uprising. The Bulgarian leader confirmed that the Russian army could count on some 10,000 to 15,000 armed supporters in the region of Tyrnovo, yet "the uprising of the Bulgarian people could break out only with the gradual entry of the Russian troops into their land." Above all, the archbishop insisted that the Russians "not surrender [the Bulgarians], as was done to the Morean Greeks at the conclusion of the peace of Kucuk-Kainarji."[34] Unable to provide such guarantees, Bagration decided not to expose the Bulgarians to possible Ottoman reprisals and dropped the idea of an uprising altogether. As a result, Major General Isaev, who operated with his detachment between Nish (Niš) and Vidin, was "strictly prohibited from inciting the Bulgarians to raise arms against the Turks" and was instead instructed to "influence them to stay calm in their villages, cultivate their fields, take care of their households, and offer the Russian troops the supplies that the latter may need."[35] In the end, the entry of Russian troops into Danubian Bulgaria in late spring 1810 was paralleled only by the distribution of Sofronii's proclamation to his compatriots, in which the archbishop declared their upcoming salvation and called upon them not to fear the Russians and not to meet them as foreigners.[36]

Although not specifically incited to rise up, the Bulgarian peasants did take up arms against the Muslims at the approach of the Russian army, as was the case in the village of Arnaut-kioi, near Razgrad, whose deputies expressed their gratitude to the Russian troops. In response, the Russian commander-in-chief, N.M. Kamenskii, declared that they were "free forever" and that, even if their current home remained in Ottoman hands, they could resettle on the left bank of the Danube, where "fertile lands await you and a brotherly nation [i.e., the Wallachians] opens its arms."[37] In the view of the Russian command, the arming of the Bulgarian population was done for the sake of their self-protection. However, in practice they joined Russian detachments in local operations, such as the capture of Dzhumla, or fight against detachments of Turkish partisans. The latter represented a considerable problem for Russian communications, as is clear from the decision to cut down the forest alongside the narrow roads that passed through the Muslim-populated areas of the Deliorman forest. The parties of 500–700 Bulgarian peasants mobilized for this task worked under the protection of Russian troops. In order to discourage Muslim villagers from supporting the Turkish partisans, Russian commanders took children as hostages.[38]

In order to deny supplies to the Ottoman army, Russian commanders would destroy villages in the areas of military operations and resettle their inhabitants. Here again, this pattern recalls the war of 1768–74. In late 1769, the advance detachment of Ch.F. von Schtoffeln burned down over 400 villages in the vicinity of the Ottoman fortresses Ibrail and Giurgiu, located on the northern bank of the Danube in formerly Wallachian territories that had been alienated by the Ottomans into so-called *reaya* districts and placed under the direct control of the fortress commanders.[39] In response to the queries of G.G. Orlov and Catherine II, who were concerned about the impact of such practices upon Russia's international image, Rumiantsev admitted that burning down villages was "the custom of barbarians rather than Europeans." At the same time, the Russian commander argued that "the present war [differed] in character from wars in other parts of Europe." The benefits of sparing settlements were lost when operating against the Ottomans, who "destroyed the villages themselves" whenever they were unable to "leave with all [their] belongings." Unless the empty villages were destroyed, argued Rumiantsev, the "inhuman enemy" (*ne znaiushchii chelovechestva*) would be able to "poison them with a deadly pestilence as they often did in the past to the ruin of humankind."[40] Rumiantsev further pointed out the military expediency of burning down villages, as it denied the Ottomans the ability to entrench themselves on the left bank of the Danube and secured the principalities of Moldavia and Wallachia. The commander also assured the empress that the Christian inhabitants of the burned villages were notified in advance and had the time to carry their belongings into the principalities, while the Muslim inhabitants, who constituted the majority of the villagers, fled beyond the Danube at the approach of the Russian troops.[41]

First practised in late 1769 in the *reaya* territories to the north of the Danube, depopulation occurred on a far greater scale to the south of the Danube after the Russian troops crossed the river in 1773.[42] After the sudden appearance of the advance detachment of Colonel Klichko in Dobrogea, Ottoman troops hastily retreated in the direction of the Balkans, forcing the local Muslim and Christian inhabitants to follow suit. The Russian parties sent in pursuit of them recaptured some of these inhabitants and had more than 3,000 of them resettled to the north of the Danube.[43] In parallel, Major General G.A. Potemkin, soon to become Catherine the Great's famous favourite, resettled Christian inhabitants from the environs of Silistria, while the even more famous Major General A.V. Suvorov transferred to the north of the Danube the Christian inhabitants of Turtukai.[44] At the end of the campaign of 1773, the Russians managed to assemble some 10,000 Christians in Turtukai and transfer them to the northern side of the Danube before retreating there themselves.[45] Rumiantsev characterized these resettlements as one of the important achievements of the 1773 campaign.[46]

Apart from organizing the resettlement of the Christian population from the southern to the northern bank of the Danube, Russian commanders also deprived the Ottomans of the ability to provision and feed their troops. To this purpose, the corps of Lieutenant General K.K. fon Ungern, positioned in Babadag in September 1773, sent out special parties into the interior of the country that, in addition to annihilating small enemy detachments, were also tasked with preventing the local inhabitants from collecting the harvest.[47] In November 1773, Russian parties were sent to devastate coastal settlements in the region of Kustenci and Varna. This made it hard for the Ottomans to maintain large numbers of troops to the north of the Balkan Mountains during the ensuing winter and thus secured the Russian army in its winter quarters.[48] The following year, the corps of M.F. Kamenskii burned down the villages in the vicinity of Shumla, although this time with the goal of provoking the grand vizier to come out of his impregnable fortress to protect the Muslim inhabitants.[49]

The campaign of 1773 thus established a pattern that would be repeated in every subsequent Russian-Ottoman war: the scorched-earth strategy of the Ottomans and corresponding measures taken by the Russians would contribute to the temporary depopulation of Dobrogea and Danubian Bulgaria. During the following Russian-Ottoman conflict in 1787–92, the burning down of villages and resettlement of Christian inhabitants from the southern to the northern bank of the Danube took place again, albeit on a much smaller scale, since the Russian troops crossed the river only in the final year of the war and did not advance beyond northern Dobrogea.[50] During the war of 1806–12, the scale of these resettlements was such that in early 1811 the newly appointed commander-in-chief of the Russian army, M.I. Kutuzov, described as "depopulated" the territory as far as 100 kilometres south of the Danube. "Having driven every inhabitant into the Balkans" the previous summer, the Russian troops now lacked supplies and, as a result, could not venture more than thirty kilometres away from the river.[51] Yet even the strictly defensive position adopted by Kutuzov at the concluding stages of the war relied on the dispatch of small parties inside Ottoman territory. "Ordered to spare the Bulgarian villages," these parties were nonetheless tasked with destroying all grain and fodder deposits.[52] In this situation, local inhabitants faced the choice of resettling in the interior of Ottoman Rumelia or following the Russian army in its retreat to the left bank of the Danube into Wallachia and Moldavia, which many of them did.

In late 1810, the retreat of the main force of the Russian army to the left bank of the Danube led to the emigration of Russia's Christian sympathizers from the environs of Razgrad and Dzhumla (Eski Cuma, Targovishte), whereas the withdrawal of the right-flank detachment of M.S. Vorontsov caused a similar emigration of Bulgarians from the areas around Plevna, Lovcha (Lovech), and Sevlievo.[53] Resettlement served as an alternative to the option of provoking an anti-Ottoman rebellion in Danubian Bulgaria that was considered by Bagration in early 1810. When delegates of the Bulgarian villages located between the Danube and the Balkans asked Kutuzov to provide them with written confirmation that Russia "will not place them in the hands of the Turks," the Russian commander rejected their demand in order "not to ruin these people, who are moved by religious fervour, by an inopportune incitation to take up arms." Instead, in the event of a crossing of the Danube, Kutuzov intended to "take measures for the transfer to the left bank of a considerable number of settlers," and issued a manifesto to that effect.[54]

The settlers were initially given lands in the former *reaya* territories of Brăila (Ibrail) and Giurgiu and were absolved from taxation for three years, though they were obliged to perform border guard service. Before long, they entered into conflict with Wallachian officials, who sought to maximize their tax returns. Reflecting the desire of the settlers to avoid the sad lot of the Wallachian peasantry, the head of the specially created settlers' administration, A.Ia. Koronelli, suggested that they be resettled in Bessarabia and given the status of a Cossack host.[55] Although the Russian authorities eventually rejected the settlers' claim to Cossack status, Bessarabia ultimately proved to be a better option for some 4,000 Bulgarian families than the *reaya* territories of Brăila and Giurgiu, after the peace treaty of Bucharest stipulated the return of Moldavia and Wallachia to Ottoman control and turned Bessarabia into a Russian province.

The Intellectual Impact of the War of 1812

The Russian-Ottoman war of 1806–12 ended less than a month before Napoleon's invasion of Russia. It was thus completely overshadowed by the first of Russia's "Patriotic Wars" (*Otechestvennye voiny*), which ultimately shaped Russian thinking on all subsequent confrontations until the First World War. Against the background of the eighteenth-century conflicts, the campaign of 1812 represented a radically new kind of experience. However important they may have been for Russian empire building, earlier confrontations with the Swedes, Prussians, Poles, and Ottomans represented peripheral wars that took place on the frontiers of Russia, or beyond its borders entirely. By contrast, the year 1812 witnessed military operations in the historical core of Muscovy for the first time in two centuries.[56] The war was a traumatic event for both the Russian elites and the masses of the population and occasioned a major surge of nationalist sentiment among the upper classes. The latter often interpreted Napoleon's invasion as a confrontation between Russia and Europe.

The outcome of this dramatic struggle helped to generate persistent myths in both Western Europe and Russia.[57] Whereas the French and other Europeans began to attribute the decisive defeat of the hitherto invincible Napoleon to General Winter, the Russians, by contrast, came to view it as proof of their military superiority. At the same time, from the very beginning there was a debate within the Russian officer corps about the relative importance of particular elements of Russia's military might that had helped to vanquish the enemy. Although all Russian officers viewed the victory as the result of the supremacy of the regular army, some of them also pointed out the importance of the partisan warfare that had been waged along the French lines of communication from the moment of the battle of Borodino in late August 1812 until the expulsion of the remainder of Napoleon's troops in December of the same year.

Both Leo Tolstoy's *War and Peace* and Soviet historiography placed such emphasis on the importance of the "clout of the people's war" in the defeat of Napoleon that it became difficult to see how controversial the subject of partisan warfare actually was for Russian military men of the nineteenth century. Russian military memoirists of the late eighteenth and early nineteenth centuries demonstrate a commitment to the humane treatment of civilians and POWs, and display a clear uneasiness about the Cossacks and other irregulars as well as the type of warfare that they practised.[58] Even when they fought on Russian soil against Napoleon in 1812, the Cossacks, in the testimony of Alexander I's aide-de-camp, A.I. Mikhailovskii-Danilevskii, found it difficult to distinguish between the enemy troops and the (this time Russian) civilian population. Mikhailovskii even alleged that the Don Cossack commander, M.I. Platov, dispatched detachments to plunder Russian villages and send booty back to the Don.[59]

The involvement of civilians in the anti-French resistance presented an equally disturbing picture to Russian officers, who had interiorized the principles of "regular" warfare. According to A.N. Muraviev, the peasants "would tie captured Frenchmen to trees and shoot them point-blank, throw them into wells, and bury them alive." Of course, these actions were a response to the ravages of French foraging parties. Nevertheless, the violent treatment to which civilians submitted the unfortunate French captives was as disconcerting as the atrocities perpetrated by the soldiers of the Grande Armée. For Muraviev, as for many other Russian officers, the "people's war" was above all a vicious circle of violence "unheard of in our age," a conflict in which the "people became worse than wild beasts and would annihilate one another with unprecedented cruelty."[60]

Mikhailovskii-Danilevskii and Muraviev were among the most remarkable representatives of the Russian military intelligentsia.[61] These people were akin to the European officer-gentlemen of the eighteenth century, who often combined military service with literary or philosophical pursuits as well as political activities.[62] Strongly patriotic, the representatives of the Russian military intelligentsia were at the same time versed in contemporary European moral and political literature and thus capable of independent judgments about the Russian army, their leaders, their fellow officers, the qualities and behaviour of their soldiers, and ultimately the virtues and vices of Russia's political and social system. This capacity for critical judgment led some of them to attempt a regime change in the failed Decembrist conspiracy of 1825. However, more relevant to the present study are their ideas about the relationship between the army and the population, which broadly followed similar developments in the so-called Military Enlightenment in France. Like the French *militaires philosophes*, the representatives of the Russian military intelligentsia sought to render warfare more humane, controlled, and rational.[63] The commitment of the best Russian officers to these principles also reflected their desire to counter the long-established European stereotype characterizing the Russians as particularly barbarous in their ways of war.[64]

Their reaction to the grass-roots resistance to the Napoleonic invasion demonstrates that the "discovery of the people" by the westernized Russian elites was just beginning in the post-Napoleonic period. The immediate nationalist reaction that the Napoleonic Wars provoked in Russia was largely an elitist, politically conservative phenomenon.[65] Its representatives admittedly sought to rally the mass of the Russian people for the defence of the faith and the fatherland, but were troubled by the politically subversive potential of such mobilization. As a result, "the people" (*narod*) evoked in the official manifestos of 1812 and subsequent years were obedient, loyal, and ready for self-sacrifice – hardly active protagonists of history.[66] In the immediate post-1812 period, religious providentialism came to predominate in official interpretations of the victory over Napoleon, further downplaying "the people's aspect" of the war.[67] While not entirely absent, representations of "the people" in literary and artistic works devoted to 1812 remained quite controlled and highly idealized, and had little in common with the sometimes shocking realities of a "people's war."

The conservative turn of Alexander I's final decade undoubtedly generated discontent among a significant portion of Russia's "1812 generation," which eventually resulted in the Decembrist conspiracy. However, "the people" hardly served as a common denominator between multiple currents that existed within the Decembrist movement, particularly between the liberal-constitutionalist Northern Decembrists and their more radical Southern counterparts. The unfinished "Russian Code" by the leader of the Southern Decembrists, Pavel Pestel, contained a program for transforming the Russian Empire into a nation state. However, Pestel's nationalism, whether Jacobin or Bonapartist in character, was a top-down phenomenon that likewise did not presuppose any active role for "the people," even though the term itself was employed quite profusely.[68] The same elitist approach characterized subsequent attempts by tsarist ideologues to instrumentalize the theme of "the people" in the wake of the Decembrist rebellion of 1825 and the Polish November Uprising of 1830–1.

The story of the formulation of the Official Nationality doctrine by Minister of Enlightenment S.S. Uvarov in 1832–3 has been told many times.[69] Older scholars have pointed out that the third element of Uvarov's famous triad – orthodoxy, autocracy, nationality –remained ill-defined and was usually understood as the loyalty of the Russian people to the Orthodox faith and the tsar.[70] More recent studies have revealed the rootedness of Uvarov's nationality (*narodnost'*) in the Western European intellectual context,[71] and, at the same time, his desire to signal Russia's "coming of age" after a period of "apprenticeship" from Europe.[72] However it may be, the top-down character of Uvarov's triad is unmistakable, and it would not be until the Slavophiles and their critical engagement with the Official Nationality doctrine that "the people" were cast in a more central role.[73] This did not happen, however, until the Crimean War, by which time "the people" had also became a key element of the emergent phenomenon of Russian populism.[74]

For these reasons, neither the tsarist military establishment nor the military intelligentsia of the first half of the nineteenth century were ready to view the people as the main protagonist of the modern war or to embrace the concept of the "people's war." At the same time, various developments in the post-Napoleonic period compelled them to pay ever greater attention to the population and recognize in its support, or lack thereof, a major factor determining the outcome of any military conflict. One of these developments was the Greek War of Independence, which began on 22 February 1821, when a detachment of Greek volunteers led by Alexander Ypsilanti crossed the Russian-Ottoman border along the Pruth River into the Ottoman vassal principality of Moldavia.

A scion of a Greek Phanariot family, Alexander Ypsilanti made a remarkable career in the Russian military during the Napoleonic Wars and became a major general at the age of twenty-five. In April 1820, Ypsilanti assumed the leadership of the secret Greek society Philiki Etaireia, founded in 1814 by Greek expatriates in Odessa with the purpose of liberating Greece from Ottoman dominance.[75] Having entered the Moldavian capital, Iași, Ypsilanti issued several fiery proclamations in which he called upon the Ottoman Greeks to rise up against the sultan, asked the local population to assist in this struggle, and alluded to the forthcoming Russian intervention. Alexander I's prompt disavowal of Ypsilanti's rebellion, as well as tensions between Ypsilanti and Tudor Vladimirescu, the leader of a parallel anti-elite uprising of Wallachian irregulars (*pandurs*), ensured the prompt defeat of Ypsilanti's movement in the principalities. Nevertheless, the Etaireia undertaking triggered outbreaks of inter-confessional violence in other parts of the Ottoman Empire. Spurred by Ottoman reprisals, the Greek rebellion in Morea continued for the following nine years, under the increasingly sympathetic eyes of the Europeans, culminating in the establishment of an independent Greek kingdom in 1830–2.[76]

Alexander Ypsilanti's venture provoked complex responses on the part of the Russian military. Like educated Russians more broadly, tsarist officers often viewed the Greek struggle for independence with sympathy and were disappointed with Alexander I's refusal to declare war on the Ottoman Empire in support of the Greeks.[77] Like the revolutions of 1820–1 in Spain and Italy, the Greek rebellion had a radicalizing impact upon some Russian military men and accelerated the formation of the Decembrist conspiracy. Although Russian officers could be sharply critical of Ypsilanti's personal qualities and his conduct during the events of 1821, the Greek uprising contributed to their appreciation of the potential of partisan action.[78]

Early Russian Theorization of Small War and Partisan Action

In early April 1821, six weeks after Ypsilanti and his followers crossed the Russian-Ottoman border, the famous partisan commander of 1812 D.V. Davydov published his *Theory of Partisan Action*, which constituted an important landmark in the development of Russian military thought.[79] Davydov (see figure 1.1) defined the scope of partisan action (*partizanskaia voina*) as "the entire space between the rear of the enemy army and its base," and its goal as depriving the enemy army of "food and ammunition" as well as "creating obstacles to its retreat."[80] Davydov pointed to the actions of Protestant German commanders of small detachments during the Thirty Years' War as the origin of partisan warfare. The operations of the Hungarian irregulars in the War of the Austrian Succession (1740–7) and the struggle of the Spanish guerrilla fighters against the French army in 1809–13 constituted the next important stages in the development of partisan action. However, only in Russia in 1812 did partisan warfare become part of the confrontation between the main forces in a conflict.[81]

Davydov argued that Russia was best placed to reap the advantages of partisan action. He proceeded from the assumption that the relative quality of an army depended on how much it conformed to the "innate abilities, qualities, and customs of the people from which it is formed." According to the Russian author, the Enlightenment, the softening of public mores, the affirmation of the right of private property, and the commerce and luxury of Europe all posed obstacles to the creation of light troops in European armies. By contrast, in Asia one found entire peoples of horsemen who had "inherited a capacity for raiding" not through agriculture, the arts, or commerce, but by virtue of "constant roving for booty amid vast deserts, cliffs, and mountains, in constant struggle with their inhabitants." Their type of warfare consisted in "sudden strikes, indefatigable mobility, and in the bold undertakings of clamorous crowds of horsemen."[82] The greatest military strength would result from a combination of a European army, that would do the actual fighting, and troops of Asian peoples, who would "deprive the enemy of food and ammunition." By virtue of its

Figure 1.1. Portrait of Denis Vasilievich Davydov by George Dawe
Source: George Dawe, *Portrait of Denis V. Davydov (1784–1839)*, before 1828, oil on canvas,
70 × 62.5 cm, Military Gallery of the Winter Palace, Hermitage Museum, St. Petersburg, Russia.
Via Wikimedia Commons.

geography, only Russia had "one of the most orderly armies" and, at the same time, commanded the Cossacks, who shared the qualities of the neighbouring Asian peoples, and yet would obey their commanders in the manner of the European troops.[83]

Davydov's thesis represented a striking example of military Orientalism, or a discourse that lumped together the styles of warfare of various non-European peoples and asserted their distinction from the European style of war in a very essentialized way.[84] His fascination with Asian warriors as ferocious, elemental, and exotic "others" of the regular, disciplined, and uniformed European soldiers is quite palpable. It demonstrates that Orientalism as a mode of thought based on the systematic opposition of East and West found expression not only in the works of poets and philosophers, but also in the writing of military men.[85] Davydov not only clearly articulated this opposition in his essay, but also echoed a central theme of the specifically Russian variant of Orientalism, namely the idea of Russia's special relationship with Asia.[86] Several years previously, this idea had been expressed by the supervisor of the St. Petersburg educational district and future minister of public enlightenment, S.S. Uvarov, in his Asian Academy project.[87] For Uvarov, as for Davydov, Russia's Eurasian geography was of paramount importance, yet there was also a difference between their arguments. While Uvarov found in Russia's geographical position an *opportunity* for the development of Oriental studies, for Davydov it *had already made* Russia militarily superior to the European great powers. None of them could boast both a regular military organization and an irregular cavalry force of a superior "Asian" type.

According to Davydov, Russia's proverbial geographical extent further cemented its advantage over the European nations at a time when war was no longer limited to duels between commanders, sieges of frontier fortresses, or the endless manoeuvring of compact masses of troops. Now "peoples rise up against other peoples, borders are quickly overwhelmed by huge armies, and military operations quickly envelop the centre of one or the other belligerent country." In these conditions, Russia's traditional disadvantage of having a particularly long and indefensible border was more than compensated for by the country's depth and breadth, as the defeat of Napoleon's army amply demonstrated.[88] It made the provisioning of the enemy army particularly challenging: the low density of the population and the readiness of the inhabitants to destroy their homes and retreat into the forests prevented the invaders from securing local supplies, while "bold and indefatigable raids by light troops" interrupted deliveries from afar.[89] Davydov was aware of the uneasiness of many Russian officers in 1812 about both partisan warfare and the idea of retreating to the centre of the country. He admitted that his proposed strategy was problematic, but argued that it was better to sacrifice property than honour and independence.[90]

Although Davydov took part in the Russian-Ottoman war of 1806–12, his thinking was clearly dominated by his experience of the Patriotic War of 1812 and may appear to be irrelevant to Russia's "Turkish campaigns." After all, Russia's wars with the Ottoman Empire took place on its southern periphery and saw offensive action on Russia's part, whereas Davydov concerned himself with the defensive war in Russia's interior against a major European invading force. However, several characteristics of Davydov's approach made it relevant to subsequent discussion of partisan action against the Ottomans. For one thing, Davydov viewed partisan warfare as part of the general action of the army. Much of his essay was devoted to establishing the principles of coordination between regular forces and partisan Cossack groups, whereby the latter positioned and repositioned themselves along a geometrical pattern defined by the front lines of the two opposing armies. Similarly, Russia's wars against Ottoman Turkey featured both regular and irregular troops, whose actions had to be coordinated, as they had been in Russia in 1812. In this respect, Russia's first "Patriotic War" and its "Turkish campaigns" were quite different from the

Spanish guerrilla warfare of 1809–13, in which armed bands represented the only fighting force opposing the French following the destruction of the regular Spanish army.

Davydov's remarks on the relations between partisan groups and the local population were even more relevant in the context of subsequent Russian-Ottoman wars. Most importantly, for Davydov, as for other Russian military writers of the first half of the nineteenth century, partisan warfare remained distinct from a "national war." Davydov's ideal partisan group was led by an officer of the regular army like himself, and consisted of Cossacks, who were irregulars distinct from both regular troops and the civilian population in the areas of military operations. Although he included the Spanish guerilla action of 1809–13 in his discussion of the emergence of partisan warfare, he viewed it "more as the case of a people who rose up for revenge" than as partisan action properly speaking.[91]

Second, Davydov argued that a partisan commander could not count on the population's unconditional and spontaneous support, even in the case of a defensive war on native soil. "The fear sown by the invaders, their encouragement of spies, suppliers, and provocateurs harmful to the defending army" could influence the people in such a way as to "make the entire occupied territory satisfy the military necessities of the invading army and become a source of recruits for it." Partisan action had to prevent this outcome by "offering to the inhabitants a point of view and a goal that satisfied their ambition and love of gain better than those offered by the enemy." According to Davydov, the capture of a trainload of grain, clothes, or army resources could attract local inhabitants to the partisans' camp and under their banners.[92]

What was true of a defensive war in Russia's interior was even more true of an offensive war in European Turkey, where Russian troops did not always enjoy spontaneous support even among their co-religionists, as the above-cited reports from Rumiantsev demonstrate. At the same time, the tools that could secure such support – the volunteer detachments created in the Russian-Ottoman wars of the late eighteenth and the early nineteenth century – were similar to Davydov's Cossack partisans of 1812 in that they were socially and sometimes even ethnically distinct from the local population. This made Davydov's theory of partisan action relevant beyond the immediate context of the Patriotic War, on the basis of which it was formulated.

Five years after the publication of Davydov's work, the subject of partisan warfare in European Turkey was discussed by A.N. Pushkin in his military review of the Ottoman Empire.[93] Pushkin's work demonstrates how Davydov's theory of partisan warfare in a defensive war on Russian soil could be applied to Russia's "Turkish campaigns," despite their peripheral and offensive character. All it took was to ignore the centuries of the Ottoman presence in South-Eastern Europe and view the Ottomans as "an army encamped in Europe rather than a nation," as Baron François de Tott had famously done in his *Memoirs on the Turks and the Tatars* (1784).[94] According to Pushkin, the Ottoman Muslims were all "janissaries" and "foreign soldiers," who kept the "true inhabitants of Turkey, the Greeks and the Bulgarians," under "military rule." In this situation, Russia's offensive wars against them were not an attempt to subjugate a nation, but rather an effort to "defeat the Turks and chase them out of Europe."[95] In order to achieve this goal, Pushkin, like Davydov, recommended the use of flying detachments on the flanks and to the rear of the enemy army in order to cut communications and supply lines. He also suggested following Wellington's strategy against the French in Spain, which consisted in turning into desert those areas through which the enemy forces were to advance.[96]

At the same time, Pushkin's discussion revealed the limits of the applicability of Davydov's theory of partisan action to European Turkey. Davydov recognized that the Cossacks remained inferior to the Asian horsemen from whom they had acquired the qualities that made them superior to European light troops. Cossack inferiority to Asian cavalrymen was not a problem as long as the Russian army confronted an invading European force. However, the Russian advantage turned into a disadvantage as soon as the Russian army faced the Ottomans, who, by Pushkin's own admission, were highly capable of small war themselves. He even cited the observation of the Swiss military theorist in Russian service A.H. Jomini, who argued that the "Turkish troops inflicted nearly the same damage upon the Russians as the Cossacks did to other Europeans."[97]

Pushkin's proposed solution to this problem consisted in combining partisan warfare à la Davydov with a popular uprising. If the Ottomans outperformed the Russians in small war, this was because of insufficient attention to the native Christian inhabitants. Pushkin suggested that the Russian army needed not only to protect them, but also to "arm them and incite a national war."[98] Apart from hampering Ottoman communications and destroying supplies, the Russian partisans had to "infuse with courage the autochthonous inhabitants, oppressed by Ottoman military despotism." Encouraged by flying detachments of Russian dragoons and mounted jaegers, the local inhabitants could "rise up in different parts of the empire and become dangerous to their masters."[99] Pushkin's contribution thus demonstrates that partisan action was not limited to defensive war, in which it served to disrupt the enemy's communications and prevent them from securing supplies and support from the population of the occupied zone. In contrast to Davydov, Pushkin saw partisan warfare as part of an offensive war, in which its role was to provoke a popular uprising to the rear of the enemy army.

At the same time, despite the difference of geographical focus, Davydov and Pushkin shared a common frame of reference that characterized early Russian thought on the place of the people in war. For them, as for other military writers of the late Alexandrian and Nicholaevan eras, partisan action and a "national" or "people's war" (*narodnaia voina*) constituted the two distinct but related types of warfare. Partisans were regular or irregular troops waging "small war" to the rear of the main fighting armies, and did so under the command of regular officers. By contrast, a "people's war" was essentially a popular uprising against a foreign invader or occupying force, in which the inhabitants themselves would take up arms under the influence of patriotic sentiments. And while partisan action could be used to spark a "people's war," most Russian military men of the post-Napoleonic period were not ready to follow Pushkin's advice to do so.

The Russian Military and the Ottoman Empire during the Greek Crisis of the 1820s

Alexander I's counter-revolutionary sentiment prevented him from declaring war against a sovereign whose rule was challenged by revolutionaries, even though this sovereign was the Ottoman sultan. However, the plight of the Orthodox Greeks during the 1820s intensely preoccupied Russian military men, who believed that another Russian-Ottoman war was imminent. The seven years that elapsed between the outbreak of the Greek crisis and the final declaration of war in April 1828 provided the Russian commanders, for the first time, with both an opportunity and an incentive to prepare a plan for the upcoming campaign.[100] In doing so, they reviewed the experiences of the previous Russian-Ottoman wars and tried to systematize their knowledge of European Turkey.

Thus, the Russian General Staff unearthed and published military topographical descriptions of the roads in European Turkey, based on data collected by Colonel Fedor Len of the General Staff, who was part of M.I. Kutuzov's extraordinary embassy to Constantinople in 1793–4.[101] These works did not offer a systematic discussion of the population statistics of Bulgaria or Rumelia. Nor could one find in them any precise data on the number of Christians and Muslims in the towns and villages located along the roads surveyed. Len had clearly paid much more attention to the physical characteristics of the roads and terrain, the width of rivers, and the strength of Ottoman fortresses. The local population interested the author inasmuch as its relative density or scarcity signified the availability of supplies. At the same time, Len did describe particular villages or towns along the two roads that he had surveyed as "Greek," "Bulgarian," "Tatar," or "Turkish." The descriptions also occasionally indicated the number of houses in a particular village. At one point, Len mentioned the existence of between 30,000 and 50,000 "industrious Bulgarian Christians, devoted to Russia" living in the area between Aidos (Aytos) and Burgas, and remarked that a descent on Burgas by a 10,000-strong Russian corps "will suffice to incite these inhabitants against the Turks who oppress them."[102] On balance, the data presented in the two descriptions was clearly incomplete and had at least in part become outdated in the three decades that had elapsed since the time of Kutuzov's mission.[103]

In the meantime, the chief of staff of the 2nd Army, P.D. Kiselev, coordinated the activities of several staff officers who in the course of the 1820s collected and analysed materials on all the previous wars between Russia and Ottoman Turkey in order to formulate the best strategy. As early as 1819, Kiselev penned a memorandum, in which he noted that despite these numerous Russian-Ottoman wars, knowledge of the Turkish territories remained poor, and that this lack of knowledge had hampered the progress of the Russian army during the war of 1806–12.[104] In order to correct the situation, Kiselev suggested dispatching Russian quartermaster officers of Greek and Moldavian origin with the commercial caravans travelling from Iași and Bucharest to Constantinople. He also suggested appointing a military agent to the Russian mission in the Ottoman capital and increasing the number of consuls in European Turkey. Kiselev's memorandum lay behind Colonel F.F. Berg's mission some seven years later (see later on in this chapter).

Kiselev's interest in the history of previous Russian-Ottoman wars was praised by the former general intendant of the Russian army in 1812–15, Lieutenant General E.F. Kankrin. Although Kankrin lacked personal experience of fighting against the Ottomans, he noted that the veterans of the Turkish campaigns rarely had sound ideas about the proper way to confront this enemy. In a private letter to Kiselev, Kankrin emphasized the changes that had occurred in the character of Russian-Ottoman wars. According to him, the early wars had been confrontations between two militias, until the military reforms of Peter the Great had transformed one of these militias into a European-style army. In the meantime, the theatre of the wars had moved from the Pontic steppe zone into the "semi-civilized region" of European Turkey. Kankrin stressed the need to produce descriptions of this theatre and of the moral state of the Ottoman "militia," including the "timariots, recruited *arnauts*, and the allied troops – Tatars, Kurds, and other militiamen brought by the pashas for the most part from Asia."[105]

After the outbreak of the Greek War of Independence, Kankrin wrote a memorandum that focused on the character of the war theatre and the likely responses of the Muslim troops and population to the appearance of Russian troops on the southern side of the Balkans. Apart from the military-statistical data collected during the grand embassy of M.I. Kutuzov, Kankrin could also draw on information provided by Colonel F.F. Berg and Major General I.F. Bogdanovich, who had been involved in the Russian-Ottoman demarcation on the Lower Danube in 1816–17. This data convinced Kankrin that the crossing of the Balkans by the Russian troops and their entry into Rumelia would cause a "national war." Some of the Turks from the villages and the countryside were likely to flee to the woods and mountains and become dangerous. Others would defend themselves in the towns and fortified castles, slowing down the Russian advance. The "best Turks" would gather in Adrianople and, if so allowed, in Constantinople; others would stay in order to protect their families, especially if they happened to live away from the war theatre.[106]

Since the Turks constituted two-thirds of the population of many Rumelian towns, Kankrin advised against taking or even blockading them without evident necessity. Instead, Russian commanders needed to try to secure the loyalty of these towns by taking the hostages (*amanats*). He also advised against inciting the "Greeks" in the territories with large Turkish populations, and counselled against accommodating Russian garrisons in the houses of local inhabitants. Russian commanders should "seek to disarm the Turks in the occupied territories, calming them with proclamations" and assurances that their "faith, property, and the harems will remain untouched." Kankrin especially urged them to "respect the class of the ulema, who [were] virtually the only ones to possess real property in Turkey."[107]

These measures had to be complemented by the organization of the new administration in these areas. According to Kankrin, the "Greek" side had to be represented by the clergy and the headmen. As far as the Muslims were concerned, Russian commanders had to act through the judges (*kadis*) and the notables (*ayans*) and organize a divan in the main town of each occupied province (*sanjak*). Kankrin also advised them "not to mix the administration of the Greeks with the administration of the Turks." He recognized that the organization of governance was "a difficult task, which did not promise quick successes, yet one could hope that many of the towns and villages would adopt a kind of neutrality."[108]

Although the capture of Constantinople never became the ultimate goal of the war, Russian military planners could not avoid the question of what was to be done once the Russian army arrived at its walls. According to Kankrin, "a great force of desperate fugitives" was likely to assemble in Constantinople, which is why Russian commanders would be well advised to postpone the taking of the Ottoman capital by several days in order "not to push these fugitives to the extreme" and give them the opportunity to move to Asia.[109] In this respect, Kankrin's suggestion concurred with that of a well-known military writer, Colonel D.P. Buturlin, who similarly warned the future Russian commander-in-chief against the idea of taking the Ottoman capital by assault.[110] According to Buturlin, Constantinople's immense population would be strengthened by the majority of the inhabitants of Rumelia, who were likely to flee from the Russian invasion. "Exalted by despair," they could offer such effective resistance that the Russians risked "losing all [their] infantry without obtaining the smallest success."[111]

Alexander I's refusal to follow up the official break in Russian-Ottoman relations with a declaration of war necessarily discouraged Russian generals from submitting more memoranda on the subject until the tsar's sudden death and the accession of his younger brother Nicholas I in December 1825. The new tsar heeded the advice of Alexander I's former envoy to Constantinople, G.A. Stroganov, to "follow a strictly national and religious policy," and became determined to resolve the Eastern Question he had "inherited" from his elder brother.[112] Nicholas I's declaration to this effect signalled the resumption of military-statistical work on the Ottoman Empire and provoked a new wave of memoranda and opinions on the best strategy to adopt in the possible war to come. Some of these memoranda concerned the subject of relations between the Russian army and the Balkan population.

The general quartermaster of the General Staff, Pavel Sukhtelen, argued that it was necessary to "pay special attention to the observation of exemplary discipline" among the troops. He also stressed the importance of "encouraging the inhabitants to be loyal and cooperative by treating them with justice and kindness, making no exception for the Turks." According to Sukhtelen, this circumspection with regard to the Muslim population was useful in view of "recent revolutions [*perevoroty*] that have taken place in Constantinople," namely, the "Auspicious Event" of 14 June 1826, which consisted in the destruction of the janissaries, who had opposed Mahmud II's military reforms. The Muslims were to be treated on par with the Christians, which entailed not only non-interference with their religious rites, but also protection "from the slightest oppression, making the commanders responsible for the strict fulfilment of this rule." These principles were to be announced in a proclamation in Greek, Turkish, and Moldavian following the occupation of Iaşi by Russian troops.[113]

According to another military adviser, Infantry General A.F. Lanzheron, strict discipline was particularly necessary in the Turkish campaigns. A veteran of the wars of 1787–92 and 1802–12, General Lanzheron pointed out that indiscipline and pillage would reduce the supplies that Russian troops would be able to find in the principalities of Moldavia and Wallachia. Mistreatment of the local population could also deprive the army of the "support and cooperation" of the Bulgarians on the right bank of the Danube, and even "push them to take up arms against [the Russians], as happened in 1809."[114] At the same time, mindful of the dangers of antagonizing the Russians' Orthodox co-religionists, Lanzheron advocated making full use of their military qualities. Specifically, he suggested raising and arming the Serbs, who could "paralyse the Turks of Vidin, Nish, and other places between the Danube and Bosnia" and thus secure the right flank of the Russian army.[115]

In other respects, Lanzheron's plan for the war presupposed rather conventional "systematic" warfare aimed at reducing the Ottoman fortresses along the Danube. In order not to weaken the main army by assigning garrisons to the captured fortresses, Lanzheron suggested razing them altogether and "transporting all their Turkish inhabitants to Russia," yet leaving the Bulgarian population in place.[116] This suggestion constituted the exact opposite of the Russian population policies in 1806–12. During that war, the garrisons and the Muslim inhabitants of the surrendered Ottoman fortresses had usually been allowed to leave for the interior of Turkey. At the same time, the retreat of the Russian troops to the left side of the Danube at the end of each campaign had triggered the emigration of Bulgarian town dwellers and villagers into Wallachia, Moldavia, and Bessarabia.

For the most part, the war planners of the 1820s continued to treat the population of European Turkey in very general terms, and more or less consistently distinguished only between the Muslims, or "Turks," and the Christians. However, one can trace the elements of a more elaborate approach that singled out particular ethnic groups within these broad categories. Thus, Lanzheron singled out the Nekrasovtsy, the Old Believer Don Cossacks who had emigrated from Russia to Turkey during the eighteenth century. Lanzheron described the Nekrasovtsy as Russia's "fiercest and cruellest enemies," and argued that their great village of Dunavets in the Danube delta had to be burned to the ground and its inhabitants destroyed.[117] For his part, General Sukhtelen suggested paying special attention to the other two groups of recent émigrés from Russia, namely, the Tatars and the Zaporozhian Cossacks, who likewise lived near the mouth of the Danube. According to Sukhtelen, the Russian command needed to "try to attract these groups with the promise of protection and even permission to settle on the left bank of the Danube."[118]

The military intelligence agent of the 2nd Army, Colonel I.P. Liprandi, likewise believed it was possible to attract both the Zaporozhians and the Nekrasovtsy to Russia's side. Liprandi noted that their emigration to the Marmara littoral in the course of the war of 1806–12, as well as their participation in the struggle with the Greek insurgents, had considerably weakened these two groups. In order to replenish their ranks, both the Nekrasovtsy and the Zaporozhians had accepted many fugitive serfs and deserters from the Russian army. According to Liprandi, one could convince these elements not to help the Turks by "treating them gently, pardoning the deserters and the fugitives, and preserving, if only temporarily, their savage liberties."[119] Liprandi also noted that there had been a change in the attitude of the Bulgarians after 1812, who had become "less savage than they used to be," while their prejudice against the Russians (for the destruction caused during the war of 1806–12) abated. According to Liprandi, "On condition of the maintenance of discipline among the Russian troops, one could hope that the Bulgarians would not abandon their habitats and would even contribute to the success of our arms."[120]

The temporary resumption of diplomatic relations between Russian and Turkey after the conclusion of the Convention of Akkerman in September 1826 led to the appointment of A.I. Ribopier as the Russian envoy to Constantinople. Alongside the diplomats, the Russian Ministry of Foreign Affairs dispatched to the Ottoman capital a military mission headed by Colonel F.F. Berg and including Staff Captain P.A. Tuchkov, Lieutenant A.O. Diugamel, and Sub Lieutenant A.I. Verigin.[121] Their task was to collect military-statistical information on the Ottoman Empire in case of war. Among other matters of purely military intelligence, Nicholas I's chief of staff, I.I. Dibich, ordered Berg to find out "to what degree one could expect an adversary zeal [*protivnago nam userdiia*] on the part of the Turkish people in case of war with Russia as well as the attitudes and resources of Christian inhabitants of the northern part of Turkey."[122] In the course of the winter of 1826–7, the members of the mission surveyed the roads in Rumelia, furnishing important information on possible routes of advance for the Russian army.[123] Berg also provided observations on the general state of the Ottoman Empire that undoubtedly helped to shape the tsar's perception of Russa's southern neighbour for the remainder of his reign.

The Russian agent was critical of the destruction of the janissary corps by Mahmud II, and of Ottoman efforts at military modernization.[124] In his correspondence with vice chancellor K.V. Nesselrode, Berg wrote about the state of "general terror" that the "Auspicious Event" had produced and noted the evasiveness with which the Turks had responded to all the questions concerning the janissaries, whose very name was officially prohibited.[125] Nevertheless, Berg recognized that "the public spirit in Turkey has undergone major changes since the revolutions that marked the reign of Sultan Selim III." Whereas the first attempt to create a European-style army had cost that sultan his life, now the people "seemed willing to support" the new military organization zealously pursued by the Ottoman government and "treated as a means of salvation what twenty years previously they had stubbornly rejected."[126]

At the same time, Berg remained unimpressed by the first measures that Mahmud II had taken in order to build a new army. The Russian agent argued that "two or three generations would have to pass before the new Turkish troops could master the learned combinations and activities of a major strategist."[127] Berg believed that the current situation of the Ottomans would oblige them to "seek their salvation in an intelligent defence of fortresses."[128] This characteristic of Turkish military strategy dictated, according to Berg, the Russian choice of a decisive offensive strategy. Since the Ottomans were bound "to avoid grand battles and resort to small war," it was imperative for the Russians "to employ a mass of troops that would be large enough to guarantee success in all directions without at the same time concentrating this mass of troops at one point because of the provisioning difficulties that would result therefrom."[129]

Like many of his contemporaries, Berg recognized the "perseveration, energy, and profound knowledge of one's country" that Mahmud II and his government revealed in the affair of the destruction of the janissary corps. Yet he argued that organizing a new army was a much more difficult undertaking for number of reasons. First, such an army would never acquire the necessary permanence as long as civil and financial administration remained in its current state and a comprehensive reform of all branches of government was undertaken.[130] The accomplishment of this task required a prolonged period of peace, which could be purchased only by great sacrifices on the part of the government. Next, in their first stage, the reforms of Mahmud II presupposed the destruction of "everything that constituted the strength of his subjects." According to Berg, the janissaries "had a national character" and, with all their obvious shortcomings, could reassemble quickly after a military defeat. By contrast, one lost battle could mean the end of the sultan's new army, which for several years would place his empire "at the mercy of the combinations of European politics."[131]

Berg also noted that Mahmud II was "impudent enough" to introduce general conscription for the Muslim population immediately after the destruction of the janissaries, which "tipped the discontent and exasperated the people." In the absence of a population census, local authorities were incapable of carrying out the recruitment in an orderly manner. As a result, the sultan's initial appeal for voluntary enrolment turned into forced conscription, which the local governors implemented in order to prove their loyalty to the ruler.[132] The sorry state of the empire's finances further aggravated the situation. As a result, in Berg's estimation, it would take more than a generation for the Ottoman government to be able to maintain a regular army of some 100,000 or 120,000 troops.[133] Overall, Berg's early assessment of the Ottoman military modernization efforts indicated the poor compatibility of their traditional and their modern sources of strength, as well as the danger of losing the former before securing the latter. His reports also implied that the people constituted the ultimate source of the country's military organization, and that military modernization could not be successful unless the army retained its "national character."

When the Russian military began to review their past confrontations with the Ottomans, their thinking about relations between the army and the local population was conditioned by the experience of the Patriotic War of 1812, and the Napoleonic Wars more broadly. These conflicts alerted Russian officers to the importance of small war and partisan action and, at the same time, made many of them apprehensive of the dangers of a "national" or "people's war" involving a general uprising of the population. In fact, Russian military literature of the post-Napoleonic decades reveals the tendency of tsarist officers to differentiate between partisan action and national war. Although the idea of raising the Balkan Christians for an all-out struggle against Ottoman rule was not entirely absent in the writings of Russian officers during the 1820s, the tsarist military establishment was generally apprehensive of the prospect of a "people's war."

Such was the predominant attitude among the Russian generals who submitted their memoranda to Alexander I and Nicholas I during the Greek crisis of the 1820s. In order to avoid an uprising by the Muslim population for a "national war" against Russia, they stressed the importance of sending them a reconciliatory and reassuring message, as well as maintaining strict discipline among the troops. They generally favoured the idea of keeping both the Muslims and the Christians of the eastern Balkans pacified in their places of residence instead of engaging with the Ottomans in a war of depopulations and resettlements, which had proved to be so devastating in 1806–12. At the same time, population – its numbers, qualities, and political attitudes – began to occupy an ever larger place in the military-statistical information that the Russian officers collected during the 1820s in preparation for a new war with the Ottoman Empire. Particularly remarkable was the place that the head of the Russian military mission in Constantinople, F.F. Berg, assigned to the political attitude of the Ottoman Muslims in response to the destruction of the janissary corps and the military reforms of Mahmud II. These new sensibilities of the Russian military conditioned their choices during the war of 1828–9.

2 The Russian Army and the Eastern Balkan Population during the War of 1828–1829

The conclusion of the Convention of Akkerman in September 1826 brought about the restoration of Russian-Ottoman diplomatic relations, which had been suspended by the outbreak of the Greek War of Independence, yet developments in Greece ultimately caused another break little more than a year later. In 1824, Mahmud II secured the assistance of his Egyptian vassal, Muhammed Ali, whose Western-style army, commanded by his adopted son Ibraghim Pasha, proceeded to subdue the Greek strongholds one by one, so that by 1827 the Ottoman-Egyptian forces were on the verge of suppressing the revolt entirely. As the military fortunes of the Greek rebels waned, their efforts to provoke foreign intervention began to bear fruit. In March 1826, the Duke of Wellington, dispatched to the Russian capital to congratulate Nicholas I on his ascension to the throne, signed the Protocol of St. Petersburg. The protocol effectively separated Russian-Ottoman tensions over the Danubian principalities from the Greek question, for which it prescribed concerted Anglo-Russian mediation.

Developed in the Treaty of London of July 1827, to which France and Austria likewise acceded, the principle of collective mediation by the European powers in the conflict between the sultan and his Greek subjects was rejected by the Ottomans. There followed an official break between the Porte on the one hand and Russia, Great Britain, and France on the other, after a joint Anglo-Franco-Russian squadron entered Navarino Bay and destroyed the Ottoman and Egyptian fleets, poised, it was rumoured, to deport the rebel Greek population of Morea. Mahmud II responded by proclaiming a holy war (*jihad*) against the infidels.[1] Although the Treaty of London prevented Russia from acting unilaterally against the Ottoman Empire on the Greek question, the Ottomans provided Nicholas I with an alternative pretext for such action when they repudiated the Convention of Akkerman and closed the straits to Russian shipping.

Following the Russian declaration of war on 14 April 1828, the 6th Infantry Corps of L.O. Rot occupied Moldavia and Wallachia.[2] The main operational line of the Russian army ran from Bessarabia, across Dobrogea to Shumla,

Silistria, and Varna, bypassing the principalities, and their occupation represented a digression meant to secure the inhabitants against a possible Ottoman incursion from Vidin. The brigade of F.K. Geismar, assigned to Little Wallachia, successfully accomplished this task in the course of the war, while the rest of the 6th Corps soon joined the main forces of the Russian army. In the meantime, the 7th Corps of A.L. Voinov besieged Ibrail, the most important Ottoman fortress on the left bank of the Danube. The garrison managed to repel the Russian assault in early June (see figure 2.1), yet the Ottoman commander decided to surrender after the Russian troops occupied Machin, located on the right bank of the Danube opposite Ibrail, which effectively deprived the defenders of the ability to receive supplies. The capture of Machin was the consequence of the successful crossing of the Danube by the 3rd Corps, commanded by A.Ia. Rudzevich, at Satunova in late May 1828, whereupon the Russians promptly occupied Isakcha, Girsov, and Tulcha, and began to advance to Bazardzhik.

From Bazardzhik, a detachment commanded by Lieutenant General Pavel Sukhtelen was dispatched east to observe Varna, while the main forces, under Field Marshal P.Kh. Vitgenshtein, moved west and blockaded Shumla. However, the capture of these strongholds (as well as that of Silistria, which was besieged by Rot) proved beyond the capabilities of the relatively small and overextended Russian forces, whose communications were actively attacked by Muslim partisans in the Deliorman forest. Only the arrival of the Guard Corps and the Black Sea Fleet under the command of A.S. Menshikov changed the situation at Varna, which fell to the Russians in late September. This, however, was the only important Russian acquisition to the south of the Danube in 1828. Despite an auspicious beginning, the campaign of 1828 thus proved unsuccessful for the Russian army. Perhaps the most important reason for this was the insufficiency of the forces initially deployed on the Lower Danube (95,000 in total), a problem that proved to be recurrent in Russia's confrontations with the Ottoman Empire. The presence of Nicholas I with his suite at headquarters in the summer of 1828 hardly helped matters, since it compromised the unity of command under the aged Vitgenshtein.

After a critical discussion of the campaign in late 1828 and the replacement of Vitgenshtein with the younger and more energetic I.I. Dibich, the Russians adopted a bolder strategy, which entailed crossing the Balkans and advancing on Adrianople and Constantinople. In preparation for this ambitious venture, the Black Sea Fleet under Admiral A.S. Greig captured the port of Sozopol, located to the south of the eastern extremity of the Balkan Mountains, and left a garrison there. Thereafter, Greig proceeded to blockade Constantinople from the north, while Russia's Mediterranean squadron, under Vice Admiral L.P. Geiden, harried grain deliveries to the Ottoman capital through the Aegean Sea and the Dardanelles. In the meantime, repeated Ottoman attempts to recapture Varna were unsuccessful, and ultimately gave Dibich the chance to defeat the

Figure 2.1. Engraving depicting the storming of Brăila by Karl Beggrov, 1829 (from the original drawing by Auguste-Joseph Desarnod)
Source: Karl Beggrov, *Assaut de Brahiloff*, 1829, lithography on paper, Russian Art and Culture, Hermitage Museum, St. Petersburg, Russia. Via Wikimedia Commons.

main forces of the grand vizier at Kulevcha on 30 May 1829. Thereafter, Dibich wisely chose not to storm Shumla and, upon the surrender of Silistria in mid-June, undertook his famous march across the Balkans, arriving in Burgos and Aidos in mid-July.

The Ottomans were clearly unprepared for this development. Expecting the Russians to storm Shumla, they had concentrated many of their forces in this stronghold, leaving the region to the south of the Balkans essentially unde-fended. Although many of his soldiers succumbed to disease, Dibich encoun-tered little resistance, and on 8 August 1829, the Russians took Adrianople without a fight. The second-largest city of Turkey-in-Europe surrendered just six weeks after the fall of Erzurum in Eastern Anatolia to Russia's Caucasian corps, brilliantly commanded by I.F. Paskevich. Forced to the negotiation table, the Ottomans at first engaged in their customary foot dragging in the hopes of an Anglo-Austrian intervention, yet Dibich sent his vanguard detachments to the outskirts of Constantinople and demanded the conclusion of a peace by early September, threatening an attack on the Ottoman capital if this was refused. With the forces of the pasha of Shkoder advancing from the west on his depleted army of just 20,000 troops, the Russian commander was clearly bluffing, yet his bluff worked. On 2 September 1829, the Ottoman representatives signed the Treaty of Adrianople, which brought the war to a glorious end.

The war of 1828–9 thus saw the first Russian crossing of the Balkans and occupation of the trans-Balkan territories. At the same time, this daring action on the part of the Russians should not obscure the politically conservative character of the war as far as Nicholas I and his generals were concerned. The Treaty of Adrianople reasserted the Russian protectorate over the Danubian principalities, consolidated Serbian autonomy, and promised the same for Greece, but left much of the Ottoman Empire in Europe intact. Even clearer proof of the tsar's conservative approach regarding both the goals of the war and the means used to achieve them can be found in the Russian declaration of war. The Foreign Ministry's note to the European governments stressed that Russia "does not seek the destruction of the Ottoman Empire" or territorial aggrandizement at its expense.[3] In his manifesto to the Russian population, Nicholas I spoke of the harrying of Russian Black Sea commerce and the violations of the previous Russian-Ottoman treaties, but did not mention Greece or Russia's Balkan co-religionists.[4]

In parallel, Nesselrode poured cold water on philhellenic passions within the country by expressly repudiating the idea that Russia was taking up arms in support of the Greek rebels.[5] These declarations, like Nicholas I's advice to the prince of Serbia, Miloš Obrenović, to maintain neutrality, leave little doubt that the tsar envisioned the war as an Old Regime "affair of kings" rather than a confrontation between peoples. The policies of Nicholas I's commanders fully corroborate this impression. Although they tried to take advantage of the pro-Russian sentiments of particular groups of Balkan co-religionists, these policies were aimed at preventing a "people's war" rather than unleashing its destructive potential.

The Russians and the Population of Danubian Bulgaria during the Campaign of 1828

The Russians' crossing of the Danube was facilitated by their contact with former Zaporozhian and Nekrasovtsy Cossacks. These groups had lived in the Danube delta since the eighteenth century and fiercely resisted the Russians during the previous two Russian-Ottoman wars. While the reason for the hostility of the Nekrasovtsy was religious (they were Old Believers), the Zaporozhians were alienated by the destruction of their *sich* on the Dnieper on the order of Catherine II in 1775. The Ottoman sultans accorded to the Nekrasovtsy and the Zaporozhian Cossacks both religious freedom and immunity from the obligations of the *reaya* population on condition of military service, which they performed as distinct auxiliary units of the Ottoman army in the wars of 1787–92 and 1806–12.[6] However, competition between the Zaporozhians and the Nekrasovtsy, fuelled by religious differences, caused vicious clashes between them in the early nineteenth century. This weakened both groups, as did their involvement in the struggle with the Greek rebels during the 1820s.

By the time of the war of 1828–9, the internal cohesion of both groups had been further undermined by tensions between the descendants of the original Nekrasovtsy and Zaporozhian émigrés and later runaways from the Russian Empire, who were of peasant rather than Cossack origin and who showed greater willingness to return to Russia on condition of pardon and recognition of their Cossack status.[7] When the Russian authorities offered this pardon in early 1828, some 1,000 Nekrasovtsy and over 2,000 Zaporozhians, headed by the hetman Iosip Gladkyi, defected to the Russian side, helping the tsarist troops to cross the Danube. Their subsequent settlement in Bessarabia as the Danubian Cossack Host and in the area of Melitopol as the Azov Cossack Host can be seen as the continuation of the Russian policy of resettlement of the Christian population from the southern to the northern bank of the Danube, which was practised on a particularly significant scale in 1806–12. Although the vast majority of Nekrasovtsy and most of the Danubian Zaporozhians rejected the Russian offer, defections weakened the two communities and reduced their military value for the Ottomans.[8]

Following the Russian crossing of the Danube, the Muslim population of the northernmost part of Dobrogea promptly fled. According to the testimony of A.O. Diugamel, conditions in the region were in stark contrast to what they had been prior to the war. In 1826–7, Diugamel crossed Danubian Bulgaria and the Balkans four times, as a member of F.F. Berg's mission charged with surveying the roads in European Turkey. Having entered Dobrogea in 1828 with the Russian army, he found an empty territory, in which the reign of "deadly silence was disturbed only by the howls of hungry dogs." On the order of the local Ottoman authorities, all Muslim and Christian inhabitants had left their homes, and the once "populous villages and well-cultivated fields" were now deserted. According to Diugamel, "[If] Bulgaria suffered severely in the course of this war, if its villages were gradually devastated and destroyed, it has to be attributed mainly to the flight of the inhabitants."[9]

An inspection of sixteen villages in the area of the Nekrasovtsy settlement of Dunavets in Northern Dobrogea revealed that eight of them, which had been populated by Turks and Tatars, were now completely deserted. Of the remaining eight, the two villages of the Zaporozhian Cossacks were likewise empty, while the rest, populated by Moldavians and Bulgarians, had some inhabitants.[10] The depopulation was organized by the Ottoman authorities, who would even fire cannon to force the inhabitants to retreat with them, if one is to believe the testimony of Major General P.Ia. Kupreianov.[11] As in 1806–12, the depopulation was part of a scorched-earth strategy alongside other measures taken to deny the Russian army the ability to provision itself. Both Kupreianov and the head of the Russian political police, A.Kh. Benkendorf, who accompanied Nicholas I during the war, claimed that the Ottomans had spoiled all fountains and wells in the area by throwing animal carcasses and packs of soap into them. The deserted settlements offered a "clear example of devastation and death."[12]

Apart from this scorched-earth strategy, the Ottomans unleashed partisan forces to the rear of the Russian troops advancing towards the fortresses of Varna, Shumla, and Silistria. As Diugamel reported, "The Turks would relentlessly attack our detachments from behind every bush, tree, and stone, and the war with such an invisible enemy was highly tiring. We constantly had to send out large detachments for reconnoitring."[13] As he accompanied Nicholas I on his way across the Deliorman forest to Varna, besieged by Russian troops, Benkendorf feared an attack on the tsar's carriage by the Turks or by the Bulgarians themselves, and was especially wary of the Nekrasovtsy, those "professional thieves."[14] According to the colonel of the General Staff, I.P. Liprandi, the entire Deliorman forest was occupied by mounted Turkish partisans "assisted by the ferocious local inhabitants," who terrorized Russian foraging parties, attacked small detachments, and killed patrols. Particularly active groups of the Turtukai-native Kolchak-Oglu and Shiraz-Oglu "moved freely from one part of the forest to another, often conducting raids on the left bank of the Danube." They also "informed the Ottoman commanders in Shumla and Silistria of the movement of Russian troops by means of signals and messengers."[15]

From the outbreak of the war, the Russian command was aware of the dangers of partisan warfare in a region heavily populated by Muslims. Following the transfer of the 6th Corps from the principalities to the right of the Danube, the commander-in-chief, Prince P.Kh. Vitgenshtein, instructed the corps commander, L.O. Rot, to "use all possible means to provide the most perfect security of the persons and property of the Muslims of the Deliorman forest." Every item taken from them had to be paid for in cash, all oppression prevented, and any offence punished unfailingly.[16] Vitgenshtein stressed that Russia was waging war not against the Muslim population, but against the Ottoman government, and Rot had to do everything in order to "keep the inhabitants in the villages, secure the provision of the troops, and avert a national war [*narodnuiu voinu*], the consequences of which would be pernicious for the army and perilous for the people."[17]

Despite the declared intention to avoid a "people's war," the Russian commanders often ended up practising the same scorched-earth strategy as was employed by the enemy. Thus, having occupied the town of Pravodi (Provadia), strategically located at the intersection of the roads connecting Shumla, Varna, and Aidos, Russian troops burned down 600 houses. The Russian soldiers who were stationed at Pravodi during the winter of 1828–9 undoubtedly regretted this measure, yet this regret did not prevent them from "devastating and burning to the ground" four neighbouring villages in order to deny the enemy the option of entrenching themselves in the vicinity of Pravodi.[18] Unsurprisingly, groups of armed Muslim inhabitants harassed Russian foraging parties and patrols, to which the Russians responded by sending out detachments of twenty or thirty soldiers for night raids.[19] Nevertheless, by the spring of 1829, the actions of the Turkish partisans were threatening Russian communications to the point of making it necessary to assign an entire battalion to each supply train.[20]

The measures taken by Russian troops were not particularly sparing with regard to the Bulgarians either. In the winter of 1828–9, Russian outposts (*peredovye posty*) were ordered to prevent the return of the Bulgarian inhabitants of the right bank of the Kamchik (Kamchia) River, who had been driven away by the retreating Ottomans the previous summer. The returning inhabitants could cause "considerable diminution of the available supplies," as well as spreading plague among the troops.[21] Needless to say, such measures antagonized the Bulgarian population, so that by the end of the campaign of 1828, according to Liprandi, "many Bulgarians were suspected of killing the Russian soldiers."[22]

Small war unleashed by the Ottoman partisans undoubtedly contributed to the lacklustre performance of the Russian troops in 1828 against the main Ottoman forces that entrenched themselves in Shumla, Silistria, Varna, and their environs. Like Rumiantsev in 1774 and Kamenskii in 1810, Vitgenshtein had no chance of capturing Shumla in 1828, admirably protected as it was by both nature and some 40,000 Ottoman troops and armed inhabitants. Unable to effectively blockade the sprawling fortress, the main force of the Russian army spent much of the summer and early fall "observing" Shumla. During this time, it lost some of its soldiers to a surprise Ottoman sortie and many more to disease. The great difficulties that the Russians experienced in supplying their troops at Shumla also prevented the timely delivery of siege artillery to Rot's 6th Corps, which was blockading Silistria, which is why the Russians failed to capture that fortress before the onset of winter.

The ambiguous results of the campaign of 1828 provoked another round of memoranda, in which Russian generals gave their versions of what had gone wrong and what would make the following year's campaign more successful.[23] P.D. Kiselev, Vitgenshtein's chief of staff, did not believe it was possible to end the war in 1829 given the improved position of the Ottomans. According to Kiselev, the latter could amass more numerous forces since the hitherto rebellious Bosnia and Albania had come to terms with the Porte and promised considerable support to Vidin, Nikopol, Sistova (Svishtov), and Rushchuk. The Ottoman forces were no longer tied down in Morea, which was occupied by the French. The sultan could also depend on some support from the governor of Egypt, Muhammed Ali. "Incited by the illusory successes of the previous campaign and the sultan's calls for a general rising," the Muslims, according to Kiselev, "could make greater effort, which would make the mobilization of the population more general."[24] These considerations, among others, led Vitgenshtein's chief of staff to argue that a crossing of the Balkans by the Russian army in 1829 would be impossible. Instead, it would need to focus on capturing the Ottoman fortresses in Danubian Bulgaria, thereby preparing the ground for more decisive actions in 1830.[25]

Kiselev's memorandum was in line with the initial ideas of Nicholas I about the campaign of 1829, formed in the context of the disappointing results of 1828.[26] However, by the time Kiselev wrote his memorandum, the tsar had been swayed in favour of a much more decisive plan of action. This change was brought about by the bold criticism of the campaign of 1828 formulated by Adjutant General Ilarion Vasilchikov. In a memorandum addressed to Nicholas I, Vasilchikov attributed the poor results of the campaign to the insufficient number of troops on the Danube; the presence of the tsar in the army; the indecisiveness of Vitgenshtein; and the utter incompetence of the general on duty, the general quartermaster, and the general intendant. Vasilchikov also criticized Kiselev, Vitgenshtein's chief of staff, who "based the preparations for this war on erroneous data" about "local circumstances and the potential resistance that we had to expect." "How could one fail to know," asked Vasilchikov in particular, "that on its way to Varna and Shumla the army would enter into rugged and mountainous terrain and, apart from fighting the Ottoman troops, would have to deal with an armed and fanatical population?"[27]

On Vasilchikov's suggestion, Nicholas I ordered the formation of a committee, which included, alongside the tsar and Vasilchikov himself, the chairman of the State Council, Count V.P. Kochubei; the war minister, Count A.I. Chernyshev; and Adjutant General K.F. Tol. The fruits of its deliberations were summarized in memorandum by Chernyshev that rejected the idea of systematic warfare within the confines of Danubian Bulgaria and argued that only the crossing of the Balkans could achieve the goal of the war. According to the committee, crossing the Balkans was necessary, since "only bold and unexpected strikes could have an impact on a people like the Turks, undermine their self-confidence and fanaticism, and cause the decline of their spirit [*upadka dukha*]."[28]

To this end, the committee recommended making a surprise attack on Shumla in March 1829, before the irregular Ottoman troops "that usually disperse for the winter" were assembled there.[29] After Shumla was captured, or at least closely blockaded, the Russian army would need to capture Silistria and secure its right flank, "which in no case should extend beyond this fortress on the Danube and beyond Shumla in the mountains."[30] After that, the Russian troops were to cross the easternmost part of the Balkans, capture Burgas in close cooperation with the Russian Black Sea Fleet, and advance in the direction of Aidos and Karnobat. According to the committee, the "terror" that the Russian crossing of the Balkans was likely to cause in Constantinople would make it appropriate to offer peace to the Ottoman government.[31]

The proposed operational line thus cut across the easternmost part of the Balkans in close proximity to the Black Sea littoral. The planners chose to keep to the coastal peripheral areas of European Turkey and rejected the idea of advancing deeper into the Balkan land mass. They pointed to the danger of pursuing several disparate goals in one campaign and stressed the necessity of keeping the scarce Russian forces concentrated. For the same reason, the committee explicitly suggested not provoking an uprising among the Serbs, pointing to the impossibility of providing them with sufficient support and citing the political inconvenience of such a measure: apart from impinging on the interests of Vienna, enlisting the Serbs would lead to an increase in their demands, which would in turn complicate peace negotiations with the Ottomans.[32] In practice, this choice meant that the Russian army would be operating in areas with a relatively high concentration of Muslims in the population and, at the same time, would be avoiding the areas with more dense Orthodox Slavic populations located further west.

The rejection of "systematic" warfare in Danubian Bulgaria and the choice of a decisive strike across the Balkans led to the replacement of the aged Vitgenshtein by I.I. Dibich, Nicholas I's chief of staff, on 9 February 1829. Even before his appointment, Dibich composed a plan for the campaign of 1829 based on Chernyshev's summary of the committee's deliberations. This plan presupposed the capture of Silistria, Giurgiu, and Turnu to secure Russian communications across the Danube. There would follow a strike across the Balkans in the direction of Aidos and Burgas, with a possible extension to Phaki and Karnobat. Dibich did not consider the capture of Shumla necessary, yet envisaged a prompt pre-emptive strike against the Ottoman forces that would venture from Shumla or Rushchuk to relieve Silistria. This provision of Dibich's plan anticipated the actions of the grand vizier, which gave the Russians an opportunity to defeat the main Ottoman force at Kulevcha on 30 May 1829, and successfully cross the Balkans soon thereafter.[33]

The Battle of Kulevcha completely changed the situation in Danubian Bulgaria. The detachments that had hitherto constituted the advance units of the Russian army, and in this capacity had had to fend off the attacks of the Ottoman forces, turned into rearguard units, whose task now was to secure the communications of the Russian army advancing across the Balkans. In particular, this was the case with the detachment of Major General P.Ia. Kupreianov, which had continuously occupied Pravodi. Having repelled the onslaught of a superior Ottoman force in May 1829, it turned to "exterminating the roaming bands of armed inhabitants, prevention of any harmful assemblages in the mountain gorges, and close observation of the valley of Kamchik."[34]

The activity of the Muslim guerillas in the Deliorman continued during the campaign of 1829. To secure Russian communications, the commander of the Russian corps observing Shumla, Lieutenant General A.I. Krassovskii, dispatched a detachment of 400 jaegers and 100 Cossacks under the command of the corps quartermaster, Stikh. The detachment entered Deliorman and found in it sixteen villages located for the most part in deep ravines (*uschelia*) surrounded by a very thick forest. Almost all these villages were inhabited by Turkish families, who fired muskets at the Cossacks and disappeared in the surrounding forest as soon as they saw the infantry approach. All these villages were destroyed at Krassovskii's order. The Russians found a great number of Russian uniforms in the main refuge of the partisans, the village of Gushchekioi. They also captured thirty women and three men, two of whom were hanged. Before they were released, the women and children had to swear to persuade their relatives not to attack the Russian lines of communication. The Russians also warned the captives that if the attacks on Russian communications continued, the troops would not spare anyone, regardless of sex or age.[35]

Two weeks later, Krasovskii reported that he had released five male hostages taken by Stikh in order to carry the same message to the partisans. Some time later, three of these returned in the company of the headmen of the villages Gulerkioi, Klakova, and Irn-dere, "who unanimously pledged to live peacefully in their villages," and even promised to capture the small groups of bandits that often appeared in the vicinity and to report on the larger groups to the Russian camp. In return, Krassovskii gave the Muslim headmen "safe-conduct passes" (*okhrannye listy*) and copies of Dibich's proclamation to the Muslim population, "which they received with liveliest joy and gratitude."[36] Nevertheless, peace in Deliorman was still not an immediate prospect, and before long another Russian punitive detachment, under the command of Lieutenant Colonel Kern, found the inhabitants of the villages of Chainlar, Ianipache, Osulkioi, Safular, and Pamukchiu collecting their harvest and preparing it for dispatch to Shumla. Having encountered "rather strong resistance on the part of the inhabitants," Kern ordered nine villages to be burned down and the harvest collected in the fields.[37]

Policies towards Muslims and Christians after the Crossing of the Balkans

As the Russian army prepared to cross the Balkans, Dibich had to decide on the policy to be followed with regard to the trans-Balkan population, both Muslim and Christian. In April 1829, he passed to Nicholas I the intelligence about the Ottoman mobilization. In addition to detachments from Bosnia and Albania, the Russian commander-in-chief reported the formation of a Rumelian "militia of sorts, out of all people capable of bearing arms." According to some rumours, "the bellicose mood of the population of the capital [met] the expectations of the sultan," and although Dibich took this information with a pinch of salt, he nonetheless confirmed that the Ottomans were "actively and rather successfully arming themselves."[38] Somewhat intimidated by the scale of the military objectives that he had to achieve, Dibich looked for ways to flesh out the limited forces that he commanded. In this situation, he returned to the idea of arming the local Christian population.

Despite the initial decision not to use Christian volunteers, various proposals for the creation of such a force began to resurface almost immediately after the opening of hostilities.[39] The most ambitious of these projects belonged to the military governor of Ismail, Major General S.A. Tuchkov, who became the land commissar for northern Bulgaria after the beginning of the war. It presupposed the creation of a Bulgarian land militia, which would be little less than a full-fledged army. This project, like the idea of Serbia's involvement in the war, was rejected, yet the commander of the 6th Corps, L.O. Rot, and the commander of the Russian brigade in Little Wallachia, F.K. Geismar, did secure the tsar's authorization for the establishment of small detachments of Christian auxiliaries. The Little Wallachian *pandurs* effectively fleshed out Geismar's tiny force, which helped him to score an important victory against the far larger Ottoman force at Băileşti. Similarly, the detachments of some twenty to thirty Bulgarians formed under the supervision of the governor general of the Babadag region, Adjutant General E.A. Golovin, "were of great use to the Russian troops due to their knowledge of the territory, language, and customs of the country."[40]

In May 1829, the Russian Black Sea Fleet, commanded by Vice Admiral A.S. Greig, helped a Russian detachment to capture Sozopol, the first coastal town to the south of the Balkan Mountains. Dibich used this occasion to raise the question of the Balkan Christian volunteers with Nicholas I. The commander-in-chief stressed that his plans for war against the Ottoman Empire had never included any "revolutionary movement." This case, however, concerned "a people who share our religion, origin, and language." According to Dibich, Bulgarians could no longer bear "the yoke of unprecedented oppression" and were revolting "without the least provocation on our part," not so much against the Ottoman government as against "their oppressors," by which the Russian commander apparently meant the local Ottoman notables (*ayans*). At the approach of the Russian troops, these people faced a stark choice between "leaving their cabins and fields on the order of their tyrants, and moving to places where ruin and death awaited them" and resisting this forced migration. According to Dibich, in this situation it would be "merciless" to deny weapons and ammunition to Christian co-religionists, who were otherwise "calm and extremely obedient people."[41]

Dibich asked the tsar for permission to "use the attitude of the Bulgarians" following the crossing of the Balkans by the Russian army. Since Nicholas I had publicly renounced any territorial acquisition and any changes in the internal organization of the Ottoman provinces, the commander-in-chief suggested finding beforehand a place of settlement for the tens of thousands of Bulgarian families who would have to leave European Turkey together with the Russian army after the war. According to Dibich, the best places for this purpose were the lands of the Ekaterinoslav and Taurida *gubernias*, as well as the territory between the Lower Danube and Trajan's Wall.[42] The tsar foresaw the difficulty of securing semi-independent status for these lands, as was suggested by Dibich, yet gave his consent to Dibich's other proposals, which eventually led to the emigration of around 50,000 Bulgarians to Bessarabia and New Russia.[43]

The defeat of the grand vizier's army at Kulevcha in late May 1829 and the capture of Silistria in mid-June gave Dibich the opportunity to concentrate his main forces for the crossing of the Balkans, which took place the following month (see figure 2.2). Relations between the Russian army and the local population of Rumelia were considerably different from those that had existed between the Russian troops and the inhabitants of Danubian Bulgaria a year before. A.O. Diugamel, who crossed the Balkans soon after the Russian army, could see the Muslim and Christian population "calmly cultivating their fields as if amid the most perfect peace," which Diugamel attributed to the outstanding discipline of the Russian troops. According to Diugamel, the Ottomans did not expect the Russians to cross the Balkans, which they considered an insurmountable obstacle. As a result, they did not take measures to depopulate the region as they had done in Danubian Bulgaria. At the same time, Diugamel argued that such a measure would be difficult to implement in Rumelia, where "the population, its habits, and mores are completely peaceful," and where the inhabitants "looked with complete indifference at the events that were taking place and did not care about the outcome of the war."[44]

Although somewhat impressionistic, Diugamel's assessment of the difference between the campaigns of 1828 and 1829 did contain a kernel of truth. Dibich made a great effort to place relations between the Russian army and the local population on the right footing. His chief of staff, Tol, began issuing guidelines to that effect to the division and regiment commanders. Thus, Colonel M.A. Timan of the St. Petersburg Ulan regiment was instructed to "treat as gently as possible" the inhabitants of the village of Fundukli, which he was responsible for occupying, and guarantee them "the perfect protection of the Russian government on condition that they remain in their places of residence, continue their economic pursuits, and do not resort to banditry." Timan had to make sure that the Cossacks dispatched on various errands "do not cause any harm or offence to any of the inhabitants … for only in this way can one convince them to stay calm in their places."[45] Similar instructions were given to Major General K.L. Montrezor, who was tasked with occupying Rusokastro with two cavalry regiments. Montrezor had to attract the inhabitants of the area to the Russian

Figure 2.2. Engraving showing the passage of Russian troops through the Balkan Mountains on 20 July 1829, by August Friedrich Andreas Campe, 1830

Source: August Friedrich Andreas Campe, *Übergang der Rußen über den Balkan, den 20ten July 1829*, 1830, engraving. Via Wikimedia Commons.

side as much as possible by persuading them that the peaceful and unarmed villagers would not be treated as enemies and that the Russian command was ready to offer them any protection if they quietly continued to pursue their agricultural and commercial activities.[46]

Assurances of protection were part of the psychological campaign that the Russian command pursued to capitalize on their recent victory. Thus, Major General Terentiev, who occupied Yambol and Slivno with his Ulan Brigade, was instructed to spread rumours among the inhabitants that the Ottoman army had been comprehensively defeated, that it had lost its artillery, and that it was in a dire condition and could no longer even think of challenging the Russians. Like Montrezor, Terentiev had to promise the local inhabitants "high protection" and "convince them that, while [the Russians] are fighting the war against the Sultan, [they] are not fighting against unarmed inhabitants." The detachment also had to "attract the inhabitants back to their homes and assure them that the Russian troops not only will not cause them any violence, but also will protect them from the violence of the remnants of [the Ottoman] army, who have become disordered, lost discipline, and are wandering in throngs not knowing where to go in order to avoid complete destruction."[47]

In early July, Dibich reported to Nicholas I that due to the promptness of the Russian advance, "the Greek and Bulgarian inhabitants of the southern side of the Balkans remained in their villages [and] received the victors with great joy." Dibich also notified the tsar of his order to the troops to spare their properties and "pay in cash for whatever they are ready to sell."[48] However, the reality was not as rosy. As was the case with the campaign of 1828 and the previous wars, the local population often fled at the approach of the Russian troops. According to the report from Colonel Timan to Tol, Dibich's chief of staff, the patrols (*raziezdy*) sent to occupy the villages of Borundzhik and Ororman found only a handful of Bulgarians. The latter told the Russians that "all the Turkish inhabitants of their villages, including the better part of the non-armed ones, [had] fled to Yambol and Adrianople."[49] Following the occupation of Rusokastro by the cavalry regiments of General Montrezor, his immediate superior, Lieutenant General P.P. Palen, reported to Dibich that according to the testimony of one local resident, "a considerable number of Turks from Burgas" passed the town on their way to Yambol and Fundukli, "suffering a great want of food."[50]

Many Bulgarian settlements were similarly empty, albeit for different reasons. According to the above-mentioned report by Palen, the Bulgarians of Rusokastro had left their dwellings in the fall of 1828 because of Turkish oppression, and were now wandering in the woods yet hoping to return to their hearths. Bulgarian inhabitants in the environs of Slivno were driven into the mountains by the Ottoman troops, as had been the practice in the previous Russian-Ottoman wars.[51] Other reports confirmed the pro-Russian sympathies of the Christians who had supposedly suffered from the excesses of Ottoman troops and/or Muslim inhabitants on the eve of the Russian occupation of a given town. Thus, the commander of the 7th Corps, Lieutenant General Ridiger, reported from Karnobat that "the town was completely devastated" and that "the excesses [*neistovstva*] of the Turks are difficult to believe," which was why "the local inhabitants are justly angry with them and received us as their deliverers."[52]

Following the occupation of Aidos by the main corps of the army, Dibich himself reported to Nicholas I about the destruction of the town's Orthodox churches, "despite the fact that we had not touched the mosques." According to Dibich, the Ottoman troops "robbed those inhabitants who did not manage to escape," whereas his own army "offered them protection," so that soon after the arrival of the Russian troops the population began to return from the mountains and the woods. The Russian commander argued that it was not always possible to follow the retreating Ottoman troops closely in order to prevent them from devastating the settlements. Nevertheless, the feelings with which the inhabitants met 500 Russian Cossacks at Karnobat gave Dibich hope that the "population will return and that the harvest, which has already been partially collected, will be completed and will give us a chance of having ample supplies at our winter quarters."[53]

To attend to this and other matters, Dibich set up a local administration headed by the bishops and "other spiritual authorities."[54] Whereas local Christians for the most part remained in their settlements (albeit in great poverty), "the Turks, with a few exceptions, all left."[55] In order to counteract this tendency and reassure the Muslims of Rumelia, Dibich addressed a special proclamation to them, professing the Russians' desire to prevent their ruin, "which is inevitable if out of fear of the approaching troops they follow the pernicious intention to leave their habitats, villages, and towns."[56] The Russian commander invited all Muslim town dwellers to stay with their wives, children, and property. They were required to surrender their weapons, which were to be kept in a depot until the conclusion of peace.

The proclamation specially guaranteed complete liberty in the profession of Islam. Led by their imams, the Muslims would "pray as before for Sultan Mahmud II, their padishah and caliph, for it goes without saying that the Muslims who remain in the territories occupied by the Russian troops are not obliged to become Russian subjects, but remain the subjects of the sultan, as before."[57] All town governors and local authorities were invited to stay on their posts and continue to carry out their functions "in order to take care of the well-being of the Muslims and protect them." All their affairs were to be settled in accordance with local laws without any interference on the part of the Russian authorities. The local inhabitants were also invited to collect their harvest for their own provision and sell any unwanted surplus to the Russian troops. The Russian command claimed all the property of the Ottoman government, yet guaranteed the absolute inalienability of private property. Similarly, Russian soldiers were not to occupy Muslim houses in the towns or villages, and "the strictest measures [were to] be taken in order to protect the Muslim inhabitants with their wives and children against the least offence or oppression on the part of the troops."[58]

The proclamation must have had an effect, since several days later, Palen reported to Dibich that the inhabitants of the villages of Kaibelar, Karabunar, and Iumurkioi had returned from the woods and put down their weapons, in return for which they received safe-conduct passes (*okhrannye listy*) from General Montrezor. The mullahs of the first two villages "acknowledged in writing that the troops treated them peacefully."[59] Similarly, the commander of the 6th Corps, Lieutenant General Rot, reported that representatives of three villages (Hadzhi Meglesi, Kazyklar, and Kair Meglesi) had approached his subordinate Major General M.T. Zavadovskii at Chenghi with the request that their villages be given protection, and had surrendered their weapons in return. Chenghi itself was empty, yet the inhabitants began to return soon after Zavadovskii's arrival. Numerous Bulgarians who had hitherto taken refuge in the mountains asked the Russian general for permission to return to their villages in the environs of Pravodi.[60] Before long, Dibich wrote to Nicholas I about the "complete calm" that now reigned on the southern slope of the Balkans as a result of the return of the inhabitants of all Bulgarian villages and the majority of Turkish ones, with the latter also agreeing to surrender their arms and provide hostages (*amanats*).[61]

The Russian commander-in-chief similarly managed to control the inter-confessional violence in Slivno. Although the city was taken "by a bayonet charge," Dibich reported to the tsar that there was "not the slightest disorder." According to his testimony, the local Bulgarians sat quietly in their houses until some of the Turkish inhabitants fled, and then came out to meet the Russian army "like brothers … with bread and salt." A considerable proportion of the Muslim population likewise chose to stay, "apparently being reassured about our behaviour." Although the Bulgarians began to "take revenge on the Turks for their earlier oppression," the head of Dibich's diplomatic chancellery, P.A. Fonton, managed to "bring them back to their senses." During his stay in Slivno, Dibich sought to convince many local Bulgarian armourers to resettle in Russia, in accordance with the plan that he had earlier proposed to Nicholas I. However, the Russian commander was not certain of success, given the attachment of the Bulgarians to their land, which was "beautiful in the highest degree."[62]

The Bulgarian inhabitants often complained of "Turkish robbers," apparently deserters from the Ottoman army. In response, Dibich's corps commanders F.V. Ridiger and P.P. Palen asked for his permission to arm the Bulgarians.[63] Dibich agreed to the proposal, on the condition that the Bulgarians elect their headmen, who would be responsible for maintaining order among the volunteers. The Russian commander-in-chief also underlined that the Bulgarians should be allowed to take up arms "only for the defence of their property against the

Turks and that they should not take any other initiative."[64] The volunteers were to be armed with the weapons that had been surrendered by the Muslim inhabitants, who had to receive appropriate compensation.[65] Dibich also asked the tsar for permission to add Bulgarian volunteers to those Russian regiments that had suffered the greatest losses to disease and to use them "in the way we had used the St. Petersburg militia in 1812." However, the commander-in-chief himself meant this as an extreme measure to be implemented only if the obstinacy of the sultan made another campaign necessary.[66]

Soon, 400 Bulgarian volunteers joined the brigade of General Montrezor, which, after the departure of the main army to Adrianople, was charged with remaining in Aidos and assuring the security of the inhabitants. Dibich ordered Montrezor to "treat these Bulgarians as kindly as possible, instil in them feelings of loyalty towards Russia, and never use them as regular troops."[67] Placed under the command of Golovin, the Russian governor general of north-eastern Rumelia, Montrezor was instructed to form volunteer detachments in Slivno and Karnobat that were likewise "destined only to protect their own property."[68] At the head of this security force, Montrezor was to watch over Yambol, Slivno, and Kazan (Kotel), and prevent the coalescing of the dispersed Ottoman troops.[69]

Alerted about one such Ottoman regrouping effort on the road between Kazan and Shumla, Montrezor dispatched a Cossack detachment, upon whose arrival the Turks "promptly surrendered their weapons and asked for protection in the secure possession of their properties." As the detachment proceeded further, the Cossacks could see more Turkish inhabitants hiding in the unassailable gorges (*ushchelia*) nearby, who made no hostile moves towards the Cossacks. This episode convinced Montrezor that the local Turks "are not disposed to fight against the Russian army and flee to distant villages only out of fear." According to Montrezor, the majority of the inhabitants of the area under his control "surrendered their weapons and peacefully enjoy the possession of their property without the least revolt."[70]

In fact, Montrezor had more trouble with the Bulgarian volunteers. According to the general, these people were motivated by a "thirst for booty [*zhazhdoiu dobychi*]" and joined the detachments only to acquire a pistol, after which they would disappear, with the volunteer leaders unable to determine their whereabouts.[71] Before long, Montrezor was asking headquarters for permission not to arm any new Bulgarian volunteers, "whose parties [were] attacking and robbing Turkish villages in the mountains and [were] causing trouble."[72] As might be expected, the Muslims did not fail to retaliate and, at the end of August, Montresor had to report an attack by a band of 500 robbers on the village of Erizar that left twenty-eight Bulgarians dead.[73] Dibich agreed with the suggestion not to increase the number of volunteers further and ordered Montrezor to keep the Bulgarian detachments permanently attached to the Russian infantry, as well as to prevent them from deserting by treating them with a "kind [*laskoiu*] and condescending attitude."[74]

The Management of Inter-confessional Relations after the War

In the meantime, the main corps of the Russian army had advanced further, and on 8 August 1829 it took Adrianople. The psychological effect of the first successful crossing of the Balkans by Russian troops was apparently so great that the second capital of the Ottoman Empire surrendered without any resistance on the part of its 10,000-strong garrison or 40,000 Muslim inhabitants (see figure 2.3). According to the conditions of capitulation, the Ottoman troops were required to put down their weapons and banners and were free to go wherever they wanted. The Muslim inhabitants of the city were invited to stay peacefully, as long as they abided by the conditions stipulated in Dibich's earlier proclamation to the Muslim population of Rumelia, or else leave with their families and properties on condition of surrendering their arms.[75] In his report to Nicholas I, Dibich praised the

> good organization and strict discipline of the Russian troops, which won the complete confidence of all inhabitants, whether Christian or Muslim. The former are readily taking up arms for the protection of their houses and families, as well as joining our Cossacks in chasing the regroupings of the dispersed enemy troops. The latter entrust themselves to our protection as soon as we appear, out of fear of their own disorganized troops.[76]

Following the pattern already established in north-eastern Rumelia, units of Russian troops were assigned to particular locations to ensure that the remnants of the Ottoman troops, who had put down their weapons, did not regroup and commit violence against the local inhabitants, particularly the Christians. More broadly, the Russian regimental commanders were expected to "use all means of gentle treatment [*laski*], condescension, and unfailing justice to attract the inhabitants, whether Christian or Muslim, to peaceful life, and the disarmed [Ottoman] troops to calm and harmless behaviour."[77]

As was the case in north-eastern Rumelia, the reaction of the Muslims of Thrace to the appearance of Russian troops was twofold. On the one hand, some began to present themselves to the Russian regimental commanders proposing that they put down their weapons in return for safe conduct, often promising that more of their co-religionists would follow suit.[78] In other places, such as Demotika (Didymoteicho), the local Muslims dragged their feet with the surrender of their weapons. In the end, the commander of the Russian cavalry detachment in Demotika, Colonel M.G. Khomutov, entered the city and captured the cannons of the garrison, but did not feel strong enough to

Figure 2.3. Russian troops enter Adrianople, 8 August 1829 (engraving from a drawing by an unknown artist, 1830s)
Source: Unknown artist, Vstuplenie russkoi armii v Adrianopol' 8 avgusta 1829 goda (s risunka s natury ochevidtsa). Originally from N.A. Epanchin, *Ocherk pokhoda 1829 goda v Evropeiskoi Turtsii*, vol. 3 (St. Petersburg: Glavnoe upravlenie udelov, 1906). Runivers via Wikimedia Commons.

confiscate the weapons from some 1,000 armed inhabitants and many armed refugees. Khomutov chose to "treat them peacefully" and took representatives of the Demotika Muslims to Adrianople so that they could see "our good disposition towards the inhabitants [of that city] and follow their example."[79]

A week later, a brigade of the Ulan Bug division dispatched to Demotika was instructed to "destroy all armed people without any mercy" should the latter "threaten Christian families with ruin." The commander of the detachment, Major General V.K. Sivers, advised the Muslim population that any such action on their part would "receive an exemplary punishment according to all the strictness of the war laws." At the same time, Sivers told the Christian inhabitants "not to raise arms against the Turks, nor give them any pretext for retaliation [*raspravy*], but live peacefully with them, or else face strict punishment."[80] Except for the testimony of one Bulgarian, Sivers could not find proof of any hostile intention on the part of the Muslims towards the Christians, and proceeded to disarm the former.[81]

Following the capitulation of Adrianople, the Russian command continued to respond to reports about regrouped Ottoman troops, including those that had surrendered at Adrianople and had subsequently been released. One such report came from the town of Hermanli (Harmanli), where stray Ottoman soldiers had supposedly "committed different kinds of violence against the Christians." Accordingly, Tol instructed Rot to dispatch an Ulan division to Hermanli to attack the town and kill all armed people "as lawbreakers [*kak narushitelei ustavov*]," if the report was confirmed. At the same time, the commander of the division had to make sure that the Christians "did not offer any cause for strife with the Turks" (*so svoei storony ne podavali nikakoi prichiny k raspriam s turkami*) and tried to live peacefully with them.[82]

According to the report of the commander of the Kharkov Ulan regiment, Colonel I.K. Anrep, who carried out the investigation, "a considerable number of armed Turks" from the villages of Drapova, Sivrika, Tekeli, and Aniklar turned to the Ottoman commander Alish Pasha, who happened to pass through Hermanli, with complaints about their Bulgarian neighbours. The Bulgarians had supposedly "demanded that [the Muslims] give them their weapons with the intention of taking [Muslim] property and even the lives of those who put up any resistance." Alish Pasha reportedly responded to this complaint by ordering the Turkish inhabitants of these villages to "treat the Bulgarians as strictly as they want," whereupon a crowd of armed Turks that included almost all the Turkish residents of Hermanli went to Drapova, massacred most of the Bulgarians, plundered their houses, and took their livestock. A smaller group then went to the village of Aniklar, where they killed eight more Bulgarians, which brought the total number of victims to 126. The town governor of Hermanli was away during the incident and, upon his return, "immediately proceeded to restore order and return the survivors' property to them."[83]

Upon his arrival in Hermanli, Anrep found its inhabitants "obedient and unarmed" and decided to "adopt peaceful measures" on the condition that they surrender both their weapons and the instigators of the massacre. He also made all Turkish headmen in the surrounding villages responsible for disarming their villagers and guarding their weapons. If the results of Anrep's investigation were accurate, the immediate cause of the massacre was Alish Pasha's response to the Turkish complaints, yet Anrep himself became convinced that "the Bulgarians, whenever [they are] armed, themselves offer the pretext for clashes."[84] This observation confirmed the above-cited reports of Major General Montrezor about the tendency of the Bulgarian volunteers in north-eastern Rumelia to turn against their Turkish neighbours the weapons that they received from the Russians. The Muslim complaints to Alish Pasha in the Hermanli episode must not have been completely unfounded, since ten days later, the commander of the 3rd Bug Ulan regiment, Colonel Compan, reported from Chermen the complaints of the local *ayan* about the devastation of fifteen villages under his jurisdiction and his desperate determination to defend himself.[85] One can therefore assume that excesses such as that which took place in the Hermanli region were the consequence of the temporary breakdown in power relations between the Muslims and the Christians that accompanied the Ottoman retreat and the arrival of the Russian troops.

The Russian command viewed the disarmament of the Muslims as a precondition of peace in the occupied territories. At the same time, the scarcity of the Russian troops strongly advocated the transfer of the weapons surrendered by the Muslims to their Bulgarian neighbours to enable them to protect their property from the bands of dispersed Ottoman soldiers who would periodically assemble to the rear of the Russian army. As soon as they were given the weapons, the Bulgarians were not averse to seizing Muslim property. This could not fail to alert the Muslims and eventually caused the Hermanli massacre. Muslim refugees were another factor complicating the pacification of the local population. Unlike those Muslims who remained in the vicinity of their settlements and responded to Dibich's proclamation by putting down their arms in return for safe conduct, those who fled kept their weapons and were naturally interested in seeing the Muslims of other Ottoman towns do the same. The armed refugees who gathered in Demotika must have been a factor in the way in which the inhabitants of the town dragged their heels when surrendering to the Russians in late August. At times, refugees would even form bands of robbers, as happened in the area of Irepoli, where they reportedly attacked even Muslim villages.[86]

Although the Bulgarian population could become the victim of attacks by stray Ottoman soldiers or armed Muslim inhabitants, armed Bulgarians ultimately caused the Russian command no less of a headache, especially after the Peace of Adrianople dispelled their hopes for liberation. Lead by Georgii Mamarchev, one of the commanders of the volunteer detachments in 1829, some 500 former Bulgarian volunteers tried to spark an anti-Ottoman uprising in Rumelia in April 1830, but were promptly disarmed by Russian troops. Placed under house arrest in Bucharest, Mamarchev managed to escape in 1833 and attempted another uprising, but was captured again by the Russians and handed over to the Ottomans, ending his days in exile in Asia Minor. In parallel, a secret society of former volunteers pursuing an anti-Islamic and broadly pan-Slavic agenda under the leadership of "Grifon D" planned to assemble a force of 1,000 men in northern Bulgaria and attack Shumla in the spring of 1830, before being discovered by the Russians.[87]

While anti-Ottoman sentiment was a feature of the leaders of the Christian volunteer detachments above all, the broader masses of the Bulgarian population of Rumelia were more likely to fear Ottoman retribution for their real or imagined pro-Russian sympathies. After the capture of Sozopol, Vice Admiral Greig reported to Nicholas I that "the inhabitants of the neighbouring territories, fleeing from the disasters that threaten them, are coming to the captured city and placing themselves under the protection of Russia."[88] It will be remembered that this fear led Dibich to justify to Nicholas I the policy of arming the Bulgarians on the eve of the Russian crossing of the Balkans. To assuage this fear, the Russians introduced into the Treaty of Adrianople a clause that allowed for the emigration of all those who "either by their conduct or by their opinions" expressed attachment to the opposite power.[89]

This clause sanctioned the emigration of large numbers of Bulgarians to the Russian Empire, which had already begun during the war. After it became clear that the political status of Danubian Bulgaria and Rumelia would remain unchanged, tens of thousands of Bulgarians asked for permission to resettle in Bessarabia and New Russia. Since there was little empty land in these regions after half a century of intensive colonization, the Russian authorities sought to limit the numbers of settlers. Nicholas I and Dibich also did not want to reduce the numbers of potential sympathizers in Rumelia in case of a future confrontation with the Ottomans. They decided to let in only those who had directly or indirectly taken part in military action against the Ottomans. This policy represented a continuation of the one adopted by Kutuzov in 1811, whereby some 4,000 Bulgarian volunteers and their families were resettled in Bessarabia. In parallel, the first Russian consul was appointed to Adrianople to reassure the Rumelian Christians, while the Porte officially pardoned everyone, allocated a considerable sum for post-war relief, and ordered the Greek Orthodox hierarchs to pacify their flock. In the end, some 66,000 Bulgarians still resettled in Bessarabia and New Russia, although up to half of them returned within a year to the Ottoman Empire.[90]

Both the resettlement of those who had the greatest reason to fear the Ottomans and the measures taken by both the Russian and the Ottoman authorities to prevent the emigration of the rest undoubtedly contributed to the pacification of Rumelia in the aftermath of the war of 1828–9. Although the unprecedented appearance of the Russian army to the south of the Balkans did contribute to outbreaks of inter-confessional violence, such cases remained limited, as did the dislocations of the local Muslim and Christian population. One can judge the latter from the "Statistical Table of Northern Rumelia" composed by A.O. Diugamel in March 1830. By "Northern Rumelia," the author understood the area south of the Balkan Mountains that was occupied by Russian troops, which consisted of the districts of Mesembria (Nesebar), Rusokastro, Karnobat, Kizilendzhi, Slivno, Yambol, Yeni Zagra, and Aidos, as well as a small part of the district of Adrianople.

According to Diugamel, the population in the area amounted to 105,053, including 88,724 Greeks and Bulgarians and 15,864 Turks. In addition, some 9,272 Turks had fled and were likely to return after the departure of the Russians, which would bring the total population to 114,325 and the ratio of Christians to Muslims to 3.5:1.[91] Of the nine districts under review, only Aidos and

Adrianople had majority Muslim populations, although in Karnobat and Slivno the correlation was close to parity. The towns of Karnobat, Slivno, Yambol, and Yeni Zagra, meanwhile, had sizable Muslim minorities.[92] In general, Diugamel noted that the Christians "were cultivating the valleys," whereas the Turks lived in the mountains. He was also the first Russian observer to note that the Turkish villages were poorer than the Christian ones.[93]

The author noted the "extreme difficulty" of collecting demographic data given the "conditions of constant population movement" that accompanied and followed the Russian crossing of the Balkans. According to Diugamel, among those Turks who had fled at the Russian approach, only a small number returned to their places of origin. The Bulgarians had likewise been moving from one village to another. Neglecting their fields and vines, they were "living in the present and [were] preparing to follow the [Russian] army."[94] The accuracy of Diugamel's data was further compromised by the fact that not all the villages within the Russian-Ottoman demarcation line were occupied by Russian troops, which is why the author expected the actual numbers to be slightly higher than those he listed.

Whereas Diugamel's description focused on the districts and towns, E.I. Enegolm's *Notes on Trans-Balkan Towns Occupied by the Russian Troops during the Memorable Campaign of 1829* (1830) provided data on larger centres such as Adrianople and Kirk Kilise (Kirklareli) and discussed the moral-political qualities of the major ethnic and religious population groups. Published immediately after it was composed, his work was not limited to military statistics, but also contained historical forays and descriptions of local architecture. The population data presented by Enegolm sometimes differed significantly from the numbers reported by Diugamel. According to Enegolm, Muslims constituted a majority of the population in the towns of Karnobat, Slivno, and Yambol, and not a minority, as reported by Diugamel.[95] The same applied to Kirk Kilise, Chermen (Çirmen, Ormenio), Demotika, Lule-Burgas (Lüleburgaz), and Chorlu (Çorlu), which Diugamel did not discuss.[96] Together with the overwhelming majority in Adrianople (13,281 Turkish houses against 4,674 Christian ones), this made Muslims the dominant group in the urban population of Rumelia.[97]

Like Diugamel, Enegolm was a staff officer with even more experience of composing military-statistical surveys. For over fifteen years he had served in Transcaucasia, participating in the Russian-Persian wars of 1804–13 and 1826–8, joining several military missions to Persia, and contributing to the delimitation of the Russian-Persian border in 1824–5. By the time of his transfer to the Danube in 1828, Enegolm had thus had ample opportunity to develop a military Orientalist perspective, which we have already encountered in Davydov's *Theory of Partisan Action* and which was well established among Russian veterans of the Russian-Ottoman wars of the late eighteenth and the early nineteenth century.[98] Accordingly, Enegolm's portrayal of the Ottoman Muslims was predictably Orientalizing: they lived in "calm complacency"; rarely bothered with trade or industry; and drew their revenue from public offices, possession of land, and the oppression of Christians. "Plundering the Bulgarians in cold blood" and "imposing their prices upon the wares of the Greeks," the Ottoman Muslims were "ferocious in war," but "honest, dutiful, and hospitable" in peaceful life. Idleness, fatalism, and terseness of expression completed the clichéd image that the author presented to his readers.[99]

Enegolm's portrayal of the Greeks similarly followed the early nineteenth-century stereotypes that resulted from the collision of high classicist ideals with the realities of late Ottoman and post-Ottoman Greece. According to the Russian author, the descendants of the "virtuous warriors" and "artful sculptors" were "obediently bending their heads under the Ottoman yoke." Enegolm found the Greek inhabitants of Rumelia as careless, vain, quarrelsome, vengeful, envious, and avid as their famous ancestors, yet saw no evidence of the "spirit of independence" that had characterized the latter. Greek attachment to Orthodoxy coexisted with the remnants of pagan customs, while their proclivity for self-enrichment often trumped their sense of beauty. Being in control of virtually all commerce and industry of the region, the Greeks, according to Enegolm, feared being robbed of their possessions and therefore hid their fortune. At the same time, obedient compliance with the demands of the Turks did not prevent them from "fooling [their masters] in commercial affairs."[100]

Enegolm was writing at a time when Russian philhellenism was still stronger and more widespread than Russian interest in other Slavic peoples. For this reason, he devoted less space to the Bulgarians than to the Turks, whose fields they cultivated, or the Greeks, at whose factories they worked. Whereas the Bulgarian inhabitants of the plains and valleys were cultivators and farmers, "as befitted the peaceful inhabitants of a blessed country," those living in the mountains were "inhuman bandits." According to Enegolm, they were not content to rob and steal and often tortured travellers, enjoying the torment of their victims "in a frenzy of brutal savagery."[101] As the following chapters demonstrate, this rather unflattering image of the Bulgarian *hajduks* would give way to a more positive depiction by the middle decades of the nineteenth century, undoubtedly as part of the mounting popularity of pan-Slavic ideas among the Russian elites.

Despite the reflection of the Russian military on its experiences in the previous Russian-Ottoman confrontations and the efforts of the Russian command to avoid a war with the Muslim population from the very beginning, the campaign of 1828 reproduced the pattern of 1806–12. The Ottomans depopulated Dobrogea and employed Muslim partisans, while the Russians tried to resettle particular groups of Danubian Christians in Russia and often burned down and devastated Muslim settlements. On balance, the campaign of 1828 was rather unsuccessful, in terms of both the attainment of Russia's strategic objectives and the army's relations with the local population. One wonders whether this scenario was not predetermined by the geography and demography of Danubian Bulgaria, as well as the memory of the previous Russian-Ottoman confrontation in the region.

This impression is confirmed by the campaign of 1829, during which the Russian army unexpectedly crossed the Balkans and occupied Adrianople. The Christians in the territories to the south of the Balkans were not driven away by the Ottomans at the approach of the Russian troops, and the Muslim partisans hardly harassed the Russian army. In contrast to Danubian Bulgaria, this region had simply not been prepared by its previous historical experiences for such drastic resistance efforts. In addition, the readiness of the Muslim population to rise up for a "national war" against the *ghiaurs* must have been greatly dampened by the effect of the westernizing reforms of Mahmud II on the provincial Osmanli, which was noted by the Russian military men.

Mindful of the negative experience of the campaign of 1828, the Russian command adopted a particularly circumspect attitude towards the Muslim population the following year, and certainly avoided calling on the local Christians to stage an all-out rising against the Ottomans. Attacks by Muslims upon Christians, such as the massacre at Hermanli, did take place, but were fairly limited in scale. Overall, the Russians had to invest more effort into containing the Bulgarian radicals than in protecting them from Muslim reprisals. The outbreaks of inter-confessional violence after the evacuation of the Russian troops were minimized by the prior emigration of some 60,000 Rumelian Bulgarians; the Porte's pardoning of wartime collaborators; and its relief efforts, supplemented by the presence of the Russian consul newly appointed to Adrianople. In general, the first crossing of the Balkans by the Russian army proved to be much less disruptive to Muslim-Christian relations in European Turkey than the entry of the small detachment of Philiki Etaireia into Moldavia and Wallachia eight years previously.

Such an outcome was, among other things, the consequence of the consciously restrained approach adopted by the tsar and his commanders in the late 1820s. The first visible manifestation of this restraint came at the moment of the tsar's declaration of war on the Porte in April 1828, which expressly renounced the desire to destroy the Ottoman Empire. Nicholas I's recommendation to the Serbian leader Miloš Obrenović to remain neutral during the conflict likewise revealed his unwillingness to unleash a "people's war" in the Balkans. Nicholas I at first even avoided using Christian auxiliary detachments, as had become customary in the "Turkish wars" of Catherine the Great and Alexander I, and authorized the formation of the volunteer detachments only after the unsuccessful campaign of 1828. Even then, this authorization came with multiple restrictions and was counterbalanced by Dibich's reconciliatory gestures towards the Muslim population.

This consciously conservative approach of Nicholas I and his commanders during the Russian-Ottoman war of 1828–9 was part of the broader reaction of Russia's Old Regime military establishment to the challenge of the French Revolutionary and Napoleonic wars. Having first encountered "the people" as a factor of modern warfare, tsarist strategists and commanders tried to return to the principles of Old Regime warfare and restore their control over armed conflict by maintaining a strict separation between the army and the civilian population and by confining fighting to the battlefield. Inasmuch as they were successful in this, the Russian-Ottoman war of 1828–9 can be seen as an aspect of the broader restoration of the political monopoly of the monarchies and aristocracies in the immediate post-Napoleonic decades. However, this return to the principles of Old Regime warfare proved to be just as short-lived as did the political restoration properly speaking. During the middle decades of the nineteenth century, Russia's conservative military establishment was forced to admit the centrality of "the people" in modern warfare and modify its approach accordingly. The theoretical and practical manifestations of this change of attitude are examined in the next three chapters.

3 Partisan Warfare and the Statistics of European Turkey: The Case of I.P. Liprandi

The occupation of the European provinces of the Ottoman Empire gave Russian officers an opportunity to continue the collection of military-statistical information that they had begun in the late eighteenth and the early nineteenth century. In 1828–30, E.I. Ditmars composed a military-statistical survey of Moldavia and Wallachia, which was complemented by that of Colonel E.V. fon Ruge, Lieutenant Colonel A.I. Bergengeim, and Staff Captain J. Chodzko in 1834–5.[1] In parallel, A.G. Rozalion-Soshalskii and several other Russian officers composed a military topographical survey of Serbia and of those six districts that according to the Treaty of Adrianople were to augment Serbian territory.[2] Military-statistical information was also collected on the eastern Balkan region, as the above-cited surveys of A.O. Diugamel and E.I. Enegolm suggest. As a result of the war of 1828–9, the Russian military acquired a better knowledge of the numbers, geographical distribution, and political attitudes of the Balkan Muslims and Christians.[3]

In parallel, the period between the Peace of Adrianople and the outbreak of the Crimean War saw the further development of military literature in Russia – a process that received its initial impetus from the Napoleonic Wars. The first Russian histories of the Napoleonic Wars appeared at this time, as did the first major Russian treatises on strategy and tactics. Russian contributions to military science and military history during the 1830s, 1840s, and 1850s reflected the definitive assimilation of the principles of modern European warfare by the tsarist officers and, at the same time, helped to construct a Russian national tradition of military art. The latter crystallized in the second half of the nineteenth century, and the reflection on the experience of Russia's Turkish campaigns played an important role in this process.[4]

These parallel developments manifested themselves in the oeuvre of I.P. Liprandi, a veteran of the Russian-Ottoman war of 1828–9, who tried to turn his experience into expert knowledge of European Turkey and place it at the disposal of the Russian command at the beginning of the Crimean War. The *problématique* of small war, partisan action, and relations between the Russian army and the population of European Turkey were central to Liprandi's interests and constituted the focus of his voluminous writings during the Nicholaevan period. Although the Russian command failed to profit from Liprandi's expertise, his case illustrates well the two-way connection between knowledge of a population and practices of warfare that stood at the basis of the nascent politics of population.

The son of Pedro di Liprandy, a Piedmontese noblemen of Spanish origin who entered Russian service under Catherine the Great, I.P. Liprandi began his career in the Russian army as a dashing young officer during the Swedish campaign of 1808–9.[5] Having fought at Borodino against Napoleon, he later participated in the European campaigns of 1813–14, and remained in France with the Russian occupation corps commanded by M.S. Vorontsov until 1818. From this period onwards, Liprandi became increasingly involved in espionage. As the head of the military police of the Russian occupation corps, Liprandi had the opportunity to learn the techniques and methods of the French police, headed by the notorious criminal turned police agent Eugène François Vidocq.

Upon his return to Russia, Liprandi was reassigned to the Kamchatka regiment stationed in Bessarabia as punishment for his participation in a duel. In 1822, he temporarily retired from the army, with the rank of colonel, and a year later entered the civil service as a special agent (*chinovnik osobykh poruchenii*) of Vorontsov, who became governor general of New Russia and Bessarabia. From his arrival in Bessarabia, Liprandi devoted his time, money, and extraordinary linguistic abilities to what became his lifetime pursuit – the study of European Turkey. The library that he had begun to build up around 1820, according to his own proud testimony, included all European works on the Ottoman Empire published since 1800, and in the 1830s was already known to a number of major European scholarly societies. During his years in Bessarabia, Liprandi closely observed the Greek Etaireia rebellion that broke out in 1821 in the Ottoman vassal principalities of Moldavia and Wallachia.[6] On the order of the commander of the 6th Corps, I.V. Sabaneev, and the commander of the 16th Division, M.F. Orlov, Liprandi visited the Ottoman fortresses on the Danube in order to collect information about the movements of Ottoman troops in the principalities and Danubian Bulgaria, a mission that he repeated in 1826 at the time of the Akkerman Congress.

In 1827, Liprandi re-entered the military and convinced the chief of staff of the 2nd Army, P.D. Kiselev, of the necessity of a thorough intelligence operation for the successful planning of the upcoming campaign.[7] Having secured Kiselev's support, Liprandi entered the principalities and, with the help of a network of agents recruited from various social strata, collected information about the Ottoman fortresses, the disposition of the Austrian troops in neighbouring Transylvania, and the attitude of the Romanian boyars, as well as that of the Bulgarians, Tatars, Nekrasovtsy, and Zaporozhian Cossacks who populated the right bank of the Danube.[8] Like the Russian consuls in the principalities, Liprandi supplied Russian occupation authorities with lists of boyars classified according to their sympathies for the Ottoman Empire, Austria, or Russia.[9] Liprandi combined military-statistical observations with the study of the history of previous Russian-Ottoman wars. To this end, he obtained unpublished diaries and memoirs from a number of veterans of the war of 1806–12, including I.V. Sabaneev, A.F. Lanzheron, S.A. Tuchkov, I.M. Garting, and M.I. Ponset.[10]

Liprandi participated in the war of 1828–9 as a colonel of the General Staff, working under the supervision of Kiselev and I.I. Dibich, the chiefs of staff of Vitgenshtein and Nicholas I, respectively. Following the outbreak of hostilities, he rushed to Iași at the head of a small detachment and captured the Moldavian *hospodar*, Ioan Alexandru Sturdza, before the latter had the chance to flee to Austria, as did his Wallachian counterpart, Grigore Ghica. In the campaign of 1828, Liprandi accompanied the Russian columns advancing through the Babadag region and then remained at the headquarters of the Russian army near Shumla, interrogating Ottoman deserters and gathering intelligence for the Russian army through his network of agents. As a result of these activities, Liprandi was perhaps better positioned than anyone else to say what was wrong in relations between the Russian army and the inhabitants of Danubian Bulgaria.

Liprandi's Partisan Detachment in 1829

Amid the discussion of the results of the first campaign of the war, Liprandi submitted a memorandum in which he attributed Russian failures to the activities of the numerous "insolent and ferocious" Muslim inhabitants, incited by "ignorant superstition, religious fanaticism, and the appeals [of the Ottoman government]," who used the advantages of the mountainous terrain covered by woods and rugged with gorges against the Russian army.[11] Neither the numerousness of the Ottoman troops nor their desperate bravery presented a problem for the Russians, yet the victories of the Russian armies in the field and the capture of the Ottoman fortresses did not have decisive consequences. "Crowds of angry inhabitants, insolent Turkish horsemen, and marauders" would hide in woods and gorges (*stremniny*) and would cut Russian lines of communication, capture trains, attack hospitals, and endanger supply depots. According to Liprandi, this "upset and depressed the Russian troops and killed their good spirit, which is the first quality of the soldier."[12] The lack of adequate information about the war theatre further complicated the situation, as all available topographical surveys proved to be unreliable.[13]

Liprandi argued that supremacy in "small war" was no less important than successes in the field and siege warfare. This supremacy could be achieved by means of partisans who would "spread in swarms around our army and could protect it against unexpected attacks, night alerts, secure the supply trains, dispose the local inhabitants in favour of the Russians or retain the refractory and rebellious ones by fear." At the same time, the partisans could "inspire terror by the suddenness of their appearance and the quickness of their attacks on the enemy camp," which would be easy to achieve given the disorder that reigned among the Ottoman troops.[14] According to Liprandi, this was the best way "to influence the enemy's imagination," which was a precondition of success "in a war against the Asians." Such measures were sure to sow "horror and confusion in the Turkish army," which "was not used to strict and permanently maintained order and lacked a systematic intelligence service."[15]

Although partisan action in European Turkey had had its advocates before Liprandi, the latter stands out as someone who put this idea into practice. To that end, Liprandi proposed forming "a flying corps of partisans." This corps would not be in a position as advantageous as that of the Russian partisans around Moscow in 1812, who, "accustomed to the climate, familiar with the terrain, and supported by the inhabitants," had fought the French, who had "lacked the means to conduct a small war."[16] At the same time, partisans in Turkey would be much more useful than Russian partisans had been in Germany in 1813 and 1814, where the local population had likewise been in favour of the Russians and the French had abandoned the countryside to retreat behind fortified positions.

In view of the peculiarity of the conditions of European Turkey, the principles adopted in the formation of the proposed partisan force necessarily had to differ from those followed in Russia or in Germany. In 1812–14, the partisan detachments had consisted only of cavalrymen strengthened by some light artillery, and had fought in well-known and open terrain against a regular army, whose cavalry had been weak. By contrast, the territory to the south of the Danube was mountainous, the attitude of the inhabitants depended on the circumstances, and the enemy was "wild and numerous and strong in regular cavalry." In such conditions, argued Liprandi, cavalry partisans alone could easily fall prey to ambushes organized by "insolent and treacherous" local inhabitants in the woods (as many Russian Cossacks did in 1828). Therefore, the proposed flying corps would have to include infantry and be more numerous than the usual partisan detachments. Liprandi proposed assembling 900 foot soldiers and 300 cavalrymen, in addition to 600 Cossacks and several guns.[17]

Liprandi argued that it was necessary to be careful in the choice of volunteers. He suggested recruiting former Etairists, who included the Suliots, Albanians, and Montenegrins, as well as "other inhabitants of rocks and mountains, who grew up in banditry, are accustomed to war in the mountains, and know well the tricks and ploys of the Turks, whose implacable enemies they are." According to Liprandi, many of the former Etairists were still present in Bessarabia, Moldavia, and Wallachia, to whom one could add the inhabitants of the districts of Mehedinți, Gorj, and Vilkov of Little Walachia (Oltenia), who were known to be sharpshooters.[18] Although all these people had so far shown little desire to offer their services, the Russian colonel believed that they would gladly flock to the Russian banner if "treated gently and in accordance with their spirit." Liprandi revealed his knowledge of the Balkan *hajduk* tradition when he recommended that 900 infantry volunteers be divided into thirty detachments of thirty people each (which corresponded to the usual size of the Balkan *cheta*) and that the commanders of these detachments be independent from one another and receive their orders only from the commander of the entre corps.[19]

Bringing such diverse people under one banner would be no easy task, and would require special qualities on the part of the commander. According to Liprandi, the latter could not treat "the Asians or their neighbouring semi-savage Christian peoples" as he would treat a regular soldier. Instead, he had to "understand the spirit and qualities of each of them, know to win their allegiance, be their commander in combat, their comrade at the bivouacs, as well as be ready to tame their impudence and their mutual and frequently pernicious quarrels by means of calculated severity." Capable of communicating with all of his polyglot soldiers, the ideal commander of the flying corps emerges in Liprandi's memorandum as a military *uomo universale* of sorts, "competent in all the branches of the military of science," and performing the functions of "recruiter, quartermaster, engineer, intendant, and commander of his party" – all at the same time.

Liprandi believed that the sudden appearance of the flying corps in the Balkan Mountains would "scare the inhabitants of Muslim confession and would subject them to the influence of their Christian neighbours or else drive them away from the war theatre." In any case, Liprandi expected that it would "eliminate their bloodthirsty ferocity and prevent the possibility of a national war [*narodnoi voiny*], which is so dangerous and entails harmful consequences for the invading army," as the Spanish and Russian war against Napoleon had proved.[20] Spread across small parties over vast terrain, these partisans would "sow fear, the only means of taming the barbarians." They would drive away the Muslim inhabitants and would instil a positive view of the Russians among the Bulgarians and other Christian peoples living beyond the Danube. With such advance detachments, the Russian army would find more support among the co-religionist population in the course of its advance into the interior of the Ottoman Empire.

According to Liprandi, the experience of the campaign of 1828 contained *a contrario* proof of this assumption. Following the arrival of the Russians at Shumla, numerous Bulgarian, Greek, and Turkish defectors from the fortress and deputies from the surrounding villages had turned up asking for protection and offering their services. However, soon after the Russian army had halted its advance and failed to occupy fully the territory that had remained to its rear, the stream of defectors and deputies had dwindled and, in the end, Bulgarians had even been suspected of robbery and killings of the Russian soldiers.[21] Had the proposed detachment of partisans already existed in 1828, argued Liprandi, the Muslim inhabitants would not have dared to threaten the Russian army from their hideouts in the woods. The favourable disposition of the Bulgarians towards the Russians would have been preserved, which would have "turn[ed] against the enemy the weapon of the small war that caused us so much harm."[22]

In March 1829, I.I. Dibich, who had just been appointed commander-in-chief, accepted Liprandi's project and charged him with the execution of the plan.[23] However, the recruitment of volunteers for the detachment proceeded slowly, and sometimes those who had signed up would later refuse to turn up under various pretexts. The volunteers expected money, which Dibich did not allocate. They also closely followed the course of the war, and only Dibich's decisive success at Kulevcha in late May 1829 finally swayed them in favour of joining. By early June, Liprandi had managed to assemble 950 people at Calafat (650 infantry and 300 cavalry).[24] These included veterans of the First Serbian Uprising, former Etairists, and the *kirdzhali*, who had operated in the vicinity of Olympus, Shar-dag, Kara-dag, and the environs of Pristina and Prizren in the first decade of the nineteenth century. At the head of this diverse and polyglot force, Liprandi was placed at the disposal of Major General V.Ia. Rupert, whose forces occupied Silistria. At Rupert's suggestion, Liprandi's patrolled the roads across the Deliorman forest, which had become impassable due to the activities of Muslim partisans.[25]

As Liprandi had foreseen in his memorandum, handling his detachment was a daunting task, particularly since Russian headquarters did not satisfy his request for an additional Cossack force because of the shortage of troops. Liprandi was thus left in sole command of these people who were "animated by unbridled passions, savage, prone to plots and riots, to murder and all evil deeds."[26] There was constant drunken carousing in the camp, and the volunteers frequently wounded each other with their incessant shooting. According to Liprandi, any attempt to suppress this disorder would cause complaints about violation of the soldiers' customs, whereupon the detachment would dissolve. Fortunately, Liprandi already knew their idiosyncrasies well enough and became their "chieftain." Initially, he was the first to enter the dangerous gorges, until his volunteers came to appreciate his courage and began to cover him every time. On several occasions, Liprandi's personal bravery helped him to prevent a riot and dispersal of the detachment.

Before long, Liprandi received Kiselev's order to begin "a systematic cleansing of the Deliorman forest." According to Liprandi, one way of doing this consisted in chasing the inhabitants out of fortified gorges and woods and burning down their villages in order to deprive them of shelter for the winter and thereby force them to retreat to the western part of the Balkans. However, this was not an easy task in view of the size of Deliorman and of its population, which is why Liprandi adopted a different strategy.[27] Having captured 140 Muslim men and 80 women from the village of Kaurgi, he gave them food and reprimanded his own *hajduks* for their actions against the women that had insulted Muslim sensibilities. At the same time, Liprandi tried to shame the captive Muslims for leaving their homes, which according to him represented a violation of *sharia*, as it prevented them from fulfilling the *namaz* and the *abdest* properly.[28] Combining psychological pressure and mercy, Liprandi made the captives repent in their actions (he pretended to pardon them because the day of their capture was the day of the Russian emperor Nicholas I). Liprandi dispatched four of the captives to spread his message to other inhabitants of the Deliorman, who were still hiding in the ambush. The goal of these measures, according to Liprandi, was to evoke feelings of "gratitude" (*priznatel'nosti i blagodarnosti*), which had far greater force among the Ottomans than among other European peoples.[29]

As a result of Liprandi's propaganda among the Deliorman Muslims, the inhabitants of eleven villages returned to their homes. Each village surrendered their weapons in exchange for safe-conduct passes (*okhrannye listy*), on which the commanders of nearby Russian detachments would attest each week that the inhabitants had remained peaceful, and accepted responsibility for maintaining peace in the local area.[30] Liprandi also managed to transfer the villages that were located in the most dangerous spots to the environs of Silistria, where they were under the control of Russian troops. However, this apparently successful pacification of the Deliorman Muslims came at the cost of mounting tensions within Liprandi's detachment. His forgiving treatment of the Turkish inhabitants deprived his own volunteers of booty. Before long, there came the news of the conclusion of the Adrianople peace treaty. However, demobilization and rewards were postponed due to the refusal of the pasha of Shkodra to recognize the treaty. This necessitated the dispatch of Kiselev's corps from the Danube across the Balkans to Sofia, which left precious few units in the rearguard of the main army. At an encampment near Turtukai, Liprandi struggled desperately to hold his detachment together, despite mutinies, deadly cold, and his own illness, until early December 1829.[31]

Liprandi's Writings on Partisan Warfare

The experience of creating and leading a volunteer detachment in 1829 provided the basis for Liprandi's analysis of partisan warfare in the decades that followed. The first product of this reflection was a manuscript entitled "On Partisan Warfare," written in the 1830s. This consisted of the above-quoted description of Liprandi's volunteer detachment in 1829, preceded by a discussion of partisan action in the Russian-Swedish war of 1808–9, Russia's Patriotic

War of 1812, and the campaigns of 1813–14 in France and Germany. This work critically engaged with Davydov's *Theory of Partisan Action*, and represents an interesting yet altogether neglected aspect of nineteenth-century Russian reflection on the role of the general population in war.

Himself a veteran of the Patriotic War of 1812, Liprandi accepted Davydov's basic notion of partisan warfare, in which strategic triangles defined the positioning and action of irregular detachments with regard to both one's own regular force and the enemy army. At the same time, he disagreed with Davydov in his interpretation of concrete historical examples of partisan warfare. Whereas Davydov considered the campaign of 1812 as the paradigmatic example of partisan warfare, Liprandi considered it to be closer to a "national war" akin to Spanish guerilla warfare. According to Liprandi, the Cossack party that was dispatched to the rear of Napoleon's armies following the battle of Borodino "acted in the centre of its fatherland, amid inhabitants who took an active part in the defeat of the enemy." Liprandi argued that the inhabitants threatened the enemy detachments and foraging parties at least as much as the Cossacks and acted out of "attachment to religion, loyalty to the monarch and love of fatherland" rather than "strategic considerations." He therefore considered the action to the rear of Napoleon's army in 1812 to be closer to Spanish guerilla warfare than to partisan action proper.[32]

Liprandi viewed partisan warfare as a more sophisticated type of action than guerilla warfare, and in fact considered it a means of counteracting and neutralizing a "national war." Whereas many contemporaries and later scholars viewed the national movements of the European peoples against Napoleon's dominance as proof of a certain degree of national development, Liprandi attributed the capacity for "national war" to "uncivilized peoples" and argued that the "enlightened" nations were incapable of it. Having received his baptism of fire in the Russian-Swedish war of 1808–9, Liprandi pointed to the guerilla-type resistance of the Savolak (Savonian) inhabitants of New Finland in 1808, while the inhabitants of Western Bothnia were "more enlightened, settled, appreciative of family life, neatness, and cleanliness, and therefore incapable of a national war."[33] He also pointed to the failure of Napoleon's attempts to organize a "national war" in France in early 1814. Although "detachments of artisans and factory workers harried the Austrian and Prussian armies in the Vosges and temporarily stalled their advance," the issuing of threats of death to anyone found to be armed and the burning down of villages "greatly softened the patriotism of the Frenchmen," in "striking contrast to the Spaniards and the Russians."[34]

Liprandi's divergence from Davydov revealed a different understanding of the place of partisan action within the broader context of wars between Russia and other powers. For Davydov, partisan warfare on Russian soil, within the areas that constituted the historical core of Muscovy, represented a crucial element of national defensive strategy. Admittedly, Davydov's concrete recommendations left little place for spontaneous popular uprisings against the enemy, as the events of 1812 would later be portrayed in Soviet historiography. Nevertheless, his account of the development of partisan warfare did include the Spanish guerillas, even though he considered this "national war" (*nar-odnaia voina*) to be somewhat *sui generis*. By contrast, for Liprandi, partisan warfare could well form part of a wider offensive action, as was the case with the campaign of 1813 in Germany, which distinguished it from fundamentally defensive guerilla warfare.[35] Whereas guerilla-type action involved the mass of the population being moved by nationalist sentiment to oppose the invader, partisans *senso strictu* were guided by strategic considerations and often operated among an initially hostile population. In fact, turning a hostile population into a loyal or even friendly one was one of the most important functions of partisan action from Liprandi's perspective. This was precisely the transformation that Liprandi's volunteer detachment helped to secure in 1829.

The distinction between partisan warfare and national war suggested by Davydov and emphasized by Liprandi was shared by a major Russian military writer of the Nicholaevan epoch, A.I. Mikhailovskii-Danilevskii. A former adjutant of Alexander I and an important memoirist, Mikhailovskii-Danilevskii undertook the task of writing the history of all the wars in which Russia had been involved during the first fifteen years of the nineteenth century. His writings contained few theoretical observations and instead provided a factual account of the wars that focused on the actions of the main armies. Nevertheless, Mikhailovskii-Danilevskii did make a contribution to the discussion of small war inasmuch as his concrete historical descriptions either confirmed or disproved the more theoretical arguments advanced by other writers.

Not unlike Liprandi, Mikhailovskii-Danilevskii questioned the effectiveness of the partisan detachments of 1812 that were so central for Davydov. He recognized their usefulness, yet claimed that "the Patriotic War offered no example of a partisan feat that could compare to the capture of Berlin, Luneburg, Kassel, Bremen, Amsterdam, and Soissons in 1813–14."[36] At the same time, Mikhailovskii-Danilevskii attributed far more importance than did Davydov or Liprandi to the anti-French resistance of the population of the Smolensk and Moscow *gubernias* and treated it separately from partisan warfare. Although "national war" emerges in Mihailovskii-Danilevskii's account as a manifestation of mass patriotism, he also mentioned cases when armed groups of Russian peasants attacked Cossack partisans, whom they took for foreigners.[37] This confirmed Liprandi's implicit counterposition of partisan action and "national war." Mikhailovskii-Danilevskii's history of the Russian-Swedish war of 1808–9 likewise validated Liprandi's opinion of the small war in Savonia as an example of a "national war."[38] Finally, Mikhailovskii-Danilevskii's history of the Russian-Ottoman war of 1806–12 described the grand vizier's effective use of "parties" (*partii*) and "armed Bulgarians" to disrupt Russian lines of communication between Silistria, Razgrad, and Bazardzhik and hamper Russian supply trains in 1810.[39] This historical episode illustrated both the traditional strength of the Ottomans in small war and Liprandi's argument that the local population, including the Christians, would support the Ottomans unless neutralized by effectively organized partisan action on the Russian side.

Despite his retirement from military service in 1832 with the rank of major general and his subsequent employment as a special agent of the Ministry of the Interior, Liprandi kept abreast of new developments in military science and military history, and published many critical reviews of publications in this domain during the 1850s and 1860s. One of these reviews was devoted to the studies of small war published in 1850 by Lieutenant General A.E. Engelgardt and I.V. Vuich, a professor of the Military Academy. Engelgardt approached his subject from the point of view of partisan action organized by the officers of the regular army rather than from the perspective of a spontaneous "national war."[40] Inasmuch as the local population figured in Engelgardt's study, it was as the object of small war rather than its agent. Not unlike Davydov and Liprandi, the author assumed that the partisan detachments had to win over a neutral or potentially hostile population. They had to "restore and maintain a good disposition towards us" as well as "acquire a certain degree of authority over the inhabitants in order to enjoy all the local advantages through their cooperation." Engelgardt also suggested that "spreading false rumours of a popular uprising to the rear of the enemy" was a useful stratagem that could further undermine the moral forces of the enemy when they began to retreat. It is noteworthy that the author did not recommend provoking a popular uprising in earnest.

By contrast, Vuich placed popular uprisings fully within the scope of "small war." According to him, such uprisings could succeed in harming the enemy only if their dispersed forces made "frequent attacks and constant alerts in mountainous, woody or marshy countries," which made "virtually all their actions nothing but small war."[41] Like Engelgardt, Vuich devoted most of his work to the partisan detachments of Davydov's type, that is, those led by army officers and consisting of either regular or irregular soldiers. At the same time, Vuich believed that the provocation of a popular uprising behind enemy lines could be one of the functions of the partisans. According to Vuich, spontaneous popular uprisings such as those that happened in Spain and Portugal required a "strong national sentiment," which was something of a rarity. For this reason, small partisan detachments of either regular or irregular troops were the best way to provoke an uprising in those areas where "the inhabitants are well disposed towards us." Vuich pointed to the example of northern Germany in 1813, where "all were weary of French dominance and ready for a rebellion," yet this arose "only with the arrival of the [Russian] partisan detachments."[42]

Liprandi praised Engelgardt's and Vuich's efforts, yet criticized them for focusing "all their attention on the war with the Western European peoples."

According to him, Russia could not made do with "general military regulations" and "general tactics" as did France, Prussia, and various other countries. Liprandi pointed out that Russia was "surrounded by peoples of different origin, religion, character and customs" and thus had to adopt special "rules, tactics, and even strategic considerations" for each of its potential enemies. These had to be based on "precise and perfectly practical knowledge of the character, customs, mode of life, and way of war of the inhabitants of the country to which we transfer our military operations."[43] Liprandi proceeded from the assumption that the different qualities of each people were particularly important to know in war, on the day of battle, when "human beings revealed all their particular passions, abilities, shortcomings, and weaknesses." According to him, "Things that could intimidate some could excite courage in others."[44]

The knowledge of the qualities of different people in war was all the more important in view of the fact that enemy armies were rarely homogenous.[45] While the Austrian army surpassed all others in terms of the "completely opposite characteristics and political opinions" of its constituent ethnic elements, the Ottoman army came a close second in this respect. Drawing on his experience in European Turkey between 1820 and 1832, Liprandi stressed the differences that existed between "Albanians of the two Albanian provinces, the Bosnians of three different confessions, Macedonians, Rumelians, Thessalians, the Bulgarians of the highlands and those of the valleys, the Tatars of Dobrogea, the inhabitants of Deliorman, the Nekrasovtsy, the Zaporozheans, [and] the different tribes of Anatolya and Egypt," all of whom comprised the Ottoman army.[46] Liprandi also noted the frequency of Russian-Ottoman wars in the preceding century and a half, which made the absence of special military instructions or guides on Turkey particularly regrettable.[47] As the following discussion demonstrates, much of Liprandi's effort during the 1830s, 1840s, and 1850s was devoted to a military-statistical description of European Turkey that had to compensate for the lack of Russian knowledge of the region and the peoples that inhabited it.

The first fruit of Liprandi's effort was a monumental compendium called "The Ottoman Empire: A Lexicon," in which the retired partisan leader matched his veteran experience of 1828–9 to his extensive readings in Western European literature on the Ottomans. Organized as an encyclopedia of 8,000 entries, this work included a great deal of geographical, historical, and ethnographic information, in addition to data on the Ottomans' military organization and their manner of making war.[48] Since much of this information, in Liprandi's own view, represented a military secret, he consciously renounced the idea of publishing his magnum opus, which he completed in 1836. In all likelihood, therefore, the information contained in the "Lexicon" did not reach many Russian officers until early 1854, when Liprandi used the data from his compendium in order to produce a thematically organized survey of European Turkey, which will be discussed later on in this chapter. Nevertheless, a brief discussion of the entry in the "Lexicon" on Adrianople is useful, if only in order to provide a more complete picture of the Russian officers' perspective on the region during the 1830s.

In his description of the second capital of the Ottoman Empire, Liprandi drew on E.I. Enegolm's *Notes on Trans-Balkan Towns* (1830).[49] To Enegolm's observations on the moral qualities of the Turks, Greek, and Bulgarians, Liprandi added his own observations of inter-ethnic relations in the region.[50] Whereas Enegolm's critical perspective on modern Greeks was based on a comparison between them and their classical ancestors, Liprandi revealed their mistreatment of their Slavic co-religionists. According to Liprandi, the Greeks not only "obediently complied with the demands of [the Ottomans]," but also demonstrated their loyalty by denouncing the Slavs. They followed the Ottoman armies as interpreters and spies and "did not lose a single opportunity to burden the Slavic tribes even more." Accordingly, the Slavs "hate the Greeks more than the Turks and attribute to them all the travails that have afflicted them ever since their settlement in this region at the time of the Byzantine emperors, who often reneged on their promises" to Slavic rulers.[51]

Liprandi's next contribution to the military statics of European Turkey was his "Review of the Theatre of the Russian-Ottoman War of 1806–12," written in 1841 as a supplement to A.I. Mikhailovskii-Danilevskii's history of that war. In this document, Liprandi highlighted the significant Muslim presence in Danubian Bulgaria. The Tatars and Turks numerically predominated in Dobrogea and Deliorman, which constituted, respectively, the eastern and central parts of the region. Liprandi particularly singled out the bellicose inhabitants of the Deliorman forest, whom he identified as the descendants of the frontier Turks resettled from Anatolia by the early sultans.[52] According to Liprandi, the inhabitants of Deliorman were distinguished from their co-nationals by their "rude mores [and] unbelievable fanaticism and were considered bloodthirsty bandits who did not differentiate between friend and foe."[53] Although Christians were more numerous further west, the westernmost extreme of Danubian Bulgaria near Vidin likewise accommodated a considerable number of Muslims, including the warlike émigrés from rebellious Serbia.[54]

Apart from the major Ottoman fortresses, the entire territory between the Danube, the Balkans, and the Black Sea was covered by field fortifications (*palanka*) and towers (*kule*), whose small garrisons, "composed of the richer and more courageous [Turkish] inhabitants themselves," served to control the local Christians.[55] According to Liprandi, the sizable presence of Muslims as well as Greeks and Armenians had had an adverse effect upon the moral qualities and political attitudes of the Bulgarians living in the eastern part of the region. The latter, according to Liprandi, had become "duplicitous, avid, perfidious," and had "lost their warlike spirit and ancient customs."[56] By contrast, the Bulgarian population of western part of the region, who remained separate from the Muslims, Greeks, and other nations, "retained their military spirit and courage," as well as the purity of their language, their old customs, and the memory of their ancient kings.[57]

Between Orientalism and Occidentalism

Liprandi's attempt to establish himself as a military Orientalist was not very successful. His overview of Danubian Bulgaria was generously rewarded by the tsar, yet came out only in 1854, during the Crimean War.[58] The fate of his "Lexicon" was even more problematic. By Liprandi's own account, in 1832 he submitted to the president of the newly founded Military Academy of the General Staff, Grand Duke Mikhail Pavlovich, a memorandum entitled "Some Considerations on Military Science." The memorandum received the approval of the tsar, who ordered Liprandi to work on a study of the "peculiar characteristics and political opinions of the Turks." In 1834, Liprandi dispatched the first completed part of his "Lexicon" to the tsar by way of the war minister, A.I. Chernyshev. However, the work apparently did not reach the addressee and was instead examined by the Military-Scientific Committee of the General Staff. The latter noted the usefulness of Liprandi's compilation from numerous and often poorly accessible works. At the same time, the committee criticized Liprandi for adopting an alphabetical rather than a thematic principle for organizing his material and declared him free to publish this work, without, however, providing any funds to this purpose.[59]

The lukewarm reception of the "Lexicon" can be attributed to Liprandi's ambiguous status as an author. Despite his veteran experience and his working knowledge of Turkish and the Balkan languages, he lacked the credentials of an academic Orientalist. By the 1830s, Russia had several centres for Oriental studies, most notably at St. Petersburg and Kazan Universities.[60] The fact that Liprandi did not have formal training in Oriental languages must have been a disadvantage. Nor did he have much formal military education. From the beginning of his military service in 1807, Liprandi was a staff officer, yet he was too old to be a student either at the Moscow or St. Petersburg schools of staff officers (*uchilishche kolonnovozhatykh*) that functioned in 1816–26, or at the Military Academy of the General Staff, founded in 1832. In this, Liprandi was different from later Russian military Orientalists (*vostochniki*), who usually graduated from the Academy and had formal training in Oriental languages.[61]

Another reason for Liprandi's failure to establish himself as a military Orientalist had to do with the main object of his expertise. Russian military men of the first half of the nineteenth century routinely referred to the Ottoman army and the Balkan population, whether Muslim or Christian, as Oriental, exotic, and Asian.[62] In this respect, Russian diaries and memoirs of the "Turkish campaigns" offer an example of Orientalism as a style of thought based on a set of dichotomies between East and West.[63] However, taken within the broader time frame of the long nineteenth century, Russian representations of "Turkey-in-Europe" underwent a certain evolution, which set them apart from the Russian perspectives on the Asian part of the Ottoman Empire and beyond.

The root of this difference can be traced to François de Tott's infamous comparison of the Ottoman Empire to an army encamped in Europe, whose "commanders" and "soldiers" still viewed the territory and the local population as a conquered country, centuries after the fall of Constantinople. De Tott's metaphor was unmistakably Orientalist with regard to the Ottoman Muslims, who were cast as Asians foreign to Europe and therefore subject to expulsion. The early popularity of this metaphor in Russia is attested by Catherine the Great's "Greek project," which sought to do just that – expel the Ottomans into Asia and restore the Greek Empire on the shores of the Bosphorus.[64] At the same time, the representation of the Ottomans as alien invaders implied that the European territories of the Ottoman Empire were non-Asian, at least in prospect, and thus subject to be reclaimed by "civilization."

Later, the "failure" of this "civilizing mission" – whether Austrian, Russian, or Western European – resulted in the emergence of the discourse of Balkanism, emphasizing the backwardness of the region and the inherent violence of its inhabitants.[65] Before this happened, however, Russian perspectives on "Turkey-in-Europe" were akin to the eighteenth-century Western European portrayals of Eastern Europe described by Larry Wolff – namely, a discourse about a transitional space, both in the geographical sense of a middle ground between West and East, and in the temporal sense, as a midpoint between an Oriental past and a European future.[66] The ostensible proof of this transition consisted in the transformation of particular Ottoman provinces into independent states (Greece) or at least their broad autonomy from the Porte (Moldavia, Wallachia, and Serbia).

The Europeanizing reforms of the Ottoman sultans likewise confirmed the impression that genuinely Oriental Turkey was either disappearing or turning into something else. And while the Russian observers of the Tanzimat were usually sceptical of its potential to save the Ottoman Empire, they also recognized the actual material changes that were taking place in Ottoman society in the middle decades of the nineteenth century, when European fashions and goods were displacing authentically Oriental vestments and wares.[67] In a similar way, the efforts of the nineteenth-century sultans to create a European-style army, however fitful and uncertain they may have been at first, ultimately transformed the traditional Ottoman military organization that Russian officers had perceived as distinctly Oriental.[68]

Liprandi did not pay much attention to the Tanzimat or the earlier reforms of Selim III and Mahmud II, interested as he was in the situation on the ground rather than in the policies of the central government. For this reason, the image of the Ottoman Empire and Ottoman warfare that Liprandi offered in the 1830s and the 1840s was rather static and did not quite account for the changes that were taking place. In this, his military-statistical descriptions reproduced the generic feature of Orientalist literature – its tendency to represent the Orient as frozen in the past, ossified, and stagnant, if not declining.[69] However, ignoring the changes meant that Liprandi's accounts of the Ottoman Empire and its military organization were somewhat outdated from the very beginning, and the progress of the Tanzimat made them even more obsolete. This helps explain why subsequent Russian strategists and commanders on the Danube had relatively little use for Liprandi's military Orientalist expertise.[70]

At the same time, Liprandi's military-statistical descriptions of the Ottoman Empire can serve as an entry into the mental world of a Russian officer of the Nicholaevan epoch. In particular, they illustrate how Orientalizing representations of Ottoman Turkey were intertwined with the Russian elites' increasingly critical perspective on Europe. The heated debate around Edward Said's famous study of Western concepts of the Orient led, among other things, to a discussion of occidentalism, or negative images of the West articulated by representatives of non-Western societies.[71] Russian literature has its fair share of occidentalist texts, the earliest of which in fact date from the peak period of Russian elite Gallomania in the late eighteenth century.[72] This critical attitude towards the West steadily gained ground after 1815, and especially in the decades preceding the Crimean War.

In a sense, the ghost of the Crimean War was present in the early 1830s, in the context of yet another revolutionary wave in Europe. The revolution of July 1830 in France triggered the Belgian revolution the following August and was echoed in the Polish November Uprising of the same year. The result was a new political and ideological split between the Western part of Europe (composed of parliamentary monarchies with an increasingly liberal public sphere) and the territories further east, dominated by the still absolutist regimes of Austria, Prussia, and Russia.[73] The surge of Russophobia in Britain and France that accompanied the Polish uprising and its suppression provoked a reaction in Russia, whose strength cannot be explained by anti-Polish sentiment alone.[74] After all, the "Slanderers of Russia" castigated by Alexander Pushkin in a famous verse were not the rebellious Poles, but the liberal deputies of the French National Assembly, who at the time of the uprising called for French intervention.[75] As Pushkin's close companion during the latter's Bessarabian exile in the early 1820s, Liprandi could not have missed this widely circulated piece and must have shared the sentiment it helped to express.

It is tempting to interpret the Russian intellectual atmosphere of the 1830s and the 1840s in terms of a nationalistic *ressentiment* that supposedly characterized the elites of the more or less "backward" countries to the east of the Rhine, or, indeed, the Channel.[76] Recognizing the superiority of Western European material civilization, the German writers of the late eighteenth and the early nineteenth century famously juxtaposed it with the superior spiritual qualities of the German people, establishing an intellectual pattern that would be followed by other Eastern European nationalists.[77] This attitude is certainly found in the writings of the Russian Slavophiles and the later Russian nationalists, yet it would be a mistake to ascribe it to the Russian officers of Liprandi's generation. If anything, recent experience must have convinced them of their material – that is, military – superiority.

Too often, the Nicholaevan epoch is interpreted through the prism of the Crimean defeat and the growing developmental gap that it revealed between the industrial or industrializing countries of Western Europe and the still pre-industrial Russia. However, their country's objective backwardness was not necessarily a factor in the consciousness of the Russian elites during the 1830s and 1840s. Having successfully repelled Napoleon's invasion in 1812 and triumphed once more over the Ottomans and the Poles in 1829–31, the Russian military men, and the educated subjects of the tsar more broadly, had some reason to look with confidence at the current state and the future of their country – particularly when they compared the apparent stability of Russia both to the crisis-ridden Ottoman Empire, and to a Europe shaken by the revolutionary waves of the early 1820s, 1830, and 1848.[78] Inasmuch as Europe figured as a source of danger in the minds of the Russian military men of the Nicholaevan epoch, it did so not in a purely military sense, but on account of the revolutionary "subversion" radiating from the Western European capitals.

A preoccupation with this "subversion" is certainly manifest in Liprandi's writings of the 1830s, 1840s, and early 1850s. Upon disbanding his partisan detachment in late 1829, Liprandi remained in military service for several more years, providing intelligence for P.D. Kiselev. In October 1829, the latter was appointed the head of the Russian provisional administration in Moldavia and Wallachia with the task of supervising the elaboration of the organic statutes for these principalities and carrying out the comprehensive reform of local administration.[79] Liprandi's reports to Kiselev helped the latter cope with the significant opposition of the Moldavian boyars, some of whom were influenced by the July Revolution and the Polish Uprising.[80] Upon retirement from military service with the rank of major general in 1832, Liprandi continued to monitor the situation in the principalities, which, after the completion of Kiselev's mission and the evacuation of the Russian troops in 1834, became exposed to the "subversive" influence of Western European consuls and travellers.[81]

One of the agents of "subversion" was Saint-Marc Girardin, a Sorbonne professor of literature, whom Liprandi met in Moldavia in 1836.[82] According to Liprandi, Girardin exercised a "pernicious influence" upon the younger people in the principalities, "enticing them into the realm of Utopia" and "sowing the idea of acquiring independence through creation of a Dacian Kingdom."[83] In his *Voyage à Constantinople par le Danube* (1836), portions of which Liprandi personally copied from the *Journal des débats*, the French writer expressed the "interest of the whole of Europe" that "the new peoples of Serbia, Wallachia, and Moldavia are born for civilization" and "enter in the political balance of Europe." Some time ago, wrote Girardin, "one of those audacious and savage spirits, a perfect child of old Russia, Suvorov, in his campaigns against France" was able to conceive a plan for mobilizing the peoples of Bulgaria, Bosnia, Serbia, and Hungary "to precipitate upon France all the Slavic hordes docile to the command of a Slavic general." According to the French writer, "In 1798 this was possible [because] the politics of the Russian name was deeply embedded in these countries; today this is less likely and will become impossible when civilization and commerce convert these peoples to the spirit of Western Europe."[84]

The events of 1848 in Moldavia and Wallachia confirmed Girardin's analysis and demonstrated that the political and intellectual development of the principalities had indeed become synchronized with that of Western Europe. Three months after the outbreak of the revolution in France and Central Europe, the French-educated Wallachian intellectuals toppled the pro-Russian prince Gheorghe Bibescu, proclaimed national self-determination for the Romanians living under Ottoman, Russian, and Austrian rule, and denounced the regime of the Russian protectorate over the principalities consolidated by the Peace of Adrianople in 1829. The Wallachian revolutionaries confirmed their anti-Russian sentiments by publicly burning a copy of the organic statute shortly before their government was dispersed by Ottoman troops, who had occupied Bucharest on the tsar's invitation.[85] By that time, Liprandi was busy fighting political subversion in Russia itself: after almost a decade in retirement, he re-entered into state service as an official of the Russian Ministry of the Interior. His most important accomplishment as a government spy was the discovery of the Petrashevtsy conspiracy in 1849, which nearly cost the young Dostoyevsky his life, alongside a score of other Russian followers of Charles Fourier.[86]

Liprandi fully shared Girardin's appreciation of the importance of the struggle between Russia and Western Europe for the minds of the Balkan peoples, just as he recognized the role of religious and linguistic ties with them as Russia's only weapon in this struggle. Although pan-Slavic ideas had entered Russian literature in the late eighteenth century, during the 1830s and the 1840s they still did not constitute a systematic and well-articulated ideology.[87] Moreover, the Slavic dimension of "the Springtime of Nations" – the First Slavic Congress, convened in Prague in June 1848 – had rendered pan-Slavism ideologically suspect in the eyes of Nicholas I. For this reason, the Russian officials could articulate their pan-Slavic sentiments only in private, as did the Moscow University professor M.P. Pogodin in a letter to the future tsar Alexander II, or incognito, as did the Russian diplomat and poet Fedor Tiutchev in a series of French publications in the European press.[88] Nevertheless, the growing currency of these ideas among educated Russians on the eve of the Crimean War is undeniable, as is their interest in the Southern Slavs.

Like pan-Slavic sentiments, accounts of Southern Slavs were hardly a novelty in Russian literature by the middle decades of the nineteenth century.[89] Nevertheless, the war of 1828–9 and the first crossing of the Balkans did represent a new stage in the Russian discovery of the Balkans inasmuch as it helped refocus the attention of Russian writers and readers from the peoples who populated the more peripheral territories of Turkey-in-Europe to those who lived in its less accessible interior regions. In this manner, the earlier interest of educated Russians in the Serbs and the Montenegrins came to be supplemented by their interest in the Bulgarians.[90] And while such authors of this period as Iu.I. Venelin and A.F. Veltman explored the early history of the Bulgarians and Russian-Bulgarian ties,[91] Liprandi was the first to emphasize the importance of the Bulgarians of the interior Balkan regions from a military-strategic point of view.

Liprandi and the Crimean War

The outbreak of the Crimean War occasioned Liprandi's last and most significant attempt to place his knowledge of European Turkey at the disposal of the Russian command. In January 1854, he composed a confidential manuscript containing general considerations on the war theatre, ethnographical and military-statistical surveys of different parts of European Turkey, and a variety of strategic, tactical, and logistical recommendations. Composed of twelve chapters of uneven length, the manuscript incorporated portions of Liprandi's "Lexicon" as well as of various memoranda that he had written in the late 1820s and early 1830s. As was the case with his "Lexicon," Liprandi viewed his manuscript as containing confidential information, and it was only decades later that he considered it possible to publish it as a series of military, historical, statistical, and ethnographic notes.

Parts 1, 5, and 6 of the manuscript discussed the climatic and epidemiological challenges of the war theatre, identified particularly unwholesome areas, and described hygienic measures that could neutralize their pernicious effects. Parts 2 and 3 addressed the peculiarities of the Ottoman way of war and emphasized the importance of using volunteer detachments.[92] Part 4 stressed both the necessity of collecting military-strategic information on European Turkey and the difficulty of doing this in practice. Part 7 provided a brief overview of the means of provisioning that the Russian army could expect to find in the region.[93] Part 9 argued for the necessity of collecting military intelligence on both sides of the Danube by means of a specially established foreign military police.[94] Part 10 offered an overview of the present theatre of military operations and the possible assistance that the Russian army could receive in Bulgaria.[95] Part 11 treated in greater detail the food and foraging that the Russians could obtain in Bulgaria if they "respected the local conditions."[96] Part 12 contained Liprandi's remarks on military communications, hospitals, and means of transportation.[97]

The most interesting section of Liprandi's manuscript in the present context is part 8, entitled "Brief Overview of the Ethnographic, Political, Moral, and Military State of the Christian Provinces of European Turkey." The "Overview" represented the largest portion of Liprandi's manuscript and was further subdivided into sections on the Danubian principalities, Bosnia, Albania, Rumelia, Thessaly, Macedonia, and Bulgaria.[98] The survey of Bulgaria was by far the most detailed and offered a wealth of information on Muslim-Christian relations in the prospective war theatre. It began with a description of "geographical Bulgaria," defined on all contemporary European and Russian maps as the territory between the Danube, the Black Sea, the Balkan Mountains, and the eastern borders of Serbia along the Timok River. Despite its name, the country was only partially Bulgarian and included considerable numbers of Turks and Tatars in addition to Russian and Ukrainian Cossacks, Greeks, Jews, Armenians, Roma, and Romanians. According to Liprandi, the local Muslim population nearly equalled the Christians, and even if the Bulgarians were slightly more numerous than the Turks, the former "would always be dependent upon [the latter], because the Muslim population is armed and concentrated" and amounted to two-thirds of the inhabitants of the towns.[99] Moreover, all non-Bulgarian Christians, with the possible exception of the Romanians, had a stake in the continuation of the Ottoman dominance and were thus likely to take the side of the Turks in the event of a conflict. According to Liprandi, all these factors gave Danubian Bulgaria the aspect of a "large, fortified barracks," in which the Muslims, even if they were somewhat less numerous than the Christians, were in command by virtue of being armed and concentrated in the cities and strategically located rural areas.[100]

Liprandi went beyond the discussion of the ethnic and religious composition of the local population and paid attention to the moral qualities and political attitudes of different population groups. He argued that the Turks of Danubian Bulgaria were unparalleled in their bellicosity and numerousness among of all their co-nationals in European Turkey and, as guerilla fighters, had systematically disrupted the communications of the Russian armies operating on the right side of the Danube during the wars of 1806–12 and 1828–9.[101] Similarly, the Turks who had come to the Vidin area from Serbia after the uprising were distinguished from the rest of the Muslim population by being "well-off, well-armed, and brave."[102] Although the Turks of Deliorman and Vidin on occasion defied the Porte's authority, this potential advantage from the point of view of the invaders hardly outweighed the threat that they could constitute in the rear of the Russian army.

Liprandi pointed out, as he had done in his 1841 review of the war theatre, that the significant presence of Muslims and other ethnicities had an adverse effect upon the moral qualities and political attitudes of the Danubian Bulgarians. The latter, according to Liprandi, were often "drunk, acrimonious, unfaithful, always ready for insolent disobedience and robbery." The heavy Muslim presence infringed upon their religious freedom to a greater extent than was the case for the Christians in other parts of European Turkey, and yet unrestrained trade and low taxes had reconciled them to the injustices of the Ottoman town notables (*ayans*). If anything, the devastating Russian-Ottoman wars, during which they had resettled away from the areas of operation of the Russian armies either on the order of the Ottoman commanders or by their own decision, had made the Danubian Bulgarians "hostile to the Russians."[103]

The distinction between geographical and "ethnographic Bulgaria" represented the greatest novelty of Liprandi's 1854 "Overview," as compared to both contemporary geographical literature and his own survey of the war theatre composed in 1841. Whereas geographical Bulgaria was in some respects a misnomer, Liprandi's "ethnographic Bulgaria," located to the south of the Balkans, was a country that lacked a proper name. Liprandi defined it as a triangle with its base in Tyrnovo, Sofia, or even Nish and its tip near Serres in Macedonia. According to Liprandi, this territory represented "the core of the Bulgarian nation," where Bulgarians were four times as numerous as in Danubian Bulgaria, lived segregated from the Turks, and had made the latter respect them by means of repeated uprisings. The almost exclusively urban Turkish population in this region did not exceed 100,000, "and there were entire districts in which there was not a single Turk."[104]

Within "ethnographic Bulgaria," Liprandi distinguished between "Mountainous Bulgaria" (*Nagornaia Bolgariia*), with its centre at Sofia; "Transmountainous" (*Zagorè*) Bulgaria, with its centre in Philippopolis; and Macedonian Bulgaria, with its centre at Serres.[105] In addition, a considerable (and often predominant) Bulgarian population was found along the southern slopes of the eastern part of the Balkans, the valley of Maritsa from Philippopolis to Adrianople and beyond, and in Macedonia and Thessaly to the south, where, in Liprandi's estimation, the Bulgarians were at least as numerous as the Greeks. As a result, Bulgaria emerged in Liprandi's description as a plant whose branches extended north, east, and south from its core in Mountainous Bulgaria.[106] According to the Russian author, the overall number of Bulgarians exceeded 5.5 million and was constantly growing. By contrast, the number of Ottomans was steadily declining due to the internal strife that had enveloped the Ottoman Empire since the late eighteenth century and the recurrent epidemics of plague that had affected the Ottomans much more than they had their Bulgarian subjects.[107]

Liprandi argued that despite five centuries of Ottoman rule, the inhabitants of Mountainous Bulgaria had not lost their original qualities and enjoyed a degree of freedom that was unparalleled among their co-nationals along the Danube and in eastern Bulgaria, or among other Christians in European Turkey. Liprandi attributed this freedom to the proliferation of *hajduks*, who were ready to avenge any wrongdoings committed against their families. In contrast to other military authors, who had earlier presented the Bulgarian *hajduks* as "inhuman bandits," Liprandi portrayed them as defenders of the commoners against all sorts of social injustices on the part of the Muslims or their Greek and Armenian collaborators. This made the Bulgarian *hajduks* different from their Albanian, Bosnian, Serbian, and Greek counterparts, who, in Liprandi's opinion, were more or less common highway robbers.[108] Liprandi estimated the number of Bulgarian *hajduks* at 50,000 and called them "the military force of Bulgaria" and "the representatives of the people," who alone could be used to "unite [the Bulgarians] and incite their sympathies."[109]

At the same time, Liprandi did not overestimate the readiness of the Bulgarians for a national revolt and argued that it was "rather difficult to incite in them the general sentiment of nationhood." According to him, Bulgarians of different regions had their own particular interests, which left their attachments to family life, agriculture, horticulture, and livestock as their only common denominators.[110] Although the environs of Nish, Sofia, and Philippopolis had witnessed mass uprisings of the population, these movements were provoked by the oppressions of local pashas and the incitements of the Serbs, rather than national self-consciousness. The Bulgarians had remained largely passive during the national liberation struggles of the Serbs and the Greeks (apart from several notable Bulgarian *hajduks*), while the aborted uprising of 1838 at Tyrnovo, the movement at Sar Kioi in 1839, and the Nish uprising of 1841 had remained local movements against the rapaciousness of the pashas, which had proclaimed loyalty to the sultan and had not manifested "any desire for liberation from the yoke of the infidels."[111]

Liprandi explained the birth of nationalist sentiment among the Bulgarians as the result of changes in their religious organization, which had been under the control of Phanariote Greeks for centuries.[112] Dominated by the Greek hierarchs, the ignorant and corrupted Bulgarian parish priests not only failed to instil a sense of nationhood among the people, but in fact restrained it from any moves towards independence.[113] Liprandi viewed with greater optimism the proliferation of popular schools, the first of which was established in Gabrovo in 1834 by the Bulgarian expatriates to Russia N.S. Palauzov and V.E. Aprilov. However, the direction of educational policies remained uncertain in the context of competing Russian, Austrian, and Western influences. Although both Russia and Austria promoted monarchical principles among the Bulgarians, the latter also sought to spread Catholicism, building upon the earlier efforts of the Papacy, which had resulted in a sizable population of Catholics in Postrum district.[114]

Liprandi also wrote about the "utopian theories" propagated among the Bulgarians by the French authors Saint-Marc Girardin, Alphonse de Lamartine, Jérôme-Adolphe Blanqui, and Cyprien Robert, as well as the plans for Bulgarian autonomy on the model of Serbia or the Danubian principalities advocated by the British writers and travellers David Urquhart, Adolphus Slade, James Henry Skene, and Jane Webb Loudon. He also mentioned the visits of the French agents Eugène Perruchot de Longeville and Jules Berthemy to eastern Bulgaria and of their British counterparts to the south-western region in 1853.[115] According to Liprandi, "Western propaganda" was attempting to "sow dissent between Bulgarians and the heads of their family" (i.e., the Russians) as well as to "destroy their present way of life to throw [Bulgarians] into the chaos of political turmoil."[116]

Although Liprandi endowed trans-Balkan Bulgaria with a central role in any Russian effort to incite small war in European Turkey, other Ottoman provinces could also play a role in this respect. Most educated Russians in the mid-nineteenth century would think of Serbia in this respect, mindful as they were of the First Serbian Uprising (1804–13) under the leadership of Karageorge Petrović, which had occasioned joint Russian-Serbian action against the Ottomans during the Russian-Ottoman war of 1806–12. By contrast, Liprandi saw in Serbia little potential for an anti-Ottoman movement. He argued that Serbia was no longer what it used to be in the early nineteenth century, when it was filled with the *hajduks,* who were the best Serbian leaders. Once surrounded by impassable woods, Serbia was now more accessible by virtue of new roads and bridges. In the meantime, the Serbs fell out of the habit of using weapons, turned into more or less prosperous peasants, and devoted themselves to politicking in their national assembly (the Skupshchina).[117]

Liprandi found greater potential for an anti-Ottoman struggle in Bosnia and Albania. Although the population of Bosnia was divided between the Orthodox (a diminishing majority), the Muslims, and the Catholics (both growing minorities), Liprandi argued that the Orthodox had converted to Islam to secure their land titles rather than out of conviction. The converts retained family ties with the Orthodox, kept their Slavic names, and continued to venerate Orthodox saints. Accordingly, the Muslims of other regions of Turkey viewed their Bosnian counterparts as "heretics and dissenters" who "failed to respect even the most important rules of Islam."[118] More populous than Serbia and covered by castles, forts, and towers, Bosnia presented a major complication not only to the Hungarians and Austrians, but even to the Ottoman government itself, which "still does not have an unconditional dominance over the country."[119]

To prove his point, Liprandi mentioned the difficulty that Mahmud II encountered in convincing the inhabitants of Sarajevo to accept the Ottoman governor, whose predecessor they had chased out decades previously. Having had the greatest number of co-nationals enrolled as janissaries, the Bosnians could not have been happy about the destruction of the janissary corps in 1826 and remained largely uninvolved in the Russian-Ottoman war of 1828–9.[120] While no fewer than 100,000 "brave, valiant, glory-seeking, and bloodthirsty" Bosnian warriors were ready to fight in their own land, hardly more than 10,000 could be mobilized by the Ottoman government, in Liprandi's estimation, and even these "were likely to disperse at the first opportunity."[121] At the same time, some Bosnians, both Orthodox and Muslim, did join Liprandi's volunteer detachment in 1828–9, which led him to conclude that "out of all the provinces of the Ottoman Empire populated by the Muslims, Bosnia alone could easily be moved not only to refuse support to the Ottoman army, but even to act directly against the Porte." Liprandi argued that if one were to "acknowledge the rights of the Bosnians, which they vindicate with weapons in arms before the sultan, they would easily fall away from the Porte." At the same time, Liprandi warned against using the Greeks or Serbs to influence the Bosnians, since the Bosnians mistrusted or hated them.[122]

Liprandi argued that the Russians could achieve the same effect in Albania, albeit with greater difficulty. Although many Albanians were Muslims, Liprandi attributed their conversion to material interests (preservation of land titles and tax exceptions) and to their "inborn desire to oppress their neighbours."[123] Viewed as heretics by the stricter followers of Islam, Albanian Muslims (both Sunni and Shia) shared with their Orthodox and Catholic counterparts a deep hatred of the Osmanli.[124] Liprandi further noted that, as an age-old nation of mercenaries, Albanians of all confessions were ready to fight against their co-religionists under the command of the infidels.[125] As in Bosnia, the Porte's control in Albania remained highly limited and extended only to the valleys, while the inhabitants of the mountains "have been at war with the Ottomans for four centuries" and "served the pashas as independent mercenaries rather than as their subjects."[126] Liprandi also noted that, similarly to the Bosnians, Albanians remained largely uninvolved in the Russian-Ottoman war of 1828–9.[127]

Liprandi recognized that by virtue of its presence on the Ionian Islands, Britain had acquired the ability to mobilize the Albanians against the Russians. At the same time, "if the Greeks began to move," Liprandi expected the Albanians to hurry home and clash with them (as they had done many times in the past) so that no one would be able to retain them in the Ottoman army on the Danube confronting the Russians.[128] The ability of other powers to manipulate the Albanians was even more limited, in Liprandi's opinion. He noted the failure of Napoleonic authorities in Illyria to acquire some influence upon the Catholic Albanians in the northern part of the country, while the death of Ali-Pasha of Ioannina ended whatever influence the French agents might have exercised in the south.[129] The Austrian efforts in this respect were even less successful. Liprandi pointed out that Southern Slavic and Turkish words referring to the Austrians remained terms of abuse, and was convinced that the Austrian attempt to occupy Albania was bound to have perilous consequences for the Austrian army. According to him, Russia could secretly contribute to such an outcome by influencing "some notable individuals in that country."[130]

Liprandi attributed the failure of George Castriot and Ali-Pasha to make Albania independent to lack of support on the part of the Orthodox Albanians, whom he wrongly considered to be more numerous than either their Catholic or their Muslims counterparts. Liprandi also believed that the majority of Albanians were Slavs and argued that in order to be successful, the centuries-long struggle of Albanians for independence required the awakening of both Slavdom and Orthodoxy from their slumber. When awoken, these "two powerful engines of the country" would help to overcome the divisive effects of "the treacherous policy of the Papacy, Venice, Naples, England, France, and Austria" and would "fuse the Albanians into one." Assisted by the Bosnian *uskoks*, the Bulgarian *hajduks*, and the Thessalian *klephts*, Albania, in Liprandi's representation, would "join the Orthodox Slavic family."[131]

Liprandi's extensive ethnographic and military-statistical survey of European Turkey served as an addendum to an overview of the war theatre that he submitted to the Russian commander on the Danube, M.D. Gorchakov, in January 1854. The extent to which the latter was influenced by Liprandi's ideas will be examined in the next chapter. Here, it is necessary to stress that his case illustrates the two-way connection between the experience of the Russian-Ottoman wars and systematic military-statistical knowledge. Liprandi was one of those military Orientalists who built their expertise through both extensive reading of the available literature and direct personal involvement in intelligence gathering and military operations in European Turkey. The experience of organizing and leading the detachment of Balkan Christian partisans became the foundation of his expertise on the region, which he tried to articulate in a series of military-statistical descriptions and memoranda intended to inform the strategy and actions of the Russian army in its next confrontation with the Ottoman Empire.

The overview of the provinces of European Turkey that Liprandi placed at the disposal of the Russian command in early 1854 contained much more detailed information on the numbers, way of life, political attitudes, and military qualities of the Balkan peoples than was available to Russian commanders in the war of 1828–9, let alone earlier. Few people in the Russian army at mid-century placed a greater emphasis on the importance of the population factor in the wars with the Ottoman Empire. Similarly, few people attributed a greater importance to partisan action for relations between the army and the local inhabitants, whether Christian or Muslim. At the same time, for Liprandi, as for other Russian military men of the Napoleonic and post-Napoleonic periods, partisan warfare was not synonymous with a "people's war." Instead, Liprandi viewed partisan action rooted in sound military-statistical knowledge of the region as a way of preventing a "people's war" by the Ottoman Muslims against the Russian army. Bearing in mind Liprandi's involvement with the Russian political police, one could say that partisan action for him represented a policing operation of sorts that was crucial to the successful outcome of the war.

Liprandi's emphasis on the importance of military-statistical study of the Balkan population and his conceptualization of partisan action as a form of policing in wartime conditions speak of the predicament experienced by the Russian military establishment in the middle decades of the nineteenth century. The Old Regime paradigm of warfare that left no place for "the people" clashed with a creeping realization of just how important "the people" could actually be in modern war. The first reaction of the conservative tsarist military to the emergent contours of future warfare consisted in identifying ways of preventing a "people's war." The choices and decisions of Nicholas I and his commanders during the Russian-Ottoman war of 1828–9, just like Liprandi's use of partisans to police the Deliorman forest in the summer and fall of 1829, constitute concrete manifestations of this conservative approach. However, what seemed to work in the late 1820s proved to be impracticable a quarter of a century later, which forced the most conservative of the Russian tsars and his military advisers to consider radically different solutions.

4 Russia and the Balkan Peoples during the Crimean War

The Crimean War represented the eruption of the tensions that had been building in relations between Russia and the Western European powers since the early 1830s.[1] After the surrender of Adrianople to the Russian army in August 1829, the British and French ambassadors in Constantinople could do little but express their fear that the empire of the sultan would "cease to exist" should the Russian army march further on the Ottoman capital.[2] Less than four years later, the Russians once again surprised Great Britain and other European powers when the Russian Black Sea Fleet carried the Russian troops to the shores of the Bosphorus in response to the last-minute appeal of Mehmed II for help against the army of his rebellious vassal Muhammed Ali, which camped at Bursa after defeating the sultan's army in Syria and Asia Minor. Russia's temporary predominance in Constantinople was sealed by the treaty of Unkiar Iskelessi of 1833, which for the following eight years obliged the Porte to close the straits to the warships of any other country in case of war between them and Russia.

Apprehensive of Russia's supposed threat to their communications with India, the British worked hard to undermine the Russian position in Constantinople and essentially achieved this goal by the end of the 1830s, when the death of Mahmud II and the succession of his young son Abdul-Mejid I caused another crisis in relations between the Porte and Muhammed Ali. In 1841, the London Straits Convention re-established the Porte's traditional right to close the straits to the warships of all nations. The Ottoman government embarked on a new round of westernizing reforms known as the Tanzimat (or Reorganization) with the moral support of Britain and France. After a period of support for Muhammed Ali against the Porte, which caused its diplomatic isolation, France rallied behind the British position on the Eastern Question, which better corresponded to the general Franco-British rapprochement made possible by the July Revolution of 1830.

This was the context in which the Franco-Russian conflict erupted around the Holy Places. Although, by the early 1850s, the July Monarchy had given way to the regime of Louis Bonaparte, the nephew of Britain's greatest enemy was very far from resuming the old struggle. Louis Bonaparte's desire to win French Catholic votes in order to become Napoleon III led him to support the Catholic monks in their clashes with the Greek Orthodox clergy for control of the Holy Places. Presented with these competing claims, which were supported, respectively, by France and Russia, the Porte decreed in favour of the former at the end of 1852. Nicholas I responded by dispatching his minister of the navy and personal friend, A.S. Menshikov, on an extraordinary mission to Constantinople with the task of restoring the rights of Russia's Orthodox co-religionists and extracting from the Porte a definitive guarantee thereof in the form of a convention. Menshikov succeeded in the first part of his task, but failed in the second. Encouraged by the British ambassador, Lord Stratford de Radcliffe, the Porte refused to sign a convention, which amounted to an official recognition of the Russian protectorate over the entire Greek Orthodox *millet* of the Ottoman Empire. Menshikov's subsequent departure from Constantinople signalled an official break in Russian-Ottoman relations and made a new war imminent.

On 3 July 1853, Nicholas I (see figure 4.1) sent his troops into Moldavia and Wallachia in an attempt to force the Porte to accept the demands that he had earlier presented through Menshikov.[3] However, the Ottoman government had become quite accustomed to the temporary loss of the principalities to the Russian armies and, at the same time, could reasonably expect to regain them after the end of hostilities, as had indeed happened under the conditions of each previous Russian-Ottoman treaty. This is why the entry of the Russian troops into Moldavia and Wallachia was patently insufficient to force upon the Ottoman government as great a concession as the recognition of Russian protectorate over the entire Greek Orthodox *millet*. Instead, the occupation of the principalities only served to provide the Porte, and later the governments of France and Britain, with a pretext for the declaration of war on Russia.[4]

As a bargaining strategy, therefore, the tsar's decision to occupy Moldavia and Wallachia was a total failure. Nor was this move successful from the military-strategic point of view after the outbreak of hostilities between Russia and the Ottoman Empire in October 1853. Constrained by Nicholas I's unwillingness to precipitate the collapse of the Ottoman Empire (which he considered imminent), the limited Russian force that occupied the principalities maintained a passive defensive position along the insalubrious marshy left bank of the Danube until March 1854. Lack of initiative on the part of the commander-in-chief, M.D. Gorchakov, and his subordinate generals resulted in the Russians' suffering two reversals from the Ottoman forces at Oltenița and Cetatea, before the army finally crossed the Danube in order to lay siege to Silistria (but ultimately failed to capture the fortress).[5]

The passivity of the Russian army on the Danube contrasted with the bold action of the Russian Black Sea Fleet under Admiral P.S. Nakhimov, which

Figure 4.1. Portrait of Nicholas I by Georg von Bothmann, 1850s
Source: Georg von Bothmann, *Portrait of Emperor Nicholas I (1796–1855)*, 1850s, oil on canvas, 84.7 × 67 cm, Russian Art and Culture, Hermitage Museum, St. Petersburg, Russia. Via Wikimedia Commons.

destroyed the Ottoman fleet at Sinope in late November 1853. The Russian naval victory spurred anti-Russian sentiment in Britain and France and motivated the governments of these countries to support the Ottoman Empire. After Nicholas I rejected the Franco-British demand to evacuate the principalities, London and Paris declared war on Russia in March 1854. What began as yet another Russian-Ottoman war turned into a broader conflict between Russia and a European coalition that had important consequences for international relations.[6] For the first time in the history of the Eastern Question, the great powers that had vied for influence over the embattled Ottoman Empire actually went to war with each other in order to settle their differences. The alliance of the two leading Christian nations to protect the domains of the Ottoman sultan against the encroachment of the Russian tsar contrasted with the joint Anglo-Franco-Russian diplomatic intervention on behalf of the Greeks during the 1820s.

The Franco-British landing at Varna, as well as the Austrian ultimatum, forced the Russians to lift the siege of Silistria in June 1854 and evacuate the principalities by the end of the summer of 1854. In September 1854, the Western allies bombarded Odessa, landed at Evpatoria in the Crimea, defeated Menshikov's army in the battle of Alma, and besieged Sebastopol, Russia's main naval base on the Black Sea. Taking advantage of the slow progress of the Franco-British troops after Alma, the Russians managed to throw improvised fortifications around the city, blocked the harbour by sinking the outdated sailing ships of the line, and held out for ten months under massive allied bombardment. Their heroic defence contrasted with the indecisive actions of the main Russian forces under Menshikov's command, which failed to relieve Sebastopol on three occasions. The siege and capture of Sebastopol in August 1855 was accompanied by British bombardment of other Russian ports in the Black Sea, the Baltic, and the Pacific. However, none of these proved decisive, and only the Austrian threat to join the Western coalition forced St. Petersburg to sue for peace, which was concluded in March 1856 in Paris.

The Crimean War was one of the first global wars. While the Crimean peninsula was indisputably its main theatre, it also witnessed action in the Baltic sea, the Arctic, and the Pacific, not to mention the already customary Transcaucasia, where the Russians were overall the most successful. It was also the first modern war: it spelled the end of the age of sail, demonstrated the superiority of French and British rifles over the smoothbore Russian muskets, and became the first major conflict to be telegraphed and photographed.[7] However, for the present study, the most important aspect of the Crimean War was the Danubian campaign of 1853–4 and, specifically, the place of the Balkan population in the plans of Nicholas I and his commanders. This chapter examines the tsar's perspectives on the Ottoman Empire on the eve of the war, his growing openness to the idea of mobilizing the Balkan Christians, and the half-hearted attempts to implement this idea in the winter and spring of 1853–4.

The Reports of Russian Military Agents in Constantinople on the Eve of the War

The tsar's choice of an aggressive stance towards the Ottoman Empire was informed by the reports of his military agents in Constantinople. Their assessment of Ottoman military potential had undergone a certain evolution since the time of F.F. Berg's mission in 1826–7. Despite his criticism of the reforms of Mahmud II, Berg did not exclude the possibility, however slim, of Turkey's successful military modernization. The same applied to those agents of Nicholas I who visited Constantinople in the context of the temporary Russia-Ottoman rapprochement in the early 1830s. At the time of Mahmud II's confrontation with his Egyptian vassal, Muhammed Ali, the tsar positioned himself as the saviour of the Ottoman Empire and his military envoy, N.N. Muraviev (Karskii), enjoyed being a model to follow for the Ottoman officers.[8] However, the death of Mahmud II and the beginning of the Tanzimat period with the ascent of his less charismatic son, Abdul-Mejid I, made Great Britain and France rather than Russia a reference point for the Ottoman military reforms. Turkey's reorientation towards Europe's two liberal monarchies manifested, among other things, in the Porte's decision to offer political asylum to Polish and Hungarian political émigrés in the 1840s.[9] In view of Nicholas I's efforts to suppress the revolutionary movements in Eastern Europe, this action of the Ottoman government could only deepen the negative attitude of the tsar's agents towards the Tanzimat reforms, which were otherwise acclaimed by the British and French diplomats and commentators.

With time, the earlier focus of the Russian observers on the personality of the sultan and the actions of his government gave way to their interest in the political attitudes of his Ottoman subjects. Particularly remarkable in this respect was the attention given by the Nicholaevan agents to the Muslim population of the Ottoman Empire. On the eve of the Russian-Ottoman war of 1828–9, the reports of Berg apprised the tsar and his commanders of the disconcerting impact of Mahmud II's destruction of the janissary corps upon Rumelian Muslims. This theme was developed after the war by M.P. Vronchenko in his *Review of the Present State of Asia Minor* (1839–40). Vronchenko pointed out that with the destruction of the janissaries, "the population has lost the last support against the rapaciousness of the local administration, without gaining a new one in the form of justice and solicitude from the supreme government."[10]

The European-style army created by Mahmud II and Abdul-Majid I in place of the traditional military establishment was likewise unpopular with the Ottoman Muslims. The Russian military agents in Constantinople in the late 1840s and the early 1850s stressed above all the alienating impact of conscription. Thus, the author of a military survey of the Ottoman Empire composed in 1847 recognized the European inspiration behind the new system that presupposed a five-year service on active duty for the able-bodied Muslims, whereupon they formed the reserve (*redif*) that could be mobilized in wartime.[11] However, according to the author of the survey, the parallels between the new Ottoman militia and the European army reserves were superficial:

> One cannot imagine that some semi-savage Kurd, Bedouin, Turcoman, or unbridled [*neobuzdannyi*] Albanian or Bosnian could become true soldiers in the European sense of the term or be compared to the Prussian Landwehr. The latter requires the development of a sense of duty in the mass of the people, attachment to the fatherland, without which the militia will be a chaotic crowd that is difficult to keep in subordination. It will take a complete political and civil revolution [*perevorot*] for Turkey to fulfil this condition.[12]

According to the "Review," one could find in the Ottoman Empire "entire tribes consisting of armed warriors who are always ready to fight." Besides the above-mentioned groups, the review mentioned in this category Serbs, Bedouins, Lazes, Druzes, and Maronites. At the same time, the author stressed that the bellicosity of their spirit and national character did not render these populations fit to serve in a regular army. While Bosnians, Turcomans, and *arnauts* "were ready to serve only as mercenaries," the rest "would fight only on their own territories for their independence or under the influence of tribal hostility" and were more likely to turn against the Ottomans than join them. The experience of the previous confrontations with Russia demonstrated that the Ottoman government could not count on the cooperation of the Bulgarians in a European war, or of the Armenians in an Asian one.[13] The military reserves available to the Ottoman government thereby became limited to the native Turks. Although the author recognized the fitness of the Turks for military service, as well as their endurance and courage, he also argued that the latter "was not real valour instilled by a sense of honour and homeland, but rather the fury of fanaticism resulting from the belief in fate," which made them likely to flee after their first attack had been repulsed.[14]

The Russian agent in Constantinople in the early 1850s, K.I. Osten-Sacken, continued this critical analysis of Ottoman military organization and its relation to the population of the empire. According to Osten-Sacken, the general state of the Ottoman army reflected "the false direction that the reforms of Mahmud II had taken," whereby "the imitation of European education" boiled down to "drunkenness and disrespect for the ancient canons of Islamism." Like Berg before him, Osten-Sacken argued that the destruction of the janissaries had deprived the Ottoman state of its original source of strength. Unlike Berg, he had no doubts about the ultimate failure of the sultans' efforts to replace the traditional Ottoman military organization with a new European system. While in the capital the efforts of the Western instructors succeeded in giving the Ottoman army a more or less regular shape, in the Asian provinces the regiments acquired only the elements of the manual of rifle and marching step from those who had earlier served in the capital regiments. Incapable of stopping "even the smallest force," the Asian army, in the words of Osten-Sacken represented "chaotic and useless regiments of vagabonds with the worst intentions, in which the imitation of the European uniform passes for the knowledge of the military profession."[15]

The Russian agent stressed that the conscription to the new regular army came to weigh as a great burden upon the Ottoman Muslims. "It made them leave the calm and careless life and renounce their habits, including their greatest pleasure – complete inactivity – in order to undertake the troubles of the military profession."[16] According to Osten-Sacken, the people were repulsed by the life in the barracks, the European-style military drill, and the mistreatment of soldiers in the regiments, which were stationed away from the capital. He argued that the recruitment system caused resistance everywhere it was introduced and pointed to the Muslim uprisings in Bosnia and Herzegovina as well as to the difficulties of extending subscription to Syria.

The weakness of the population base aggravated the situation even further. The Russian agent questioned the accuracy of the official Ottoman statistic that suggested that the population of the Ottoman Empire amounted to 35.2 million and argued that the actual figure might have been as low as 18 million, of which Muslims amounted to one-half.[17] With recruitment numbers in Rumelia in decline, Osten-Sacken estimated the real strength of the Ottoman reserve (*redif*) at only 50,000 people instead of the official figure of 140,000.[18] The only way to correct this situation was to impose the military duty upon Christians, which the Ottoman government considered many times. However, this would mean liberating them from the capitation tax (*harac*), a major source of revenue that the sorry state of the Ottoman finances did not allow it to sacrifice. Nor was this the only inconvenience that explained the hesitancy of the government to incorporate Christians of all ranks into the army. According to Osten-Sacken, "Muslim fanaticism would not tolerate that Turks and *reayas* be treated as equals and that they perform a service in common, that they inhabit the same barracks, that the Christians be promoted together with the Turks and command the latter."[19]

Osten-Sacken argued that the military value of the Ottoman Empire did not have anything to do with the efforts of the sultans to create a European-style army. Inasmuch as Ottoman Turkey was still an entity to be reckoned with, this was solely on account of "the richness of the land, the remnants of erstwhile bellicosity, and the possibility of *levée en masse*."[20] The Russian agent found the population of the Ottoman Empire composed of "people of strong constitution, who were perfectly capable of performing military service," but who were totally alienated by government policies. In the eventuality of war, it was thus highly important for the Russian government to play on this disposition of the Ottoman Muslims. According to Osten-Sacken, the latter "[knew] from hearsay about the good treatment of the local population by the Russian armies in 1829," so that in the end not only the Christians but also the Muslims were "well disposed" towards the Russians.[21] The Russian agent even claimed that he could frequently hear in private conversations expressions of desire to be under of the authority of the "Moscov *reaya*" as soon as possible, before the Ottoman government robbed them of everything. More realistically, Osten-Sacken suggested paying special attention to the numerous nomads of Asiatic Turkey, who, with their rebellious attitude towards the Ottoman government, could provide the Russian army with "resources that could not be expected anywhere else."[22]

Compared to the reports of Berg of the late 1820s, those of Osten-Sacken demonstrate a significant change of perspective. Berg's somewhat contradictory description of the policies of Mahmud II reflected the ambiguous attitudes of the broader Russian educated public towards the sultan who managed to make Ottoman westernization irreversible. A ruler who heroically overcame the resistance of fanatical traditionalism was undoubtedly a familiar figure for the post-Petrine Russian military men, yet it contradicted the already established perception of Ottoman Turkey as an Oriental society that was fundamentally inimical to Western models of political and military organization.[23] With the death of Mahmud II in 1839 and the end of Russian-Ottoman rapprochement, the Russian military observers of the Ottoman Empire refocused their attention from the policies of the government to the responses of the Ottoman subjects to westernization. The discovery of the Muslim population and its supposedly negative attitude towards the Tanzimat served as proof of the incompatibility of traditional Turkey with the Western borrowings. In this respect, the reports of Osten-Sacken on the eve of the Crimean War complete the Orientalization of the Ottoman Empire that began in the early decades of the nineteenth century.

Nicholas I and the Idea of Raising Russia's Orthodox Co-religionists

Reassured by these reports, Nicholas I was considering the possibility of a new war as early as January 1853 and discussed different military options with both Menshikov and Field Marshal I.F. Paskevich. The tsar's initial idea consisted in capturing the Bosphorus by means of a naval expedition akin to the one that took place in 1833, when Russia's Black Sea Squadron brought 10,000 soldiers for the protection of Constantinople against the army of the rebellious Egyptian pasha Muhammed Ali.[24] After Menshikov expressed his doubts about the success of such an operation,[25] the emperor considered the possibility of an amphibious assault against Varna and Burgas, which would provide the Russians with a foothold on the southern side of the Balkans. In the meantime, the Russian 4th Army Corps was to enter the principalities, cross the Danube at Girsov, blockade Silistria, and establish communication with the assault force in Varna and Burgas (see map 4.1).[26]

Map 4.1. *Outline Map of Turkey from the Time of the Crimean War* by J.M. Adye. 1860
Source: John Adye, *A Review of the Crimean War, to the Winter of 1854–5* (London: Hurst & Blackett, 1860), 32. Map lithography by J. Netherdrift. British Library, Digital Store 9077.f.46. Original held and digitized by the British Library. Via Wikimedia Commons/Flickr.

Paskevich expressed his reservations concerning the latter plan. He pointed to the difficulty of successfully neutralizing the Ottoman fortresses on the Lower Danube and taking Adrianople with anything less than three army corps. Back in 1829, he wrote, it was easier to take the old Ottoman capital, since "the entire military population of Turkey was against the sultan because of the destruction of the janissaries. It would suffice only to demonstrate that we sympathize with the janissaries and the cities would open their gates to us. Today, we do not know the population's attitude towards the sultan."[27] According to Paskevich, there were 30,000 armed inhabitants in both Adrianople and Krik Kilise. Should they offer resistance, even five Russian divisions would not suffice, particularly if the pashas of Bosnia and Dalmatia were to threaten the Russian right flank. Another precondition of success was the complete Russian control of the Black Sea (as was the case in 1828–9). Under the best possible circumstances, only one-third of the Russian army would be able to reach Constantinople. Even if it were successful in taking the Ottoman capital, the three Russian army corps would have to stay in European Turkey for three or four years before it would be possible to replace them even partially "by the formation of indigenous Christian tribes and their integration into our ranks." This made Paskevich wonder whether the remainder of the Russian army would be sufficiently numerous in the eventuality of a general European war.[28]

Instead, the field marshal suggested to limit the Russian actions to the occupation of Moldavia and Wallachia by a much smaller force of two or three divisions. The regular armed forces of the principalities created during the Russian occupation of 1828–34 were to serve as "a nucleus of the Christian militia of Turkey." Eventually, the volunteer battalions were to be attached to the Russian regiments as sharp shooters and irregular cavalry, "following the example of Wellington in Portugal in 1811 and Mikhelson in Serbia in 1807."[29] A veteran of the 1806–12 Russian-Ottoman war on the Danube, Paskevich, by his own admission, did not know how much influence Russia retained over the Balkan Christians. However, he believed that as long as "Muslim contempt towards the Christians" persisted, this influence would not disappear entirely, even though Russia repeatedly surrendered its co-religionists to the Ottomans, who punished them for pro-Russian sympathies.

Even if their attachment to Russia had waned, argued Paskevich, the Serbs and Bulgarians were bellicose by nature. There would always be people willing to join the anti-Ottoman struggle for the sake of revenge, due to personal grievances, or out of love of war.[30] Paskevich suggested attracting such people through their co-nationals already enrolled in the Moldavian and Wallachian militias. These volunteer companies and battalions would be placed under the command of the best Russian officers to make them steadier in battle. Once their strength reached 30,000, it would become clear that the Christians, who constituted two-thirds of the population of European Turkey, "could not fail to threaten the Muslim rule in Europe given an active support on our part."[31]

Paskevich's opinion must have convinced the tsar to confine himself to the occupation of Moldavia and Wallachia as a means of pressuring the Porte to recognize Russia as the protector of all its Orthodox Christian subjects.[32] Following the entry of Russian troops into the principalities in July 1853, the field marshal further developed his idea of Christian militias. In a memorandum submitted to the tsar in September, Paskevich argued that the readiness of the Christians to rebel against Ottoman rule was directly connected to the state of the Muslim population. According to Paskevich, "The greater the excitement of Muslim fanaticism, the easier it would be to convince the Christians to take up arms, if only for their own self-protection."[33] The field marshal suggested spreading proclamations among the population of the right bank of the Danube that would invite all Christians to join the volunteer detachments of their co-nationals in the principalities. These proclamations would need to stress "the insecure situation of the Christians given the exasperation of the Turks and the dangers threatening Christendom." Encouraged by generous remuneration and ammunition, the volunteers could form an army of 30,000 or 40,000, or even more, which would consist of "daring sharpshooters, who know the terrain and the local way of war." Employed in an intelligent way, this force would greatly help the Russian army, which would inevitably suffer losses from diseases and local climate.[34]

The field marshal's attention was fixed on the Lower Danube, where he suggested a crossing near Girsov with a subsequent attack on Varna. Mindful of the Ottoman habit of depopulating Danubian Bulgaria in the earlier Russian-Ottoman wars, Paskevich suggested establishing the army stores there to sustain the subsequent Russian crossing of the Balkans. In his plan, "the space from Bucharest to Girsov, Varna, Shumla, Silistria, and Rushchuk [had to] be the quadrant of our first actions," as was the case in 1828–9. At the same time, Paskevich advised against occupying the whole of Wallachia and argued that "although the Turks could invade Little Wallachia and plunder the Christians, we cannot defend them all." According to him, occupation of the entirety of Wallachia, including Little Wallachia, was a recurrent mistake that had been committed by all earlier Russian commanders from Munnich to Rumiantsev and Kamenskii in view of the limited Russian forces.[35]

Before the Ottoman declaration of war in October 1853, Paskevich fully shared the tsar's unwillingness to take offensive action in European Turkey, albeit for a different reason. Whereas Nicholas I did not want to provoke the collapse of the Ottoman Empire, the field marshal was primarily concerned with the attitude of the European powers. However successful the Russian offensive could be, it would only incur senseless casualties, argued Paskevich, since "Europe would not allow us to reap the fruits of our victories." By contrast, a defensive position adopted by Russia would not antagonize the European powers. Instead of direct military attack, Russia could employ "an even deadlier weapon against the Turkish Empire that no European power could contest, namely, our influence upon the Christian peoples of Turkey." Mindful of the tsar's legitimist principles, the field marshal argued that his proposed mobilization of the Ottoman Christians "had nothing to do with exciting the subjects to rebel against their ruler." According to Paskevich, the Christian inhabitants of the Ottoman Empire were not only subjects of the sultan, but also often "voiceless victim[s] of the fanaticism and whims of every vizier, pasha, and even of any *ayan*" so that the "white tsar" remained their last resort.[36]

The field marshal recognized that there was "nothing new" in his idea and that in every war with the Ottoman Empire, attempts had been made to attract Christian volunteers. In Paskevich's own admission, none of these attempts had brought Russia any advantage. Although the approach was fundamentally correct, a nucleus for an effective volunteer force had been lacking during the previous wars: "There were no instructors who could give the correct shape to a desperate, yet disorganized crowd." However, this time the situation was different, since the troops of Moldavia and Wallachia created under the provisional administration of P.D. Kiselev in 1829–34 "could become the nucleus of our Christian militias in Turkey." According to Paskevich, these militias would make it possible to limit the Russian troops on the Danube to one or two corps, which would minimize the losses that the Russian army had traditionally suffered through climate and disease. This would also enable Russia to keep the bulk of its army on the western frontiers.[37]

Although suppression of revolutionary movements at home and abroad had been Nicholas I's credo throughout his reign, Russia's evident diplomatic isolation in the fall of 1853 led him to change his traditionally negative attitude towards the anti-Ottoman movements of the Balkan peoples. In early November, the tsar suspected that the British, despite their ostensible support of the Porte, anticipated the collapse of Ottoman rule in Europe and sought to "lead the cause of emancipation of the European Christians."[38] To thwart these designs, Nicholas I considered declaring to all powers that "the moment has come to re-establish the independence of Christian nations who fell under the Ottoman yoke centuries ago." In this scenario, "Moldo-Wallachians, Serbs, Bulgarians, Bosnians, and Greeks would be governed by the rulers of their choice, elected among their co-nationals." An appeal to join Russia in her struggle would thereupon be addressed "not only to our Greek Orthodox co-religionists, but to all Christians under Muslim rule in Europe." The tsar expected, rather unrealistically, that these actions would "quickly change the attitude of the entire Christendom" and would make continued British support for the Ottomans impossible.[39] Nicholas I proposed to "sound out the disposition of the [Christian] provinces" of European Turkey by dispatching "intelligent individuals" who would "obtain as fast as possible exact data on the actual spirit of these provinces and the help that one could expect from them." In particular, the tsar intended to dispatch E.P. Kovalevskii to the Serbs and the Bosnians. Nicholas I also intended to call to St. Petersburg "a deputation of Moldavian and Wallachian notables selected among the most reasonable boyars and clergymen in order to communicate to them my intentions and secure their support for this project."[40]

Chancellor Nesselrode hurried to dampen the tsar's sudden surge of radicalism. According to him, the hope of resolving the crisis by diplomatic means was not yet entirely lost. In this situation, it was particularly inopportune to proclaim the independence of Balkan Christians, as it would confirm Europe's worst fears about Russia's designs with regard to Turkey. Having opposed the national emancipation of Poles, Hungarians, Italians, Caucasian highlanders, and "Daco-Romanians," how could Russia "contradict its professed doctrines and call on the European nations to support the insurrection of the Christian provinces of the Ottoman Empire?" What principles would Russia evoke if the sultan decided to follow suit and proclaim the independence of the Circassians and other Muslim peoples of Russia's Transcaucasian provinces?[41] As long as the Russian force on the Lower Danube was too small to render effective support to the Balkan Christian insurgents, the proposed proclamation would only make Russia's co-religionists vulnerable to Ottoman fury and atrocities and would expose Russia itself to "the most virulent recriminations." At the same time, Nesselrode expected the Christians to "rise up in large numbers" without Russian provocation, should Russia be forced to conduct "an all-out war" (*une guerre à outrance*) against Turkey in the spring of 1854. Once the uprising had flared up spontaneously, argued the chancellor, "it would be natural for us to consider it a matter of honour not to deliver our co-religionists to the brutal and bloody vengeance of the Muslims, whose yoke they had endured." By then, the proclamation of the independence of the Balkan Christians would no longer have a subversive character and would have become a statement of fact.[42]

Nicholas I never fully embraced the idea of a Christian insurrection. Thus, in the summer of 1853 the commander of the Russian troops in Moldavia and Wallachia, M.D. Gorchakov, requested 10,000 old muskets from the War Ministry in order to arm the Bulgarians in case of necessity, yet the tsar noted in the margins of his letter that he "did not want to incite an uprising."[43] In response to Gorchakov's reports on the progress of the Greek Etaireia in preparing an uprising in Thessaly and Epirus, the tsar wrote that these designs "stink of revolution, particularly since [Etaireia] wants to begin the insurrection against the wishes of the Greek king."[44] Whereas Gorchakov presented the Serbs as valiant fighters, Nicholas I confessed that he "did not have much faith in them since they have a lot of moral corruption."[45] In October 1853, the tsar authorized Gorchakov to recruit Greeks and Serbs, although the Russian commander still had to avoid enrolling the "rascals" (*canailles*).[46] In the end, Nicholas I did have a place for a movement of co-religionists in his war plans, yet this movement would begin only when the tsar deemed it necessary and remain fully under his control.

Small War and the Planning of the Danubian Campaign of 1854

The initial plan of the campaign of 1854 drafted by Nicholas I bore the influence of both Paskevich's idea of stirring up a Christian uprising and Nesselrode's reservations about it. After initial "demonstrations" on the Lower Danube, the main corps of the Russian army had to cross the Danube near Vidin and use the Serbs and, possibly, the Bulgarian forces to harass the Ottomans. Nicholas I accepted Paskevich's idea of the Christian militias, yet, mindful of Nesselrode's objections, viewed it only as a last resort. His plan presupposed issuing proclamations to Russia's "co-religionist and Slavic peoples" (*edinovertsam i edinokrovnym narodam*) in European Turkey only at the end of 1854, should the actions undertaken by the Russian army until then fail to force the Porte to accept the Russian peace conditions. The same applied to the formation of volunteer detachments, to which the tsar intended to devote the winter of 1854–5.[47] By early 1855, it should be clear whether Britain and France remained hostile to Russia. It would also become clear how much hope the Russians could place in the Christian population of Turkey. Nicholas I intended to advance only "if the popular uprising for independence acquires the most general and comprehensive character." In the tsar's plan for 1855, "the fighting had to take place between the Christians and the Turks," while the Russian army had to serve as the "reserve force" supporting the former.[48]

Paskevich praised the idea of crossing the Danube upstream as a way of establishing contact with "the most bellicose tribes" in European Turkey, such as Serbs, Bulgarians, and Montenegrins. "By turning against Turkey its own population," this plan, in the words of Paskevich, would preserve Russian forces and "spare Russian blood."[49] However, Paskevich deemed it necessary to prepare the upstream crossing through the capture of Silistria, which would secure Russian communications in Wallachia from a possible Ottoman counter-attack.[50] In the meantime, the Serbs and Bulgarians were to be prepared for an uprising that would coincide with the opening of the campaign in April. Whereas only small detachments of Russian troops had been sent to assist the Serbs in previous confrontations with the Ottoman Empire, this time the dispatch of an entire corps would make it possible to capture not only Vidin, but also Belgrade. According to Paskevich, the Serbs would thereby "feel the possibility of independence from the Turkish yoke."[51]

Paskevich's response to the tsar's plan of the campaign revealed his tendency to slip into conventional fortress warfare on the Lower Danube and thus deviate from his own earlier advocacy of mobilizing the Balkan Christians. The tendency was even more pronounced in the plan of war proposed by Adjutant

General F.F. Berg in November 1853. It will be remembered that Berg co-ordinated the reconnoitring of European Turkey on the eve of the Russian-Ottoman war of 1828–9, and now essentially suggested re-enacting this successful campaign. He recognized that the hostile attitude of Britain and France prevented the Russian Black Sea Fleet from supporting the army as it had in 1828–9, which rendered impossible the capture of Varna. Otherwise, Berg followed the thinking of the planners of the previous war and suggested capturing Silistria and Rushchuk in order to establish a "solid base of operations."[52] This would provoke the Ottomans to come out of their impregnable military camp at Shumla into the field. Their likely defeat in this case would "deliver to us the better part of Bulgaria." Although his plan presupposed the allocation of a secondary corps to operate between Little Wallachia, Vidin, and Sofia to "raise the Serbians and arm the Bulgarians," Berg was against directing the main force of the Russian army into this area. According to him, this would place the army at a dangerous distance from Russia, and make it victim of the uncertain attitude of the Serbs, as well as of the barrenness of their country and the adjacent territories. After all, the route to Adrianople by way of Silistria was almost twice as short as that by way of Vidin and Sofia.[53]

Nicholas I's first reaction to these ideas illustrates the mounting importance of the population factor in war planning. In his response to the field marshal, the tsar recognized the importance of Silistria, particularly "if our direction were Shumla, Varna, or the Balkans, as in 1828 and 1829." At the same time, the tsar pointed out that a crossing at or near Rushchuk would be "more reasonable" if Russia's goal was to mobilize its Christian co-religionists, as Paskevich had himself suggested. Nicholas I remarked that such a crossing would place the Russian army "in the midst of Bulgarians and closer to the Serbs." The tsar still conditioned the further advance of the Russian army upon "a general uprising of Christians." From this point of view, the capture of Rushchuk was more likely to provoke such an uprising than the capture of Silistria, located at greater distance from the areas most densely populated by the Christians.[54]

The idea of crossing the Danube at Rushchuk was first suggested by Gorchakov, who pointed out the difficulty of doing so in the environs of Vidin, which were heavily occupied by the Ottomans. Upon crossing the river, the 40,000-strong Russian corps had to stay in western Bulgaria for the winter of 1854–5, "which would have the most positive influence upon the uprising of the Orthodox peoples."[55] The Russian detachments were to "probe into [*rasprostranit' poiski*] the direction of the Balkans and Serbia in order to incite and support the uprising of the local Orthodox peoples."[56] Gorchakov also argued that the dispatch of a Russian detachment from Little Wallachia to Serbia could be necessary as early as spring and summer 1854, "if the Serbs rise up against the Turks on their own." According to Gorchakov, this measure would not contradict the tsar's intention not to address any fiery proclamations to Russia's

Orthodox co-religionists until 1855. In Gorchakov's opinion, the Balkan Christians were quite likely to take up arms on their own initiative before that time. The arrival of Russian troops would encourage them further without "compromising the Russian government in the eyes of neutral European powers."[57] In parallel, the Russian commander hoped for an anti-Ottoman uprising in Thessaly bordering on the Greek kingdom. Reports about the preparation of this uprising had been coming since the fall of 1853.[58] In the meantime, Gorchakov proceeded with the formation of Bulgarian volunteer detachments and praised the bravery of the Wallachian border guards who patrolled the left bank together with the Russian Cossacks.[59]

Gorchakov may have been influenced by I.P. Liprandi, who accompanied his overview of the ethnographic, political, statistical, and military state of the Christian provinces of Turkey, discussed in the previous chapter, with a survey of the theatre of war as of the end of 1853. In this survey, Liprandi argued that the concentration of the Ottoman forces at Vidin represented a stratagem whose goal was to prepare the actual strike across the Lower Danube at the border between Moldavia and Wallachia, a point at which the Russian communication lines were at their most vulnerable. Liprandi also believed that the mock concentration of the Ottoman forces at Vidin aimed at inciting the anti-Russian uprising of *pandurs* in Little Wallachia. He was certain that the leaders of the Wallachian revolution of 1848, suppressed by Russian-Ottoman intervention, were present in Vidin for the same purpose.[60]

To counter this stratagem, Liprandi suggested unleashing a "small war" in the rear of the Ottoman forces at Vidin. Conducted by means of volunteer detachments of Bulgarian *hajduks*, such a war would prevent the concentration of the Ottoman forces on the Lower Danube and counter the French and the British efforts to set Bulgarians against Russia. According to Liprandi, the recruitment of *hajduks* would spare "the masses of Bulgarian population from the revenge of the Turkish government." Small war by means of Bulgarian *hajduks* was also likely to attract the Bosnian *uskoks*, Orthodox Albanians, and even their Muslim co-nationals, as well as the Turks of the Deliorman forest.[61] According to Liprandi, detachments of *hajduk* volunteers were also indispensable in case the Russian command decided to transfer military operations to the right side of the Danube, particularly into the core of the purely Bulgarian agricultural population located in the south of the Balkans.[62]

A small war using Bulgarian *hajduks* could also help Russia in case of a possible landing of French and British troops in European Turkey, as Liprandi argued in another memorandum submitted to the Russian command in early 1854.[63] To begin with, Liprandi doubted that the French and British armies could be of any significant assistance to the Ottomans. Given the religious differences and the rivalry that existed between these three nations, any attempt to establish a joint camp at Adrianople could lead to open conflict between them. Partisan action by means of Bulgarian *hajduks* would land the allied force in a similar situation to that of the French army in Moscow in 1812, while advancement of this force towards the Danube would expose the French and the British troops to diseases, which would "shake the strength of their spirit to the very foundation."[64] The smallest reversal suffered by this force in confrontation with Russian troops, or any attempt to retreat, would have the same consequences as the French retreat from Moscow in 1812. Bashi-bazouks, *deli*, Albanians, the inhabitants of Deliorman, and *hajduks* and *klephts* would not miss the opportunity to profit from it.[65]

Liprandi considered similarly ineffective a possible landing of the British troops in Southern Albania or of the French ones at Shkodra. The former could be countered by provoking the Slavic element among the Albanians, which would turn the Albanians against the British and would render their position on the Ionian Islands precarious.[66] An even greater strength of the Slavic element in northern Albania would render the latter undertaking even more hazardous. Were the French to disembark at Shkodra and advance eastwards, the Montenegrin, Serbian, and Bulgarian *hajduks* would harry the French column just as effectively as the Montenegrins had stopped the French attempt to penetrate from Illyria into Serbia during the Napoleonic Wars. Liprandi assumed that the Russian operation line would cut across the western part of Danubian Bulgaria and the trans-Balkan territories, which is why he anticipated little difficulty for the Russian army in case of the allied landing at Varna or Burgas. In both cases, the French and British troops would lack cavalry and would be harassed by the Bulgarian *hajduks* if they were to advance westwards in order to meet the Russian army.[67]

The proposed mobilization of the Bulgarian *hajduks* for a small war in the ethnically Bulgarian territories was fully in accordance with the character of the ongoing confrontation as envisioned by Liprandi. In his opinion, this confrontation had to decide whether the Orthodox Slavs would acquire "freedom of religion" and whether they would remain "under the political yoke of the Muslims." It also had to decide whether the West would "acquire at least an indirect influence over the Slavs" or whether Russia would "attain full political and religious predominance over them." According to Liprandi, these questions were to be solved neither in the Northern Sea nor in the Baltic, nor even at the Black Sea, but on the banks of the Danube and in the space between this river and the Bosphorus, the Sea of Marmara, and the Adriatic, "in the core territories of the Bulgarian people."[68] This drew all eyes to the Bulgarians as "the only agricultural and truly industrious people of European Turkey," and endowed them with "a central role" in this struggle. In Liprandi's opinion, "The sympathy of Bulgarians towards Russia resulting from common religion and origin, linguistic proximity, and historical memories [was] not yet shaken by the vices and intrigues of Russia haters." If inspired, Bulgarians could "crush Turkey by the sheer weight of their numbers" and thereby put an end to both the Ottoman Empire and the alliance of the Western powers.[69]

Gorchakov's assumptions about the attitudes of the Balkans peoples also bore the influence of N.Kh. Palauzov, one of the leaders of the Bulgarian community in Odessa.[70] As early as July 1853, Palauzov sent the Russian commander a memorandum entitled "On the Present State of Bulgarians in European Turkey." In this document, he painted in the darkest colours the lawlessness that reigned in the Ottoman countryside, decried the heavy taxation exacerbated by tax farming, and bewailed the efforts of the Greek clergy to stifle the progress of education among Bulgarians. He also stressed the desire of the Bulgarians to acquire political autonomy on the model of Serbia, Wallachia, and Moldavia and emphasized their loyalty to Russia and the tsar.[71]

In January 1854, Palauzov sent another memorandum to the Russian command, in which he treated the Bulgarian issue from a specifically military-political point of view. He began by pointing out that Bulgaria was repeatedly "forgotten" in Russian-Ottoman peace negotiations after being the sight of horrible clashes (*strashnye poboishcha*). Although this did not undermine the loyalty of Bulgarians towards Russia, Palauzov pointed to persistent propaganda efforts by "Western European renegades and enemies of public order," as well as British, French, and Austrian agents who sought to achieve just such a goal. Having maintained correspondence with his co-nationals in the Ottoman Empire, Palauzov assured the Russian command that the Bulgarians "are all ready to rise up and overthrow the Turkish yoke, yet they base [their plans for] rising up on Russian aid and assistance."[72] According to Palauzov, if Russia provided them with weapons, as many as 100,000 Bulgarian cavalrymen could join the Russian war effort, and their number would increase several times in case of a general uprising. Such an uprising was neither possible nor desirable before the Russian troops crossed the Danube, yet the Bulgarians could be prepared for it via specially dispatched emissaries. In the meantime, it would be useful to appoint Bulgarian representatives to the army and corps headquarters, and to the volunteer detachments to be recruited in Moldavia and Wallachia.[73]

Assigned to the Russian headquarters in Bucharest "for the relations with Bulgarians," Palauzov contributed to the creation of the volunteer detachments recruited from the Bulgarians of Moldavia, Wallachia, and Bessarabia with the goal of unleashing a small war after the Russian crossing of the Danube. Whereas Liprandi's partisans of 1829 served to pacify the Muslim population, Palauzov envisioned a small war by means of the volunteer detachments as a way to spark an uprising of the Bulgarian population. In the words of N.Kh. Palauzov's cousin S.N. Palauzov, who likewise served at the Russian headquarters, "The necessity of a people's uprising in Bulgaria is evident: the uprising will not only facilitate our military operations in Danubian Bulgaria and the crossing of the Balkans, but will also make it possible to achieve the goal of liberating the oppressed Christians of Turkey."[74]

For the Palauzovs and other activists of the Bulgarian community in Russia, the new Russian-Ottoman war was above all an opportunity to secure political autonomy, if not complete independence, for Bulgaria, which had been a cherished goal since at least 1829.[75] Similar opportunism in the name of this higher objective can be seen in the actions of the Bulgarian revolutionary firebrand Georgi Sava Rakovski, the leader of the failed anti-Ottoman uprising in Wallachian Brăila in 1843. Having served a term in an Ottoman prison, Rakovski then worked as a lawyer and merchant in Constantinople.[76] After the Russians occupied the principalities, he began negotiations with the Ottoman war minister, Mehmed Ali Pasha, and the foreign minister, Reshid Pasha, with the suggestion to arm the Bulgarians and use them against the Russian army.[77] After the Ottomans rejected this idea, one of Rakovski's emissaries contacted the Russian consul in Belgrade, N.Ia. Mukhin, informing him of the existence of a secret Bulgarian society that had managed to collect nearly a million piastres and used it to arm 3,600 volunteers in Kazanlyk (Kazanlik, Kazanlak), Gabrovo, Elena, and Sistova. In December 1853, Mukhin reported to Gorchakov that this force could easily serve the nucleus of a 10,000-strong army, which could cut the Ottoman communications and supply lines with Thrace near Gabrovo and Kazan after the Russians crossed the Danube. In order to carry out this plan, the conspirators needed more money and several Russian officers for the training of the partisans.[78]

Rakovski apparently expected that the Russian army would cross the Danube at Sistova in the direction of Gabrovo – in other words, in the areas most densely populated by Bulgarians, where partisan warfare had the greatest chance of success.[79] These hopes were dashed when the Russians renounced their original intention of crossing the Danube in the upper course (whether at Vidin or at Rushchuk) and instead chose to focus on the lower course of the river and Silistria as they had done in the earlier wars. Although all Russian war planners recognized the perils of engaging the Ottomans in the fortress warfare, their eyes were fixed on the Lower Danube after the entry of the European powers into the war became imminent. By the end of November, Gorchakov was aware that the Russians would not have control over the Black Sea and would probably have to encounter a European force either at the approaches to Constantinople or even on the northern side of the Balkans. In this situation, Gorchakov considered it inopportune to attempt to cross the Balkans, yet he still deemed it necessary to conduct military operations on the right side of the Danube in order to "provoke the uprising of the Orthodox peoples, who will not raise arms until we cross [the river]."[80] The prospect of a Franco-British landing at Varna made the Russian commanders refocus on the Lower Danube, which necessarily called into question the plans of inciting a uprising in the more ethnically Bulgarian territories to the west.[81]

The new plan drafted by the tsar in early February presupposed the crossing of the Danube in the low course and the capture of Tulcha, Isakcha, Machin, and Girsov. The Russian army then had to take Silistria and besiege Rush-chuk. At this point, the Serbs and Bulgarians would have to rise up against the Ottomans, although Nicholas I did not expect their contribution to be more than a "useful diversion" that would distract some of the Ottoman forces. Having secured a firm position on the right bank of the Danube, the tsar did not plan to advance further "until the extent of the Christian uprising and its influence upon the situation becomes clear."[82] In practice, such an uprising had to "threaten the Ottoman communications, particularly in the mountains."[83] The greatest weakness of this scenario was the lack of connection between the planned actions of the Russian army in the first months of the campaign and the expected movement of the Balkan Christians. In the words of General P.Kh. fon Grabbe, the Russian army was to enter "the most desert-like and insalubrious region of Turkey and besiege the Danubian fortresses, which the Turks, who are awkward in the field, defend very well…. This does not facilitate an uprising of Greeks and Slavs in any way."[84]

Before long, the increasingly hostile position of Austria called this new plan into question by paralysing the Serbs and threatening the right flank of the Russian army in Little Wallachia. At one moment in mid-February, the tsar decided to maintain a defensive position until June, by which time it would become clear whether Austria was staying neutral and whether the Greek uprising in Thessaly "could provoke an uprising in Herzegovina, and, perhaps, in Serbia and Bulgaria, despite the Austrian efforts to restrain the latter."[85] In this case, the "decisive strike," or the capture of Silistria and Rushchuk, would have to be postponed until August and September. Misleadingly reassuring news subsequently received from Vienna led Nicholas I to resume his original intention to besiege and capture Silistria in late spring. Whereas the tsar underestimated the Austrian threat, Paskevich, by contrast, became overly concerned with it. Appointed commander-in-chief of the Danubian army in late February, the old field marshal renounced any idea of an offensive war and no longer talked of capturing Silistria or mobilizing the Balkan Christians. Fearful of being squeezed between the Austrians and the Ottomans, who were soon to be strengthened by a Franco-British force at Varna, Paskevich increasingly considered the possibility of evacuating the principalities altogether.[86]

Gorchakov, who became Paskevich's second in command, likewise considered abandoning the principalities, yet argued against premature evacuation, which "would have a disastrous impact upon the uprising of the Christians that seems to be on the way."[87] In Gorchakov's opinion, the evacuation of Little Wallachia, long advocated by Paskevich, would similarly undermine the spirit of Russia's Orthodox co-religionists. It would allow the Ottomans to enter the region and would reanimate the anti-Russian resistance movement that Gorchakov had quelled the previous fall.[88] According to the former commander-in-chief, any evidently defensive moves on the part of the Russian army would "paralyse the activities of the co-religionist peoples" that constituted "our main hope."[89] In this situation, it was essential to maintain an offensive posture while taking precautions against both the Austrians and the possible appearance of a French corps at Varna.

However, even this semblance of offensive strategy advocated by Gorchakov was increasingly at odds with Russia's international situation, and in particular with Russian-Austrian relations. In an attempt to placate Vienna, tsarist diplomats promised that the Russian troops would not enter Serbia or any adjacent territories. Having received this news, Gorchakov still considered making a foray to the right bank of the Danube near Vidin with a detachment of regular troops strengthened by some volunteers. In order not to stir up the Serbs, the volunteers were supposed to consist entirely of Bulgarians. Instead of provoking an anti-Ottoman uprising, the volunteers had to reassure their co-nationals that Russians were coming to deliver them from "Turkish excesses."[90] Always mindful of the strategic importance of Austria and always sceptical of military operations in Little Wallachia and near Vidin, Paskevich questioned the rationale of the measures proposed by Gorchakov, particularly since both Serbs and Bulgarians "so far remained indifferent and no real effort was made to incite them anyway." According to the field marshal, an operation against Vidin would make sense only as a means to raise the Serbs, which was no longer Russia's goal. At the same time, the importance of Silistria grew by the day, and Paskevich suggested focusing as many forces as possible on capturing this fortress.[91]

Military Operations in Danubian Bulgaria and the Local Population

As the Russian troops crossed at Galați (see figure 4.2), General A.N. Liders called on the soldiers to be "merciful towards the unarmed inhabitants and spare them regardless their confession." He also called on them to treat their Orthodox co-religionists as brothers, whose rights, "long acquired by Russian blood" but recently violated by the infidels, the Russian army had to restore.[92] Gorchakov instructed Liders to support the favourable attitude of the Bulgarians towards Russia and encourage them to contribute to the Russian war effort. The Bulgarians were to "deny the enemy supplies, weapons, and rest in their villages and towns; report on their movements; and prevent the Turks from plundering their homes, attack and capture their small parties and in general harm them in any possible way." Aware of the tsar's desire to postpone official appeals to Russia's Orthodox co-religionists, Gorchakov instructed Liders not to "issue any promises [to Bulgarians], especially written ones." He also did not allow the enrolment of volunteers that turned up on the right bank of the Danube into the volunteer detachments formed in the principalities.[93] Nor were they to receive any pay or many weapons.[94] Gorchakov's expectations of Bulgarians were thus clearly unrealistic, in the light of how little he could offer in return.

Figure 4.2. The Russian crossing of the Danube, March 1854
Source: "Vostochnaia voina 1853–56 gg.," in *Voennaia entsiklopediia*, vol. 7, ed. K.I. Velichko et al. (St. Petersburg: I.D. Sytin, 1912).

The same applied to Nicholas I. The entry of the Anglo-French fleet into the Black Sea and the increasingly hostile posture of Austria forced the tsar to issue his proclamation to Russia's Orthodox co-religionists much earlier than he had originally intended. Having appointed Paskevich to replace Gorchakov as commander-in-chief on the Danube, Nicholas I found that "it was time to call Bulgarians to arms" and personally wrote an appeal to "our co-religionist brothers in Turkey."[95] In this appeal, the tsar proclaimed the "defence of the Christian Church and its outraged Orthodox sons" as his only goal and reminded his co-religionists of the Russian blood that had been shed on many occasions for the rights of those who were now "less constrained in their way of life than others." Having thus referenced the Russian contribution to the autonomy of Moldavia and Wallachia, the proclamation declared that it was time "for other Christians to obtain the same rights" and called them to "unite in a common deed [*podvig*] for the Faith."[96] By means of this proclamation, Paskevich had to try to "raise the Bulgarians for a guerrilla warfare, if only to complicate [the enemy's] communications between Shumla and the Danubian fortresses."[97] The tsar also expected the Serbs to rise up on their own and envisioned a clash between them and the Austrians, which would this neutralize the latter.[98]

The change to the plan of the campaign and the new focus on the Lower Danube and Silistria necessarily modified the objectives that the Russian command set before the volunteer detachments that had been formed in the principalities since the fall of 1853.[99] Instead of acting in the more ethnically Bulgarian territories between Vidin and Rushchuk, the detachments of Hadji Stavri Koinov and Simeon Boichin were assigned to the Deliorman forest "for the opening of the small war" against the local armed Muslim inhabitants.[100] The same applied to the detachment of Captain Grigorii Zabalkanskii, which was initially destined to operate further west in the area of the Kara Lom River and Razgrad, "from where they could [have] lias[ed] with the inhabitants of the Balkan Mountains and incite them for an uprising."[101] As a result of the army's focus on the Lower Danube, the small war was again unleashed in Deliorman rather than in the more ethnically Bulgarian areas further west, as had been suggested by Liprandi and envisioned by the Palauzovs. In May 1854, S.N. Palauzov still believed in the possibility of igniting Bulgarian uprisings in Gabrovo, Tyrnovo, and Elena, by means of some 1,000 volunteers that had been concentrated in Little Wallachia to aid the detachment of I.P. Liprandi's younger brother, Lieutenant General P.P. Liprandi.[102] However, this plan was never implemented, because of yet another change in the Russian plan of the campaign.

Having arrived at the Danubian theatre, Paskevich reported with the timidity of an octogenarian, but also much greater sense of realism, that Austria's entry into the war would make Russia's position on the Danube untenable. The field marshal no longer advocated capturing Silistria or inciting Russia's Christian co-religionists to rise up against the Ottomans. Instead, he suggested evacuating the principalities in advance of any hostile moves on Austria's part in order to meet the enemy at much stronger positions inside Russia.[103] Nicholas I reacted with evident displeasure to Paskevich's proposal, which rendered senseless all Russian actions of the previous ten months,[104] yet the old field marshal continued to press his point. Paskevich even acknowledged the lukewarm attitude of the local Christians, which otherwise discredited his earlier advocacy of mobilizing their co-religionists. According to him, one could not place much hope on Bulgarians: "Those living between the Balkans and the Danube are oppressed and disarmed; they are like the Negros accustomed to slavery." Although those Bulgarians who lived in and beyond the mountains were reportedly more "independent-minded," they lacked unity and weapons, and it would take time and the presence of the Russian army to unite and arm them. In Paskevich's appreciation, "nothing was to be expected from the Serbs under their current ruler" (Prince Alexander Karageorgievic), while the 2,000 or 3,000 Serbian volunteers that could be mobilized would only "irritate Austria."[105]

The field marshal's foot dragging seriously slowed the progress of the siege of Silistria, which finally began in May 1854. Having suffered or feigned a concussion, Paskevich was replaced by Gorchakov, who by this point was no more enthusiastic about Russian prospects on the Danube. Although he still found Russian presence at Silistria useful for sustaining the hostility of the Christian population towards the Porte, Gorchakov nevertheless wrote that "these peoples do not demonstrate the readiness to take up arms in earnest." According to Gorchakov, Balkan Christians "pray to God for the Russian tsar, yet they are not ready to sacrifice themselves for the success of the holy cause."[106]

Gorchakov may have downplayed the actual extent of the Bulgarian struggle in June, just as he had exaggerated their willingness to fight the previous winter. According to the testimony of N.I. Ushakov, Gorchakov's general-on-duty, the local Bulgarians in fact "took every opportunity to prove their boundless zeal." They supplied the Russian army besieging Silistria daily with food and fodder "at the fairest prices," and many asked for arms and ammunition. Assisted by Greek, Serbian, Moldavian, and Wallachian volunteers, they "not only managed to protect their villages from the Turkish squads, but also captured the enemy marauders and fugitive Russian religious dissenters, who served as Ottoman Cossacks."[107] Bulgarian volunteer detachments formed in Bessarabia and the principalities were indeed usefully employed against the Muslims of the Deliorman forest, yet they numbered only 2,000 people.[108] Overall, the extent of this partisan warfare fell far short of full-scale mobilization of the Balkan Christians, which Paskevich suggested in the summer and fall of 1853, and this must have contributed to Gorchakov's low spirits.

The lacklustre performance of the Russian commanders prevented the Russian army from taking Silistria before June, when the Austrian ultimatum indeed forced Nicholas I to evacuate the principalities. This effectively put an end to any projects of raising the Balkan peoples for an anti-Ottoman uprising. As the foregoing discussion demonstrates, there was much talk about the Balkan population in the correspondence of the tsar, his commanders, and their advisers in 1853–4, and very little concrete action. Moreover, the plans of using partisans on a large scale to provoke an uprising of Balkan Christians were definitively subordinated to the overall strategy of the Russian command, which kept changing in response to the progressive worsening of Russia's position on the Danube in the second half of 1853 and the first half of 1854. Despite Paskevich's early idea of limiting the role of the Russian army to the support of a large-scale movement of the Balkan peoples, in practice, the mobilized co-religionists were a small appendage to the Russian army that was deployed in a way that was hardly conducive to a large-scale uprising.

Nonetheless, the Danubian campaign of 1853–4 is important to this story inasmuch as it demonstrates a clear change in attitude towards the idea of a "people's war" in the Balkans. Whereas in 1828–9 a national war, whether of Muslims or of the Christian peoples of the region, was something that the Russian commanders sought to avoid at all costs, a quarter of a century later they viewed it as a possibility and even hoped to see it break out. To be sure, Nicholas I and his commanders remained apprehensive of any policy that smelled of revolution. Nevertheless, the increasingly desperate situation in which they found themselves in the second half of 1853 and in 1854 explains their greater readiness to call on Russia's co-religionists to join it in the struggle against the Ottoman Empire and its Western European allies. The paradox of the situation was that this new attitude towards a "people's war" in the Balkans was at odds with the strategic choices that the tsar and his commanders made in response to the menacing moves of the Western powers that effectively precluded the successful ignition of the anti-Ottoman uprising. And yet, however inconsequential, the military-political options that were first considered in 1853–4, were de facto implemented a quarter of a century later in the circumstances to the discussion of which we now turn.

5 The Russian Army and the Ottoman Empire, 1856–1877

Alexander II's ascension to the throne in February 1855 and the conclusion of the Crimean War a year later announced a major change in the history of the Russian Empire and its military organization. The two decades that followed came to be known as the Great Reforms, which included the emancipation of the Russian peasantry from serfdom in 1861, the creation of the modern judiciary, and the introduction of elected district and *gubernia* administration (*zemstva*) in 1864, as well as the municipal reform of 1870.[1] While these reforms had a lasting impact upon Russian politics and society, their initial rationale arguably involved rendering the Russian social structure compatible with modern military organization based on universal military service and a system of national reserves.[2] This explains why the military reform of 1874 was the last to be implemented, even though military modernization was always at the top of the agenda of the tsar and his associates.[3]

The military reform of 1874 was the product of a generational change in the Russian high command and military administration. The commanders of Nicholas I – Paskevich, Menshikov, Gorchakov, Liders – were veterans of the Napoleonic Wars, all of them older (and sometimes considerably so) than the tsar himself, who was almost sixty when he died. By contrast, the notable military figures of Alexander II's reign belonged to the next generation of officers – the first to receive higher military education at the Imperial Russian Academy of the General Staff, created in 1832. This was certainly the case for Dmitrii Alekseevich Miliutin and Nikolai Nikolaevich Obruchev (see figures 5.1 and 5.2), who will feature prominently in the pages that follow. A closer look at the intellectual background of these officers is necessary to grasp some of the problems that preoccupied the leading military men in the era of the Great Reforms.[4]

These people represented a new type of Russian officer, whom one might call the military intellectual. In contrast to the morally conscious and versatile – but also amateurish – representatives of the Russian military intelligentsia of the early 1800s, whose representatives figured in the early chapters of this study, the military intellectuals who came of age around the middle of the nineteenth century were more firmly focused on the army and the problems that confronted it. Military service, which used to be one of the markers of noble status, became for them the main source of their identity. Systematic military education helped them to compensate for their relative lack of combat experience in a period (1815–53) that witnessed no major European war. It also defined the comprehensive and systematic manner in which they formulated the problems of the army. Higher military education effectively turned them into scholars, whose research into military history, statistics, logistics, tactics, or strategy was always the basis of policy that they formulated and implemented during the 1860s and the 1870s.

This chapter explores the intellectual background of this new generation of Russian military men and their perspectives on Russia's traditional rival, the Ottoman Empire, during the post-Crimean period. It begins by examining the discipline of military statistics, which emerged during the 1850s and the 1860s as the main tool of both reform and empire building. Military statistics reflected a growing appreciation of the role of population as both a factor of relative strength or weakness of a country's army and a potential challenge that it could confront in the war theatre. Confirmed by the experience of the war in the North Caucasus, this assumption became common to both the Russian reformers and their critics during the 1860s and 1870s, influencing their responses to the Eastern Crisis of 1875–8. The population factor figured prominently in both the proposals of some Russian officers to ignite a "national war" among the Balkan Christians, as well as in the actual war planning of the Russian General Staff at the time of the Eastern Crisis.

The Development of Military Statistics in the Post-Crimean Period

In the early nineteenth century, statistics was a branch of political science focused on the collection, classification, and discussion of facts pertaining to the condition of state and community. In contrast to "political arithmetic," which dealt with quantitative data, statistics provided qualitative descriptions. Over time, the discipline began to acquire its modern quantitative character in response to the growing desire of European governments to turn the population in general and specific groups within it into the objects of policy.[5] The task of singling out such groups on the basis of economic activity, way of life, or language became the task of the transformed science of statistics during the 1830s and 1840s, a period that one scholar has characterized as the age of "statistical enthusiasm."[6]

Inasmuch as the French Revolution abolished the medieval estates, corporations, and communities, it rendered necessary the discipline of statistics as an alternative tool for organizing the mass of atomized individuals.[7] Having emerged in the early modern period as a largely descriptive discipline that assessed the relative strengths and weaknesses of particular states, over the course of the nineteenth century statistics increasingly evolved in the direction of a quantitative science of population.[8] Applied to the military domain, population statistics helped above all to measure the manpower of one's own country and of its likely adversaries.[9] It also increasingly took note of such formal characteristics as confession, language, ethnicity, and the moral-political profile of the inhabitants of a given region as indicators of their likely attitude towards the army in question. The necessary corollary of this approach was the substitution of the abstract confessional and ethnic categories for the actual local communities that historically combined diverse (and unequal) individuals.

Military statistics, which developed during the same period, proceeded from the assumption that population was an important factor both of the overall military strength of a country and of military operations in a specific theatre of war. The earlier focus of the staff officers on the armed forces of a country gave way to their concern with a much broader range of factors contributing to the nation's military might. As defined by Miliutin, who effectively introduced military statistics into the curriculum of the Imperial Russian Academy of the General Staff in 1847, the "currently existing military forces of a state" were not limited to its "armed forces," but included "all means that a state has at its disposal to assure its external security or to achieve its political goal by the force of arms." According to Miliutin, military statistics thus had to "embrace virtually the entire composition of the state [*sostav gosudarstva*] and consider all of its elements from the military point of view, i.e., in relation to the means of conducting a defensive or offensive war."[10] Alongside its territory and political organization, the "elements of the state" included factors related to its population: its numbers, distribution, level of well-being, and moral qualities. All these characteristics of the population defined not only the size of the military forces but also their essential qualities, and indicated "to what extent the government could rely upon the cooperation of the people and the loyalty of the army in the case of war."[11]

Although Miliutin's own military-statistical study was devoted to Prussia and Germany,[12] the primary focus of the early Russian practitioners of this discipline was the Russian Empire itself. Ever since the 1830s, the officers of the General Staff had been composing and updating military-statistical descriptions of Russia's European provinces and the neighbouring territories.[13] The novelty introduced by Miliutin and his associates and disciples consisted in elaborating uniform criteria for the execution of military-statistical surveys, as well as making the latter an important means of the military reform that Miliutin pursued after his appointment as war minister in 1861. Beginning in 1863, the Military-Scientific Committee, with Miliutin's disciple Obruchev as its executive secretary, made information gathering a constitutive part of reform.

Figure 5.1. Portrait of Dmitrii Alekseevich Miliutin, 1860s
Source: Unknown artist, *Dmitry Alekseevich Milyutin, Adjutant General. Minister of War (1861–1881)*, oil on canvas, 63 × 72 cm, Military Historical Museum of Artillery, Engineers and Signal Corps, St. Petersburg, Russia. Via Wikimedia Commons.

This reform involved separating army command from military administration and supplies, and resulted in the division of Russia into fourteen military districts. The more precise and reliable data collected by the General Staff officers in the post-Crimean period helped the new war minister to overcome the formidable opposition that he encountered in his efforts to move the Russian army closer to a system of reserves and universal military service. Miliutin's efficient use of statistics in lobbying for the interests of his ministry and his proposed reforms in turn stimulated other Russian ministries to intensify their own statistics-gathering efforts and similarly use them for the defence of their institutional interests.[14]

One of the problems that plagued Russia's military-statistical efforts during the middle decades of the nineteenth century was the absence of a clear definition of strategic objectives. In order to be really effective, data gathering and analysis had to be informed by a shared understanding of which country represented Russia's most likely adversary and the greatest security threat.[15] Despite the frequency of the Russian-Ottoman wars in the preceding century and a half, the crisis-ridden Ottoman Empire could not be that country, as the Crimean War had demonstrated only too clearly. This uncertainty disappeared only following the emergence of Germany as the greatest European power in 1871. Germany's potential threat to Poland, the western borderlands, and even the Russian core lands was set out in a memorandum that Obruchev submitted to the Secret Strategic Conference in March 1873.[16] Obruchev's memorandum allowed Miliutin to overcome the final resistance to his proposed introduction of "universal" military service, which took place in 1874, thereby fulfilling the objectives of the military reform that Miliutin had pursued since 1861. With the final identification of Germany as Russia's greatest security threat during the 1880s, the criteria for data collection in military statistics finally became clear, making possible the elaboration of Russia's first general mobilization plan in 1887.[17]

Despite its focus on the European part of the empire, Russian military statistics played an important role in empire building on Russia's eastern peripheries, as well as in the policies that St. Petersburg pursued with respect to its southern and eastern neighbours. The graduates of the General Staff Academy played a prominent role in the Imperial Russian Geographical Society, founded in 1845, and joined the expeditions that it organized into Siberia, the Urals, Tian-Shan Mountains, Northern China, and Tibet.[18] Some of their surveys literally charted the course of Russia's territorial expansion. Thus, Miliutin's disciple M.I. Veniukov personally explored the course of the Ussuri River and thereby helped the governor general of Eastern Siberia, N.N. Muraviev (Amurskii), to annexe the Primorie region. Another one of Miliutin's students, A.I. Maksheev, combined his surveys of the Aral Sea and the Syr Daria River with construction of forts and the participation in the military expeditions against the Central Asian khanates of Kokand and Khiva in the late 1840s and the early 1850s.[19] In 1867, after the Russian conquest of Tashkent and the creation of the Turkestan province, Maksheev went there to undertake a geographical, ethnographical, and statistical survey.[20]

Practitioners of Russian military statistics had their greatest policy impact in the North Caucasus, where Miliutin received his baptism of fire in the late 1830s and to which he returned in 1856 as the chief of staff of the Caucasian viceroy, A.I. Bariatinskii.[21] The Crimean War revealed the precariousness of the Russian hold on the Caucasus, caused by the anti-Russian resistance of the mountain tribes, led by Imam Shamil. In the words of the veteran of the Caucasian war Colonel Rostislav Andreevich Fadeev, the bulk of the 270,000-strong Caucasian corps was tied up against Shamil's forces, leaving the remaining troops barely sufficient to confront the Ottomans in Asia Minor and certainly insufficient to oppose the expedition corps of the Western allies.[22] The demilitarization of the Black Sea stipulated by the Paris Peace Treaty of 1856 exposed the Russian littoral and gave the tsarist military authorities cause to fear communications between the British and Shamil, as well as the mountain tribes of the north-western Caucasus.[23] In 1857, Miliutin came up with a plan of pacification of the rebellious region through the policy of systematic expulsion of the natives from their habitats in the mountains and their resettlement in the lowlands. This was tantamount to recognizing that the native population in its entirety rather than particular armed groups represented a security challenge to the Russian Empire. Accordingly, the proposed solution was demographic rather than purely military: the hostile population was to be replaced by Cossack settlements, which Miliutin designated as the "Russian element." Approved by the tsar in 1858, the plan was put into operation by the commander of the Western Caucasian defence line, Lieutenant General N.I. Evdokimov, whose troops between 1860 and 1864 burned down and otherwise destroyed native settlements, forcing over 400,000 tribesmen to resettle on the plains of Kuban and Stavropol regions or emigrate to the Ottoman Empire.[24]

The essence of this war was best expressed by Fadeev. Located on the shore of a European sea that connected it to the entire world, the Western Caucasus, according to Fadeev, "could only become firmly attached to Russia if it was turned into a Russian land."[25] In Fadeev's opinion, there was no hope of "changing the feelings of a barbarian people numbering half a million, which had always been independent, hostile, armed, defended by an inaccessible geography, and exposed to the constant influence of all the interests inimical to Russia."[26] Fadeev frankly admitted that the war conducted in order to turn the region into a "Russian land" had caused "desperate resistance" and therefore required "annihilating a considerable part of the trans-Kuban population in order to force the other part into unconditional surrender."[27] The last four years of the Caucasian war consisted, in Fadeev's definition, in chasing the Western Caucasian mountaineers from their wilderness and in their replacement by Cossacks, whose settlements were "meant not just to crown the region's subjugation," but "served as one of the main means of conquest."[28]

The challenge of overcoming the resistance of warlike inhabitants in a mountainous region made the Russian officers look into how other European powers dealt with cases of staunch native resistance to conquest. They became particularly interested in the response of the French army to the guerilla warfare waged by Abdelkader in Algeria during the 1830s and 1840s. According to Fadeev, both the Russians and the French encountered "amid the corrupt states of the Asian world" two peoples who "equalled the Europeans in courage," while the wilderness in which they lived "rendered the superiority of regular weapons fruitless by making it impossible to advance in closed ranks."[29] In his quest for alternatives to the difficult and largely fruitless Russian expedition against Shamil's headquarters at Akhulgo in 1839, Miliutin was the first to become interested in the French plans for military settlements in Algeria in the early 1840s.[30] The study of the French experience became systematic in the wake of the Crimean War, when several graduates of the General Staff Academy travelled to Algeria to compose military-statistical descriptions of the region and overviews of the French policies there.[31]

The Russian War Ministry continued to follow closely the situation in the Ottoman Empire in the post-Crimean period. The Russian military agent in Constantinople, V.A. Frankini, supplied Miliutin's predecessor as war minister, N.O. Sukhozanet, with reports on the settlement of Muslim émigrés from the Caucasus and Crimea in the Ottoman domains. Frankini mentioned the interest of the Porte in settling the émigrés in European provinces, "where the Muslim population is very sparse and much inferior to the Christians." According to Frankini, "The Caucasian Tatars [*sic!*] constantly refused to comply with this desire of the Ottoman government."[32] Except for a very small number of those who agreed to settle in Dobrogea, the great majority preferred Asia where they had spread out along the entire coast and even in the Anatolian interior towards Sivas and Karpout. Frankini also noted that the Crimean Tatars "[had] accepted the offer of the Ottoman government and the majority of them are settling today in European Turkey, for the most part in Bulgaria, in the environs of Adrianople, Varna, and Dobrogea." Despite the high mortality among the émigrés, Frankini believed that the Crimean Tatars would "be able to make use of the lands that the Ottoman government accorded to them," since they were "more industrious and less poor than the Tatars of the Caucasus." Of all the emigrants, only the Crimean Tatars benefited the Ottoman Empire, according to the Russian military agent.[33]

Frankini also monitored the attitudes of the indigenous Muslim and Christian population of European Turkey. In May 1860, he reported the large-scale recruitment of Bosnian irregulars (bashi-bazouks) and the difficulty of the Ottoman government in doing the same in Albania.[34] Frankini noted that the Porte "could count only on the fanaticism of the bashi-bazouks" in suppressing a possible uprising of Slavs and Greeks, and he "shuddered to think of the excesses that will take place in case a conflict occurs."[35] At the time of the Greek uprising on Crete six years later, the Russian agent noted that "the state of spirits in the Turkish provinces ... was very hostile towards the government."[36] With the exception of the Bulgarians, whom Frankini described as "a passive people who have got used to the yoke," all the other Christians, whether Orthodox or Catholic, "Greeks, Myrdita, Herzegovinians, Bosnians, would be ready to make common cause against the Turks." According to Frankini, "In all these provinces one finds the seed of deep, radical, irredeemable discontent that lacks only a spark to explode," while in Albania and Herzegovina "the authority of the government [already] does not extend beyond the walls of the forts, blockhouses, and fortified places occupied by the troops."[37]

Apart from Frankini's reports, the War Ministry's main sources of information on the Ottoman Empire were the military-statistical studies of Russia's southern rival prepared and published by the officers of the General Staff. These studies reveal the mounting interest of the Russian military men in the ethnic composition of the empire of the sultan in general and of its European provinces in particular. As a result, traditional evocations of Muslim-Christian antagonism came to be combined with references to the overwhelming ethnic and racial diversity of the sultan's domains. This diversity figured as yet another aspect of the weakness of the Ottoman population base, a subject that had attracted the attention of the Russian military observers even before the Crimean War. Thus, Colonel A.V. Lavrentiev, a graduate of the General Staff Academy and the author of the military survey of the Ottoman Empire published in 1862, not only provided data on the numerical strength of each subject people of the Porte, but also evaluated the relative size of the broader Turkic, Slavic, Semitic, and Greek-Latin "families." In the author's estimation, the members of the first group amounted to only one-third of the empire's entire population and constituted only one-eighth of the inhabitants of European Turkey.[38]

The data on the religious composition somewhat spoiled the reassuring effect of the reassessment of Ottoman demography on the basis of ethnicity and race. Like so many observers before him, Lavrentiev pointed to religious divides as a major factor in the weakness of the Ottoman Empire, and yet, he could not fail to recognize that the same divides reduced the strength of the Ottoman subject peoples, in particular the Slavs. The majority of the Slavs of Bosnia and Herzegovina "unfortunately [belonged] to the most fanatical followers of Islam," while the total number of Muslim Slavs, in Lavrentiev's estimation, amounted to over half a million, or one-twelfth of Turkey's Slavic population. Added to some 2.1 million Turks and more than a million Muslim Albanians, the Muslim Slavs brought the pool of potential Ottoman loyalists in European Turkey to one-fourth of the entire population, while the Catholic-Orthodox religious divide reduced Russia's possible sympathizers there to just over two-thirds of all inhabitants.[39] This group of potential supporters was further weakened by the fact that "the egoistical interests of the ethnically Greek Orthodox clergy often led it to act in support of the Muslim government." In Lavrentiev's appreciation, "All this produces a melee of inter-ethnic relations [*mezhduplemennykh sootnoshenii*], the clarification of which is difficult to foresee, particularly since one cannot expect religious indifferentism and a clear manifestation of ethnic tendencies from an ignorant population living at a low stage of civilization."[40]

Whereas Lavrentiev focused on the moral-political attitudes of the Christian and Muslim population, others adopted a more objective approach and tried to arrive at the best possible estimation of the actual numbers of the various religious and ethnic groups. In the works of such authors politics took the form of denunciation of what they considered to be the Ottoman statistical

Figure 5.2. Photograph of Nikolai Nikolaevich Obruchev
Source: *General-adiutant Nikolai Nikolaevich Obruchev*, [1888?], photograph, The Miriam and
Ira D. Wallach Division of Art, Prints and Photographs: Photography Collection, The New York
Public Library, New York, https://digitalcollections.nypl.org/items/510d47db-ad6e-a3d9-e040
-e00a18064a99. Originally published by Fototipiia V. Shteina i S. Lapteva in St. Peterburg, Russia.

misrepresentations, the goal of which was to present the Muslims as having a
greater share of the total population of European Turkey than they in fact did.
Needless to say, in doing so, these authors often went to the opposite extreme
and unduly overestimated the number of Christians in general and particular
ethnic groups thereof in particular.

The most authoritative of these was the chapter on the Ottoman Empire in
the *Military-Statistical Collection*, compiled by Obruchev in the late 1860s. As
the target of his attack, Obruchev chose the statistical compendium published
by Salaheddin Bey, the Ottoman representative at the 1867 World Exhibition in
Paris.[41] Obruchev exposed discrepancies between the latter and the generally
respectable works by Jean Henri Abdolonyme Ubicini as the products of the
Ottoman author's self-serving fantasies.[42] According to Obruchev, a 3.5 million
increase of the number of the European Muslims, as suggested by Salaheddin

Bey, "had nothing to do with the natural movement of population," and the Circassian emigration (amounting to 595,000 people between 1855 and 1866, according to official Ottoman data) could explain only a fraction of this increase.[43]

In the end, Obruchev noted that despite their different estimations of the absolute numbers of the Turks in Europe, Western authors agreed that overall "the Turkish tribe … is rapidly declining."[44] The Russian author used the reports of the British consul in Danubian Bulgaria, Lieutenant Colonel Edward Neale, and his counterpart in the Adrianople province, Henri Blount, to illustrate the decline of the Turkish population in these two regions, where the Turkish settlement was "the most developed and exist[ed] in compact masses."[45] Obruchev attributed this demographic decline to a system of military recruitment that fell only upon the Muslims and the wasteful manner in which the Porte conducted its wars, as well as the "internal lifestyle of the Osmanli," their "lack of moderation in the pursuit of the physical pleasures," "apathy towards regular healthy work," and the "disgusting vices" reigning among the upper classes.[46]

As was the case in other areas of military-statistical work of the Great Reforms period, the study of the Ottoman Empire lacked a sense of purpose. Whatever the strengths and the weaknesses of the data that the Russian military men collected, it remained of limited usefulness as long as the objectives of Russia's "Eastern policy" remained undefined. Following the conclusion of the Peace of Paris of 1856, Russia lost its exclusive protectorate over the Danubian principalities, which it had tried to extend to the entire Orthodox community of the Ottoman Empire on the eve of the Crimean War. The severe limits imposed by the peace treaty on Russia's coastal defences and naval force on the Black Sea greatly reduced the threat that the tsars had earlier represented to the sultans. According to Chancellor A.M. Gorchakov, Russia was "composing itself" in the post-Crimean period and maintained a correspondingly low profile in the affairs of European Turkey for around fifteen years. After 1864, the Russian ambassador to Constantinople, N.P. Ignatiev, had to confront the difficult issues posed by the Cretan Revolt of 1866–9 and the Greek-Bulgarian church schism of 1870–2 in a way that would not compromise Russia's prestige within the community of its Orthodox co-religionists, which was increasingly plagued by internal tensions.[47] It took a major crisis within the Ottoman Empire and the mounting pressure of pan-Slavism at home to make the Russian government in general and the War Ministry in particular come up with a definitive policy towards European Turkey.

The foregoing discussion demonstrates that Russian military reform and the development of Russian military statistics in the middle decades of the nineteenth century were in many ways associated with the person of Miliutin. Admittedly, both phenomena were too complex and comprehensive to be viewed as the work of one man, however able and energetic he may have been. Nevertheless, Miliutin's personality can be seen as their most characteristic expression. To recapitulate: both the reform and the development of military statistics were the products of a new generation of Russian officers born in the wake of the Napoleonic Wars. Their education and, in some cases, subsequent teaching at the Academy of General Staff turned these people into intellectuals who viewed research as a means to formulate and solve the problems that confronted Russia's army, its broader military organization, and, ultimately, Russian society itself. They shared the assumption that the military forces of a country were not limited to its standing army, and instead represented the sum total of its territory, political system, and population, including the latter's moral qualities, principles of social organization, and economic activities. In this perspective, the army had to be a natural expression of the society that it was supposed to defend, and an increase in the national military might ultimately depended on demographic growth and socio-economic development.

Criticism of Reform and Pan-Slavism

However important Miliutin's disciples and associates at the War Ministry and the General Staff may have been to Russia's military organization in the second half of the nineteenth century, they were not the only significant group. The Russian army in the mid-1800s was too complex for that. Alongside the intellectually impressive military professionals, it included more conservative and/or radical elements who could not fail to be critical of the main direction of Russia's military transformation. Influential aristocratic elements in the military saw in the reforming efforts of the war minister and his disciples a manifestation of dangerous liberalism or even some revolutionary subversion. One finds an extreme example of such attitude in the in the persistent hostility towards Obruchev on the part of Alexander II's younger brother Grand Duke Nikolai Nikolaevich. The latter claimed that Obruchev secured for himself a transfer to the General Staff in early 1863 to avoid participating in the suppression of the Polish uprising of the same year and did so supposedly out of sympathy for the rebels.[48]

As the editor of the War Ministry's *Voennyi sbornik* (Military Almanac) in the late 1850s, Obruchev had indeed rubbed shoulders with Nikolai Chernyshevskii, the guru of the young Russian radicals, whose programmatic novel *What Is to Be Done?* (1862) had a major influence on all subsequent Russian revolutionaries, including Lenin.[49] Moreover, Obruchev's cousin V.A. Obruchev was a member of the revolutionary organization Land and Freedom (1861–4), a prototype of the People's Will, whose members would eventually assassinate Alexander II.[50] Nor was Obruchev alone among Miliutin's disciples and younger associates to be suspected of leftist sympathies. M.I. Dragomirov, Obruchev's fellow student at the General Staff Academy and a major Russian military theoretician of the late nineteenth century, allegedly had a portrait of

Alexander Herzen, the father of Russian socialism, in his room and was "an atheist and a political liberal."[51]

To adequately assess such allegations, one would have to know that their author, Mikhail Veniukov, another graduate of the General Staff Academy, himself wrote for Herzen's London-based magazine *Kolokol* (The Bell). Moreover, in the late 1850s, Herzen counted among his readers the minister of the interior, P.A. Valuev, and occasionally even Tsar Alexander II. Convinced of the necessity of thorough reforms, Obruchev, Dragomirov, and other disciples and younger associates of Miliutin could have some common ground with the philosophical and literary critics of the Nicholaevan system, but only for as long as these critics did not cross the red line of radical politics. Chernyshevskii's call for peasants to rebel against the land reform of 1861 and Herzen's support of the Polish uprising of 1863 were just such a red line as far as Miliutin's disciples were concerned, whereupon their support for and loyalty to the Russian state was unequivocal.[52]

Alongside the attacks of conservative aristocratic elements, Miliutin and his associates had to deal with the critics of a different kind. Of the same age as the war minister and his younger associates, these people played a dissident yet remarkable role in Russian military history of the 1860s and 1870s. Some of them (M.I. Cherniaev, M.D. Skobelev) were of petty noble origin, while others were descended from prominent and even aristocratic families (A.I. Bariatinskii, N.P. Ignatiev, R.A. Fadeev). Their educational background was likewise mixed, and included some graduates of the General Staff Academy (Cherniaev, Skobelev) alongside others who owed their promotion to alternative educational paths and distinguished service in the Caucasus (Fadeev). Their common denominator was their weariness with the academic and administrative approach of Miliutin, personal adventurousness, and a populist pan-Slavic public posture that often placed them at loggerheads with the conservative foreign policy of Chancellor Gorchakov and the sober-minded approach of the war minister.

Whereas the General Staff officers involved in the military reform and military statistics can ultimately be seen as the disciples of Miliutin, the dissenters lacked a single mentor and master mind and thus hardly represented a single party. Nevertheless, many of their attitudes and ideas found expression in the work of R.A. Fadeev, who became the most important intellectual opponent of the war minister in the late 1860s and early 1870s. Born to a distinguished noble family, Fadeev was a dropout from an artillery school who compensated for his lack of systematic education by broad reading, natural inquisitiveness, and an imaginative writing style. Having distinguished himself by his service in the Caucasus, Fadeev became a member of A.I. Bariatinskii's suite at the crucial stage of the Caucasian war in the late 1850s and the early 1860s. Charged with the task of writing the first semi-official account of the Caucasian war, Fadeev sympathetically commented on Miliutin's activities as Bariatinskii's chief of staff. Fadeev's subsequent *Letters from the Caucasus* (1865) likewise justified Miliutin's plan for the large-scale expulsion of the natives of the Western Caucasus and their replacement by Cossacks.

Upon retiring from military service in the rank of major general, Fadeev turned to journalism. In 1867, he published in the *Russian Messenger* a study of the Russian armed forces which revealed both the assumptions he shared with Miliutin and a highly critical perspective on the pre-reform Russian army that owed much to the Slavophile criticism of "the Petrine period of Russian history." Similar to Miliutin, Fadeev defined "national forces [*narodnye sily*]" as the "sum total of the moral, political, and material power of nations."[53] According to him, in order to be effective, military organization had to "correspond to the social order" of a nation and "represent its actual, living social relations in all their naturalness." Inasmuch as the national forces had to be "a reproduction of the nation," the question of military reform became "a question about the nation itself, its spiritual and material foundations" and thus "a political question that entered the sphere of public consciousness."[54] Having thus justified a public examination of Russia's military development, Fadeev proceeded to criticize Russia's pre-reform military organization for its lack of a native basis and attempts to imitate the old Prussian model that had already revealed its inadequacy with Napoleon's defeat of the Prussian army at Jena in 1806.[55] According to him, a million-strong Russian standing army that "placed into a hereditary military estate any person it once touched … burdened the people much more than it could protect them."[56]

Although Fadeev praised the military reform for overcoming the most evident shortcomings of the Petrine system,[57] he was increasingly critical of the social transformation of the Russian officer corps and of the tendency of the military administration to sideline the army.[58] In a series of articles published in the journal *The Russian World* in 1874, he attacked the reform of the military educational institutions, which thereby lost their exclusively noble character and began to admit people of all social backgrounds who met the educational requirements. According to Fadeev, the educational reform was tantamount to "a fundamental reordering of the Russian army," whereby the officer corps lost its erstwhile noble character and came to be filled with the sons of petty civil servants and seminary dropouts who lacked the moral qualities necessary for an officer.[59]

Fadeev also criticized the introduction of universal military service, which further diluted the noble leadership and increased the "all-estate character" of the army. He considered obligatory military service unnecessary for all social groups in view of the size of Russia's population, yet argued for making it mandatory among noblemen, who had become increasingly reluctant to serve alongside the officers of lowly origin.[60] The essence of Fadeev's proposed measures consisted in "replacing the present artificially nurtured command hierarchy of the Russian forces by a natural hierarchy" that had its roots in Russian social organization. Turning "each Russian nobleman into a born officer of a national force" (*prirozhdennyi ofitser narodnoi sily*) was, according to Fadeev, a precondition of the transformation of the former "recruit army" into "a Russian people organized for battle [*ustroennyi dlia boia russkii narod*]."[61]

Reminiscent of the conservative utopia of the Slavophiles, Fadeev's attack on Miliutin's policies and the Great Reforms more broadly coincided with the surge of pan-Slavic sentiments among the Russian educated society.[62] Between the Crimean War and the Eastern Crisis of 1875–8, these ideas served the representatives of the Russian elites to reconceptualize their country's foreign policy after the evident failure of the Holy Alliance strategy that the tsars had pursued since 1815. One should not forget, however, that the vision of Russia as the leader of the all-Slavic coalition had its negative mirror image, namely, the nightmarish prospect of the loss of Russia's borderlands and its reduction to the status of second-rank power that the pre-Petrine Muscovy had been.[63]

This tendency is very much evident in the work of Russian pan-Slavism's most original thinker, N.Ia. Danilevskii. A fringe participant of the Petrashevtsy "conspiracy" exposed by Liprandi in 1849, Danilevskii was exiled to the Volga region and eventually became an official of the Ministry of Interior contributing to the legal regulation of fishery and conducting meteorological research. A natural scientist by training and vocation, Danilevskii nevertheless entered the history of the Russian thought as the author of *Russia and Europe* (1869), a historical and sociological treatise that became a reference point for anti-Western intellectuals. Danilevskii argued that Russia was "foreign to the European world by its internal organization" and, at the same time, "too strong and powerful to be one of the European great powers and play the role of a member of the European family." According to Danilevskii, Russia could occupy a place worthy of itself only by becoming "the head of a different, self-sufficient system of states" that would serve as a counterweight to Europe in its entirety. He predicted that unless Russia realized its historical role, it would have to submit to the demands of Europe and would suffer the fate of an "outdated, redundant, and unnecessary" entity.[64]

In this case, according to Danilevskii, Europe would not only "put an end to Russian influence on the East" and "create bastions undermining Russia's ties with its Western Slavic relatives." It would also try to "dilute the Slavic spirit to the point when Slavdom becomes dissolved in the Europeanness and turns a simple fertilizer of the European soil." In doing so, Europe could use its "Turkish, German, Hungarian, Italian, Polish, Greek, and perhaps Romanian collaborators, who were always ready to corrode the unconsolidated body of Slavdom." In the meantime, Russia would "lose its *raison d'être*, its living essence and its idea," and would spend the rest of its miserable days as a "rotting historical trash deprived of any sense and meaning." Or else it would become "a lifeless mass, a soulless body" that in the best possible case would "turn into ethnographic material for new historical combinations."[65]

Fadeev's *Opinion on the Eastern Question* published in the same year as Danilevskii's treatise was another attempt to envision a pan-Slavic super-Russia. In contrast to Danilevskii's historical and cultural analysis, Fadeev's approach was more concrete and pragmatic – he was a military man, after all – which is why it had greater contemporary resonance. Fadeev argued that ever since Muscovy became the Russian Empire and extended beyond the purely Russian lands into ethnic cross strip (*cherespolositsa*) of Eastern Europe, its western border became "an arbitrary and accidental line contingent on the first major political event."[66] According to Fadeev, "the historical force of Russia consisted in the huge sympathetic population that lived alongside our south-western borders." This population could be mobilized not by last-minute manifestos (as had been attempted in 1854), but by promoting the "intellectual and moral communication" between Russia and the Slavs before the new war breaks out.[67]

Fadeev warned that Russia's procrastination in unifying the Slavic peoples threatened to aggravate its internal complications in Poland, the Black Sea region, and even the Caucasus. In other words, the failure to integrate external frontiers (consisting of the Austrian and Ottoman Slavs) could result in the loss of the internal frontiers, that is, of Russia's western borderlands. The Polish uprising of 1863 revealed the fragility of Russian rule in these territories as well as the existence of a "hostile intelligentsia." In case of a war between Russia and the Germanic powers, this intelligentsia "will immediately resume its erstwhile influence and will force the local population" neutralized by the peasant reform of 1861 "to work for the benefit of our enemy."[68] Russia's likely defeat in this case would mean a retreat to the Dnieper and the restoration of Poland in the borders of 1772, as well as opening the prospect of the loss of Finland, Livonia, Bessarabia, Crimea, and the Caucasus.[69]

Fadeev evoked this scenario to demonstrate that Russia could not become entrenched in its current limits and argued that its fate depended upon the resolution of the Slavic question. The pan-Slavic general expected Russia either to "extend its dominance to the Adriatic" and become the centre of the Slavic and Orthodox world or to "retreat to the Dnieper" and contract to the limits of "national [*pomestnyi*] Russian state."[70] The stark historical alternative formulated by Fadeev was based on the assumption that the actually existing Russian Empire was either too large or, however strange it might appear, not large enough. In other words, the actually existing Russia, despite its vastness, was for Fadeev an unstable transitional entity, which could contract, if not disappear altogether, unless it becomes a still larger body.

This approach conditioned Fadeev's view of the Ottoman Empire. In contrast to the majority of contemporary commentators, who viewed the Eastern Question as the problem of the Orthodox and Slavic population of the

Ottoman Empire, Fadeev considered it part of the broader Slavic question defined by the struggle between Russia and the German powers for influence over the Slavs of Eastern Europe.[71] For Fadeev, as for the majority of Russian pan-Slavists, this struggle was pregnant with the possibility of another war between Russia and a European coalition. In contrast to the majority opinion, Fadeev considered Austria-Hungary and Prussia rather than Britain to be Russia's main opponents. This meant that the question could not be solved through yet another war with the Ottomans, but required a head-on battle with the Germans on the middle Danube.[72] Fadeev thus suggested preparing for war with Austria-Hungary and Prussia still before Obruchev arrived at the same conclusion in his memorandum submitted to the Secret Strategic Conference of March 1873, which became one of the starting points of Russia's war planning during the 1880s.[73]

The Eastern Crisis, Russian Perspectives on Islam, and Plans for the Mobilization of Balkan Christians

By virtue of their shared focus on Russia's western frontier, Fadeev and Obruchev had little to say about the Ottoman Empire until the outbreak of the Eastern Crisis in 1875 challenged each of them to come up with a plan of action. The uprising in Bosnia and Herzegovina of 1875, followed by the uprising of April 1876 in Bulgaria and the Serbian-Ottoman War of the same year caused a great resonance in Russian society and posed a problem for Alexander II and his advisers.[74] The tsar and the Russian Foreign Ministry's reaction to the uprising of the Balkan Christians was quite reserved at first and consisted in cooperation with Vienna within the framework of the Alliance of the Three Emperors. In December 1875, Austrian foreign minister Gyula Andrassy and the Russian ambassador in Vienna, E.P. Novikov, negotiated the so-called Andrassy Note, which sought to reconcile the Porte and its Orthodox subjects through the regularization of taxation and the promise of religious freedom in Bosnia and Herzegovina.[75] However, this moderate approach could satisfy neither the Herzegovinian or Bulgarian rebels, nor the Moscow Slavic Benevolent Committee, whose thundering condemnation of the Ottoman "barbarities" increasingly resonated with the Russian public opinion.[76] Under its pressure, Alexander II began to adopt an increasingly bellicose attitude, even though the fear of the repetition of the Crimean scenario never completely abandoned him.

This time, however, the political situation in Europe was very much different from what it had been a quarter of a century earlier. Both France and Austria-Hungary were still recomposing themselves after recent defeats by Prussia, whereas the triumphant Bismarck was loath to antagonize Russia, whose benevolent neutrality had helped him unify Germany. This made the task of creating an anti-Russian coalition much more difficult for London. Equally different was the state of the European public opinion. In the immediate aftermath of the failures of the 1848–9 revolutions, the European liberals and radicals were united in their hatred of Russia as the "Gendarme of Europe," and, at the same time, sympathetic towards the Ottoman government, whose westernizing reforms included a liberal-constitutional component.[77] Two decades later, this sympathy gave way to the condemnation of the "Turkish atrocities in Bulgaria" that helped the British liberal leader William Gladstone in his struggle with the conservative and Turcophile policy of Prime Minister Benjamin Disraeli.[78]

According to Cemil Aydin, the anti-Ottoman sentiment in Britain and other European countries during the Eastern Crisis constituted an important stage in the process of racialization of Muslims that helped produce the hegemonic and monolithic narratives of Islam versus the West.[79] This broad interpretation finds some support in the studies of Russian policies towards the Muslim population in the middle decades of the nineteenth century. A politicization of Islam in the context of anti-Russian resistance in the Caucasus contributed to the erosion of Catherine the Great's tolerant approach and brought about attempts to contain the spread of Islam within the Russian Empire.[80] On the level of state policy, the tolerance or even encouragement of Islamization of the heathens gave way to attempts to Christianize them, by making the Orthodox message accessible in native languages.[81] Meanwhile, representations of Islam and of the Muslims in the Russian press increasingly stressed fanaticism, oppressiveness, and ignorance at the expense of moral virtues and Oriental aesthetics.

And yet, Russian perspectives on the Ottoman Empire and its Muslim population arguably retained a measure of nuance. The anti-Islamic turn of the mid-nineteenth century was somewhat offset by the development of critical perspectives upon both the European society and the westernizing reforms in the Ottoman Empire. Echoing the Slavophile critique of Peter the Great's reforms in their own country, some Russian observers of the Tanzimat argued that attempts to create a European-style Ottoman army and equalize the rights of the Muslim and the Christian subjects of the sultan contradicted the fundamentals of Islam and undermined the national spirit of the Ottomans.[82] As has been demonstrated, reports of the Russian military agents in Constantinople since the late 1820s had indeed stressed the unpopularity of the reforms among the provincial Muslim population and treated the latter with some degree of sympathy, which was replicated by conservative Russian publicists later in the century.[83]

The Russian "discovery" of the provincial Muslims, distinct from and often opposed to the Ottoman government, manifested in an increasingly nuanced treatment of this religious group in Russian military-statistical descriptions of European Turkey during the 1860s and the early 1870s. As has been demonstrated, these surveys distinguished between the autochthonous Muslim population of the eastern Balkans and the recent émigrés from Crimea and the Western Caucasus. Russian observers of the Ottoman Empire attributed to each of these categories of Muslims different moral-political qualities and different attitudes towards Christians. As the subsequent discussion demonstrates, both the Russian war planners in 1876–7 and the Russian provisional authorities in Bulgaria in 1877–9 adhered to this nuanced approach, even though particular generals could succumb to excesses of anti-Muslim sentiment.

Predictably, such excesses characterized above all the authors of various plans of mobilization of the Balkan Christians for an anti-Ottoman struggle. The first of such plans belonged to Major General I.K. Kishelskii. An ethnic Bulgarian who had studied in Russia on a stipend established by Nicholas I, Kishelskii entered Russian military service following the outbreak of the Crimean War. He participated in the defence of Sebastopol as a commander of a detachment of Russian chasseurs (*okhotniki i plastuny*) and later took part in the "pacification" of the North Caucasus. Since then, he served as Russia's "secret agent in the affairs of Turkey's Christian provinces," in the testimony of War Minister Miliutin.[84] In January 1876, Kishelskii wrote a "Temporary Project for the Organization of an Uprising in Bulgaria for Independence and Freedom of Life," which represented a collection of organizational and tactical principles addressed to the Bulgarian volunteers. The author noted that the Bulgarians were the only people of European Turkey that did not have "their military language, their libraries, and military statutes," which could help them be "successful on the battlefield." Writing before the Ottoman suppression of the Herzegovinian uprising, Kishelskii argued that the Bosnian and Herzegovinian Serbs were successful against the Turks not only due to their personal courage, but also due to their familiarity with the Serbian military statutes. Accordingly, the author's goal was to "render the Bulgarian brothers familiar with the military art."[85]

Kishelskii argued that the best initial strategy against the Ottoman regular troops and the bashi-bazouks was to remain dispersed in the mountains, which would in turn force the Ottomans to disperse their forces and would weaken them. This strategy would also help protect "hundreds of thousands of women and children" from "Turkish fanaticism." Just as the Turkish population was likely to hide in fortresses or in the vicinity thereof, Kishelskii suggested hiding the masses of Bulgarian families in places specially prepared by the heads of the volunteer detachments. As they retreated into the mountains, the inhabitants of the villages had to take with them life essentials, food, and church utensils.[86] With the gradual multiplication of the volunteer detachments, Kishelskii envisioned the formation of three "people's armies" (*narodnye armii*). Two of them would occupy Danubian Bulgaria and Eastern Rumelia, respectively. The third, or western, army would operate in the territory extending to Nish and the borders of Serbia and Bosnia in the north, Albania in the west, and Thessaly and the Mediterranean in the south.[87]

In early April 1876, Kishelskii met Miliutin in order to transmit to him the "sad news" on the situation in Bulgaria. Kishelskii argued that Bulgaria was worse off than other provinces of the Ottoman Empire because the Muslim minority there was armed, whereas the Christian majority was unarmed and "feared total annihilation." Miliutin advised Kishelskii to restrain his co-nationals from premature uprising and temporize until the situation around Bosnia and Herzegovina became clear. "Should the question be decided by force of arms," argued Miliutin, "Bulgaria had to be the last to join in."[88] However, Kishelskii pursued his project and actively participated the collection of funds for the Bulgarian militia. In June 1876, he asked Miliutin to release from the Odessa customs a load of rifles purchased for Bulgarians several years previously.[89] Having retired from the Russian service, Kishelskii left for Serbia, which had just declared war on the Ottoman Empire, in order to organize the Bulgarian detachments on Serbian territory and lead them into Bulgaria.

Despite Kishelskii's ardent Bulgarian patriotism, not all of his co-nationals in Russia supported his plan. Thus, the governor of the Southern Slavic Boarding School (*Iuzhnoslavianskii pansion*) in Nikolaev, Todor Minkov, wrote that anyone who read or heard Kishelskii's projects "would think that they are written in a madhouse."[90] In the end, Kishelskii's plan was thwarted by M.G. Cherniaev, another retired Russian general, who famously, but inefficiently, commanded the Serbian army during the Serbian-Ottoman War of 1876.[91]

Cherniaev represented a paradigmatic example of an adventurer general, whose capture of Tashkent in 1865 triggered the Russian conquest of Central Asia.[92] Dismissed from his post in Turkestan in 1866, Cherniaev temporarily retired from military service to become the editor of the periodical *The Russian World*, which published Fadeev's criticisms of Miliutin's military reform. Having established connections with the Moscow pan-Slavists, led by I.S. Aksakov, Cherniaev became an enthusiastic supporter of the Slavic cause during the Eastern Crisis and accepted the invitation of the Serbian Prince Milan to head the Serbian army in June 1876.[93] According to the hostile Miliutin, Kishelskii's project was the victim of Cherniaev's personal ambitions. Cherniaev supposedly seized on Kishelskii's idea of Bulgarian militia as a way to become a Bulgarian *hospodar*. However, Cherniaev killed the project upon learning that Bulgarians had contacted Fadeev, his erstwhile associate turned competitor, with the proposal to become their military leader.[94]

Having fallen out with Cherniaev and seeing no chance that his proposed principles would ever guide Russia's internal or foreign policy, Fadeev left in 1875 for Egypt, to act as a military adviser to the khedive, whom he expected to clash with the Porte one day. Following the outbreak of the Eastern Crisis, Fadeev returned to Russia, actively joined the Slavic cause, and attempted to influence the direction of Russian foreign policy in a series of memoranda. In one of these pieces, submitted to the deputy foreign minister, K.F. Girs, in May

1876, Fadeev outlined what he considered to be the right strategy for Russia on the Eastern Question. As so many of his Russian contemporaries, Fadeev considered the Ottoman Empire to be terminally ill, pointing to the recent *coup d'état* that replaced Abdul-Aziz I by Murad V, the collapse of Ottoman finances, and the weakness of the Ottoman army. According to him, the formally dominant Muslim element in European Turkey was rapidly diminishing in numbers and becoming so impoverished that they "had long had to sell their pistols and scimitars to buy their daily bread." The Muslim population of Asia Minor was similarly burdened with taxes and exhausted by military draft, and "will not move a finger on its own to sustain Turkish dominance in Europe." In Fadeev's assessment, the balance of internal forces of the empire had shifted decisively from the centripetal to the centrifugal:

> In the south, the numerous Arabian people strives to liberate itself from the yoke and, by way of the leading sheikhs, asks the khedive to raise the Arabian banner. In the north, a million and a half Muslims (not counting the neutral Albanians) have to keep in check ten million Christians. In the middle, the Turks of Asia Minor want to get rid of the hated privilege of military service for the maintenance of a multiethnic state that they do not care about.[95]

Whereas all the other powers could "deal only with the Ottoman government," Russia alone, in Fadeev's view, was "in close connection with internal living forces of the [Ottoman] Empire, its subject peoples who have become cumulatively more powerful than the official Porte." In these conditions, Fadeev believed, Russia's real interest consisted in preventing any *diplomatic* interference into the "Turkish strife." Given Russia's advantage over other European powers, diplomatic non-interference would effectively exclude "everyone, but Russia" from deciding the Eastern Question.[96] Fadeev suggested encouraging the anti-Ottoman uprising of the Greeks in Epirus, Thessaly, and Western Macedonia, and in the Balkan Mountains, which would distract the Ottoman forces and make them "unable to oppose the regular forces of Serbia, Montenegro, and the Greek Kingdom for a very long time."[97] In parallel, the Russians had to encourage the khedive to pursue "the creation the Arab kingdom" and "the termination of the secular authority of the sultan" by means of "the Russian party" that Fadeev claimed he had created in Egypt.

According to Fadeev, unhampered access to southern seas had to be the main goal of Russian policy in the Eastern Question, since the larger part of the Russian population lived in the southern part of the country (between the Oka River and the Black Sea). From the point of view of Russian pan-Slavism, Russian presence in the Dardanelles was all the more central because the power that controlled the straits would inevitably "directly influence the fate, organization, as well as internal and external relations of the peoples [*plemena*], who would break out of the Turkish yoke."[98] In contrast to his *Opinion on the Eastern Question*, Fadeev argued that Russia's control of the Dardanelles was worth allowing Austria to "decide for the time being the organization of the neighbouring Turkish provinces as she wanted." It mattered little whether Austria "split them into small possessions, took some of them under her guidance or even direct authority – the greater the Austrian oppression is felt in these countries the better it will be for us in the nearest future."[99] This solution would also be "least disturbing" for Germany, with which Fadeev suggested concluding an alliance in order to thwart the formation of an anti-Russian coalition.[100] Complemented, if possible, by a Franco-Russian agreement securing French interests in the Mediterranean, the Russian-German alliance would leave Britain without an ally on the continent, whereupon Russia could "move the Turkish Christians for a general uprising" and capture the Dardanelles.[101]

Whereas Kishelskii's projects were criticized as hare-brained by the more sober-minded of his fellow Bulgarians, Fadeev's proposals received a similar evaluation by Miliutin. The war minister considered Fadeev a "windbag and a schemer," no doubt because of the many critical pieces that Fadeev had earlier written on the subject of military reform.[102] Miliutin described Fadeev's plan of a Russian expedition to the Dardanelles, despite the presence of the British fleet at Bezik Bay as "a chimerical proposal reminiscent of delirium."[103] The war minister similarly dismissed Fadeev's view of the Egyptian khedive as a potential supporter of the Slavs in their struggle with the Porte. At the same time, Miliutin noted with surprise and bewilderment that Fadeev's plan was received by the tsar "with some sympathy," which undoubtedly encouraged the pan-Slavist general to persist in the advocacy of his approach to the Eastern Question.

In October 1876, Fadeev submitted another memorandum to the head of the General Staff, F.L. Geiden, in which he offered a more detailed justification for inciting an uprising of the Ottoman Christians.[104] In the five months that had elapsed since Fadeev submitted his memo to Girs, the Serbian army had been effectively defeated, while the Russian and the European public became apprised of the April Uprising in Bulgaria and its brutal suppression. The disappointing performance of the Serbs and the martyrdom of the Bulgarians led the Russian pan-Slavists to shift attention from the former to the latter for the rest of the Eastern Crisis. Fully in line with this tendency, Fadeev viewed Bulgaria as "the centre of all Russian interests," a country that determined the fate of Constantinople and the straights. At the same time, Fadeev argued that these interests could not be attained by purely military means "without an energetic rising of the Bulgarian people that has to be prepared in advance."[105]

Fadeev insisted on a speedy Russian occupation of Bulgaria. Unless surprised by a rapid strike, the Ottomans would be able to offer staunch resistance, which would complicate Russia's position in relation to the European powers.

However, such a staggering blow was impossible without the Bulgarians. According to Fadeev's calculations, the Ottomans could concentrate up to ten divisions on the Danube, supported by the armed inhabitants in the fortresses. Even if a superior Russian force were able to promptly overwhelm the Ottoman army and force the sultan to accept the desired conditions, it would still be dealing with the Porte and not with the scattered Muslim population that represented, in Fadeev's estimation, "the stumbling block of the Eastern Question."[106] In the likely case of stanch resistance on the part of the Ottomans, the Russian troops would have to stay concentrated and advance "along the well-trodden road past Shumla to Adrianople," without spreading its detachments and penetrating into the interior of the country. As a result, five-sixths of Bulgaria would remain "untouched by the Russian campaign" at a time when "the Muslim population is organized as an army keeping in check completely unarmed Christians."[107] Fadeev feared that "on the day of the conclusion of peace it will turn out that the greater part of Bulgaria is loyal to the sultan and petitions to stay under his benevolent rule," which would immediately be supported by "Europe that is always ready to juggle the cards in the Eastern Question." For this reason, argued Fadeev, "a fundamental change in the internal way of life of Bulgaria" was impossible "without the rising of the Bulgarian people throughout the entire country."[108]

According to Fadeev, all the Ottoman forces would be engaged by the Russian army, which would leave the maintenance of the existing order in vast areas located away from the operational line in the hands the Muslim population. One therefore had to assign as much force for the provocation of the uprising as was necessary to overcome the armed Muslim inhabitants, yet this force had to be spread wide and live off the land without thinking of its base and operational line. Fadeev defined this force as something in "between the real battle troops and partisans." In contrast to the partisans, who "swoop and gallop away," the detachments suggested by Fadeev had to "swoop and stay" before moving on. At the same time, they had to be a "regular" and sizable force given the numerousness of the Muslim inhabitants and the necessity to cover entire country from the Russian operation line in the east to Bitol (Macedonia) in the west.[109]

Fadeev pointed to the inevitable weakening of Russia's western frontier should additional Russian troops be charged with occupying Bulgaria. He also argued that Russian troops were inadequate for this task: despite their loyalty to Russia, the Bulgarians, in Fadeev's opinion, "remembered only too well earlier invasions and promises … following which the Turks settled scores with them." Finally, were the Bulgarians to remain "passive onlookers of our struggle with the Turks," Russia's proclamation of Bulgarian independence would appear "a purely military measure that does not prove in the least the vitality of the people itself."[110] For all these reasons, claimed Fadeev, only the Bulgarians themselves are able to raise the Bulgarian banner successfully and with full significance for the world as well as carry it around the country. Only they can prevent the mass slaughter of Christian villages that one otherwise has to expect after the beginning of the military operations. In this case, the war will become easier for us through the distraction of the Turkish forces and our designs will become a *fait accompli* by the day of the final treaty.[111]

Fadeev suggested that the Bulgarian squads had to be organized promptly, still before the war was declared. In his opinion, this was a relatively easy task. Fadeev pointed to the reports of the Bulgarian committees, according to which an unlimited number of Bulgarian volunteers could be attracted from Romania and from the right bank of the Danube. Together with the majority of the 5,000 Bulgarian volunteers assembled in Serbia as of October 1876, the Bulgarian force could reach 20,000. Fadeev suggested assigning Russian soldiers, NCOs, and officers on leave, as well as all Bulgarians who were currently serving in the Russian army to the task of training the new militia.[112]

Armed by the Chassepot rifles purchased by Fadeev with the financial assistance of the Moscow Slavic Benevolent Committee, this force had to be "sufficient for the liberation of the vast country between the Danube and the mountains as well as the capture of the Balkan gorges without the distraction of the Russian army, which will go down its usual war road."[113] Fadeev believed that the "timely capture of the Balkan Mountains by armed rebels supported by the regular Bulgarian regiments" would deprive the Ottomans of the ability to maintain their main defensive line between Varna and Shumla. Following this success, it would be easy to "double or even to quadruple the Bulgarian troops and move them in the very centre of the southern part of the country to Philippopolis and Tatar Bazardzhik (Pazardzhik) – the area of the recent Bulgarian uprising."[114] According to Fadeev, the benefits of preparing in advance a large Bulgarian force would not end with the conclusion of the war and the acquisition of independence for Bulgaria. The latter would "assume its rights as a ready army," and a "russified one" at that. The Russian cadres among the militia who would settle in Bulgaria after the war could counteract "anti-Russian propaganda that constantly, even if uselessly, besieges this tormented country," as well as provide the Bulgarian troops with ready NCOs in the likely case of a new confrontation.[115]

Russian War Planning in 1876–1877

However critical he may have been of Fadeev, the war minister was himself increasingly convinced of the inevitability of war and thus of the necessity to prepare for it. In February 1876, after the news of the suppression of the Herzegovinian uprising and the formation of the Serbian-Montenegrin alliance reached St. Petersburg, Miliutin approached Alexander II for the first time on the question of possible preparations for war. The tsar decisively rejected the idea out of fear that any preparations would be interpreted as signs of Russian aggressiveness and told the Serbian and the Montenegrin princes not to count on Russia's help.[116] However, Miliutin was increasingly sceptical of the possibility of resolving the question of the Ottoman Christians through diplomatic pressure on the Porte and the good will of the sultan and his ministers. He attributed the crisis to "the complications inherent in the very form of the Muslim state" that could only be resolved by a "complete political and social overhaul": one had to "cut the Gordian knot."[117]

In late March 1876, Miliutin conferred with Obruchev on the need to elaborate several alternative plans of mobilization in response to "the most probable eventualities" and "different political circumstances."[118] At the end of June 1876, the war minister questioned the principle of non-interference, given the support rendered to the Ottoman Empire by England and Austria-Hungary as "Turks and Circassians [were perpetrating] revolting atrocities in Bulgaria, killing unarmed and defenceless population by the thousands."[119] Amid the talks about Russia's unpreparedness for war, Miliutin presented to the tsar the reports of the Mobilizational Committee of the General Staff, which showed that "despite numerous shortcomings remaining in our military organization, the Russian army was ready for war as never before."[120] In July, Miliutin noted that Serbia had organized partisan detachments and a "national war" (*narodnuiu voinu*).[121]

In the spring and summer of 1876, Alexander II continued to fear that a war with the Ottoman Empire could lead to the formation of another anti-Russian coalition. At the same time, the tsar's growing sympathies for the Slavic cause manifested in the granting of permission to Russian officers to take leave from the army in order to join the Serbian army as volunteers. Among the many officers who took advantage of this permission there were even several Muslims from the tsar's suite led by a son of Imam Shamil. Miliutin reported, sceptically, the latter's promise "to assemble a band [*shaiku*] of Circassians for actions against the Turks."[122] In September, following the defeat of the Serbian forces under the command of Cherniaev and the Porte's unwillingness to accept Britain's official demand for an armistice, Alexander II abruptly changed his attitude and no longer considered impossible either a break in Russian-Ottoman relations or an outright war.[123] Miliutin gave the green light to the General Staff for the elaboration of a plan of war.

Obruchev played the main role in this process. In the mid-1870s, he wrote an overview of European Turkey as a potential war theatre for the Academy of the General Staff. This overview summarized available military-statistical knowledge of the region, evaluated the experience of the past Russian-Ottoman wars and identified the best strategies for future confrontations.[124] Obruchev may have consulted the manuscript of Liprandi's surveys from the 1840s and the 1850s, since in his own memorandum, he followed the latter's subdivision of Danubian Bulgaria, noting the barrenness of the Dobrogea steppe, the difficult terrain and the warlike Muslim population of the Deliorman forest, and the predominantly Bulgarian population of the western part of the region and their strong national sentiment.[125] He also noted that the trans-Balkan territories represented a more hospitable terrain for the Russian army both because of their predominantly Bulgarian population and greater availability of food and fodder.[126]

As to the possible operational line for the Russian army, Obruchev consciously departed from the strategic choices made by the Russian command in 1828–9. He rejected the shortest route to Constantinople by way of eastern Bulgaria, which had been taken by the Russian troops fifty years earlier. He pointed to the bareness of Dobrogea, "the warlike, fanatical population" of the Deliorman, and the difficulty and limited usefulness of taking Shumla and Varna, all of which was confirmed by the negative experiences of 1828–9.[127] By contrast, the route across central Bulgaria, although longer, had the advantage of circumventing Shumla and "cutting across a country sympathetic to us."[128] The westernmost route, which was the longest, offered similar advantages, as it would bring the Russian troops to the valley of Maritsa by way of Sofia, where their appearance would have "such an impact upon the moral state of the Turks and the population of the peninsula that would guarantee the success of the campaign" (see map 5.1).[129]

Obruchev's memorandum contained an early formulation of the strategy that the Russian army would adopt, yet the final war plan was the product of collective thinking, which examined alternative possibilities. Following the outbreak of the Eastern Crisis, other Russian officers came up with their own ideas on the best strategy to adopt in a war against the Ottoman Empire. The most original of them belonged to the Russian ambassador in Constantinople, N.P. Ignatiev. Yet another graduate of the Academy of General Staff, Ignatiev switched to the diplomatic track early on and made a spectacular career that included highly successful missions to the Central Asian khanates and China. This earned him promotion to the rank of major general and eventually an appointment as the Russian envoy (and later ambassador) to the Porte. Not unlike Fadeev, Ignatiev combined pan-Slavic sympathies with opposition to the conservative policy line of his ministry pursued by Chancellor A.M. Gorchakov. In contrast to Fadeev, he had a considerable (though by no means decisive) influence upon the emperor.

Ignatiev's first published work was a review of the history of the Russian-Ottoman wars composed during his studies at the Academy on the eve of the Crimean War. In this work, the future ambassador contrasted the enormous losses of the Russian armies to disease in the European theatre of war to the

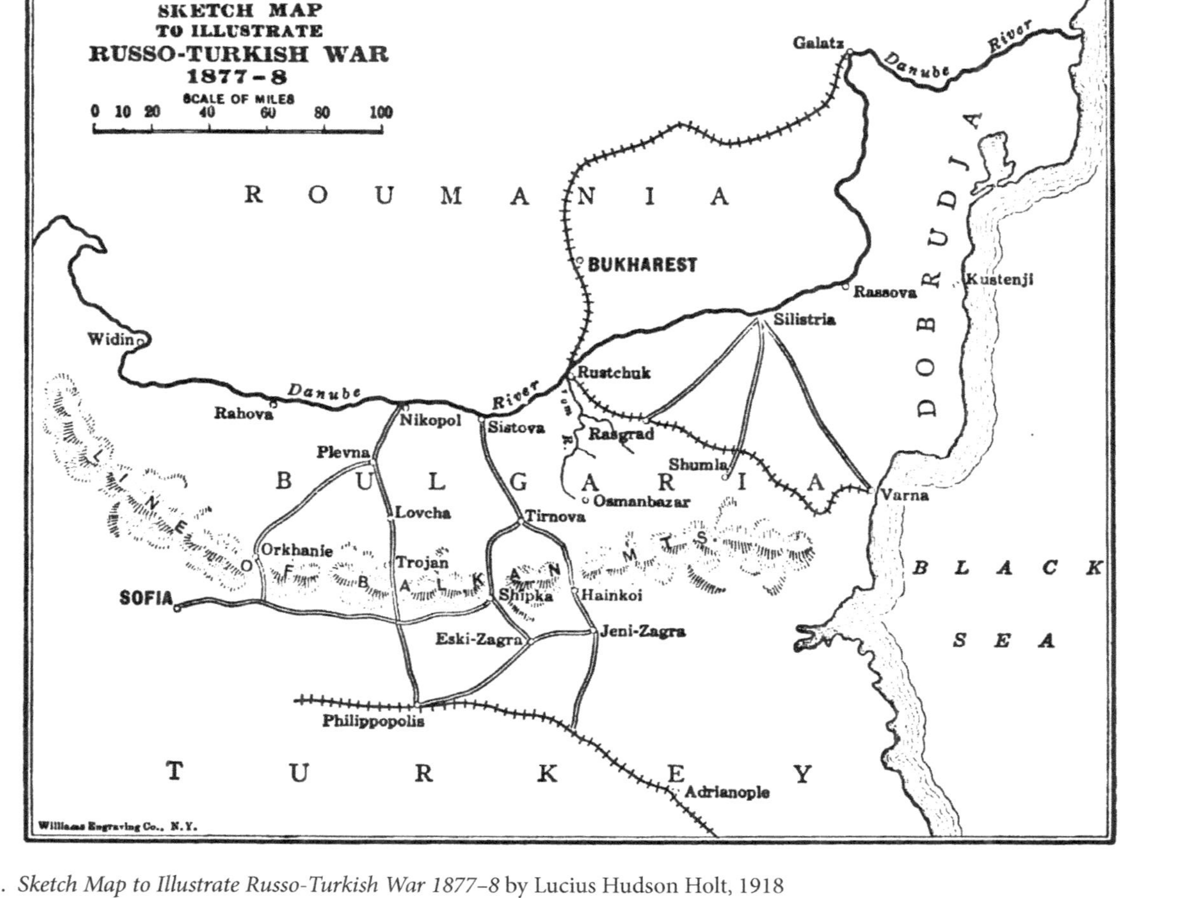

Map 5.1. *Sketch Map to Illustrate Russo-Turkish War 1877–8* by Lucius Hudson Holt, 1918

Note: The original map appeared in colour. The red for the Turkish population was converted to white for legibility in black and white.

Source: Lucius Hudson Holt, *The History of Europe from 1862 to 1914* (New York: Macmillan, 1918), 198. Map originally printed by Williams Engraving, New York. Originally held by the New York Public Library and digitalized by Google. Via the Internet Archive (user tpb).

remarkable success of the small army of Prince Paskevich in Asiatic Turkey in 1828–9.[130] Since then, Ignatiev had become convinced that in the future the Russian army should focus its efforts on the Asian theatre. During his diplomatic service in Constantinople, Ignatiev "used every opportunity" to convince the officers of the General Staff dispatched to Turkey by the Caucasian viceroy of the necessity to concentrate on the Asian frontier of the Ottoman Empire "a force capable of promptly obtaining startling and decisive results."[131]

Apart from climatic considerations, Ignatiev's proposals had far-reaching demographic implications, which were well expressed by the sympathetic Miliutin. In late July 1876, the war minister supported the suggestion of ambassador Ignatiev and Colonel A.S. Zelenoi to concentrate the troops of the Caucasian corps on the Ottoman border near Aleksandropol "in order to keep in Asiatic Turkey at least part of the Ottoman troops and those semi-savage hordes that were going to rush into the Balkan Peninsula against the poor Slavs." Miliutin only regretted that the opposition to this idea on the part of Caucasian viceroy Grand Duke Mikhail Nikolaevich had caused the Russians to lose time, so that "all the Asian scum has already fallen on the Balkans."[132]

In addition to the unwillingness of the grand duke, Ignatiev's idea encountered counterarguments of other Russian officers. One of them was Colonel N.D. Artamonov, who had surveyed European Turkey in the late 1860s.[133] In May 1876, Artamonov composed a memorandum summarizing the experience of the previous Russian-Ottoman wars and suggesting the most advantageous strategic choices. For Artamonov, the resolution of the Eastern Question equalled the abolition of the Ottoman Empire in the Balkans, which is why the Asian theatre of war could have only secondary importance.[134] Artamonov fully shared Ignatiev's concern about the perilousness of the Danubian and Balkan region for the Russian troops, yet his proposed solution consisted in securing the quickest possible strike across the Balkans to the Ottoman capital.[135] Artamonov reproduced verbatim Obruchev's earlier considerations on the preferability of the operational line across the middle part of Danubian Bulgaria and stressed the perils of engaging the Ottomans in the fortress warfare on the Lower Danube.

As so many Russian authors before him, Artamonov pointed to the difficulty of capturing the Ottoman fortresses. Although they usually failed to follow the principles of modern fortification, Ottoman fortresses, according to Artamonov, would attract all Muslim inhabitants from the environs, "of whom all those capable of carrying arms were soldiers who would daily appear on the walls." Imbued with "the spirit of struggle against the infidels," the Muslim inhabitants constituted "the most important force of defence" of the Ottoman fortresses, which made it particularly important to "shake their morale."[136] Since the Ottoman Muslim population was both brave and prone to panic, Artamonov argued that the desired result could be achieved by sudden investment and massive bombardment. Here again, the earlier failure of the Russian commanders to supply the besieging troops with sufficiently strong siege artillery served as an *a contrario* confirmation of Artamonov's thesis.[137]

Obruchev attached Artamonov's memorandum to his own first draft of the campaign plan submitted first to Miliutin and, eventually, to the tsar in October 1876.[138] As a result of Ottoman suppression of the April Uprising, Obruchev defined the war aims as "wrenching from the dominance of the Turks that country (Bulgaria), in which they have committed so many atrocities." Although Russian championship of the rights and interests of their Orthodox co-religionists had long figured as one of the leitmotifs of Russia's Eastern policy, Russian war planning rarely took the actual security of Christians into consideration. By contrast, Obruchev did just that when he insisted that the "extreme rapidity of the Russian operations" was essential to "[saving] the Christian population" that was the object of Russia's intercession.[139] Taking into consideration "the bitter experience of the previous war," Russia had to avoid fortress warfare. Having quickly crossed the Danube, the Russian army ought to "get beyond the Balkans" in a single coup and "take only those fortified places that were absolutely necessary for securing [its] rear." Obruchev recommended employing numerous Cossack cavalry, which alone was able to endure the shortage of fodder in Bulgaria and, at the same time, secure a "quick and more or less scattered [*razbrosannyi*] occupation of the country."[140]

Obruchev also rearticulated his earlier arguments in favour of the operational line across the more western parts of Bulgaria. In previous "Turkish" wars, he argued, the Russian army would cross the Danube in the lower course and besiege the powerful fortresses of Rushchuk, Silistria, Varna, and Shumla. Only in 1829 did the Russians manage to get beyond this quadrangle of Ottoman strongholds, cross the eastern Balkans, and occupy Adrianople. However, on that occasion their army had kept close to the Black Sea coast and had been supported by the Russian fleet, which was no longer there in the 1870s due to demilitarization of the Black Sea in the wake of the Crimean War. The insecurity of the littoral apart, argued Obruchev, eastern Bulgaria was to be avoided because of the preponderance here of the Turkish and émigré Circassian population "capable of stubborn resistance." The Russian strategist suggested using a secondary force to occupy the Galați bent on the Lower Danube and "conducting the main operations on the middle Danube and in the central Bulgaria." Here the river went farthest into European Turkey, which would place the Russian army at the shortest distance from its goal. An operational line across the middle Danube would allow the Russian army to render prompt assistance to the Bulgarian population to the east, west, or south, as well as to coordinate its actions with the Serbian and Montenegrin forces.[141]

The only similarity between Obruchev's approach and that of the planners of the earlier "Turkish" campaigns was the assumption that the Asian front was clearly secondary. In contrast to Ignatiev, Obruchev argued that an expedition into the depth of Anatolia was costly, while the occupation of the frontier territories could not have a decisive impact upon the Ottomans in view of the distance that separated the Caucasus from Constantinople. For this reason, Obruchev suggested limiting Russian goals here to the occupation of Kars and Batum and concentrating the bulk of the available Russian forces in the European theatre. Mindful of the role that Austria played in aborting Russia's Danubian campaign in 1854, Obruchev suggested making provisions for the formation of a Galician army, "should Austria join the British policy."[142]

Dated 1 October 1876, Obruchev's plan presupposed the launching of the military operations that same fall and their completion within two or three months. The advantages of catching the Ottomans unprepared during the time of the year when they were least disposed to fight would outweigh the difficulties of such a campaign. However, the element of surprise that could allow Russia to achieve its goals in European Turkey with limited forces disappeared in the midst of the diplomatic negotiations of the fall and winter. Ignatiev, who represented Russia at the Constantinople Conference in December 1876, informed the Russian headquarters in Kishinev of the growing Ottoman effectives in Europe, their improving quality and organization as well as of the preparation of the Ottoman fortresses in the north-eastern Balkans.[143] By the time the Constantinople Conference came to an unsuccessful end, the Ottomans had relocated their forces from defeated Serbia and Montenegro to the Danube and the Asian frontier and mobilized not only the reserve of the regular troops (*redif*), but also the land militia (*moustafiz*), so that "virtually all the able-bodied Muslim population was armed and called to the colours."[144] Upon returning to St. Petersburg in February 1877, Ignatiev declared that "the favourable moment for dealing the Ottoman Empire a decisive blow had been irrevocably lost."[145]

At this moment, Ignatiev submitted a memorandum to the minister of war in which he once again tried to draw the attention of the Russian military to the necessity of concentrating efforts on the Asian theatre of war. In contrast to the Danubian army, which had to cross Romania and the Danube before it entered Ottoman territory, Russian troops in the Caucasus could enter Turkey immediately after the declaration of war, which "could not fail to have an impact both on the Ottoman government and the population of the country." According to Ignatiev, the fact that the Muslims constituted the majority of the population of the Asian war theatre was an advantage. The Russian invasion would thereby have "a much greater influence upon the dominant element of the Ottoman Empire" than an invasion in the European theatre, where the Muslims were less numerous than the Christians. The forces of the sultan consisted primarily of their Asian subjects, which was why the desired result could be more easily achieved by threatening "the source of their power" than by challenging them in Bulgaria.[146]

Ignatiev also argued that the triumphs of the Russian troops in Asia were likely to have a greater impact on Europe, and especially on England, where "concerns about the routes to India trampled any other consideration." While they were unable to stop the advance of the Russian army to Erzerum and Sivas, the British "could always count on Austria-Hungary and the jealousy of the other great powers to restrain our hand in Europe." Once they entered the Asian provinces, Russian Caucasian troops would attract the Ottoman reserves and facilitate the Russian operations on the Danube. According to Ignatiev, this represented the best means of "defending the Caucasus" and "preventing the Turks and the English agents from raising the uprising of our mountaineers and intriguing among our Transcaucasian Muslims."[147] Ignatiev argued that it would be wrong to limit the numerous Caucasian corps to secondary operations in Kabulistan (as was the intention of the Caucasian viceroy, Grand Duke Mikhail Nikolaevich). According to Ignatiev, the goal of the war in Asia was to "beat and disperse the Ottoman forces in Armenia, penetrate Anatolia and, by a decisive movement to Sivas (and even beyond, if necessary), force the sultan to demand peace and have his friends and counsellors to pressure him to submit to our demands in order to save his empire from definitive collapse."[148]

Although the General Staff found Ignatiev's reported figure of 600,000 mobilized Ottoman troops exaggerated, Obruchev realized that the limited Russian force envisioned in his October plan could no longer quickly occupy Bulgaria and capture Constantinople. After all the preparations that the Ottomans had the time to make over late fall and winter, the realization of these goals could be secured only if the Russian forces in the European theatre were doubled to allow a full-fledged army of some 100,000–120,000 to make a breakthrough across the Balkans and another one of comparable size to secure its rear in Danubian Bulgaria.[149] The choice of operational line across the middle Danube into central Bulgaria remained the same, yet Obruchev suggested that the army assigned to operate in Danubian Bulgaria not only occupy Babadag and besiege Rushchuk, but also make forays into Dobrogea and Deliorman, control the Slinvo and Gabrovo passes across the Balkans, and, possibly, even attack Shumla.

Obruchev's updated plan can be seen as a partial return to the patterns of Russian strategic planning during the earlier wars, inasmuch as it presupposed active operations on the Lower Danube and in the quadrilateral of the Ottoman fortresses. Obruchev once again recognized the dangers of fortress warfare and acknowledged that the dispersion of the Russian forces between Silistria, Shumla, and Varna made the campaign of 1828 largely futile. Nevertheless, he believed that the Rushchuk-Varna railway line constructed in the wake of the Crimean War made a difference, by enabling the transportation of heavy artillery to Shumla and Varna.[150] As in the fall of 1876, Obruchev viewed the Asian theatre as a secondary one, yet he concurred with Ignatiev that the Caucasian army would similarly have to be doubled if the capture of Constantinople from the European side proved to be impossible (e.g., if the British intervened decisively). In this case, the realization of the war goals could be achieved only by "the destruction of the land possessions of Turkey in both Europe and Asia," which necessitated the advance of the augmented Caucasian army deep into Anatolia.[151]

The impossibility of effectively doubling its forces in the European theatre led the Russian army to pursue a strategy that was closer Obruchev's original suggestions of October 1876. As will be shown in the next chapter, the lack of coordination between different Russian detachments after their successful crossing of the Danube on 10 June 1877, fatally undermined Obruchev's goal of rapidly occupying trans-Balkan Bulgaria and protecting the Christian population. As a result, Obruchev's strategy, designed to maximize the security of Russia's co-religionists, had the opposite effect of making the Bulgarian population more vulnerable to the reprisals of the Ottomans. As will be shown, the unsuccessful pursuit of Obruchev's plan also turned out to be a factor that increased the vulnerability of the local Muslim population. Transferred to the Asian theatre on the insistence of his enemy, commander-in-chief Grand Duke Nikolai Nikolaevich, Obruchev had no control over the implementation of the strategy in Europe that he had helped to design and thus hardly bears responsibility for these unexpected outcomes, which will be addressed in the next chapter.

In Obruchev's thinking, the co-religionist population figured as potential victims who had to be protected while his choice of operational line in principle minimized the contact between the Russian army and the masses of the Muslim population of the eastern Balkans. In other words, Obruchev hardly envisioned raising the Bulgarians for a national war against the Muslims, which was advocated by Kishelskii and Fadeev. At the same time, Obruchev's war planning, like the contribution of Artamonov and Ignatiev to this process, reveals the much greater role that the population factor played in Russian strategic choices in 1876–7 than was the case in either 1828–9 or 1853–4. For all the differences of style and perspective, the Russian war planners at the time of the Eastern Crisis were not unlike the pan-Slavist generals in recognizing the importance of the inhabitants of the war theatre for the military and political outcomes of the confrontation. Reflecting the mounting role of population in contemporary military statistics, Russian war planning in 1876–7 in turn had a major impact upon different religious and ethnic groups of European Turkey during and after the Russian-Ottoman war of 1877–8.

6 Russian Population Policies during the War of 1877–1878

While the Russian army prepared for war, the diplomats made last-minute efforts to find a peaceful solution to the crisis. The principal fruit of these efforts was the Constantinople Conference, convoked in December 1876, at which the representatives of the European powers and Russia presented to the Porte a plan of reconciliation with its Balkan Christian subjects. The collective intervention of the European diplomats was based on prior agreement that was reached between Ignatiev and the British extraordinary and plenipotentiary ambassador to Constantinople, Lord Salisbury, to which other European representatives soon adhered. According to this plan, the defeated Serbia had to regain the territories that had been occupied by the Ottoman army, Montenegro had to incorporate the rebellious districts of Herzegovina, while the rest of Herzegovina and Bosnia had to form an autonomous province. Most importantly, the plan presupposed the formation of two autonomous Bulgarian provinces that would include the Bulgarian-majority territories both to the north and to the south of the Balkan range.[1] Even though the British thwarted Ignatiev's proposal for a single autonomous Bulgaria, the plan presented to the Porte for the first time followed the "ethnographic principle" of territorial delimitation.

The Porte countered the proposals of the Constantinople Conference with the new Ottoman constitution, which supposedly assured the rights of the Christian population and their adequate political representation in the prospective Ottoman parliament.[2] After the failure of the plan became evident, the Russian Foreign Ministry focused its efforts on the diplomatic preparation of the war, namely on securing the Austrian neutrality. In late June 1876, Alexander II met Franz Joseph I at Reichstadt for an informal discussion of the political restructuring of the Balkans after the prospective Serbian-Ottoman War. The Russian-Austrian bargaining eventually resulted in the secret military and political conventions of January and March 1877 signed by the Russian ambassador in Vienna, E.P. Novikov, and the Austrian foreign minister, Gyula Andrassy. The conventions assured Austria-Hungary's "benevolent neutrality" in the upcoming Russian-Ottoman war on condition of the Austrian occupation of Bosnia and Herzegovina. The political convention also excluded the creation of "a big Slavic state" in the Balkans, a stipulation that was subsequently interpreted very differently by the Russians and the Austrians.[3]

In parallel, St. Petersburg applied pressure on Romania to assure the passage of the Russian troops through its territory, as well as its eventual entry into the war as Russia's ally. The principal difficulty here was the question of Southern Bessarabia, which Alexander II had been forced to cede in 1856 under the conditions of the Treaty of Paris and was now determined to recuperate. Having visited the tsar in Crimea in October 1876, the Romanian prime minister, Ion C. Brătianu, was well aware of Russia's intention to reannex the territory, which Brătianu, as any Romanian nationalist, considered to be Romanian. In contrast to the Turcophile faction within the Romanian parliament, Brătianu and Romanian foreign minister Mihai Kogălniceanu realized the impossibility of opposing Russia by force yet prepared for a diplomatic battle for Southern Bessarabia after the war. Accordingly, the Russian-Romanian convention, concluded after some hard bargaining on 16 April 1877, affirmed Romania's territorial integrity.[4]

On 12 April 1877, Alexander II declared war on the Ottoman Empire. Having paraded before the tsar in Kishinev, the Russian troops crossed the Pruth River by the new railway bridge designed by Gustave Eiffel and entered the territory of Romania, which soon proclaimed independence from the Ottoman Empire and became Russia's ally. Six weeks later, the Russian forces under the command of Grand Duke Nikolai Nikolaevich crossed the Danube at Zimnitsa (Zimnicea) and rapidly occupied the central part of Danubian Bulgaria, leaving the eastern and western parts of the province under the control of significant concentrations of the Ottoman forces. On 24 June, the Russian vanguard of Lieutenant General I.V. Gurko captured Tyrnovo, the capital of the medieval Bulgarian kingdom that had fallen to the Ottomans five centuries earlier.

At this point, Nikolai Nikolaevich came up with the idea of a rapid advance across the Balkans that could force the Ottomans to abandon Rushchuk, Shumla, and Varna and retreat to the south of the mountains in order to defend Constantinople.[5] The grand duke thereby reproduced the logic of Obruchev's initial plan of the campaign, which, as will be remembered, presupposed a rapid strike across the Balkans on Adrianople through the country with the overwhelmingly Bulgarian population. Given the grand duke's enmity towards Obruchev and his role in the removal of the latter to the Asian theatre of the war, an attempt to implement what was de facto Obruchev's idea appears ironic. It also proved to be quite tragic since Nikolai Nikolaevich was certainly not up to the task of assuring supreme coordination of the Russian forces that this ambitious plan required.

Nikolai Nikolaevich's immediate subordinates were likewise problematic. His chief of staff, A.A. Nepokoichitskii, was one of the first graduates of the General Staff Academy and a veteran of the Caucasian and the Crimean wars. However, he was well over sixty at the time of the war, lacked initiative, and soon became quite unpopular in the army because of his association with the company of "Gerger, Horwitz and Kogan," which was contracted to assure the provision of the Russian troops, but often failed to do it properly. Nepokoichitskii's immediate subordinate, deputy chief of staff Major General K.V. Levitskii, belonged to the same generation as Obruchev and was one of the best in his class at the General Staff Academy. In the months preceding the war, he coordinated the intelligence gathering activities of colonels G.I. Bobrikov and P.D. Parensov in Romania and the Lower Danube.[6] At the same time, Levitskii lacked Nepokoichitskii's steadfastness and, in Miliutin's view, was rather scatterbrained. That both Nepokoichitskii and Levitskii were of Polish origin did not add to their popularity in the Russian army, although, in all fairness, their loyalty was beyond doubt.

In November 1876, in a memorandum written on Nikolai Nikolaevich's invitation, Levitskii followed Obruchev and Artamonov in the choice of the operational line. He argued that the shorter route taken by the Russian armies in the past across the Lower Danube was to be avoided because of the Silistria, Varna, and Shumla fortresses, the threat of the British navy along the Black Sea coast as well as the sparse population of the country. By contrast, crossing the Danube between Rushchuk and Vidin would enable the swift capture of the Balkan passes. According to Levitskii, the appearance of even the light cavalry troops in the valley of Maritsa could have a "big moral impact" on both the Ottoman troops that still confronted the Serbians and upon the Bulgarian population, which would allow to "proceed immediately to the formation of the Bulgarian militias [*druzhiny*]." Having incorporated these elements of the "people's war" into the proposed strategy, Levitskii nevertheless gave a nod in the direction of the old strategic thinking by pointing to the paramount importance of Rushchuk. He warned that "it would be highly dangerous to advance across the Balkans before the capture of this fortress."[7] This concession to the fortress warfare explained the strengthening of the left flank of the Russian army and the relative weakness of its right flank, which proved to be quite fateful.

To make matter worse, the circumstances of summer 1877 were no longer those of the fall of 1876, when Obruchev formulated his bold plan. Over the winter, the Ottomans managed to concentrate considerable forces in Europe as well as fortify their positions. It will be remembered that Obruchev recognized this and his updated plan for the campaign of March 1877 combined a strike across the Balkans together with a more systematic investment of the eastern part of Danubian Bulgaria. However, the forces under the command of Nikolai Nikolaevich were some 50,000 soldiers short of what Obruchev deemed necessary to implement in his updated plan. This meant that Nikolai Nikolaevich was de facto trying to implement Obruchev's initial idea of rapid offensive with limited forces in conditions than were much less propitious than before. Dispatched to the Caucasus, Obruchev did not have the ability to alert the tsar and others to the perils of such an undertaking.

In retrospect, Obruchev's plan could have worked in the summer of 1877 only if the Ottoman forces concentrated on Russian flanks had remained entirely passive. Although this was largely the case of Abdul Kerim Nadir Pasha, who commanded the Ottoman troops in the quadrilateral, the commander of the Vidin corps, Osman Nuri Pasha, showed greater initiative in his actions against the weaker right flank of the Russian army. In the first half of July, Osman Pasha's forces left Vidin and captured Plevna, from which they could threaten the Russian communications in the central parts of Danubian Bulgaria. The advance of the main part of the Russian army across the Balkans was impossible until Plevna was recaptured. Since two Russian attempts to do so were unsuccessful, Gurko's vanguard had to retreat to the north of the Balkans. The effective failure of the Russian campaign plan caused considerable dislocation of the population of the eastern Balkans by fall 1877. It fell upon the provisional Russian administration in Bulgaria to deal with consequences of this dislocation, which necessitates an overview of its formation and early activities.

The Formation of the Russian Provisional Administration in Bulgaria

In November 1876, Alexander II designated V.A. Cherkasskii as the head of the Russian provisional administration to be established in the occupied territories after the outbreak of the war. One of the Moscow Slavophiles, Cherkasskii (see figure 6.1) worked alongside D.A. Miliutin's younger brother N.A. Miliutin and Iu.F. Samarin in the editorial committee that prepared the peasant reform of 1861. Several years later he joined the younger Miliutin and Samarin as a member of the Commission of Internal Affairs in the Kingdom of Poland. In the wake of the Polish uprising of 1863, this commission tried to make the Polish peasants loyal to the Russian tsar by liberating them from the tutelage of the rebellious Polish landlords. Cherkasskii was then elected mayor of Moscow, in which capacity he contributed to the municipal reform of 1870. This remarkable career came to halt when the prince signed an "inappropriate" petition to the tsar that asked for greater liberty of expression. However, this incident must have been forgotten by the time of the outbreak of the Eastern Crisis when the tsar summoned Cherkasskii on Miliutin's suggestion and instructed him "do beyond the Danube something similar to what we had done in Poland."[8]

Cherkasskii's activities as the head of the civil administration in Bulgaria demonstrate that a convinced Slavophile was not necessarily and uncritically pan-Slavist. The prince kept at arms length numerous Bulgarian activists who

Figure 6.1. Portrait of Prince Vladimir Aleksandrovich Cherkasskii by I.N. Kramskoi, 1879

Source: I.N. Kramskoi, *Portrait of Prince Vladimir Alexandrovich Cherkassky (1824–1878)*, 1879, oil on canvas, 108 × 85 cm, State Historical Museum, Moscow, Russia. Via Wikimedia Commons.

viewed the war and the Russian presence in the eastern Balkans as an opportunity to implement their visions. In the course of 1877, Cherkasskii's irritable personality was like a cold shower for many Bulgarian hotheads and their pan-Slavist sympathizers among the Russians. His critical perspective upon the Bulgarians transpires in his self-defined duty of "protection of the freedom of religion of foreigners, including Muslims, from the manifestations of local fanaticism."[9] At the same time, Cherkasskii's Slavophile background made him view the conflict as a confrontation between Orthodox Christianity and Islam. Although the prince could be quite critical towards the Bulgarian "brothers," he had no soft spot for followers of the Prophet, whom he considered to be fundamentally the guilty side. This explains his approach to the management of inter-confessional relations in the territories occupied by the Russian army following the outbreak of the war.

In the seven months that elapsed between his appointment to the new post and the Russian crossing of the Danube, Cherkasskii preoccupied himself, among other things, with gathering statistical information on the region.[10] Reflective of his experience with statistics in the context of the Great Reforms, Cherkasskii's efforts paralleled and replicated the statistical studies of the Russian General Staff cited in the previous chapter, as well as the intelligence gathering efforts of Grand Duke Nikolai Nikolaevich's staff on the eve of the war.[11] The prince in fact acknowledged the expertise of the military men in this domain and appointed a General Staff Academy graduate, Colonel L.N. Sobolev, as the head of special statistics gathering commission that he set up in Bucharest after the formal declaration of the war in April 1877.[12] In the 1860s, Sobolev spent several years in Turkestan and produced a statistical study of one of the provinces that received an award from the Russian Geographical Society.

The fruit of Sobolev's efforts in 1877 was the five-volume *Materials for the Study of Bulgaria,*[13] which revealed the uncertainty of the ethnographic and statistical data necessary for the resolution of the problem of the Christian population in European Turkey. The Russian officials refused to believe that the difference between the number of Muslims and non-Muslims of European Turkey constituted only 1,118,138 people, as the most recent Ottoman official data presented by Abdolonymph Ubicini had it.[14] According to Sobolev and his subordinates, this "gross inaccuracy" utterly destroyed the credibility of the official Ottoman statistics.[15] At the same time, Sobolev did not want to unduly undercount the actual number of Muslims of Bulgaria. He doubted that the latter were only 600,000, as some Russian authors argued, for this would bring the number of the Osmanli Turks to only 150,000 after one deducted some 300,000 Pomaks and at least 150,000 Tatars and Circassians.[16] The numbers on Bulgarians ranged, according to different sources, between 2 and 7 million, as did the populations counts of the Greeks (between 900,000 and 2,900,000).[17]

In a report submitted to Miliutin on the eve of the Russian passage of the Danube, Cherkasskii argued that the difficulties of reorganization of the country were proportionate to a greater or smaller share of the Turkish population in a given region and suggested to tailor the length of the Russian post-war occupation accordingly.[18] As Liprandi and Obruchev before him, Cherkasskii pointed to the heavily Muslim eastern region of Danubian Bulgaria, and Slivno *sanjak* to the south of it, as potentially the most troublesome territories. The commissioner was much less concerned with the small, predominantly urban, Muslim minority in the rest of Danubian Bulgaria and in the trans-Balkan territories. Nor did Cherkasskii expect many problems in the Rhodope Mountains and Macedonia, whose relatively numerous Muslims were of Bulgarian, Albanian, or Serbian origin.[19]

Cherkasskii believed that disarmament of the Muslim population was necessary in order to "avoid in future bloody clashes between different ethnic groups of the Balkan Peninsula." The commissioner found support for such a measure in the protocols of the Constantinople Conference of December 1876, as well as in the practice of the Russian administration in the Caucasus and parts of Asia Minor that were being occupied by the Russian troops.[20] At the same time, Cherkasskii advised against house searches that could provoke the Muslims. Instead, he suggested introducing a system of fines for the non-delivery of a specified number of weapons determined for each locale on the basis of the number of Muslim houses and the testimonies of the "worthiest local Christians." He argued that there was no need to disarm the Bulgarian population, for, "having already been disarmed by the Turks themselves, they [had] only a very small number of weapons, which they [needed] badly in order to protect themselves from possible attacks by the Muslims."[21]

Cherkasskii's approval of proposals for the disarmament of the Muslims was based on reports about the clashes between the Muslim and Christian populations on the right bank of the Danube that immediately followed the Russian declaration of war.[22] According to one such report from Tulcha, the Circassians who immigrated to Dobrogea in the early 1860s were "mercilessly plundering the Christian properties" and desecrating the churches. The author of the report, M.D. Tivchev, the order of the local Ottoman authorities to evacuate the city helped "Circassians and Turks" to "plunder and ruin" local Christians. Having formed a committee, the Tulcha Christians refused to follow the order and took up arms to defend their homes, yet feared that their rich region "will turn into a desert" unless the Russian army promptly came to rescue.[23]

Another report presented the wretched Bulgarians as "victims of the abuses of the ferocious Turks" and "playthings of the freakish Circassian fiend [*igrushka prichudlivogo zlodeia-cherkesa*]."[24] According to the authors of the report, plunder of Christian property, desecration of churches, and arson happened not only in Tulcha, but also in Isakcha, Machin, Babadag, and their environs. From the communication of the Russian consul in Galați, A.S. Romanenko, it appears that the ferocity of the Circassian repressions increased as a result of the resistance that the Bulgarian population initially put up to such raids. The consul questioned the sincerity of the Ottoman declarations of powerlessness in the face of this religious fanaticism and insinuated that the Ottoman government itself was doing everything to "stoke the fanaticism" of the Muslim masses.[25]

Although Romanenko blamed the Ottoman government, his report placed into doubt the reality of the straightforward Christian-Muslim divide by mentioning that the Bulgarians sought and found protection from Circassian raids not only in the villages of the Russian Old Believers, but also in the settlements of the Crimean Tatar emigrants in Dobrogea.[26] In fact, following the outbreak of the war, the Circassian raids became a problem not only for the right-bank Christians, but also for the local Muslims, as is clear from petition of both Bulgarian *and* Turkish population of the villages of Batak, Dolnii Studen

(Karaesene, Dolna Studena), and Gornyi Studen (Gorna Studena) to "protect them from the attacks and banditry of the Circassians."[27] Although the Russian command readily identified the Circassians as quintessential troublemakers, it largely failed to recognize that Circassian raids could be as much a problem for the eastern Balkan Muslims as they were for the local Christians.[28]

The Russian authorities perceived the problem of tensions between the Muslims and Christians almost exclusively as the problem of the security of the latter. The head of the Russian intelligence network in Romania and Bulgaria, P.D. Parensov, went as far as to propose the distribution of weapons to the Bulgarian population by the advance detachments of the Russian army. According to Parensov, the Christian inhabitants who greeted the Russians could fall victim to the revenge of their Muslim neighbours and the bashi-bazouks in the period between the departure of the Russian vanguard detachments and the arrival of the main army.[29] Although Nikolai Nikolaevich rejected this proposal as extreme, he likewise tended to overestimate the Muslim threat to the Christian population and, at the same time, to underestimate both the possibility of Christian attacks on Muslims and conflicts within the Muslim population.

Concerns with the protection of the Christian population also informed the approach of the Russian command to the question of Bulgarian militia. The War Ministry retained Fadeev's proposed mode of organization of the militia, yet redefined its goal from that of a large vanguard combat force to a much smaller military police agency that had to prevent banditry, provide military intelligence, and liaise between the Russian army and the local population. "The Foundations for the Organization of Bulgarian Militia" noted that regardless of the future political status of Bulgaria, it would need a local armed force that would "protect the population from the banditry of Turks and Circassians." The document referred to the example of the militia that was formed in 1861 in Syria for the protection of Christians against the "predatory attacks" (*khishchnichestvo*) of the neighbouring Muslim tribes.[30] Rather than taking part in field battles, this force would have to "protect the local population from small parties of brigands" perform "escort and military police service in place of the currently existing Turkish *zaptii*, as well as aid the Russian troops as scouts by providing intelligence, discovering local resources [*raskrytiem sedstv strany*], and liaising with the local population [*sviazi s mestnym naseleniem*]."[31]

The "Foundations" presupposed the formation of militia units for western, central, and eastern Bulgaria, composed of local volunteers. They first had to assist the Russians in the occupation of these parts of the country and stay there to become the "ready element" (*gotovyi element*) for the organization of the military administration and of the land police as well as for the "development of the Bulgarian militia on a larger scale."[32] In this form, the project of the militia received the approval of the tsar, who entrusted its implementation to Major General N.I. Stoletov, a veteran of the wars in the Caucasus and Central Asia. Soon after the declaration of the war, the chief of the General Staff, F.L. Geiden, suggested enrolling in the Bulgarian militia those Bulgarian and Serbian volunteers who participated in the Serbian-Ottoman War of 1876 and were now returning to St. Petersburg together with the Russian volunteers.[33] However, Nikolai Nikolaevich found that "the right organization and combat force of any militia" depended on the "homogeneity of its composition." The grand duke decided to limit the recruitment pool to the local population of Bulgaria and exclude "any foreign elements," whether "Serbs or other Slavic or non-Slavic nationalities."[34] He thereby helped make the militia a specifically Bulgarian national force, whose appearance on the right bank of the Danube would have a polarizing impact on the local Bulgarian and Muslim population.

Remarkably, the Bulgarian leaders themselves were not unanimous in their attitude towards the militia that the Russians were about to create. In particular, the highly influential leader of the Bulgarian minority in Romania Evlogii Georgiev advised the Russian military agents in Bucharest to include a certain number of Bulgarians into the regular Russian units and use them as scouts, in particular for the crossing of the Balkan Mountains, rather than recruit Bulgarian volunteers into a separate national military force. Although Georgiev's extensive network of business agents greatly helped the officers of the General Staff to collect intelligence on the eve of the war, the leader of the so-called "Old Bulgarians" may have sensed the disruptive potential of a separate Bulgarian militia and preferred that the Russians rely on the traditional Balkan *hajduks*.[35] However, the Russian military men, even those who were not as hot-headed as Kishelskii and Fadeev, were increasingly looking in the direction of "people at arms" and ignored Georgiev's counsel.

Before long, Stoletov challenged the War Ministry's view of the function of the Bulgarian militia as an aid to the field army (*deistvuiushchaia armiia*) in "[protecting] the peace and order in the trans-Danubian region."[36] Instead, he believed that the militia had to join the Russian vanguard detachment and take part in battles. In the words of Stoletov, the Russian command had to "direct the activity of the Bulgarians who will take up arms against the Muslims and thereby regulate the national uprising [*narodnoe vosstanie*] according to the laws and customs of war."[37] Although the militia was not among the troops that were the first to cross the Danube, Stoletov's viewpoint ultimately prevailed, and the Bulgarians were assigned to the vanguard detachment of General I.V. Gurko, which captured Tyrnovo and the Balkan passes and eventually entered trans-Balkan Bulgaria in early July 1877.[38] As the following discussion demonstrates, this decision had important consequences for the Christian-Muslim relations after the outbreak of the war.

Inter-confessional Violence and Population Dislocations in the Summer and Fall of 1877

It soon became clear that the Christian population was thinking not only about self-protection. According to Cherkasskii's aide, Major General D.G. Anuchin, as soon as the Russians crossed the Danube near Sistova on 15 June 1877, all local Muslims fled, while the Bulgarians entered "some kind of intoxication" and began plundering their properties with "elemental anger." Having fraternized with the Bulgarians, some Russian soldiers joined in the pogrom that soon ceased to be "an expression of popular hatred" and came to be animated by "the basest inclinations." The chaos also spread to the surrounding countryside where deserters from the Bulgarian militia, "various local riffraff" and even occasional Orthodox priests formed the real bands of robbers.[39] The Muslim inhabitants responded by fleeing eastwards to Shumla and southwards across the Balkans, so that within a week of the Russian crossing very few of them were left in the entire territory between Nikopol, Plevna, Tyrnovo, the Yantra River, and the Danube.[40]

In view of the expected arrival of the tsar at the front, these outbreaks of violence greatly embarrassed the Russian command. Having arrested some 140 soldiers at Sistova for "various disorders [*bezobraziia*]," Nikolai Nikolaevich threatened to punish further breakdowns of discipline "with all the severity of the martial law."[41] The commander-in-chief also placed within the jurisdiction of the military courts the cases of murder, rape, banditry, robbery, and arson.[42] However, it was easier to restore discipline in the army than to prevent the Bulgarians from attacking the Muslims and their properties. Ten days later, a similar pogrom took place in Tyrnovo at the approach of Gurko`s vanguard detachment.[43] In the countryside, the Bulgarians would put on fire the villages that were abandoned by the Turks and the Russian advance units sometimes had to protect from "the vengeance of the Bulgarians" those Muslim elders, women, and children who failed to flee.[44] However, this protection could only be temporary as the Russian army continued its offensive leaving the Muslims and their emboldened Bulgarian neighbours in its rear. Minister of War Miliutin, who arrived in Bulgaria together with Alexander II, immediately pointed to the glaring contradiction between the spirit and letter of the tsar's proclamation to the population of Bulgaria on the one hand and the actual situation of the Muslims since the appearance of the Russian army on the other.

Under this criticism, Nikolai Nikolaevich's chief of staff, General A.A Nepokoichitskii, and Cherkasskii first tried to blame each other.[45] However, the arguments that each of them offered in self-defence ultimately complemented rather than contradicted one another. Nepokoichitskii pointed to "much hatred [that] had built up" between Christians and Muslims and claimed that "the Turks did well to go away." He admitted that "lapses are inevitable in wartime" and, at the same time, assured Miliutin that those Muslims who remained in the region "suffered no offences."[46] For his part, Cherkasskii declared his helplessness to do anything without a policing force "given the fervently hostile attitudes of the two populations that hate each other for reasons of faith and [ethnic] origin." Not unlike Nepokoichitskii, the head of civil administration asserted that the departure of Muslims was a good thing. "Given our exposed communications, he wrote to Miliutin, our only salvation is the absence of the Turks between the Danube and Tyrnovo. If they come back, we are much worse. Believe me and do not encourage them to return."[47]

Miliutin nevertheless insisted that something had to be done with the hundreds of Turkish families that were kept in the open field near the imperial headquarters at Bela (Byala).[48] Cherkasskii's proposal to send Ottoman prisoners of war to Russia, argued Miliutin, could not possibly be applied to the Muslim civilians arrested in this way, for their numbers were likely to increase to "thousands and hundreds of thousands of families" as the Russian army moved into the Ottoman interior. The minister of war observed that as of mid-July there was no supreme governing body that would have any instructions in this respect and that as soon as the headquarters moved to a different place, they would have died or fled.[49] He suggested appealing to the population to moderate their actions and creating a strong Bulgarian police force to restore order.[50] In the end, the troops were prohibited from treating unarmed Muslims, and especially women and children, as prisoners of war; instead, they had to be brought back to their villages and placed under the supervision of the village heads.[51]

Cherkasskii responded to the Bulgarian attacks on Muslim property and lives by demanding from the commander-in-chief some troops to serve as a police force. In early July, he admonished Nikolai Nikolaevich on the necessity of providing the emerging civil administration with the necessary military police means (*voenno-politseiskie sredstva*) "for the preservation of order and peace in the region."[52] Cherkasskii specifically urged the grand duke to specify "when exactly and on what scale the army will render this help … without which no civil administration will be able to do anything."[53] Cherkasskii argued that even in the completely peaceful Russian regions the civil authorities could not do without armed police and the army. According to Cherkasskii, "strong and reliable Russian police" were even more needed in Bulgaria, with its "dominant and acrimonious [*strastnyi*] division in the local population between the Bulgarians and the Turks, the Christians, and the Muslims." This division would take long to disappear, and "was likely to become even deeper," as was clear from the anger of Tyrnovo Bulgarians with the head of the Russian civil administration: the latter did not arrest the town's Muslim inhabitants who came to ask him for safe-conduct passes (*okhrannye listy*).[54]

Cherkasskii was critical of the idea of employing the Bulgarian militia or a special gendarmerie recruited from the Bulgarians for the maintenance of order. The militia have not yet interiorized military discipline and "was not completely foreign to passionate national aspirations." A gendarmerie would take long to create while its personnel was unlikely to remain impartial towards the local Muslim population. If all this was true of the predominantly Bulgarian territories that were already occupied by the Russian army, argued Cherkasskii, it would be even more true of certain areas of Osman Pazar (Omurtag), Sevlievo, Kazanlyk, and Slivno, where the Muslim population was more numerous and where it would probably decide to stay rather than flee.[55] Cherkasskii pointed out that all these considerations made the Constantinople Conference put forward the idea of an international European gendarmerie in Bulgaria. Now its place had to be taken by the Russian military force as "the only impartial mediator [*bezpristrastnyi element*] between the peoples of the Balkan Peninsula."[56]

Although he greatly overestimated the degree of impartiality of the Russian troops, the head of the civil administration identified a real problem, which only the Russian commander-in-chief had the power to solve. However, despite Cherkasskii's repeated appeals, Nikolai Nikolaevich failed to respond promptly, and here the enmity between Cherkasskii and Nepokoichitskii may have played a role.[57] In the meantime, the governors of Tyrnovo and Sistova failed to investigate the cases of the Bulgarian attacks on the Muslims due to a "lack of means to do so."[58] As the burnings of the Turkish villages continued, Miliutin feared the complications that this could create for the Russian authorities in future if the Turkish population returned to their abandoned hearths. In addition, it "gave a pretext for new accusations" against Russia.[59]

The Russian policy of disarming the Muslim inhabitants generated additional tensions. The Russian detachments advancing towards the Balkans were ordered to "disarm the Muslim population … and form an armed guard [*vooruzhennaia strazha*] from the local [Christian] population."[60] In this way, the Russian commanders sought to secure the Christian population against the attacks of Circassians and the bashi-bazouks (see figure 6.2), which were quite frequent.[61] The Muslims sometimes opposed the policy of disarmament by force, as happened in the village of Batak near Tyrnovo, where a skirmish between Russian dragoons and local inhabitants caused a fire that consumed half of the houses. In response, the Russians requisitioned the livestock of the Batak Muslims and executed six of them for armed resistance, as well as for the atrocities that they had supposedly committed against the local Christians.[62] In other cases, the Muslims surrendered only the old weapons and kept the newer ones in secret deposits, which enabled them to support the Ottoman troops when the latter regained some of their previously lost territory.[63] Finally, those Muslims who fled at the approach of the Russian troops often did so with their weapons, which turned them into targets for Russian cavalry units, who would attack them and capture their carts and livestock.[64]

Figure 6.2. *Two Hawks (Bashi-bazouks)* by V.V. Vereshchagin, 1878
Source: Vasily Vereshchagin, *Two Hawks (Bashi-bazouks)*, 1878, oil on canvas, 78.5 × 110 cm, Kyiv Picture Gallery National Museum, Kyiv, Ukraine. Via Wikimedia Commons.

In the territories further east, where the Muslims were more numerous, they were less likely to flee. Instead, they would retreat to the forests, but remained in the vicinity of their villages and offered armed resistance to the Russian troops. Thus, the troops of the 13th Army Corps, which occupied the territory between the Yantra and Kara Lom Rivers to the west of the Deliorman forest and the quadrilateral of the Ottoman fortresses, encountered sizable groups of armed inhabitants and Circassians hiding in the woods. These showed "great hostility"[65] and complicated the work of the Russian patrols and sentinels (*nabliudatel'no-okhrannaia sluzhba*).[66] In response, the Russian troops burned down some of those villages whose inhabitants offered resistance.[67]

With the sudden appearance of Gurko's vanguard on the southern side of the Balkans, many local Muslims fled, much like their co-religionists to the north of the mountains had done two weeks earlier.[68] For their part, the Bulgarians formed local militias, which attacked those Turks who did not manage to leave with the Ottoman troops. According to Anuchin, "The Muslim homes were plundered, mosques destroyed, and many Turks killed in the most merciless way."[69] One gets a sense of the lawlessness that reigned in the region during this period from the reports of the participants in the trans-Balkan raid. Thus, Second Lieutenant M.M. Chichagov wrote about daily requests from the Bulgarians for weapons, as well as frequent encounters with armed Bulgarians who "wandered everywhere, captured prisoners, fugitives, and Turkish marauders."[70] By mid-July, the inter-confessional and inter-ethnic violence in the trans-Balkan territories was out of control. According to Captain E.M. Bibikov who brought the news from Gurko to the Headquarters in mid-July 1877, "the popular hatred between Turks and Bulgarians assumed frightening proportions. Wherever the Russian troops approached, the Bulgarians would cut down the Turks and burn their houses to the ground. Elsewhere the Turks were raging over the Bulgarians and there was no possibility of calming down the passions."[71]

Events at Eski Zagra illustrate well the dynamics of the inter-confessional and inter-ethnic conflict in the context of an unstable front line.[72] Tensions between Turkish and Bulgarian inhabitants of the town had been building up ever since the abortive uprising of September 1875, organized by the Bulgarian Central Revolutionary Committee in Bucharest. The following spring, the areas to the west of Eski Zagra were affected by the much more serious April Uprising, the suppression of which made the European public denounce the "Turkish atrocities in Bulgaria." With the crossing of the Balkans by Gurko's vanguard in early July 1877, the tensions between the two communities reached a tipping point. The Bulgarian inhabitants had every reason to fear the bands of Circassians and bashi-bazouks who roamed in the environs, as well as the army of Suleiman Husnu Pasha, which marched from Adrianople to check Gurko's advance. For their part, the Muslim minority of the town feared their numerous Bulgarian neighbours radicalized by the nationalist propaganda and emboldened by the appearance of the Russian troops to the south of the Balkans.[73]

These mutual fears were further exacerbated by the events in the neighbouring towns. At the approach of the Russians, the Ottoman governor (*kaymakam*) of Kazanlyk formed a partisan band out of fugitive Ottoman soldiers and bashi-bazouks, which terrorized the Bulgarian population and even ambushed and killed a Russian officer. Having occupied Kazanlyk on 3 July, the Russians arrested the *kaymakam* together with several other "Turkish bandits." The Russians executed some of them "for the moral satisfaction of the Bulgarian inhabitants" and in order to prevent the latter from massacring the local Muslims.[74] In the meantime, the Ottoman authorities of Yeni Zagra carried out summary executions of some Bulgarians in the central square of the city for their supposedly pro-Russian attitudes.[75] Eager to avoid this fate, the Bulgarian members of Eski Zagra city council wrote a letter to "the commander-in-chief of the Kazanlyk region" imploring him to send in the troops in order to protect them from the wrath of the Muslims, who "have gone mad as a result of the events in Kazanlyk."[76]

In fact, the Muslims of Eski Zagra may have also welcomed the Russian occupation as a guarantee against a large-scale massacre. At least, they did not flee at the approach of the Russian troops as their counterparts in Sistova and Tyrnovo had done in June and there was no pogrom. However, the entry of the Russian cavalry detachments and of the Bulgarian militia into Eski Zagra on 9 July, did not calm down the passions. The Bulgarian inhabitants began to denounce some of their Muslim neighbours to the Russian commanders for real or imagined crimes.[77] The Bulgarian members of that the city council, headed by the famous nationalist Petko Slaveikov, identified the "evident bandits" among the Muslim inhabitants and expected the commander of the militia Stoletov to execute them on the spot. When the latter hesitated to do so, the Bulgarians accused him of "weakness and indecision."[78] Instead, Stoletov gave the order to arrest the families of the Muslim partisans and search the houses of other "influential and very untrustworthy" (*neblagonadezhnykh*) Turks.[79]

As in Kazanlyk, several Muslim notables of Eski Zagra had indeed left their families and formed bands that joined the bashi-bazouks and Circassians in plundering and burning down the Bulgarian villages in the environs of the town.[80] This forced the Bulgarian inhabitants of the region to gather in Eski Zagra under the protection of the Russian troops and the Bulgarian militia. In mid-July, numerous carts carrying wounded civilians began to arrive to the town daily.[81] In response, the Eski Zagra Bulgarians formed their own militia bands and urged Stoletov to give them weapons. They asked the Russian commander to permit them to collect the wounded from the neighbouring villages, bury the dead as well as assure the overall security in the environs of the town.[82]

In the meantime, the approach of the troops of Suleiman Pasha confirmed Stoletov's earlier observation that Gurko's vanguard "has gone too far and [that] retreat is no longer possible, especially for the militia, which will have to fight to the end defending the population."[83] Over the following few days, the Eski Zagra detachment fought unsuccessfully to re-establish a connection with the main forces of Gurko that had occupied Yeni Zagra. Pushed back to Eski Zagra, the Bulgarian militia put up a staunch fight, yet was ultimately unable to hold the ground against the prevailing Ottoman force. As the Ottomans forced their way into Eski Zagra on 19 July, the Bulgarian inhabitants and the militia began a chaotic retreat under the fire of the Ottoman troops and of the Muslim inhabitants of the town.[84] Up to 10,000 Bulgarians died in the process, and only the preoccupation of the Ottoman troops with plunder prevented them from inflicting still greater casualties.[85]

The second reversal that the Russian army suffered at Plevna on 18 July 1877 made it necessary to recall Gurko's forces to the north of the Balkans, whereupon the Bulgarian population of Yeni Zagra, Kazanlyk, and Eski Zagra felt the full force of Ottoman reprisals. At this time, the Ottomans also regained Lovcha and Gabrovo on the northern side of the Balkans, each time exacting severe reprisals against the local Christians.[86] Cherkasskii and his staff soon began to hear rumours about the beatings of men and children, the rape of women and girls, and even people being hung by the legs with fires set below their heads. In Eski Zagra, the Ottomans reportedly broke into a church and cut down many Bulgarians who tried to hide there. Anuchin could ascertain the veracity of these reports six months later, when he entered Eski Zagra with the Russian troops and saw a pile of rotten corpses of children in the courtyard of one of the houses.[87]

The Russian officers and civilian officials were unanimous in their denunciation of the "Turkish atrocities," yet by late July 1877, many of them were beginning to question the wisdom of organizing Gurko's expedition from both the military and the moral-political point of view. Cherkasskii wrote to Miliutin that it was wrong to "compromise the population and undermine its attachment to us" and predicted that the Bulgarians would reproach the Russians for what happened in Gabrovo, Lovcha, Yeni Zagra, and Eski Zagra.[88] The hero of the Sebastopol defence, General E.I. Totleben, who did not join the Russian army until September 1877, noted in his diary the terrible ambiguity of the Russian-Bulgarian relations after Gurko's retreat: "The Turks massacred the Bulgarians in the territories that we abandoned. We came to save the Bulgarians and yet they were dying because of our aid."[89] On the eve of the retreat, Gurko himself "[shuddered] to think that our temporary presence in these territories" would lead to "the annihilation of the entire Bulgarian population of the town of Eski Zagra and Kazanlyk and of the villages of the Tundja valley."[90]

The Ottoman reprisal measures at Eski Zagra and Yeni Zagra, caused the flight of tens of thousands of Bulgarians across the Balkans to the territory more firmly occupied by the Russians.[91] Gurko wrote to Cherkasskii about "chaos reigning on the Shipka Pass and the devastation of the fields between the Balkans, Gabrovo, and Tyrnovo caused by the fugitives, Russian transportation teams, and the troops themselves that suffered shortages of supplies."[92] The number of Bulgarian fugitives from beyond the Balkans, the environs of Lovcha, and Bebrovo, as well as the valley of the Lom, reached 200,000.[93] Their plight motivated the Bulgarian attacks on the Muslims in those parts of Danubian Bulgaria that were occupied by the Russians. Thus, at the news of the Ottoman reprisal measures to the south of the Balkans, the Christians killed the Muslims in three villages in the vicinity of Gabrovo on 28 July and burned down the large Turkish village of Trembesh near Tyrnovo on 30 July.[94]

Cherkasskii responded to this emergency by forming a special commission under Colonel P.A. Dometti that placed the Bulgarian refugees in the abandoned Turkish houses in villages and towns, fed them from the Muslim grain deposits, and distributed among them the money collected by the Moscow Slavic Benevolent Committee.[95] As early as June 1877, he authorized the Bulgarian village heads to collect harvest from the abandoned Turkish fields and retain one-third of it for the Bulgarian refugees (the rest being reserved for the Muslim owners).[96] According to Cherkasskii, the cost of assistance to the trans-Balkan refugees could not fall exclusively on the Russian administration, or on the Bulgarians of Tyrnovo and Sistova. This was a "common cause of the society" (*obshchee zemskoe delo*), and the expenses associated with it had to fall "on all proprietors and inhabitants regardless of faith and nationality." For this reason, the head of Russian civil administration believed that "the flight of some Turkish inhabitants does not absolve them from the duty to bear their share of the common burden." On this ground, the Bulgarian refugees were given not only the Turkish harvest and a one-year usufruct of the Turkish land, but also "all sorts of monetary sums and revenues obtained by the local financial departments from the sale of the Turkish movables and the leasing of their properties."[97]

Whereas in the western part of Danubian Bulgaria, the occupation of the abandoned Turkish homes by the Christian refugees from beyond the Balkans took place on the initiative of the Russian civil administration, further east, in Dobrogea, it occurred spontaneously following the pattern already established during the previous Russian-Ottoman wars. According to the Tulcha governor, Iuzefovich, the local Muslims who had fled during the earlier Russian occupations did not return either because they died or because they preferred to settle somewhere in the south. As a result, the number of the Christian settlements grew with time. In Iuzefovich's testimony, the same process occurred again in 1877; before the Russian administration could blink an eye, the abandoned Muslim villages were occupied by Christian inhabitants.[98] Although Iuzefovich authorized these occupations until the return of the owners, the squatters, mindful of the past experience, clearly expected to stay put.

The failure of the third Russian attack on Plevna in late August 1877 and the decision to undertake a systematic siege finally provided the civil administration with the law enforcement units that it asked for. In October, Nikolai Nikolaevich placed a Cossack regiment and two reserve battalions demanded by Cherkasskii at the disposal of the civil administration.[99] On Cherkasskii's suggestion, the commander-in-chief also invited some eighty officers of the St. Petersburg, Moscow, and Kiev military districts to serve in the civil administration as *sanjak* governors and heads of the districts. The staff (*shtaty*) of the Turkestan governor generalship temporarily served as the basis of this administration.[100] The Bulgarian militia, which took part in Gurko's expedition and later defended the Shipka Pass alongside the Russian troops, was likewise assigned for "the patrol and the police service" at Tyrnovo, Nikopol, and Sistova.[101] However, the participation of the Bulgarian militiamen in the maintenance of order remained minimal. Recruited from numerous Bulgarian seasonal workers in Romania, the militiamen often used their weapons for attack against local Christian as well as Muslim property and were as much a problem as a solution.[102]

Nevertheless, the reversals that the Russians suffered at Plevna and the influx of the Bulgarian refugees provided those who sought to arm the Bulgarian population with an opportunity to rearticulate their ideas.[103] Thus, the head of the Russian military intelligence service, Colonel N.D. Artamonov, argued that the Bulgarian militia was insufficient to defend all towns and villages from the raids of the bashi-bazouks as well as patrol the mountain passes and gather information on the Ottoman troops. According to Artamonov, the Ottoman government dispatched emissaries to raise the Muslim population and arm them with new weapons, which left Russians no other choice but to arm the Bulgarians in response. Apart from the local militias in particular villages and towns which had been formed since the moment of the Russian crossing of the Danube, Artamonov suggested creating small detachments (*cheta*) of Bulgarian brave men (*iunak*) that would gather military intelligence and patrol the routes in front of and on the flanks of the Russian army.[104]

In response to this project, Cherkasskii noted that the leaders of the *chetas* were "suspicious individuals," who should be placed under the supervision of the commanders of the Russian troops and who should be prohibited from operating in areas where the civil administration was already established. Since the *chetas* "will live only by plunder," argued Cherkasskii, they "should live exclusively at the expense of the Turkish population and not at the expense of those Christians whom we came to protect from violence."[105] By the time Cherkasskii expressed his reservations, Nikolai Nikolaevich had already authorized the famous *hajduk* Panaiot Khitov to form the proposed *chetas* in the region of Elena. As a result, the total number of Bulgarians enrolled into *chetas* in this area in the fall of 1877 reached 1,000 people. Some of them later crossed the Balkans together with the Russian army and fought with the Ottomans at Kazanlyk.[106]

Population dislocations, Muslim-Christian clashes and the maintenance of order were not the only challenges that the Russian military and civil authorities in Bulgaria had to face during the war. Relations with the Romanian allies as well as with the Bulgarians themselves could likewise be a source of headache as one can see from a private letter from the military governor of Nikopol, Lieutenant General A.D. Stolypin, to Cherkasskii.[107] Stolypin listed the heads of cattle and sheep as well as the amount of fodder and foodstuffs that the Romanian soldiers had taken illegally from the Bulgarian villages in the environs of Nikopol and warned that "unless one puts an end to the plundering (*maroderstvo*) of the Romanian troops, one could fear a clash between them and us."[108] Russian military governor also complained of the incompetency of the Bulgarian administrators. According to Stolypin, all Bulgarian officials he had to deal with were "swindlers" (*moshennik na moshennike*), while the governor of Sistova, Naiden Gerov, was a "colourless personality" (*bezlichnaia lichnost'*), who only compromised the Russian army in the eyes of the public (*takie gubernatory nas komprometiruiut*).[109]

Stolypin was not the only Russian administrator who criticized the Bulgarian self-government. The interim governor of Tulcha, T.P. Iuzefovich, likewise reported to Cherkasskii that the "expressions and actions" of the Bulgarians who took positions in the newly formed organs of municipal administration "provoked discontent and envy among their adversaries." Iuzefovich also wrote about manifestations of "antagonism" between the Greeks and the Bulgarians, for which the latter were responsible.[110] Before long, the Tulcha Bulgarians clashed with Iuzefovich's successor, I.V. Belotserkovets, whom they blamed for falling under Greek influence, an accusation that provoked a long and equally acrimonious refutation on the part of the latter.[111]

The relations between the Russian army and the Bulgarian population in general were not as cloudless as one might assume from reading numerous descriptions of the joy of the Bulgarians at the entry of the Russian troops. For one thing, few of them wanted to join the Bulgarian militia units that took an active role in the military operations. Stoletov praised the spirit of his men and explained the limited number of volunteers by the unexpected turn in the war after the Russian reversals at Plevna and Gurko's retreat as well as by "all those horrors that the Bulgarians have suffered" since then.[112] The Bulgarians more readily joined the local militias and municipal police units that the Russians created for the purpose of protecting the Christian population from the raids of Circassians and the bashi-bazouks.[113] However, such volunteers must have been motivated, among other things, by the opportunity to capture Muslim properties. The above-mentioned governor of Nikopol, Stolypin, reported cases of insubordination of the local Bulgarian militiamen, who used weapons distributed among them by the Russians to capture grain deposits and disobeyed the Russian instructors assigned to their units.[114]

The attitudes of the Bulgarian population towards the Russians were not uniform. Many, perhaps most, Bulgarians were genuinely supportive of the Russian troops, as was the case of the hundreds of men and boys of Gabrovo who carried water to the Russian troops, defending the Shipka Pass under a hail of Ottoman bullets.[115] At the same time, Colonel F.M. Depreradovich wrote about the repeated complains of Bulgarians about the plundering Russian Cossacks, while the painter of battle pieces V.V. Vereshchagin noted their reluctance to offer him accommodation, food, and fodder.[116] Some Bulgarians even sympathized with the Ottomans. This was the case of the village of Chumakovtsy, which was burned down by the detachment of Major General P.F. Cherevin for "the evident assistance that its inhabitants rendered to the bashi-bazouks and the Circassians."[117]

Inter-confessional and Inter-ethnic Violence in the Concluding Stages of the War

Plevna fell in late November 1877, after an unsuccessful attempt of Osman Nuri Pasha to break away from the besieged town. Marred by the deaths of large numbers of Ottoman POWs (as seen in figure 6.3), this hard-won Russian-Romanian victory was the turning point of the war.[118] Numerous Russian troops that arduously besieged the fortress for over four months could now join the forces that had been holding the Shipka Pass against the assaults of Suleiman Pasha. Having failed to break through into Danubian Bulgaria and relieve the corps of Osman Nuri Pasha besieged at Plevna, the Ottomans lost their morale before the emboldened Russians. In late December 1877, Gurko crossed the Balkans again, occupied Sofia, and advanced to Philippopolis, while another part of the Russian army defeated the Ottoman forces in the Battle of Sheinovo. With the fall of Adrianople on 8 January the war was effectively over.

After the Russian army took Plevna and began its offensive towards the old Ottoman capital, the local Bulgarians met it with requests to give them weapons for self-protection against the Circassians.[119] In response to such requests, the commanders of advance Russian units sometimes would take the initiative to arm local Bulgarians with the weapons of dead or captured Ottoman soldiers.[120] In Eski Zagra and the neighbouring villages, the Bulgarians did not wait for permission. They captured the weapons that the Russians had previously taken from the Turkish inhabitants of the town and used them to seize their land, houses, and movable property.[121] According to the report of the temporary Russian commander of the town to Gurko, neither the Bulgarian headman nor the patrols could stop them.[122] The same took place in Sofia after its fall to the Russian troops in December 1877. The hostility of the Bulgarian inhabitants towards the Muslim neighbours was so great that the Russians had to offer protection to the former "oppressors."[123]

As was the case with Danubian Bulgaria in the summer of 1877, the entry of the Russian troops into trans-Balkan towns was preceded by the flight of large swathes of the Muslim population and accompanied by the plunder of their properties.[124] In Philippopolis, captured by Gurko on 5 January after several days of fighting, the scale of these robberies was such that the consuls of the European powers submitted a formal protest to the Russian commander. The consuls reported that "the acts of violence and disorder of all kinds committed by Bulgarians" were "daily acquiring greater proportions." The consuls alleged that the Bulgarians "adroitly exploit the innocence of the Russian soldiers in order to push them … to participate in these acts as well as use them as cover." While

Figure 6.3. *The Road of the War Prisoners* by V.V. Vereshchagin, 1878–9
Source: Vasily Vereshchagin, *The Road of the War Prisoners*, 1878–9, oil on canvas, 181 × 298.9 ×
5.7 cm. Gift of Lilla Brown in memory of her husband, John W. Brown, Brooklyn Museum. Via
Wikimedia Commons.

"the acts of theft were innumerable," the security measures taken by Gurko after the first personal meeting with the consuls were insufficient. The disorder,
claimed the consuls, was without precedent either in the last two years or during the recent Ottoman retreat, even though the Turks, who were abandoning their homes, might be expected to feel some ill will towards the Christian
population, which they knew was hostile to them. The consuls asked Gurko
to assign soldiers for the protection of their consulates. They also admonished
the Russian commander to exclude from the local militia that he intended to
create "any Orthodox Bulgarian unable to prove his good behaviour," as well as
include in it "as many foreigners as possible since the latter will be motivated
exclusively by a sense of impartiality and justice."[125]

In response, Gurko ordered the Russian troops to be accommodated only
in the abandoned Muslim homes and all Muslim properties to be sealed, and
made the lower commanders personally responsible for any thefts.[126] At the
same time, neither he, nor other Russian commanders perceived the trans-Balkan Muslim population as just the innocent victims of the Christian atrocities.
According to Nikolai Nikolaevich, the Muslims who followed the evacuation
order of Suleiman Pasha fled with all their belongings after setting fire to both
their own dwellings and those of the Bulgarians.[127] The Russian battle painter
V.V. Vereshchagin, who accompanied M.D. Skobelev's vanguard detachment

advancing on Hermanli and Adrianople, reported the complaints of the local Bulgarians that their Muslim neighbours took their clothes, utensils, horses, and carts, and fled to Constantinople.[128] Sometimes, the fires and robberies went hand in hand with more serious atrocities. Thus, Lieutenant General Veliaminov, the commander of the 31st Infantry Division, found "numerous corpses of Bulgarian men, women, and children" lying near the "villages set on fire by the Turks" in the environs of Tatar Bazardzhik. The town itself was "burned and devastated" and there were "many corpses in the streets and houses."[129] Several days later, Captain Nord of the Lifeguard Hussar regiment reported from Haskioi (Haskovo) that "the Turks have committed frightening atrocities against Bulgarians and burned many houses."[130]

As earlier in the war, some of these atrocities were the work of the Circassian irregulars. Even before the Russian crossing of the Balkans, the Bulgarians of Dolni Lom complained that Circassians were putting their villages on fire and shooting the inhabitants.[131] Circassians had "plundered and massacred" the large village of Chuperlikioi in the environs of Philippopolis, so that the troops of the 3rd Infantry division that occupied it on 4 January found "a corpse in every house."[132] Circassians and bashi-bazouks were also reportedly "plundering and committing atrocities" in Yambol after the regular Ottoman troops left this town, and Slivno, which the Russians found burned and devastated with many Bulgarian inhabitants massacred.[133] In other cases, the culprits were the Ottoman soldiers, some of whom turned into marauders after the defeat of Suleiman Pasha's army at Philippopolis. Thus, the commander of the 3rd Infantry Division, V.D. Dandevil, reported about "Turkish marauders who descend from the mountains (to which they fled after the battle) and massacre and rob the Bulgarians at the distance of one- or two-hour ride from Stanimaki."[134]

Such depredations continued to the very end of the campaign: the Russian troops that occupied Adrianople and advanced into Eastern Thrace in mid-January 1878 found beheaded corpses of Bulgarians along the road.[135] At the same time, these devastations and massacres seem to be the consequences of the disintegration of the Ottoman army in the wake of the defeats at Sheinovo and Philippopolis rather than a deliberate policy adopted by the Ottoman command. Thus, Colonel V.A. Bunakov, the chief of staff of the 2nd Guards Cavalry Division, reported to Gurko's chief of staff, D.S. Naglovskii, that although the villages along the highway from Derbent (Golyam Dervent) to Kayali were "devastated, burned, and abandoned by Bulgarians," his division was able to spend the night at a village that was father away from the highway. This led Bunakov to conclude that the Ottomans did not apply a systematic scorched-earth policy and "burned only those villages through which they passed."[136] Bunakov's assessment was confirmed by Skobelev, according to whom "the panic-stricken Muslim population is fleeing and does not even think of burning anything on our way." [137]

Although most of the anti-Bulgarian atrocities at the concluding stages of the war must have been the work of the bashi-bazouks, Circassians, and stray Ottoman soldiers, the inter-ethnic violence sometimes percolated to the level of local communities. Thus, the Bulgarians of the village of Chenakievo in the environs of Tatar Bazardzhik complained to the Russian troops about the visit of some fifteen armed Turkish inhabitants of the neighbouring villages Osinovo (Osikovo), Seltse (Selcha), and Fotin (Fotinovo). Having lost several men to the armed resistance of the Chenakievo inhabitants, the alleged robbers retreated promising to amass all their fellow villagers and massacre all the Bulgarians. Helped by a company of the Lifeguard Lithuanian Regiment, the Chenakievo Bulgarians indeed repelled a bigger assault the following day, whereupon the Russian troops and some 200 armed Bulgarians attacked and destroyed the Turkish villages of Osinovo and Seltse.[138]

This episode demonstrates that trans-Balkan Muslims had as many reasons to fear their Bulgarian neighbours as vice versa. When the Russian vanguard of Major General A.P. Strukov caught up with the large crowds of Muslim refugees in the environs of Lule-Burgas and suggested that they return to their places of residence in the Russian-occupied territory, some of them agreed on the condition that the Russian general provide them with a convoy for protection against Bulgarians.[139] Emboldened by the presence of the Russian troops, the latter had indeed roamed around the caravans and would even plunder the Muslim carts claiming that they just take back what had originally belonged to them.[140] When the Russian detachments caught up with the refugees or cut off their lines of retreat, the Bulgarians, who had been hiding in the forests, in their turn "attacked these poor Turks and took their revenge upon them in the most horrible manner," reported Nikolai Nikolaevich to his imperial brother. "The scenes and sights were truly frightening: in some places there were up to five or six thousand corpses of the old men women and children scattered along the road."[141]

Whereas the grand duke presented the massacre of Muslim civilians as exclusively the work of Bulgarians, some of "the frightening scenes" that he was referring to were actually the work of the Russian army. Having defeated the troops of Vessel Pasha, at Shipka in early January, the Russian forces once again occupied Kazanlyk, while the Russian vanguard commanded by M.D. Skobelev advanced to Hermanli. The famous Russian general was seeking the remnants of Suleiman Pasha's army that was defeated by Gurko's forces in the Battle of Philippopolis on 4 January 1878. Envious of Gurko's glory, Skobelev sought to capture the Ottoman commander and his remaining forces, whom he expected to retreat to Adrianople by way of Haskioi and Hermanli. Having occupied Hermanli on 5 January, Skobelev dispatched the detachment of Colonel V.F. Paniutin westwards towards Haskioi in order to meet Suleiman Pasha's troops. The latter, however, decided to flee to the south, across the mountainous

Rhodope region. Unaware of this, Paniutin took a large caravan of some 5,000 or 6,000 Muslim refugees for Suleiman Pasha's units and destroyed them in two hours.[142]

The Hermanli massacre, as this episode came to be known in the British press, reveals an important difference between the Russian-Ottoman war of 1877–8 and the one that took place fifty years previously. In contrast to 1829, the Ottoman command ordered the evacuation of the Muslim inhabitants from trans-Balkan territories.[143] The refugees (numbering at least tens of thousands) moved in large groups of people, in which women, children, and the elderly were under the protection of armed men and some Ottoman soldiers and irregulars.[144] This necessarily blurred the distinction between the combatants and non-combatants and contributed to the large number of victims among the civilian Muslim population at the concluding stages of the war.[145] In the Hermanli episode, the irregulars that convoyed the refugees opened fire at the approaching detachment of Paniutin and then fled, exposing the women, old men, and children to the undiscriminating vengeance of the Russian troops.[146]

According to the diary of the 63rd Uglich Infantry Regiment involved in the attack, having put the armed Muslims to flight, Paniutin gave the order to assemble the elderly and children, put them on carts, and dispatch them to Hermanli to be placed under the custody of the local *chorbadzhi*.[147] This rather radiant account is however belied by the Russian battle painter Vereshchagin, who accompanied Skobelev in his advance to Hermanli, and who presented a much more sombre scene. According to Vereshchagin, after "a hot firefight," Paniutin "bayoneted [*podnial na shtyk*] the entire wagon train" so that "[for] many miles, the road was covered by the dead and the wounded, mostly women and children rather than men. The soldiers would push the people off the carts and would tear apart and scatter their belongings, looking for money. After Skobelev approached the site, he was shocked by his mistake."[148]

The Hermanli massacre was but the largest and best-known case of a Russian attack on a refugee wagon train provoked by the Ottoman irregulars or armed inhabitants. Several days previously a similar incident took place in Hermanli itself at the moment when Skobelev's cavalry vanguard commanded by Major General Strukov entered the town. Having encountered a large wagon train of Muslim refugees accompanied by some of Suleiman Pasha's regular soldiers at the approaches to Hermanli, the squadron of Major P.P. Chulkov circumvented it and crossed the railway bridge over the Maritsa River. After this, the Ottomans put the railway bridge on fire and barricaded the highway bridge with their carts cutting Chulkov's cavalrymen from the rest of the Russian forces. There followed a night of fighting, at the end of which Chulkov's unit was able to break through the bridge and rejoin the rest of Strukov's forces that routed up to 3,000 armed refugees, bashi-bazouks, and stray Ottoman soldiers. Strukov felt compelled to explain this incident to the Ottoman representatives

Server Pasha and Namyk Pasha, who passed through Hermanli the following day on their way to Nikolai Nikolaevich's headquarters in Eski Zagra, where they arrived to negotiate an armistice.[149]

Similar incidents involved Gurko's advance cavalry units as well. Thus, the Russian hussars of the 2nd Cavalry Division spotted a wagon train near the village of Stroev that was proceeding in the direction of Philippopolis, under the protection of Ottoman soldiers and armed inhabitants. The hussars approached it without opening fire on assumption that the wagon train would surrender without resistance. However, the armed inhabitants and some Ottoman soldiers opened fire on the hussars at close distance from behind the carts. Supported by the dragoons of the same division, the hussars put the Ottoman soldiers to flight and cut down nearly all the armed inhabitants.[150] After this episode, the head of staff of the 2nd Brigade of the Second Guards Cavalry Division, Colonel G.A. Kovalevskii, managed to convince another group of armed refugees retreating to Philippopolis not to fire upon the Russian detachments.[151] As a result, some of the armed inhabitants complied with the order to surrender their weapons and go back to their homes, whereas the other part proceeded to Philippopolis.[152]

Attempts to persuade the Muslim refugees not to offer resistance sometimes produced mixed results. When the units of the 2nd Guards Cavalry Division encountered another trainload further down the road to Adrianople, they used an interpreter and "an effendi" captured with the previous caravan to demand the people on the wagon train not to open fire and surrender their weapons. While the front carts complied with this demand, those behind them began to fire on Russian cavalrymen forcing them to retreat. Thereupon, the Ottoman regulars who convoyed the train and the armed inhabitants formed a skirmish line, occupied the crest of the hill near the highway and even attempted an offensive yet were eventually dispersed by several cannon shots leaving a huge number of wagons on the highway.[153] Cases of armed resistance were not limited to encounters between the caravans of the Muslim refugees and the Russian advance unites. The armed inhabitants of the villages in the environs of Philippopolis likewise would fire at the approaching Russian cavalry units.[154]

Novoe vremia correspondent V.I. Nemirovich-Danchenko attributed this resistance to the influence of the Muslim agitators (*softas*) and bashi-bazouks, who burned down villages and killed those who refused to leave. According to the Russian journalist, the propaganda of the *softas* explains why the caravans of the refugees opened fire at the approach of the Russian troops instead of surrendering.[155] Apart from the influence of religious militants, the behaviour of the trans-Balkan Muslims must have reflected their fear of Russian and Bulgarian revenge for the atrocities committed towards the trans-Balkan Bulgarians following the precipitous retreat of Gurko's vanguard in July 1877. Having reentered the "Rose Valley" around Kazanlyk in late December, the Russians indeed found the evidence of widespread Ottoman reprisals in the wake of Gurko's raid. Whereas the Muslim settlements were deserted shortly before the arrival of the Russian troops, the Bulgarian villages had lain in ruins since the summer and were full of rotten corpses of adults and children. Nemirovich-Danchenko reported the Bulgarian corpses all along the way from the Shipka Pass to Eski Zagra, which testified to the massacre of the town inhabitants by Suleiman Pasha's army after the withdrawal of Gurko's vanguard.[156] Eski Zagra itself was totally destroyed – out of 3,500 buildings only 19 remained intact, and the ruins were likewise full of rotten corpses.[157]

Clearly, religious, and nationalist passions in Rumelia in 1877–8 were much stronger than some fifty years previously, at the time of the first crossing of the Balkans by the Russian army.[158] The Russian troops themselves were likewise more prone to anti-Muslim sentiment. Whereas in 1829, Russians spared the mosques, this was hardly the case fifty years later. The Russian battle painter Vereshchagin reported the desecration of the Etritropol mosque by the solders of Gurko's detachment that occupied the town shortly before the fall of Plevna.[159] According to Nemirovich-Danchenko, the same applied to the mosques of Sistova, Tyrnovo, and Plevna. Even though the Russian correspondent found the Orthodox church in Kazanlyk similarly ravaged by the Circassians, he had to admit that the Ottomans treated churches much more respectfully.[160]

Although the commanders of the Russian detachments chasing the retreating Ottomans were usually able to keep their troops disciplined, the same was not always the case of those Russian soldiers who fell behind their units during the final offensive of the war. Thus, Colonel Rozhnov of the Lifeguard Lithuanian regiment, who was left in Tatar Bazardzhik with two companies to guard some 700 Ottoman POWs, reported to Naglovskii about numerous Russian stragglers, who were "drinking, marauding, and aimlessly destroying considerable supplies of food and fodder that were left by the Turks." The sight of this mindless destruction prompted Rozhnov to assume the functions of the military governor (*komendant*) of the town and to assign patrols, who would arrest the wrongdoers and dispatch them to their units.[161]

San Stefano and the Outline of a New Political Order

The Russian-Ottoman peace negotiations that opened soon after the Battle of Shipka-Sheinovo resulted in the preliminary peace treaty of San Stefano, signed on 19 February 1878 by Ignatiev, the former ambassador in Constantinople, and the head of the grand duke's diplomatic chancellery, A.I. Nelidov.[162] The treaty dramatically redefined the political map of the Balkans by securing the formal independence of Romania, Serbia, and Montenegro, as well as creating a de facto independent principality of Bulgaria, whose ties to the Ottoman government would be reduced to the payment of a symbolic tribute. Cherished by the Russian Pan-Slavs and momentarily supported by the tsar, Ignatiev – the main author of the San Stefano treaty – drafted a Greater Bulgaria that included Macedonia and extended to the Aegean littoral.

Although San Stefano Bulgaria looked like a rabbit drawn by Ignatiev out of his pan-Slavic hat, it did have some roots in the pre-war period, and those roots were not exclusively Russian or Bulgarian. The proposed territorial delimitation of the Balkans was based on the assumption that "ethnographic Bulgaria" was much larger than the geographical terminology of the day suggested. First expressed among the Russian military authors by Liprandi, this idea reflected the evolution of the European cartography and ethnography of the Balkans in the middle decades of the nineteenth century, a period that witnessed the publication of the first ethnographic maps of the region (see map 6.1). One of these maps, composed by the Austrian ethnographer Felix Philipp Kanitz in 1874, served the basis of the San Stefano treaty, if one is to believe an early historian of Russian provisional administration in Bulgaria, Major General N.R. Ovsianyi.[163]

Unable to brush off the "ethnographic principle" altogether, the Austrian and the British representatives had taken precautions lest its application unduly advantage Russia. Thus, in early 1877, Austrian foreign minister Andrassy conditioned Vienna's neutrality in the prospective war on the non-creation "of a big Slavic state" in the Balkans, a clause that was inserted into the secret Russian-Austrian conventions of January and March 1877.[164] For his part, the British representative at the Constantinople Conference of December 1876, Lord Salisbury, insisted on the division of the ethnically Bulgarian territories on both sides of the Balkan Mountains into two provinces with the centres in Tyrnovo and Sofia. Significant Muslim and Greek population in the Tyrnovo province would help reduce the Russian influence in the areas close to Constantinople and the Black Sea. Salisbury's plan also left Adrianople, Rodosto, and Gallipoli to the Ottomans, barred Bulgarians from the Aegean Sea, and thereby delivered the Bulgarian bishoprics in Macedonia into the hands of the Greeks.

The anti-Russian and anti-Bulgarian implications of this plan spurred Cherkasskii to draft his alternative outline of the post-war Balkans. Before the Russian crossing of the Danube in June 1877, Cherkasskii suggested tracing the western border of Bulgaria along the Bistritsa River and down to the gulf of Saloniki. He also suggested giving the Bulgarians the Aegean coast from Saloniki to the estuary of Maritsa, which would leave to the Greeks only the Saloniki and the Gallipoli peninsulas. The proposed borders, according to Cherkasskii, would "closely coincide with the historical, religious, and ethnographic limits of the two rival nations." They would "secure the economic conditions of existence of the Bulgarian principality, would put an early limit to the dangerous Greek pretensions, and prevent the Greeks and the Bulgarians from interfering in each other's internal affairs."[165]

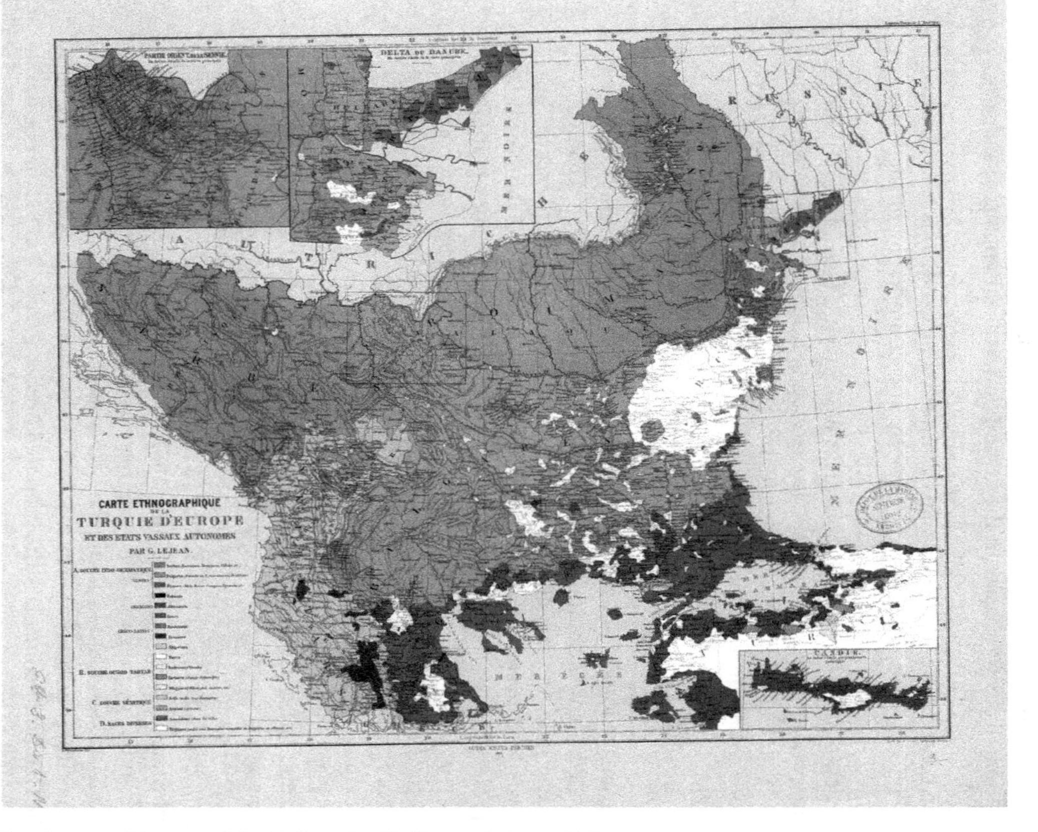

Map 6.1. French ethnographic map of the Balkans by Guillaume Lejean, 1861

Note: The original map appeared in colour. The red for the Turkish population was converted to white for legibility in black and white.

Source: Guillaume Lejean, *Carte ethnographique de la Turquie d'Europe et des états vassaux autonomes*, 1861, lithography by C. Hellfarth, in Lejean, "Ethnographique de la Turquie d'Europe," in *Mittheilungen aus Justus Perthes' geographischer Anstalt über wichtige neue Erforschungen auf dem Gesammtgebiete der Geographie*, supplementary vol. 1860–1, ed. August Petermann (Gotha, Germany: Justus Perthes, 1881). Via Wikimedia Commons and

The projected principality was expected to include 5 to 5.5 million people, with 4 to 4.5 million Bulgarians, 100,000 Greeks, and 50,000 Jews, the rest being Turks, Tatars, and Circassians.[166] Cherkasskii counted the Muslim Pomaks as ethnic Bulgarians arguing that they were "far from being fanatics" and "differed markedly from the Bosnian Serbs."[167] The same applied to the Tatars who, "have always lived in peace with Bulgarians" and even "offered them protection." Of all the Muslims, only the Turks and Circassians were dangerous, according to Cherkasskii, yet they "were hardly more than half a million."[168] The prince believed that the Porte would not oppose the resettlement of Circassians in Asia, particularly if this resettlement were partially financed by Bulgaria.[169]

Cherkasskii continued to elaborate his project during the last months of his life (he died on 19 February 1878, the day of conclusion of the preliminary peace of San Stefano, which was also the anniversary of Alexander II's peasant emancipation manifesto of 1861). According to his secretary, Colonel Anuchin, the prince envisioned the creation of self-governing village, town, and district councils that would include elected members "regardless of their ethnicity or religion" and that would take care of their local issues as well as supervise the distribution and collection of taxes.[170] Following the creation of local self-government, Cherkasskii's project presupposed the convocation of the notables (the clergymen) of all confessions to discuss the electoral law.[171]

Although the prince paid lip service to the principle of religious freedom and self-government, he sought to strengthen the Bulgarian element at the expense of the Muslims. To this end, he suggested securing for the Bulgarians a numerical predominance in the administrative councils of those districts in which the Muslim population constituted the majority. Thus, the project of the administrative councils in Philippopolis *sanjak* qualified the principle of election of the local, district and town councils "regardless of religion or ethnicity" by a two-thirds quota in favour of the predominant Orthodox population.[172] The voters were to be divided into confessional curias (of the Orthodox, Muslims, Armenians, and Catholics), the elections were to be indirect, and the heads of the councils were to be elected from the predominant Christian population.[173] Cherkasskii specifically suggested that each curia should have the right to confirm or reject the deputies elected by other curias. A deputy who received less than 50 per cent of the votes of all electors, regardless of confession, would be considered rejected, and in his place the curia that elected him had to elect another person. In this way, the more numerous Christians could bar the entry into the council of those Muslims whom they found undesirable.[174]

Cherkasskii also considered it necessary to complement the confessional principle of the organization of curia by the ethnic principle. Eager to support the Bulgarian element against the Greeks in towns with mixed Bulgarian-Greek population (such as Philippopolis), he suggested excluding from the elections non-residents; foreign subjects; and Bulgarian apprentices, whom the Greek employers would register as Greeks to inflate their own numbers.[175] Cherkasskii also suggested disqualifying the town dwellers from the elections to the district councils (limiting the latter only to the rural population). This excluded the Jews and Armenians, who lived only in towns.[176] The Russian administration pursued these principles after Cherkasskii's death. Thus, governor L.I. Iliashevich ordered the head of the Lule-Burgas and Bunar-Gissar districts, N.R. Ovsianyi, to secure the Christian Bulgarian majority in the district and municipal councils. To that effect, foreign subjects and Muslims who had fled before the advancing Russian troops (even if they returned later) could neither vote nor be elected "since their permanent residence in the given area cannot be duly ascertained."[177]

This chapter has demonstrated that some of the choices made by the Russian command and the occupation authorities during the Russian-Ottoman war of 1877–8 clearly aggravated inter-confessional and inter-ethnic tensions, while others demonstrated at least their desire to avoid such tension. Most importantly, the decision to cross the Danube further upstream and advance towards Adrianople and Constantinople across the territory located to the west of the quadrangle of the Ottoman fortresses and the Deliorman revealed the desire of the Russian war planners to circumvent the areas most densely populated by the Muslims, in which the Russian troops were likely to encounter Muslim partisans. However, in conjunction with other choices made by the Russian command as well as the political situation of the eastern Balkans in the late 1870s, this well-intended decision in fact contributed to Christian-Muslim clashes and population dislocations.

The entry of the Russian army into the more ethnically Bulgarian areas to the west of Rushchuk rendered the local Muslims vulnerable in ways in which their more numerous co-religionists in eastern Bulgaria had never been. A Russian occupation could not reverse completely the power relations between the Muslims and the Christian Bulgarians in those areas in which the former constituted a majority or at least a significant minority of the local population as the example of Deliorman and the eastern part of Danubian Bulgaria has demonstrated many times during the previous Russian-Ottoman wars. Many of the Muslim inhabitants of this region also had the option of retreating behind the walls of the Ottoman fortresses. By contrast, the relatively scarce Muslims of the central part of Danubian Bulgaria lacked such protection and had more to fear from their numerous Christian neighbours emboldened by the presence of the Russian troops.

The use of the Bulgarian militiamen likewise contributed to the ethnic clashes. As will be remembered, most of the militiamen were not local: instead, they were recruited from the Bulgarians of Bessarabia and Romania. Unintegrated into the local web of the Muslim-Christian relations and spurred by the news and sights of atrocities of the Ottoman irregulars, such militiamen were even more uncompromising in their attitude towards the Ottoman Muslims than their co-ethnics from Danubian Bulgaria and the trans-Balkan territories. The situation was further aggravated by the inclusion of the Bulgarian militia in the Russian vanguard force of General Gurko that crossed the Balkans early in the war, but had to retreat to the north after the failure of the main Russian army to quickly capture Plevna. Whereas Gurko's first foray across the Balkans towards the areas of the April Uprising uprooted the local Muslim population, his subsequent retreat made tens of thousands of trans-Balkan Bulgarians follow the Russian troops out of fear of the Ottoman revenge.

Most of the time, the Russian provisional administration in the occupied territories had to respond to the *force majeure* situation that resulted from a peculiar combination of the aforementioned strategic choices of the Russian command and the vagaries of the fortunes of war. As has been demonstrated, V.A. Cherkasskii's efforts to deal with the dislocated Muslims and Christians were greatly hampered by the absence of any effective law enforcement units under his command as well as by his tensions with Nikolai Nikolaevich and his chief of staff, Nepokoichitskii. The way Cherkasskii responded to these challenges reflected his overall perspective on the Eastern Question. This perspective had quite a few things in common with the military men who helped to plan and conduct the war with the Ottoman Empire. Not unlike War Minister Miliutin and his disciples in the General Staff, Cherkasskii grounded his policies in the study of the population of the eastern Balkans. At the same time, Cherkasskii shared a passionate interest in the Eastern Question with Miliutin's main critic R.A. Fadeev, and his approach was similarly pan-Slavic. Although Cherkasskii could be quite critical of the Bulgarians, he viewed them and not the Muslims as the primary victims of the outbreaks of inter-confessional violence that the war was likely to generate.

As a result, Cherkasskii's concrete policies aimed to strengthen the Bulgarian population with regard to both the Muslims and other groups of Christians. Thus, he was a major proponent of disarming the Muslims in order to secure the Bulgarians. During the war, the prince authorized the occupation and use of the abandoned Muslim properties by the trans-Balkan Bulgarian refugees. This measure helped alleviate their condition, but was bound to generate tensions upon the return of the Muslim refugees after the war. Finally, Cherkasskii's proposals concerning the new political settlement in the eastern Balkans made during the war likewise reveal his effort to ensure that the Bulgarian element would be politically dominant in the provincial and district administration. These policies were continued after the prince's death by the new Russian imperial commissioner in Bulgaria.

7 Population Policies after the War

The Treaty of San Stefano played a fateful role in Bulgarian history. For a brief moment, it evoked the mirage of the Greater Bulgaria that was unattainable because of the opposition of European great powers and the hostility of other Balkan peoples. The great powers, above all Britain and Austria, could not allow the complete destruction of Turkey-in-Europe, which, they assumed, would strengthen Russia. For their part, Greek, Serb, and Romanian nationalists could not look calmly at the prospect of establishment of the Bulgarian nation state on a scale that would make it naturally dominant in the Balkans. And while post-1878 Russian-Bulgarian relations demonstrated that the European fears of St. Petersburg's hegemony in Bulgaria had been rather unfounded,[1] the subsequent history of the Macedonian question revealed the strength both of Bulgarian irredentist nationalism and of the Greek and (to a lesser extent) Serbian reactions to it.[2]

Although many Russians would have liked to see Greater Bulgaria come to life, the Russian Foreign Ministry did not treat it as a real possibility from the beginning. Instead, Chancellor Gorchakov; his deputy, N.K. Girs; and the Russian ambassadors in London and Vienna, P.A. Shuvalov and E.P. Novikov, viewed the preliminary Treaty of San Stefano as, at best, a starting position in the process of bargaining with the European powers. In the course of this bargaining, they were ready to trade the inflated initial claims for more modest gains that would be accepted by the Concert of Europe and codified in the definitive treaty. This was a sound approach characteristic of the old European diplomacy, yet it squared poorly with the nationalist passions of the late nineteenth century. As a result, the definitive settlement reached in Berlin in the summer of 1878 greatly disappointed not only the Bulgarian nationalists, but also the Russian pan-Slavists, and even the later historians often interpret it as a case of Russia losing the peace after a victory in the war.[3]

Convoked in early June 1878 under the presidency of Germany's "Iron Chancellor," Otto von Bismarck, the Congress proceeded to recognize the independence of Romania, Serbia, and Montenegro.[4] The province of Bosnia and Herzegovina, the site of the Christian uprising that triggered the Eastern Crisis, was left under nominal Ottoman control, but quite real Austrian occupation (per the secret Russian-Austrian convention of January 1877). Eager to check Serbian ambitions, Austria-Hungary also occupied the *sanjak* of Novi Pazar, which constituted a land bridge between Serbia and Montenegro. Most importantly, the Congress limited the autonomous Principality of Bulgaria to the territories north of the Balkan Mountains and Sofia *sanjak*. Macedonia remained under the control of the Porte (which was obliged to carry out some reforms) and the Bulgarian-majority territories of the Maritsa valley were to constitute the autonomous Ottoman province of Eastern Rumelia under a Christian governor general (see map 7.1). Finally, the duration of the post-war Russian occupation of Bulgaria and Eastern Rumelia was reduced from two years to nine months, during which the provisional administration was to help create the institutions of the new Bulgarian state.

This work was to be carried out within the legal framework sketched out in San Stefano and amended in Berlin. An assembly of Bulgarian notables in Philippopolis or Tyrnovo was to elaborate a statute of the kind that was adopted in 1831–2 in the Danubian principalities. In the areas where the Bulgarian population was mixed with the Turkish, Greek, or Wallachian (*aromâni*), due attention was to be paid to the rights and needs of these ethnic groups.[5] The Muslim landowners who decided to emigrate from the newly established Bulgarian principality and Serbia had the right to retain their landed property, which they could lease or entrust to other persons. Mixed Turkish-Bulgarian commissions established under the supervision of Russian commissioners in the main towns were to decide any questions related to the recognition of property titles of the Muslims as well as determine within two years the mode of sale, exploitation, and use of all the lands that belonged to the Ottoman government and to religious establishments (*waqf*).[6]

As a general principle of future Bulgarian law, the Berlin Treaty asserted that "the difference of religious faith and confession cannot serve as a pretext for the exclusion of anyone or disqualification of anyone from the use of all civil and political rights, access to public office, service, and distinctions, or the exercise of liberal arts and trades in any territory whatsoever."[7] The treaty further guaranteed freedom of religion to all the natives and foreigners and prohibited any interference into the hierarchical organization of the religious communities and their communication with their spiritual heads."[8] While police and criminal cases were placed in the jurisdiction of the newly established judicial system, civil cases between Muslim subjects were to remain within the purview of the *kadi* courts.[9] However, these courts were not recreated because all *kadis* fled during the war and the majority of them did not return. As a result, the Bulgarian Muslims turned to the general Bulgarian courts, even in cases that involved family law.[10]

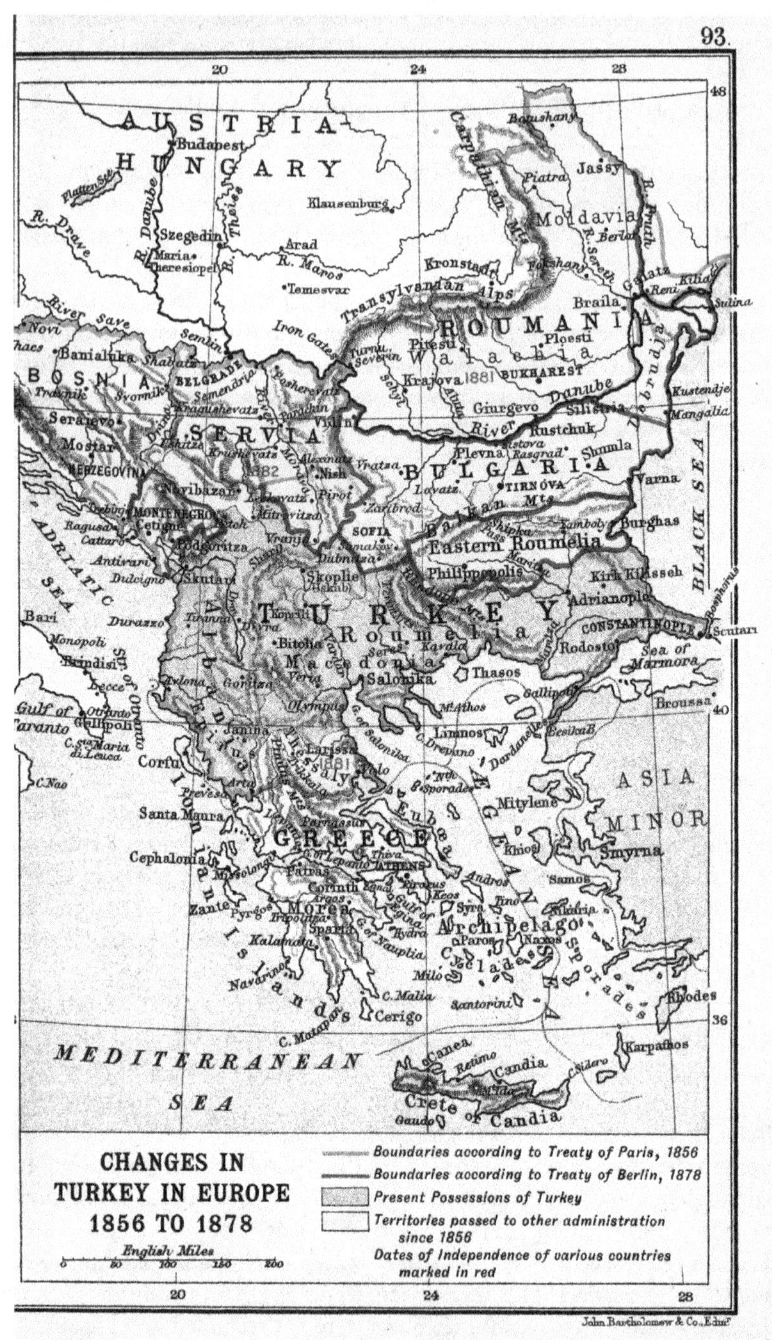

Map 7.1. *Changes in Turkey in Europe 1856 to 1878* by J.G. Bartholomew, 1914
Source: John George Bartholomew, *Changes in Turkey in Europe 1856 to 1878*, in *A Literary and Historical Atlas of Europe* (London: J.M. Dents, 1914), 93. Originally held by the University of California Libraries and digitalized by the California Digital Library. Via the Internet Archive (user scanner-ian-white).

Alexander II decided to follow Cherkasskii's advice and entrust the provisional administration of Bulgaria to a capable Russian general. Fortunately, the there was no shortage of governors general who combined civilian and military functions in the borderland regions of the Russian Empire. The tsar's choice fell on A.M. Dondukov-Korsakov, who served as the governor general of Kiev prior to the war.[11] Early in his career, Dondukov-Korsakov (see figure 7.1) took part in the Caucasian war and the conquest of Chechnya and later served as the commander of the Don Cossack Host in the early 1860s. After a brief retirement, he re-entered state service, this time at the Ministry of the Interior, and in 1869 was placed in charge of the south-eastern region. Confronted with Ukrainian nationalism, he chose to subdue it through a policy of intelligent concessions without compromising on the critical issue of mass publications in the Ukrainian language, which were banned by the Ministry of the Interior in 1863.[12] On the eve of the Russian-Ottoman war, Dondukov-Korsakov became the commander of the Kiev military district and after the outbreak of hostilities assumed the command of the 13th Army Corps that was besieging Rushchuk. This combination of military and administrative experience must have determined Alexander II to appoint Dondukov-Korsakov as his imperial commissioner in Bulgaria.

Dondukov-Korsakov's main task was to supervise the elaboration and adoption of the organic statute for the new principality, much as P.D. Kiselev had done half a century earlier for Moldavia and Wallachia.[13] Like his predecessor in the Danubian principalities, the imperial commissioner in Bulgaria was to go beyond conventional constitution-making and engage with the quasi-totality of issues related to the foundation of a new state that ranged from public hygiene to the creation of a military force. Although Dondukov-Korsakov did not have to fight with the epidemics of plague and cholera that hit Moldavia and Wallachia during Kiselev's tenure there, his task was in many respects even more challenging. He had to overcome the consequences of an unprecedently destructive war in an ethno-confessional terrain that was much more complex than that of the Danubian principalities. He also had much less time to complete his task than did Kiselev, who governed Moldavia and Wallachia for four and a half years.

During his tenure as the imperial commissioner, Dondukov-Korsakov reported to War Minister Miliutin, as well as to E.I. Totleben, who replaced Grand Duke Nikolai Nikolaevich as commander-in-chief of the Russian army in the Balkans in April 1878. A military engineer by training, Totleben first distinguished himself in the Caucasus and earned true glory as the creator of Sebastopol's defences in 1854. These enabled the Russians to hold out against the combined French, British, and Ottoman forces for almost a year before succumbing to massive shelling. After the Crimean War, Totleben was appointed the head of the Engineering Department of the War Ministry,

Figure 7.1. Photograph of Prince Aleksandr Mikhailovich Dondukov-Korsakov
Source: *General-adiutant, kniaz' Aleksandr Mikhailovich Dondukov-Korsakov*, photograph, in
Kavkazskii kalendar' na 1883 god (Tiflis, 1882). Via Wikimedia Commons.

focusing on the fortification of Russia's western frontier. On the eve of the war
of 1877–8, Alexander II placed Totleben in charge of Russia's Black Sea coastal
defences and September 1877 summoned him to organize the systematic siege
of Plevna that finally bore fruit in November of that year. As the new commander of the Russian army in the Balkans, Totleben supervised the gradual
withdrawal of the Russian troops from the walls of Constantinople and together
with Dondukov-Korsakov worked out policies with regard to the Muslim and
Christian populations of the region.[14]

Whereas Totleben was Dondukov-Korsakov's immediate superior, his most
important subordinate was Lieutenant General A.D. Stolypin, who in October
1878 was appointed governor general of Eastern Rumelia and of Adrianople
sanjak. A veteran of the Crimean War and a friend of the great novelist Leo
Tolstoy, Stolypin combined service in the artillery with several military administrative appointments. In the late 1850s and the early 1860s, he headed the Ural
Cossack host, nearly at the same time when Dondukov-Korsakov commanded

the Don Cossacks. After a stint in the civil service in the early 1870s, Stolypin was summoned to the field army with the outbreak of the war and became the commandant of the Nikopol fortress and, later, of the Plevna garrison. After the war, he briefly served as a military governor of the Philippopolis district before joining the mixed commission that supervised the transfer of the Ottoman fortresses of Shumla and Varna to the Russians in July 1878. As the commander of the 9th Corps (since August 1878) and the governor general of Eastern Rumelia, Stolypin was reporting to both Totleben and Dondukov-Korsakov. He supervised the final evacuation of the Russian troops after both the commander-in-chief and the imperial commissioner left Bulgaria in April 1879.

The Rhodope Uprising and Muslim Resistance in Other Parts of the Eastern Balkans

The first preoccupation of the Russian provisional authorities was the Rhodope Uprising, which began in the valley of the Arda and the slopes of the Rhodope Mountains and quickly spread westwards to the district of Kiustendil (Kyustendil).[15] Following the defeat of the army of Suleiman Pasha at Philippopolis, bashi-bazouks, Circassians, some regular soldiers and officers, and some Muslim refugees from the territories occupied by the Russian army fled to these mountainous territories populated by the Pomaks and some Christian Bulgarians.[16] At the first appearance of the Russian troops in the Rhodope in January 1878, the Pomaks remained peaceful and even welcoming. However, the situation quickly deteriorated after Muslim villages became the targets of the Bulgarian refugees, who had fled from Eski Zagra, Yeni Zagra, and Kazanlyk in the summer of 1877 and now followed the Russian army in its final offensive on Adrianople. Under the protection of the bashi-bazouks, the Muslim inhabitants responded in kind. Rumours about the conclusion of the San Stefano Treaty further radicalized the Muslim refugees in the Rhodope, who prevailed upon their Pomak co-religionists to join them in their raids. As a result, by the end of February, groups of insurgents had grown larger and spread their scope of operation around two principal centres at Dovlen (Dolen) and Kirdzhali (Kardzhali), the latter of which had long defied the Porte's authority in the past.[17]

The character of the Rhodopian insurgency changed over time. The commanders of the Russian detachments that were the first to enter the region noted the diverse composition of such armed bands that included, at least initially, some Roma, Bulgarians, and Greeks, alongside Turks and Circassians. At first, the bands were similarly indiscriminate in their targets and plundered both Bulgarian and Turkish villages.[18] However, the movement acquired a more distinctly Muslim character with the arrival of Muslim preachers from Constantinople, Gümülcine, and Covalla, as well as of British emissaries.[19]

The same factor helps explain the failure of the attempts of the commanders of Russian advance detachments to pacify the population with the news of the conclusion of the peace treaty. At the appearance of the Russian troops, the armed inhabitants would leave their villages and retreat to the mountains, while the few elders who remained in the villages blamed the Bulgarians and declared that the Muslims would put down their weapons and submit to the Russian authorities only if the Bulgarians were disarmed.[20]

The role of the Ottoman authorities was altogether ambiguous, and by May 1878 the Russians had become convinced that the bands of bashi-bazouks were directed by the Ottoman governor of Gümülcine.[21] The Porte was slow to respond to Nikolai Nikolaevich's invitation to send its representatives to the Rhodope to pacify the insurgents.[22] When the Ottoman representatives arrived in the area of the uprising, they devoted themselves to the collection of testimonies on the Bulgarian atrocities that supposedly caused the uprising. The military governor of Philippopolis Stolypin wrote about nightly conferences between the Ottoman representatives, the Greek metropolitan, and the English vice-consul. Stolypin considered the latter to be the main instigator of the troubles. He also politely asked the Ottoman emissaries to leave the area.[23]

By the time of Dondukov-Korsakov's arrival in Philippopolis in May 1878, Totleben could report to the tsar about the destruction of three centres of the uprising in the Rhodope Mountains by the Russian troops.[24] This, however, pacified only the districts to the north of the Arda River, along the southern border of Philippopolis *sanjak*. Both in the valley of the Arda and the areas to the south of the river the armed bands continued to grow and "receive orderly organization, weapons, ammunition, and general coordination from Constantinople and Giumiurdzhin [Gümülcine]." Totleben estimated the number of insurgents at 20,000, of which 8,000 had "a rather regular organization." In case of a reopening of hostilities with the Ottoman Empire, Totleben foresaw the disruption of Russian communications between Adrianople and Sofia unless sufficient forces were assigned to neutralize the insurgents.[25]

To better understand the early Russian perspectives on the Rhodope Uprising, one must recall international tensions between the conclusion of the preliminary Treaty of San Stefano in February 1878 and the opening of the Berlin Congress in June of the same year. The Russian command had to reckon with the possibility of a new war, this time not only against the Ottoman Empire, but also against Britain. The total size of the Ottoman army around Constantinople, at Shumla and Varna, and in Old Serbia, Macedonia, and Thessaly by early June 1878 was, in Totleben's estimation, already higher than that of the Russian forces in European Turkey. If some 60,000 to 70,000 British were to support them, Totleben foresaw the necessity to retreat from Adrianople and Philippopolis and establish a defensive position along the Balkan Mountains.

At the same time, the Russian commander-in-chief shuddered to think of the consequences of such a retreat upon the Bulgarian population:

> After six months of our occupation, after the introduction of the civil administration, after the recruitment of local Bulgarians into the national militia, after the majority of the Muslims had left their villages, and had lost their properties, the Turks would abandon themselves to all the horrors of vengeance if they re-occupy the country. One can expect a total massacre. Kazanlyk, Yeni Zagra, and Eski Zagra after the first campaign of General Gurko offer us an example thereof.[26]

The Rhodope Uprising preoccupied Totleben not only in conjunction with the possible reopening of hostilities between Russia and the Ottoman Empire supported by Britain, but also in relation to the movement of the Muslim population in other parts of European Turkey. In September 1878, the commander-in-chief wrote to Miliutin that "the Ottoman government has not only lost control over the popular masses in Bosnia, Herzegovina, Albania, and the Rhodope Mountains, but is in fact itself carried away by fanatical violence and tacitly, if not explicitly, helps sustain their bellicose mood." After the withdrawal of the Russian troops from the environs of Constantinople, the Porte was rumoured to dispatch some of its forces to Albania, whose armed population would thereby be able to put up resistance to the Austrians and assist the Rhodopian insurgents.[27]

For the Russian command, the Rhodope Uprising was thus an important element of a possible Muslim backlash, which they were determined to prevent through a combination of force and compromise. Soon upon Dondukov-Korsakov's arrival in Philippopolis, the Russians abandoned their attempts to suppress the insurgent bands to the south of the Arda and instead decided to seal off the Rhodope Mountains from the rest of Rumelia. In line with this policy, the troops along the line of demarcation were to abstain from any expeditions into the mountains and prevent any armed individuals from penetrating the Russian occupied area. The commanders of these units were to "make sure that armed Bulgarians do not attack the peaceful Muslims."[28]

These measures helped restore order and the local Bulgarians could even resume their field work and commerce with the Muslims.[29] Nevertheless, the insurgency continued to smoulder in the following months. In August, Totleben again reported to Alexander II about the agitation among the Muslim refugees and the local population of the Rhodope and the valley of the Arda. New bands were being formed under the leadership of Ueden Pasha, who called himself the commander of the People's Army of the Rhodope Mountains and planned to attack the Russian troops after the harvest time.[30] As late as October 1878, the Russians had to arm the Bulgarian population of the border districts to make them capable of self-defence against the bashi-bazouks coming from the Rhodopes.[31]

In the meantime, the Berlin Congress established an international commission for the investigation of the Rhodope Uprising composed of representatives of the Ottoman Empire, Austria-Hungary, Great Britain, France, Germany, Italy, and Russia. The commission was to find out the situation of the refugees in this region, their numbers, place of origin, ethnicity, religion, and circumstances that had forced them to leave their homes and prevented their return. It was also to propose measures that would assure the return of the refugees and could formally count on the "immediate help" of the Russian administration in securing such return.[32] The Russian ambassador in Constantinople, A.B. Lobanov-Rostovskii, noted that, philanthropy apart, the goal of the commission was to "formally accuse Russia," yet advised Dondukov-Korsakov to "avoid misunderstandings with it."[33]

Upon arrival in the Rhodope, the commission, or rather its British, French, and Ottoman members, proceeded to collect testimonies from Muslim refugees about their mistreatment by Russian troops. The Russian member of the commission, A.K. Bazili, soon sent an alarming report about the orchestrated character of such testimonies. According to him, the "witnesses" themselves had sometimes committed atrocities against Bulgarians and were now using the commission to cover up their own crimes.[34] The final report of the commission must have indeed looked biased, since the German and the Austrian representatives refused to sign it, while the Italian member of the commission, who had at first signed the report, later withdrew his signature.[35]

In his relations with the Rhodope Commission, the imperial commissioner took into account the position of the Russian representative at the Berlin Congress, P.A. Shuvalov, who declared that the Rhodope region remained outside the zone of responsibility of the Russian commander-in-chief (it had never truly been occupied by Russian troops after all).[36] Accordingly, the imperial commissioner defended himself and his predecessors against accusations of mismanaging the situation in the Rhodope. On the same ground, he opposed the efforts of the commission to bring the Muslim refugees in the Rhodope back into Eastern Rumelia. In a note addressed to the commission, Dondukov-Korsakov argued against the return of those Muslims who had become involved in the killings and robbery of the Christian inhabitants of the valley, as this would provoke "bloody revenge," which he would be "unable to prevent." In these circumstances, the imperial commissioner insisted on collecting reliable information on the refugees and suggested that only those who had been uninvolved in anti-Christian atrocities and had put down their arms should be allowed to return.[37]

Rhetoric apart, Dondukov-Korsakov perceived the Rhodope Commission to be a party to the conflict rather than a neutral arbitrator. Following the arrival of the commission's representatives to the area of the rebellion, he wrote in August, the "bands" of insurgents reached 10,000, became better organized and armed and could receive support from the Ottoman army from the Aegean littoral.[38] Accordingly, Dondukov-Korsakov would not admit the investigation of the Russian military and administrative affairs by the commission or the collection of testimonies from Russian military men. The Russian troops on the Rhodope frontier line were ordered not to communicate with the members of the commission.[39] In parallel, Dondukov-Korsakov forwarded to the Russian embassy in Constantinople the list of Bulgarian villages burned and plundered by the Turks in the *sanjaks* of Philippopolis and Slivno, as well as a list of Bulgarians killed by Muslims.[40]

While Dondukov-Korsakov confronted the Rhodope Commission in Philippopolis, Totleben protested its activities in meetings with Ottoman foreign minister Mehmed Esad Saffet Pasha in Constantinople. The Russian commander-in-chief pointed out that in the recent Austro-Franco-Italian War of 1859, the Austro-Prussian War of 1866, and the Franco-Prussian War of 1870–1, the civilian population would not flee from the occupied territory and would instead submit to the administration introduced by the advancing army. At the same time, the occupiers would take the most decisive measures to suppress armed bands when these appeared. Totleben specifically mentioned that during the occupation of the north-eastern part of France, the Germans would burn all those villages in which *franc-tireurs* ambushed their weak detachments.[41] Totleben then pointed out that the Ottoman conduct of the last war was completely different from these European precedents. The Russian commander-in-chief mentioned the atrocities against Bulgarians that preceded the war and those that followed the retreat of Gurko's vanguard from Kazanlyk, Yeni Zagra, and Eski Zagra in July 1877. He also criticized the order of the Ottoman Commander Suleiman Pasha to the civilian population to leave the territories that were about to be occupied by the Russians after the fall of Plevna and the Russian victory at Shipka.

Whereas Totleben's predecessor, Grand Duke Nikolai Nikolaevich, placed much of the blame for the plight of the Rumelian Muslims on the vengeful Bulgarians, Totleben did not mention the Bulgarians at all. Instead, the new Russian commander-in-chief stressed the responsibility of his Ottoman counterpart. In winter conditions, he argued, the retreat ordered by Suleiman Pasha made the death of many children and old people inevitable. The panic that spread among the Rumelian Muslims as a result of this order caused, according to Totleben, the chaotic situation that accompanied the Ottoman retreat from Sofia and Shipka to Philippopolis, Adrianople, and Constantinople, in the course of which regular Ottoman troops and irregulars were moving together with large masses of civilians. Totleben also blamed the Ottoman troops for firing at the advancing Russian detachments from behind the cover of the civilians and their carts. A certain number of women and children who perished under Russian fire in such conditions were, in the words of Totleben, "the inevitable victims of the consequences of war." However, these occasional deaths were "nothing in comparison with the calamities caused by the flight itself, in which tens of thousands of people perished for nothing."[42]

Totleben dismissed the numerous allegations of rape that the protocols of the Rhodope Commission contained. Instead, he emphasized the discipline of the Russian troops, as well as the compassion that they showed to the refugees and to the numerous children abandoned on the roads by both Muslim and Bulgarian parents. Totleben also argued that the horrible picture of the Russian atrocities against the Muslim refugees that the British, Ottoman, and French members of the Rhodope Commission painted in its protocols did not square with the large-scale return of these refugees to the Russian occupied territories that began in the summer of 1878. The Russian commander-in-chief found it strange that the Muslim refugees in the Rhodope refused (as the commission claimed) to return to their places as long as these were occupied by the Russians, whereas the Muslim refugees in Constantinople were desperately trying to do just that.[43] To pacify the Rhodope, Totleben demanded the quickest possible occupation of the territories on the right bank of the Arda River by regular Ottoman troops in order to exclude for the future any contact between the Russian units on the left bank of the river and the insurgents. He also demanded the expulsion of "European agitators and adventurists" from the Rhodope, and, in particular, Sinclair, the leader of the so-called People's Army of the Rhodope.[44]

The Rhodope Uprising alerted the commander-in-chief to the movement of Muslims in other parts of the Balkan Peninsula. The commander-in-chief was particularly preoccupied with the Albanian League that refused to recognize territorial concessions to Montenegro, Serbia, and Bulgaria sanctioned by the Berlin Congress. Totleben suspected that the Porte secretly encouraged the Albanian League in the last-ditch attempt to prevent the implementation of the peace treaty. Since one of the corps formed by the League was reportedly destined to aid the Rhodopian insurgents, Totleben had to act with firmness and determination. At an audience with Abdul-Hamid II, he not only dismissed Anglo-Ottoman investigations of the Russian atrocities during the war, but also conditioned Russian withdrawal from Adrianople upon the Porte's cooperation in the pacification of the Rhodope.[45]

For the last time, the Rhodopian insurgents preoccupied the Russian authorities in late September and October 1878, at the time of the withdrawal of the Russian troops from territories that did not become part of the autonomous province of Eastern Rumelia established by the decision of the Berlin Congress. Upon the evacuation of the Russian troops from the village of Big Derbent in the Rhodope Mountains, a band of 1,500 deserters from the Ottoman army, Muslim refugees from northern Bulgaria, and armed Muslim inhabitants from the neighbouring village of Demir Eren began to rob the local Bulgarians and killed three of them. The Bulgarians appealed to the commander of a Russian detachment in the nearby town of Demotika, who dispatched a score of Cossacks to help them regain their property and rescue their captured relatives. However, the inhabitants of Demir Eren opened fire at the approach of the Cossacks and Bulgarians and forced them to retreat. Two companies of the Galitskii regiment dispatched from Demotika two weeks later likewise encountered Muslim resistance yet managed to expel the bashi-bazouks from Demir Eren. Similar but smaller clashes took place in several other villages.[46]

According to Totleben, the Ottoman governor of Ferre, Makhzar Pasha, not only failed to implement the Porte's orders towards the pacification of the region, but in fact "excited the fanaticism of the Muslims by collecting their complaints against the Christians."[47] As a result, the Russian commander-in-chief had to act unilaterally by dispatching troops into the mountains in order to expel the bashi-bazouks from the villages. A specially formed detachment of Cossacks and line troops under the command of Lieutenant Colonel Bibikov chased the bashi-bazouks to the main range of the Rhodope Mountains in the second part of October. In the process, Bibikov's Cossacks burned down nine villages whose inhabitants supported the insurgents. Concerned with the public image of the Russian army, Totleben reprimanded Bibikov for the excesses of his troops and strictly prohibited the burning of villages in the future.[48]

The attempts of British diplomats to investigate cases of Russian mistreatment of the Muslim population were not limited to the Rhodope Commission. The most active in this respect was Henry Drummond-Wolf, the British member of the International Commission on Eastern Rumelia, which took over the civil affairs of this region still occupied by the Russian troops in October 1878, in accordance with the decision of the Berlin Congress. According to Stolypin, who at the same time became governor general of Eastern Rumelia, Drummond-Wolf "searched for any facts that testified to the oppression of the Turkish population" and filed official protests. However, the Muslim inhabitants whom the British representative sent to Stolypin to testify about the alleged destruction of their houses and mosques by Russian soldiers denied such incidents before the Russian governor general. If they did indeed have a grievance against the Russian troops, the Muslims probably did not have the courage to articulate it before Stolypin. As a result, Drummond-Wolff had to offer Stolypin his apologies.[49]

North-eastern Bulgaria was another region that preoccupied the Russian provisional authorities. Soon after his appointment in April 1878, Totleben also expressed to Alexander II his concerns about the quadrilateral "covered by thick forest, that has a mostly Turkish population, which in 1828 and 1829 interrupted all our communications in the rear of the army."[50] Given the continued presence of Ottoman troops in Shumla and Varna and the possibility of war with Britain, Totleben considered it untimely to withdraw any Russian troops from Bulgaria. On the contrary, he believed it necessary to prepare for the possibility of a British landing at Varna and wrote about "the agitated state of the Turkish population" in the quadrilateral. Later, in response to the local Turks' fears of Bulgarian attacks after the imminent transfer of Shumla and Varna to the Russians, Totleben believed it necessary to take in advance "the strictest possible measures for the punishment of the culprits regardless of nationality."[51]

Although the Treaty of San Stefano presupposed the transfer of Shumla and Varna from the Ottomans to the Russians, the Porte was slow to do so, apparently in the hope of getting some concessions from the Russian side. The Ottoman government delayed the appointment of special representatives, who were supposed to implement the transfer together with their Russian counterparts. In late June 1878, after the opening of the Berlin Congress, Totleben reported that the process of withdrawal of the Ottoman troops and supplies from Shumla was halted altogether. Instead, the Ottoman authorities brought some Circassian and Muslim refugees back into the fortress.[52] Even after the Berlin Congress confirmed the stipulations of the San Stefano treaty in relation to the transfer of Shumla and Varna, the Ottomans continued to drag their feet and managed to delay the transfer until October.

The areas further south likewise drew the attention of the Russian authorities. By spring 1878, many Muslim refugees had assembled in the eastern part of the Balkan range, of whom 16,000 chose to board ships and emigrate, while others asked for permission to return to their original places of settlement. In parallel, the Russian command received reports about the proliferation of bashi-bazouk bands in the region of Kotel as well as in the districts of Karnobat, Mesembria, Aidos, and Burgas. As long as the Ottomans continued to hold Shumla and Varna, it was important to prevent the penetration of Ottoman patrols from these territories beyond the demarcation line, for such expeditions supposedly contributed to the formation of the bashi-bazouk bands, some of which reached 1,000 people.[53]

Their activity continued even after the transfer of Shumla and Varna to the Russians. Thus, in December 1878, Totleben wrote about the appearance of Muslim bands in the area to the north of Aidos, where they were supported by the local Turkish inhabitants.[54] A subsequent report from Stolypin revealed that only forty Turkish inhabitants openly resisted Russian troops in one village, yet the region continued to be a source of concern for the Russians.[55] Two months later, the Russian consul in Philippopolis, A.I. Tseretelev, once again wrote of an "armed clash" (*échauffourée*) between the Muslim population of Aidos in the Slivno province of Eastern Rumelia and Russian troops. Tseretelev expected the Aidos district to become "a hotbed of Muslim agitation," since it represented an uninterrupted chain of Turkish villages connected to the Deliorman forest.[56]

Although the movement was quickly suppressed, the attitudes and possible actions of the Muslim population in the eastern parts of Eastern Rumelia and the Principality of Bulgaria continued to worry the Russian authorities. These worries made the imperial commissioner energetically protest the Ottoman occupation of the port of Burgas. According to him, such a measure would provoke the numerically predominant Turks of Pravoda, Varna, Shumla, Razgrad, and Osman Pazar into "disorders and acts of revenge" against the Christians.[57] On the same grounds, Dondukov-Korsakov opposed the request of Rauf Pasha to enter the Principality of Bulgaria with some 10,000 Muslim emigrants. The imperial commissioner called this request "an element of a hostile plan" and immediately connected it to the suspicious behaviour of the existing Muslim population of eastern Bulgaria.[58]

In March 1879, the Russian vice-consul in Varna, F.K. Lisevich, reported, with reference to the Shumla district governor, about the creation of a secret Muslim committee with connections in the Ottoman capital. According to this report, the goal of the committee was to capture the fortifications of Shumla and the mountain passes towards Aidos in order to incite rebellion in the "quadrangle" of the Ottoman fortresses. This would "give the Ottoman government a pretext to interfere with the goal of establishing its protectorate over the Turkish element, predominant in the 'quadrangle.'" In parallel, demobilized Ottoman soldiers and militiamen returning from Constantinople supposedly assured their local compatriots that "the government of the sultan would soon be reintroduced in the region, as has already happened in Edirne and as will soon be the case in Eastern Rumelia."[59] The everyday behaviour of the Muslims seemed to confirm Russian suspicions. Lisevich wrote about the respectful hospitality with which the Muslim villagers met the officials and gendarmes and, at the same time, noted their "unwillingness to cultivate their fields" and their selling of their livestock.[60]

The imperial commissioner likewise found greatly suspicious the "air of passivity and submission" that the Turks assumed particularly after their contact with the British journalist Fitzgerald and "other British agents."[61] Fearing provocations during the approaching evacuation of the Russian troops, Dondukov-Korsakov dispatched special agents in order to "penetrate the secret intentions of the Muslims and investigate external intrigues that could create regrettable complications."[62] According to the intelligence he received, the conspirators planned to "raise all Muslims of Bulgaria and bring the country back under the rule of the sultan," immediately after the withdrawal of the Russian troops. If this proved to be impossible, they intended "to put everything to fire and sword and leave for Constantinople."[63] In order to achieve this goal, the conspirators counted on the support of some 7,000 demobilized Ottoman soldiers who had returned to their native region, as well as on the stocks of rifles left in Shumla by the Ottoman troops prior to the surrender of the fortress to the Russians in the fall of 1878. In order to counteract these designs, Dondukov-Korsakov strengthened the local police by authorizing the creation of Bulgarian village patrols, who were to learn how to use 11,000 rifles from the Russian weapons deposits under the instruction of specially appointed Russian officers. Additionally, the imperial commissioner counted on 2,000 Bulgarian volunteers who had been previously allowed to study the manuals of rifles, following the example of Eastern Rumelian gymnastic societies (see later on in this chapter).[64]

The Management of Muslim and Christian Migrations after the War

In his management of the inter-confessional and inter-ethnic relations in the eastern Balkans, Dondukov-Koraskov had to take into account the commitments of the Russian military and civilian authorities made before his appointment. Thus, in his official proclamation to the Bulgarian population at the end of the war, the commander-in-chief, Grand Duke Nikolai Nikolaevich, once again affirmed that all inhabitants had equal rights to personal safety and full protection of their property "regardless of ethnicity and confession." The proclamation specifically urged the population to "receive [the refugees] as brothers and co-nationals [*sograzhdane*]," whatever their ethnicity or confession.[65] Following the publication of the Berlin Treaty, tens of thousands of Muslims indeed asked for permission to return to the Russian-occupied territories. At the end of July 1878, Dondukov-Korsakov estimated the number of returnees at between 12,000 and 15,000 in Philippopolis *sanjak* alone.[66] Two weeks later, he counted 30,000 or 40,000 people already in Eastern Rumelia, in addition to the 47,000 who had gathered in Adrianople with the intention to move further west and north.[67]

The imperial commissioner tried to stop, or at least limit, the return of Muslim refugees. Having established a special commission for the examination of the property titles of the refugees, Dondukov-Korsakov instructed it to slow down as much as possible the return of the Muslims to their former places of residence. To discourage the refugees from coming back, it was announced that only those Muslim refugees who returned to the Principality of Bulgaria before 15 June 1878 would have the right to one-half of the harvest from their lands.[68] However, the Russian ambassador in Constantinople, Lobanov-Rostovskii, realized early on the impossibility of justifying such a policy before the diplomatic representatives of other European powers. A refusal to admit Muslim refugees, he noted, could be used as a proof of Russia's "inability to govern the region."[69]

Therefore, the imperial commissioner had to modify his approach and allow all former Muslim inhabitants of the Principality of Bulgaria and Eastern Rumelia to return, with the exception of the Circassians and people whose past crimes "could provoke repressive measures on the part of the Christian population."[70] Special Russian-Ottoman commissions established in Varna and Constantinople had to supervise the process of repatriation, verify the documents of refugees, and ascertain their entitlement to return. On the suggestion of

Totleben, the imperial commissioner requested from the provincial governors lists of Muslims who had committed atrocities against their Bulgarian neighbours during the war and communicated them to Lobanov-Rostovskii so that the Constantinople commission could prevent the return of these individuals.[71]

All returnees had to surrender their weapons, except for the natives of the Shumla and Varna districts, who were nevertheless prohibited from carrying weapons in the streets. To facilitate the settlement of the Muslim refugees, Dondukov-Korsakov allocated to them one-half of the harvest that had been collected from their fields in their absence by the Bulgarian tenants (*arendatory*). In those cases when abandoned Muslim villages could not accommodate the Bulgarian occupiers and all of the returning Muslims, Dondukov-Korsakov suggested settling the latter in sheds and dugouts in the vicinity or else sending them to lands that had been inhabited by Circassians before the war.[72] The imperial commissioner was thus clearly unwilling to accommodate the Muslim refugees at the expense of the Bulgarian population.

Dondukov-Korsakov considered it unfair to expel the Bulgarians who had occupied the Muslim homes, since their own villages in the valley of the Tundzha had suffered much greater destruction in the course of the war.[73] For the same reason, he believed it "absolutely unjust and unthinkable" to use the revenues of the Bulgarian principality to aid the Turks, who had "destroyed Bulgarian villages and committed all the violence and atrocities that [had drawn] the attention of Europe on the eve of the war."[74] Instead, he hoped to cover the accommodation expenses with sums from the war contribution that the Porte had to pay according to the peace treaty.[75] At the same time, the imperial commissioner rejected outright the idea of Ottoman participation in the administration of the war damage payments in the Principality of Bulgaria and suggested limiting such involvement to Eastern Rumelia.[76]

Politically, Dondukov-Korsakov viewed the return of the Muslim refugees as a hidden attempt to "strengthen the Muslim element" in Eastern Rumelia taking advantage of the new organization of the region decided by the Berlin Congress.[77] According to the imperial commissioner, it was not even clear at the beginning whether the returning Muslims were natives of the territory, in which they wished to settle.[78] The persistence of the Rhodopian problem only deepened his tendency to perceive the Muslim returnees as a "restless and dangerous element." Dondukov-Korsakov noted that the insurgents were unlikely to advance into the Russian-controlled territories, and yet "their presence on our borders greatly provokes the Turkish masses."[79] War Minister Miliutin at least partly shared this perception and wrote about the need to "suppress and put an end to" what he called the "Muslim agitation under the guise of mass movement" that was being "artificially provoked by the Porte and its European friends." According to Miliutin, Russia's response to this tendency could consist in postponing the withdrawal of its troops.[80]

Predictably, the Russian efforts to limit the return of the Muslim refugees exasperated the Ottomans and the British. The Ottoman representative at the Bulgarian National Assembly in Tyrnovo, Petrev Pasha, protested the extremely complicated procedure whereby the Muslim refugees returning to Eastern Rumelia or the Principality of Bulgaria could reclaim their properties.[81] Frederick Dufferin, the British ambassador in St. Petersburg, denounced the "concerted intention of the Christian inhabitants of certain districts of Eastern Rumelia to drive their Mohammedian fellow citizens from their homes." In response to similar protests by the new Ottoman governor of Adrianople, Rustem Pasha, Stolypin, the governor general of Eastern Rumelia, observed that the Muslim emigration from Eastern Rumelia to the east was as natural as the Christian emigration from the Edirne *vilayet* to the west.[82]

The Russian provisional administration indeed confronted the influx of Christian immigrants from those territories of San Stefano Bulgaria that according to the decisions of the Berlin Congress were to remain under Ottoman control. In July 1878, the imperial commissioner insinuated that the Muslim "persecution" of Macedonian Christians was aimed at forcing them to resettle in northern Bulgaria, which would change the ethnographic situation of Macedonia with its currently predominant Bulgarian element, a plan that clearly interested the Greeks and the Albanians.[83] The suppression of the abortive Macedonian uprising by Ottoman troops led Dondukov-Korsakov to expect "massive emigration" of Christians from Macedonia into Sofia province.[84] Indeed, in December 1878, after the defeat of the bands that entered Macedonia from the Russian-occupied territory (as seen later on), some 25,000 Bulgarians emigrated from Macedonia to Sofia province.[85]

The beginning of the retreat of Russian troops from southern Thrace in September 1878 led to the immigration of Thracian Christians into Eastern Rumelia.[86] According to Totleben, the movement was caused by the threats of the newly reinstalled Ottoman authorities and the murder of several Christian inhabitants by Muslims. Both the threats and the number of murders were greatly exaggerated by the Thracian Greeks, who sought in this way to spread panic among their Bulgarian neighbours and make them sell their lands at a low price.[87] In order to calm the Bulgarians, Totleben even halted the withdrawal of Russian troops. However, the assurances of the Ottoman authorities and the warnings that the emigrants were going to meet the same sad fate as the Muslim refugees proved futile, and the process continued.[88] Some 8,000 emigrants had entered Eastern Rumelia by early October 1878, and two months later, the number of these resettlers had reached 30,000 and 20,000 in Philippopolis and Slivno provinces, respectively.[89]

The commander-in-chief considered it inhuman to force the Thracian Bulgarians to stay under Ottoman rule, yet feared that the impending withdrawal of Russian troops from Eastern Rumelia could cause a similar exodus of

Rumelian Bulgarians.[90] Although his estimate of the eventual number of Thracian emigrants proved to be an exaggeration,[91] by March 1879 there were already 60,000 Christian immigrants from the areas that the Berlin Congress had left outside the Principality of Bulgaria and Eastern Rumelia.[92] The influx of refugees placed further strain on the economic situation in territories already suffering from the devastation caused by the war and the transportation duties imposed by the Russian army. The Russian vice-consul in Burgas, N.G. Gartvig, wrote about "the masses of Turkish and Bulgarian refugees" in Karnobat, Semengli, and the environs of Yambol, and reported that in the first of these towns the hungry peasants even "besieged Red Cross hospitals asking for bread."[93]

As in the case of Macedonia, Dondukov-Korsakov initially opposed the resettlement of Thracian Christians in Eastern Rumelia out of a desire to preserve the Bulgarian population in Thrace.[94] However, before long the imperial commissioner changed his mind upon reading petitions submitted by the Bulgarian and Greek villagers of Thrace. The latter asked for permission to follow the Russian troops "to escape bloody Turkish revenge and the arbitrariness of the [Ottoman] authorities."[95] According to Dondukov-Korsakov, "the persecutions, killings, and robberies" of Eastern Thracian Christians began as soon as the Russian troops proceeded to evacuate the province. Unless the grievances of the Thracian emigrants were promptly addressed, the imperial commissioner feared that they might take "quite natural revenge" on the Turks living in Rumelia and the Principality of Bulgaria.

Dondukov-Korsakov viewed the influx of Christian immigrants as an opportunity to slow down or stop altogether the return of the Muslim refugees. "Would it not be expedient," he wondered, "to stop for the time being the return of the Turkish immigrants and effect the exchange of the Christian land of Adrianople *sanjak* against lands in Rumelia that belonged to Turkish villages whose inhabitants have not [yet] returned[?]"[96] Having obtained the agreement of the war minister for this measure,[97] Dondukov-Korsakov suggested that the Ottoman government prevent the return of its Muslim subjects to Slivno and Philippopolis provinces, since "all free places and the harvests of their fields will be needed by the Christian refugees."[98] Indeed, special commissions were created in Adrianople, Philippopolis, and Slivno, with money and grain funds allocated to them.[99]

As the Christian immigration gained momentum, the Russian provisional authorities intensified their efforts to scale down this process that was straining the resources of Eastern Rumelia.[100] Thus, the Russian governor general, A.D. Stolypin, admonished the Bulgarian population of Adrianople *sanjak* to stay loyal to the Ottoman administration and remain in their places of residence, while the Russian military governor of Adrianople, P.M. Molostovov, issued orders to the district commanders to limit Christian resettlement.[101] By December 1878, some of these Christian immigrants to Eastern Rumelia had begun to return to Adrianople *sanjak*, although a report by the commander of the 7th Cavalry Division, Adjutant General K.N. Manzei, led Stolypin to expect another massive influx of Christian émigrés in the near future.[102]

An opponent of Christian immigration, Stolypin weighed the ethno-political and socio-economic consequences of this process. The governor general did not take seriously the fear of Thracian Christians that they would all be massacred by the Ottoman Muslims following the complete Russian evacuation of Adrianople *sanjak* (which took place in February 1879, following the ratification of the Russian-Ottoman peace treaty). "We saw no such massacre in the districts that we have already evacuated and, unfortunately, we have to admit that a dozen murders would not compare to the hundreds of resettlers that would inevitably die in the course of the winter in the difficult circumstances of their emigration [to Eastern Rumelia]." Besides, inviting thousands of homeless and hungry people was hardly conducive to the preservation of order in Eastern Rumelia after the withdrawal of Russian troops from the province. Finally, the influx of Thracian Christians would exacerbate the disputes around the former Turkish villages that had recently been populated by Bulgarians, disputes that, according to Stolypin, were inevitable once the Turkish refugees returned.[103]

Dondukov-Korsakov generally agreed with Stolypin yet advised against the use of force to stop Christian émigrés from entering Rumelia. In December 1878, the imperial commissioner argued that their number would not be as great as had been expected the previous fall and dismissed Stolypin's concern about possible property disputes between Christians and Muslims following the return of the latter to Eastern Rumelia. According to Dondukov-Korsakov, their return was "hardly possible because of the predominant desire among the Turks to [move] to Asia Minor, which the Porte supports by all means."[104] However, Stolypin continued to sound the alarm about public agitation among Bulgarians at the prospect of the restoration of Ottoman rule. According to the general, attacks by the Bulgarians against the Muslims in the Rhodope Mountains were as likely as attacks by the Muslims against the Bulgarians in Aidos and Airabos.[105] As a result of Stolypin's reports, by February 1879 the imperial commissioner himself expected "serious clashes between the [Thracian] emigrants and the Muslim population of Rumelia" and eagerly blamed the Berlin settlement for this.[106]

Although the Russian authorities parried the British and Ottoman accusations of mistreatment of Muslims in the context of the Muslim-Christian population exchange between Thrace and Eastern Rumelia, their attitude towards Christian immigration remained ambiguous. Thus, Gartvig admitted in conversation with the local Bulgarians that their co-nationals who were flooding into the district strengthened the local Bulgarian element against the rather numerous local Turks and Greeks. At the same time, Gartvig pointed out that the Bulgarians who abandoned the "richest lands assigned to the Ottoman Empire according to the Berlin Congress thereby forgo any hope of regaining them."[107] Gartvig's remarks reflected the dilemma faced by Russian policymakers after they proclaimed the goal of strengthening the Bulgarian element in the territories that had been included within the Principality of Bulgaria by the Treaty of San Stefano, yet remained outside it according to the Treaty of Berlin.

Concerned as they were with Muslim-Christian relations in Eastern Rumelia, the Russian provisional authorities did not ignore inter-ethnic relations among Christians. From the very beginning their goal was to strengthen the Bulgarians rather than the Greeks in the region. Even before the end of the Berlin Congress, Slivno governor I.S. Ivanov argued that the international commission on Rumelia would do everything to undermine the local Slavic element and admonished Dondukov-Korsakov to counteract these designs by appointing ethnic Bulgarians as heads of district administration, opening village and municipal schools, and creating a Bulgarian national bank to aid the Bulgarian victims. Ivanov also advised the imperial commissioner to prevent the emigration of Bulgarians from southern Bulgaria and Macedonia into the principality, as "this would weaken the Bulgarian element in these places, which in this case will be forever lost to Bulgarians."[108]

Dondukov-Korsakov must have found Ivanov's last point to be particularly pertinent, as is clear from his position on the question of Bulgarian emigration from the district of Dzhumaia. During the war, Dzhumaia (Yukari Cuma, Blagoevgrad) was occupied by Russian troops, yet was to return under direct Ottoman rule in accordance with the decision of the Berlin Congress. In response, the inhabitants of Dzhumaia sent a delegation to the governor of Sofia, P.V. Alabin, which declared their intention to send their families to the Principality of Bulgaria and revolt against the Ottoman government as soon as Russian troops evacuated the district.[109] Despite Alabin's assurances that the European powers would not allow arbitrary rule on the part of the Ottomans, "it [was] impossible to convince the Dzhumaia inhabitants that on the day of retreat of the Russian troops, the bashi-bazouks concentrated on their borders [would] not unleash a bloody retribution for their support of the Russians and all the calamities that the local Muslim population [had] suffered."[110] The Sofia governor asked Dondukov-Korsakov for instructions in view of the fact that "the richest and most perspicacious" of the Dzhumaia Bulgarians were already leaving the district. Mindful of the weakening of the Bulgarian element that such emigration was likely to cause, Dondukov-Korsakov ordered Alabin to treat the Dzhumaia Bulgarians "benignly" (*sniskhoditel'no*) yet insisted on preventing their large-scale resettlement in the principality.[111]

Eager to preserve the Bulgarian element in the territories that did not join the Principality of Bulgaria, the Russian Ministry of Foreign Affairs instructed its newly appointed consul in Philippopolis, A.N. Tseretelev, to counteract all influences aiming to separate Eastern Rumelia from the principality. The ministry expected the Greeks to seek predominance over Bulgarians with the support of the local Muslims. Tseretelev was instructed to prevent the subjection of the Bulgarians by the Greeks and, at the same time, secure a rapprochement between the two warring Christian nationalities.[112] This overall goal of Russian policy informed the approach of the provisional administration towards some 20,000 Greek emigrants from Thrace. Dondukov-Korsakov found Stolypin's suggestion to settle them in the Principality of Bulgaria rather than in Eastern Rumelia "quite sound," since it was important "not to increase the Greek element in areas where the Greeks seek predominance over other ethnicities."[113] Accordingly, the imperial commissioner gave orders to settle the Greek emigrants from Demotika in Vidin province, far to the north of the Greek-Bulgarian demographic front line.

Muslim Service in the Militia and Bulgarian Gymnastic Societies in Eastern Rumelia

The formation of a Bulgarian national army constituted one of the most important tasks of the imperial commissioner according to ministerial instructions.[114] An important landmark in this process was the "Temporary Rules on the Formation of the Bulgarian Militia," which introduced the principle of universal military service. Approved by Totleben on 19 June 1878, the rules initially did not apply to the *sanjak* of Varna, where the number of Christians was lower than that of Muslims, or to Sofia and Vidin provinces, since the border with Serbia was not yet demarcated. Taking into consideration the excitement of passions among the nationalities of the Balkan Peninsula, it was decided to limit conscription to Bulgarians only.[115] At the same time, the conscription order stated that volunteers "of all nationalities and confessions" would be accepted, "if they are able to present letters from their communities testifying to their trustworthiness [*blagonadezhnosti*]."[116]

After the Berlin Congress stipulated the restoration of the Porte's supreme authority over Eastern Rumelia, Miliutin urged Dondukov-Korsakov to focus his efforts on the creation of an effective police force and gendarmerie on both sides of the Balkans. According to the war minister, only by creating a "strong and reliable national guard" could one hope that "despite the monstrosity of the child that was disfigured in Berlin, it will remain alive and, with time, grow stronger and develop."[117] For several months after the Congress, the Eastern Rumelian militia remained part of the militia (*zemskoe voisko*) of the Principality of Bulgaria, was staffed almost exclusively by Russian officers, and was placed under the command of the imperial commissioner. The arrival of the International Commission on Eastern Rumelia to Philippopolis in October 1878 prompted the Russian authorities to single out the Rumelian militia into a separate unit and replace the Russian officers with Bulgarian ones, transferred from both the Russian army and the militia of the Principality of Bulgaria.[118] In doing so, the imperial commissioner took special care to limit the appointment of foreign officers to the Eastern Rumelian militia, particularly those of Austrian Slavic (Polish) and Serbian origin.[119]

The creation of a militia and gendarmerie both in the Principality of Bulgaria and in Eastern Rumelia posed the problem of conscription of ethnic and religious minorities. An exclusively Bulgarian institution at the time of its formation, the militia soon had to be reformed in such a way as to accommodate Greek and Muslim conscripts. In accordance with Miliutin's guidelines, Dondukov-Korsakov authorized the drafting of the Greeks of Varna province before the end of 1878 and planned to draft Muslims the following year.[120] Although the Varna Greeks eventually complied, their response to the draft was characteristically lukewarm. They continued to look down upon Bulgarians and regretted the end of Ottoman rule, which had made it easier to envision the restoration of Greater Greece.[121] For their part, the Muslims of the north-east declared that they preferred emigration to service in the Bulgarian militia, and offered to pay a special tax in lieu of military service, akin to the Ottoman *bedel*.

From Dondukov-Korsakov's point of view, emigration would relieve the region of a "hostile element" and would provide lands for the settlement of a great number of Christian refugees.[122] The imperial commissioner considered the desire of the Muslims to emigrate "quite natural" since "the Quran, history, and the failure of different *hatt-i humayuns*" had all shown "the impossibility of cohabitation of the Christian and Muslim elements as soon as these elements acquire equal rights." "One has to know Islam," pontificated Dondukov-Korsakov, "in order to understand what the Berlin Congress failed to realize: a Muslim who accepts a Christian as his equal is no longer a Muslim."[123] At the same time, the imperial commissioner argued that the simultaneous emigration of the Turks and immigration of Bulgarians could "occasion the most regrettable clashes," particularly since the Muslim population was allowed to keep their firearms. In this situation, Dondukov-Korsakov considered a military tax to be workable alternative, yet he found it difficult to reconcile such a measure with the earlier abolition of the Ottoman *bedel* tax on Christians by Alexander II.[124] In the end, Dondukov-Korsakov suggested declaring a one-year delay for the military conscription of Muslims, at the end of which the latter had either to accept military service or to emigrate. The imperial commissioner expected that the majority of Muslims would choose the latter option, which would provide space for the settlement of the Bulgarian immigrants from Adrianople *sanjak*.[125]

The same question of Muslim service in the militia confronted the Russian provisional administration in Eastern Rumelia. In December 1878, Miliutin ordered Dondukov-Korsakov to elaborate new rules for the formation of an Eastern Rumelian militia (separate from those of the principality) "in such a way as to include proportionate numbers from Greek and Turkish populations of the province."[126] The imperial commissioner tried to slow down the separation of the Eastern Rumelian militia on the grounds that such a measure might exacerbate the agitation of the local population and cause disorder. He also considered the drafting of Muslims into the ranks of the militia to be more suitable for the Principality of Bulgaria than for Eastern Rumelia.[127] Stolypin, the governor general of Eastern Rumelia, similarly pointed to the "most harmful consequences" of "[drafting] Muslims into the militia so that after our withdrawal they could come back to their villages with knowledge of marksmanship and military drill."[128]

Nevertheless, both Dondukov-Korsakov and Stolypin ultimately had to comply with the policy that was pressed upon them by both the war minister and the commander-in-chief. In January 1879, Totleben wrote to Miliutin about the desirability of "giving to the Eastern Rumelian militia that final organization that it needs to have at the moment of its transfer to the Turkish authorities and which necessitates the inclusion in it of Greeks and Muslims." Even if such a measure could lead to clashes between Muslims and Bulgarians, reasoned Totleben, it would be better if these clashes took place while the Russian troops were still in place and not after the evacuation.[129] Totleben also pointed out that the Bulgarian officers whom Dondukov-Korsakov had transferred from the militia units of the principality to those of Eastern Rumelia would preserve the link between the two formations. Finally, adding Greeks and Muslims to the Rumelian militia in proportion to their presence in the ethnic composition of the province would deprive the European commission of the pretext for meddling with Rumelian forces after the Russian evacuation.[130]

The decisions of the Berlin Congress caused uncertainty on the part of Rumelian Bulgarians, who addressed several petitions to Dondukov-Korsakov.[131] The imperial commissioner assured the petitioners that the proposed organization of Eastern Rumelia would in any case be better that what had existed prior to the war and warned them that any resistence would be repressed. However, the Bulgarians agreed to observe order only as long as Russian troops remained in the province.[132] They could not imagine a local Christian militia under the command of Muslim officers and feared that the governor general might be selected from among the Greeks or Armenians, who had formerly helped the Ottomans oppress the Bulgarians.[133]

The attitude of the Rumelian Bulgarians made Totleben fear that the withdrawal of Russian troops from Eastern Rumelia would cause large-scale emigration of local Bulgarians to the principality, just as the retreat of the Russian army from Thrace had caused the emigration of Thracian Bulgarians to Eastern Rumelia. To prevent such an outcome, Totleben suggested reassuring the Rumelian Bulgarians through the creation of gymnastic societies and firearms deposits. The Russian commander-in-chief justified this measure by reference to the weakness of the Rumelian militia, which would not be able to resist Ottoman troops without the aid of an armed population. To prove the effectiveness of the proposed measure, Totleben pointed to the example of Albania, where the Prizren League had refused to cede territories to Montenegro, Serbia, and Bulgaria in accordance with the decisions of the Berlin Congress and eventually defied the Porte's authority. "The main source of strength of the Albanians," reasoned Totleben, "is in their universal possession of firearms, their good marksmanship, and their martial spirit."[134]

According to the commander-in-chief, the proposal was in line with the new political attitude of the Bulgarians. He pointed out that at the end of 1878 the Bulgarians were no longer what they had been in 1877, when they were uncertain of the successful resolution of the war and feared that they would suffer the cruel fate of their co-nationals in Kazanlyk and Yeni Zagra after the retreat of Gurko's vanguard. During the ten months of Russian rule, the Bulgarians came to value their newly regained freedom, rallied together, and repeatedly asked the Russian commanders to teach them how to handle their rifles.[135] Since the Russian army was being rearmed with Berdan rifles, Totleben suggested transferring the old Krnka rifles to the arms deposits that he suggested creating in Philippopolis, Kazanlyk, Eski Zagra, Iambol, and other places. The commanders of the militia units would teach Bulgarian civilians how to shoot but would issue them with rifles only if Muslim attacks made such self-protection measures necessary.[136]

To justify his proposal, Totleben also pointed out that the Ottoman authorities were likewise arming the Muslim population in the territories that were outside the limits of the zone of Russian occupation.[137] These measures by the Ottomans were not limited to the Rhodope Mountains, which had never been fully occupied by the Russian troops; or Thrace, which the Russians were evacuating in the fall of 1878 in accordance with the decisions of the Berlin Congress. Before surrendering Shumla and Varna to the Russians, the Ottoman commanders of these fortresses had transferred large stocks of firearms to the Muslim inhabitants of the Deliorman forest. Totleben did not fail to mention this when the British member of the Rumelian commission, Henry Drummond-Wolf, raised the issue of firearms deposits and gymnastic societies in Eastern Rumelia during Totleben's visit to Philippopolis.[138]

Dondukov-Korsakov shared Totleben's viewpoint and found the arming of the Bulgarians of Eastern Rumelia necessary in view of the prospective transfer of the province to nominal Ottoman control. As early as July 1878, the imperial commissioner found it necessary to rearm the Bulgarian population of the southern part of the province, in case the Rumelian Muslim refugees in the Rhodope Mountains were allowed to return to their places of origin with their weapons.[139] He also authorized the accumulation of 200 extra rifles by each unit of the Eastern Rumelian militia, to be distributed to Bulgarian civilians if necessary.[140] Both Totleben's idea of creating firearms deposits and Dondukov-Korsakov's preliminary measures to that effect were approved by Alexander II, who found in them a means to "prevent the emigration of the Christian population of Eastern Rumelia when the evacuation time comes."[141]

Despite the tsar's approval, this measure also had its critics among the Russian authorities, notably, the governor general of Eastern Rumelia, Stolypin. Stolypin argued that the distribution of firearms would be taken by the Bulgarian population as tacit encouragement to resist the new political order after the Russian evacuation. Stolypin advised against establishing the firearms deposits altogether and suggested rejecting the Bulgarian requests to teach them to shoot in order to "cool as much as is still possible their bellicose spirit."[142] In response, the imperial commissioner argued that even if massacres (*reznia*) took place after the evacuation of Russian troops, "they will still be smaller if the Turks know that the Bulgarians carry firearms."[143] Totleben supported Dondukov-Korsakov's approach, pointing to the role of the arming of the population in the Caucasian and Polish insurgencies. As a result, a 200,000-strong Russian army was necessary to pacify the Caucasus, while the troops in the western borderlands proved to be insufficient to suppress the uprising of 1863 and had to be supported by Russian Guards units. On the other hand, the teaching of marksmanship and the distribution of firearms, according to Totleben, was a means of "making the Bulgarians a martial people, for which the current agitation of their nationalist sentiments offers a good occasion."[144]

Stolypin himself soon accepted Dondukov-Korsakov's and Totleben's point of view. In January 1879, he reported to the Russian ambassador in Constantinople, Lobanov-Rostovskii, that regular Ottoman troops and bashibazouks occupied several districts of Eastern Rumelia and that the Ottoman authorities were arming the Muslim inhabitants of the territories along the borders of the province. These measures "greatly excited the minds of both the Turkish and the Bulgarian population" within Eastern Rumelia and forced Stolypin to distribute firearms among the latter.[145] Sentry units (*voennye karauly*) were created in order to protect Christian houses from possible Muslim attacks.[146] Russian troops and the Bulgarian militia were ordered to teach the local population how to shoot and thereby prepare them for service in the militia.[147] The gymnastic societies created to this end proved to be so popular with the Bulgarians that Stolypin found it necessary to order that the firearms be stored in special warehouses and distributed only in case of a real threat.[148] Together with the local militia, the members of the gymnastic societies in Eastern Rumelia numbered 60,000.[149]

Russian efforts to arm the Bulgarian population of Eastern Rumelia did not go unopposed. Henri Drummond-Wolf expressed his concerns as early as December 1878.[150] Before long he reported the creation of the gymnastic societies and the putative intention of the Russian administration to send "bands of this description" to Rhodope district. His protests were relayed to the Russian government by the British ambassador in St. Petersburg, Frederick Dufferin, who argued that the gymnastic societies were incompatible with the constitution of Eastern Rumelia that the international commission was about to produce. Dufferin warned the Russian Foreign Ministry that the Muslim population of the province would view such associations as mere partisan groups and not as legitimate guardians of peace and order.[151] Russian foreign minister Girs found nothing illegal in the existence of the gymnastic societies yet instructed Lobanov-Rostovskii to make sure that members of such societies stayed away from the Rhodope.[152]

Having authorized the formation of gymnastic societies and rural sentries in Eastern Rumelia, Russian policymakers viewed it as a fundamentally defensive measure that "should definitely not be taken as the arming of the population for the purposes of a future uprising tacitly encouraged by the Russian government."[153] At the same time, they realized that this measure could encourage Bulgarian nationalists to revise the decisions of the Berlin Congress by force and took special care to prevent such attempts as well as urge the Rumelian Bulgarians to comply with the established order.[154] However, the restraint that the Russian provisional administration exercised towards Bulgarian hotheads was not always effective, if only because some some policymakers themselves profoundly regretted "the monstrosity of the child that was disfigured in Berlin."[155]

This ambiguity of the Russian attitude towards Bulgarian nationalism created complications in Macedonia. Soon after the conclusion of the preliminary Treaty of San Stefano, the Russians appointed a governor of Macedonia and seventy officers with the goal of establishing a provisional administration in the territory. This administration was to rely on a Russian cavalry corps and the local *chetas*. However, these plans were soon overtaken by the Berlin Congress, which left Macedonia to the Ottoman Empire. Although Dondukov-Korsakov could do nothing to change its stipulations, he turned a blind eye to the activities of the Macedonian "committees of unity" in Bulgaria itself (first established by the Diamandov brothers in Vidin and Tyrnovo), which included numerous natives of Macedonia who had served in the Bulgarian militia during the war. In early October, two detachments of partisans (1,500 in total) led by retired Don Cossack captain Adam Kalmykov and a Polish émigré, Louis Wojtkiewicz, crossed the border into Macedonia.[156] After several successes, they were dispersed by regular Ottoman troops in November 1878, although the intermittent fighting continued until 1881.[157] This undertaking prompted a note from the

Porte to Lobanov-Rostovskii, following which Alexander II issued a reprimand to Dondukov-Korsakov for having being unaware of the activities of the committees, or else for having turned a blind eye to them.[158]

In his defence, Dondukov-Korsakov blamed the failure of the Russian civil administration to develop a definitive policy on this issue prior to his appointment as imperial commissioner.[159] According to him, the unrealized plans to introduce Russian administration in the province caused unrest among Macedonian Christians, while the decision of the Berlin Congress that left Macedonia to the Ottoman Empire prompted vehement protests on their part. Another provoking factor was the banditry of the bashi-bazouks, who in July 1878 burned down thirty villages along the demarcation line established in Berlin.[160] Spurred into action, Dondukov-Korsakov ordered the heads of the district administration on the border of Macedonia to prevent the formation of armed bands that intended to enter the province.[161] In parallel, the governors of the Principality of Bulgaria and Eastern Rumelia were to collect the information on the numbers, organization, and goals of the "committees of unity" that were sponsoring the insurgents and prevent their development, as well as the development of all secret societies that had a political character.[162]

The exchanges between Dondukov-Korsakov, Totleben, and Stolypin on the question of the Eastern Rumelian militia and the creation of firearms deposits revealed significant changes in the political attitude of the Russian military. The earlier concerns with the politically subversive character of mobilizing the Balkan Christians that transpired in the correspondence between Nicholas I and his commanders during the Danubian campaign of the Crimean War were not entirely absent at the end of the Eastern Crisis. Although Dondukov-Korsakov did a lot to arm the Rumelian Bulgarians, he found it "sad to see that such a monarchical government as the Russian one" had to turn a blind eye to "secret funds, revolutionary committees, and anarchist bombs" in order to give the Bulgarian nation "the means to re-conquer the freedom that we have failed to secure for it."[163] Nevertheless, concerns about the security of the Bulgarian population came to prevail over all other considerations after the Eastern Crisis, and the war of 1877–8 revealed the destructive potential of inter-confessional and inter-ethnic violence. Such concerns reflected both the idealistic pan-Slavic sentiment that prevailed within the Russian military and the more pragmatic interest in preserving Russia's influence among the Bulgarians after the Berlin Congress dashed hopes raised by San Stefano.

Dondukov-Korsakov's main task as imperial commissioner – to supervise the elaboration and adoption of the statute for the Principality of Bulgaria – was accomplished in February 1879 with the election of the Constitutional Assembly in Tyrnovo. The Bulgarian statute guaranteed freedom of religion to non-Orthodox Christians and followers of other faiths, "on condition that profession of their faith [*ispolnenie ikh obriadov*] does not infringe upon the existing laws."[164] The document asserted that "no one can avoid obeying the existing universal laws on the pretext of one's religious convictions."[165] The spiritual affairs of non-Orthodox Christians and other confessions were placed within the jurisdiction of their spiritual authorities, who were to act "under the supervision of the respective minister" and "within the limits of laws that would be specially issued to that effect."[166] The definitive settlement of inter-confessional relations was thereby left to the future Bulgarian government, yet the overall tone of the document was hardly compatible with the idea of far-reaching religious autonomy for Muslims.[167]

The anti-Muslim bias of the statute reflected, among other things, the policies of the provisional administration and the personal attitudes of the imperial commissioner. Appointed soon after the conclusion of the preliminary Treaty of San Stefano in February 1878, Dondukov-Korsakov encountered several problems in his management of inter-confessional relations. The most immediate and pressing of these was the Rhodope Uprising, which erupted in the spring of 1878. The Ottoman soldiers and irregulars who fled to the region following the defeat and dispersal of Suleiman Pasha's army near Philippopolis together with refugees served as a catalyst for the rising up of the local Muslim population. After attempts to pacify the insurgents or suppress them by force proved to be unsuccessful, the Russian strategy consisted in cordoning off the Rhodope region and disclaiming any responsibility for what was going on there on the grounds that it had never been properly occupied by the Russian troops. Although the crisis was ultimately resolved, the imperial commissioner remained concerned about the possibility of another Muslim uprising until the end of his tenure.

Another challenge was the return of Muslim refugees after the end of the war, and particularly after the decisions of the Berlin Congress. Dondukov-Korsakov would have preferred them not to return at all, yet he had to take into account the provisions of the Berlin Treaty and international pressure. The imperial commissioner therefore tried to reduce the number of returning Muslims as much as possible by complicating the legal procedures through which they could reclaim their properties captured by the Christians during the war. Dondukov-Korsakov also sought to prevent the return of those Muslims whom he found particularly troublesome, namely the Circassians.

Such policies reflected the imperial commissioner's belief, widespread among Russian officials, that the Muslims would not be able to accommodate themselves to the emergent Principality of Bulgaria once the Bulgarian majority assumed its political rights. The policies of the Russian authorities towards the Muslim refugees ultimately belied their assertion that the eastern Balkans were fundamentally a Christian land, and that the Ottoman conquest represented a historical injustice that the emigration of Muslims to Asia could correct. For this reason, Dondukov-Korsakov and other Russian officials were initially hostile to the idea of the emigration of the Christian population from Macedonia and Thrace to Eastern Rumelia and the Principality of Bulgaria, since this would weaken the Christian element in the former provinces and render them more decidedly Muslim.

The decisions of the Berlin Congress that truncated San Stefano Bulgaria and stipulated the transformation of Eastern Rumelia into an autonomous Ottoman province made the Russian officials fear Ottoman reprisals against the local Christian population. To secure the local Bulgarian population, the Russian authorities created the Eastern Rumelian militia, organized gymnastic societies, and established firearms deposits. This was tantamount to arming the civilian population – a measure that past Russian commanders had found too "revolutionary" even at times of war. The decision to arm the Rumelian Bulgarians was informed not only by the example of the Albanian Prizren League, but also by the experience of Russia's own struggles against the guerrillas in the North Caucasus and Poland in the late 1850s and early 1860s. Russian policymakers assumed that the Ottomans would want to avoid the pitfalls of fighting against an armed population that Russia's own experience had revealed. The Ottoman government indeed wisely avoided sending troops into Eastern Rumelia after the Russians evacuated it in May 1879, and even accepted incorporation of the province into the Principality of Bulgaria six years later.

In their response to the Rhodopian insurgency, their management of the Muslim and Christian migration, and their policies on the Bulgarian militia and gymnastic societies in Eastern Rumelia, the Russian occupation authorities continued to distinguish between the different groups of the Balkan Muslim population. Russian animosity towards the bashi-bazouks and Circassians was certainly greater than that towards the Pomaks or the urban Muslim population of Philippopolis or Adrianople, and Russian treatment of these groups was accordingly different. At the same time, the overall anti-Muslim bias of the Russian commanders and officials in 1878–9 is also evident, particularly when their pronouncements are contrasted with the accommodating rhetoric of their predecessors half a century earlier.

This difference is indicative of the already-mentioned hardening of attitudes towards Islam and the Muslims that came to characterize Russian policies after the more tolerant approach of Catherine the Great and her immediate successors. This change constituted the Russian dimension of the broader European racialization of Islam in the second half of the nineteenth century, as analysed by Cemil Aydin.[168] Ideological groupings as different as Gladstonian liberals and Russian pan-Slavists contributed to this process in the early stages of the Eastern Crisis, yet the subsequent clash of empires played a no less significant role. First, the changing fortunes of the Russian-Ottoman war helped polarize

Balkan communities into "Muslims" and "Bulgarians." After the war, Ottoman and British attempts to instrumentalize the Rhodopian insurgency had the same effect, as did Russian efforts to counter this insurgency and strengthen the "Bulgarian element."

The correspondence of the Russian occupation authorities in 1878–9 reflected their novel tendency to think of the historically and culturally distinct groups of the Balkan Muslim population as interconnected by a common political agenda of resistance to the new political order that Russia was trying to implement. When they related the Rhodopian insurgency to the activities of the Albanian Prizren League, the petitions of the returning Muslim refugees, and putative conspiratorial activities in the Varna and Shumla regions, the Russian commanders were making their own contribution to the emergent notion of the Muslim world as distinct from and opposed to Christianity and/or Europe. At a time when European and Islamic intellectuals were articulating early versions of the "clash of civilizations" thesis, Russian military men, like their British and other European counterparts, were beginning to think of the Muslim world as an entity with its own rules and logic, a potential military-political force that had to be contained and controlled unless rival great powers mobilized it against them. In this sense, the policies of Russian occupation authorities in the eastern Balkans in 1878–9 were indicative of the emergence of an altogether novel dimension of the great power struggle that would persist well into the twentieth century.

Conclusion

In one of the most forceful attempts to undermine received notions about the nineteenth-century Balkans, American demographer and historian Justin McCarthy presented the Balkan Muslims as the victims of a century-long process of ethnic cleansing carried out by Christian national-liberation movements with the assistance of foreign powers. According to McCarthy, Russia played a major role in this process, particularly during the Russian-Ottoman war of 1877–8, when it supposedly sought "to drive the Turkish race out," or even "exterminate it."[1] To the reader of this study, it should have become abundantly clear that the Russian command harboured no such intentions either in 1877–8 or at any point prior to that. Although the Western perception of the Ottoman Empire as an "encampment" in Europe and the associated idea of the expulsion of the Ottomans into Asia had reached the Russian military men quite early, it never became a practical goal for Russian commanders or occupation authorities.

The closest approximation to anything like a twentieth-century-style "final solution" to the Balkan Muslim question can be found in R.A. Fadeev's October 1876 memorandum on the Bulgarian militia. To recall, Fadeev identified the Balkan Muslim population as "the stumbling block of the Eastern Question" and thus as the primary object of Russian and Bulgarian forces in the upcoming war. As has been demonstrated, the creation of the Bulgarian militia on Fadeev's suggestion did help to give the Russian-Ottoman conflict the character of a "people's war," which led to the high number of casualties among eastern Balkan Muslims and Christians. At the same time, Fadeev had no role in the elaboration of the actual Russian war plan, which, as has been demonstrated, in fact sought to minimize the contact between the Russian army and the Muslim population. An expulsionary attitude towards the eastern Balkan Muslims can also be found in the correspondence of the imperial commissioner A.I. Dondukov-Korsakov on the question of the return of Muslim refugees in 1878. Yet neither the Russian military command nor the Foreign Ministry supported

Dondukov-Korsakov in his efforts to reduce the number of returning Muslims and his "success" in this sense should not be overestimated.

Despite the death and dislocation of hundreds of thousands of eastern Balkan Muslims, neither the war of 1877–8 nor the policies of the Russian occupation authorities in its aftermath fundamentally changed the multi-ethnic and multi-confessional character of the region's population. Muslims constituted a sizable minority of the population of Rumelia prior to the war and they remained a sizable (albeit reduced) minority in the territory ten years later, at the time of the first population census in autonomous Bulgaria. What was left of "Turkey in Europe" after 1878 would remain similarly ethnically and confessionally mixed for decades to come. The definitive ethnic unmixing of Eastern Thrace, for example, occurred only in the wake of the Balkan Wars and the First World War, a period that also witnessed a large-scale population exchange between Turkey and Greece. The principal contribution of the Russian-Ottoman war of 1877–8 to the eventual ethnic and religious homogenization of South-Eastern Europe consisted of the consolidation of several emergent nation states (Romania, Serbia) and the foundation of a new one (Bulgaria). All of these would chase the chimera of ethnic nationalism, with ominous consequences for their minorities, but only decades later.

Still, the Russian-Ottoman wars and Russian occupation of the eastern Balkans had a major impact on the ethno-confessional situation in the region. In assessing this impact, I have sought to avoid the extremes of praise and vilification that characterize much of the historical literature on Imperial and Soviet Russia's military interventions in Eastern Europe. On the one hand, one can no longer take seriously the celebration of Russia's "liberatory role" with regard to the Slavic and Orthodox population of South-Eastern Europe that characterized Soviet historiography. On the other hand, one should be equally critical of the attempts to reduce the role of the Russian army to hideous war crimes made by some historians of Eastern Europe in recent decades. The question of whether the Russian/Soviet soldier was a liberator of Eastern European peoples from Ottoman or Nazi tyranny, or an oppressor, marauder, and rapist, has been hopelessly tainted by Cold War propaganda and present-day geopolitics. Only slightly less politicized is the comparison of the Russian army to its historical adversaries: the images of Russian, Ottoman, French, or German "barbarities" generated by rival propaganda machines over the last two centuries are all quite potent (and misleading).

Sceptical of the very possibility of objectively comparing the behaviour of Russian troops to that of their Ottoman or European counterparts, I have confined myself to an examination of the changing place of the Balkan population in Russian military thought, strategic planning, and occupation policies. This examination has revealed that the choices made by tsarist strategists and commanders during the Russian-Ottoman wars of 1828–9, 1853–4, and 1877–8 reflected a general reconceptualization of the role of "the people" in modern warfare. These choices represented an important variable in the final outcomes of the Balkan conflagrations of the 1820s and the 1870s that left a significant impact upon Christian-Muslim relations. As has been demonstrated, this impact was not uniform. In both 1828–30 and 1877–9, certain aspects of the Russian military strategy and occupation policies contributed to the aggravation of inter-confessional tensions, while others helped, or at least sought, to defuse them.

Thus, on the former occasion, the choice to engage the Ottoman army on the Lower Danube and in the quadrangle of the Ottoman fortresses led to the already customary depopulation of Dobrogea and galvanized the Muslim partisans in the Deliorman forest. This certainly gave the campaign of 1828 an aspect of a war against the Muslim population, even though such a war was certainly unintended. At the same time, inter-confessional tensions would undoubtedly have been higher during the first campaign of the war had Nicholas I succumbed to the temptation to mobilize local Christians into volunteer detachments in 1828. When, a year later, the tsar finally acquiesced to Dibich's requests to arm the Bulgarians, this measure hardly contributed to inter-confessional peace in the occupied territories. This, however, was counteracted by Dibich's willingness to learn from the negative experiences of the past and his careful handling of Muslim sensibilities following the Russian crossing of the Balkans and the occupation of Adrianople.

Overall, the Russian-Ottoman war of 1828–9 had a rather limited disruptive impact upon inter-confessional and inter-ethnic relations in the eastern Balkans, particularly compared to what took place some fifty years later. To explain this, one is justified in arguing that nationalist passions among the Slavic population of European Turkey did not run as high in the first half of the nineteenth century as they would at the time of the Eastern Crisis of the late 1870s. However, no less significant was the restrained approach of the tsar and his commanders, which in fact constituted the military-strategic counterpart to the conservative politics of the first post-Napoleonic decades. The restoration era witnessed the efforts by European rulers to reaffirm their authority, which had been compromised by the principle of popular sovereignty during the French Revolution. Similarly, the kind of war that the tsar and his commanders waged in 1828–9 represented a return to the principles of Old Regime warfare inasmuch as they sought to minimize the involvement of the local population and avoid a "people's war," the spectre of which first rose during the Revolutionary and Napoleonic period.

However, just as the restoration ultimately failed to turn the clock back to where it had been before 1789, so the attempt to minimize the involvement of the Balkan population in the Russian-Ottoman confrontations proved to be short-lived. Developments in the middle decades of the nineteenth century testified to the growing importance of the people in modern warfare. One of these was the development of population statistics. Between the Greek War of Independence of the 1820s and the Eastern Crisis of the 1870s, Russian officers became increasingly interested in the confessional and ethnic composition of European Turkey, as is clear from their progressively more detailed surveys of the potential war theatre. The authors of these surveys paid more and more attention to the moral-political qualities and attitudes of different groups of the local population in an effort to identify which of these population groups were likely to be hostile to or supportive of the army during a war.

As a result, the choice of operational line for the army came to depend, among other things, upon the ethno-confessional profile of the population of the area in question. The correspondence between Nicholas I and his commanders on the eve of the Danubian campaign of 1854 during the Crimean War offers the first illustration of this tendency. Faced with an emergent anti-Russian coalition and eager to compensate for the relative weakness of the Russian army on the Danube, the tsar played with the idea of mobilizing Russia's Orthodox co-religionists and, for this purpose, planned to cross the river further upstream into the areas more densely populated by the Bulgarians. This plan represented a deviation from the familiar pattern of fortress warfare on the Lower Danube that had characterized earlier Russian-Ottoman wars. Some twenty years later, N.N. Obruchev's plan for war was based on the same choice, and, in contrast to the Danubian campaign of 1854, it was implemented.

A re-evaluation of the partisan action and of the related phenomenon of the "people's war" constituted another manifestation of the growing importance of the population in the thinking of the Russian military men of the nineteenth century. As has been argued, the tsarist officers of the post-Napoleonic period remained rather critical towards the idea of the involvement of the people in military operations. However, the experience of the Napoleonic Wars also revealed the potential of partisan warfare, especially in a region like European Turkey. Following D.V. Davydov's example in the war of 1812, I.P. Liprandi first organized a detachment of Balkan partisans during the campaign of 1829, and then related this experience to the partisan warfare of the Napoleonic epoch.

Whereas, for Liprandi, partisan action was above all a way to counter a potential mobilization of the Balkan Muslim population against the Russian army, some representatives of the next generation of Russian officers came to appreciate it as a means of mobilizing Russia's Balkan co-religionists against the Ottoman Empire in the context of the Eastern Crisis of the 1870s. In doing so, I.K. Kishelskii, R.A. Fadeev, and N.I. Stoletov essentially embraced the idea of a "people's war," which had hitherto appeared too disturbing and politically subversive. In practice, greater acceptance of the notion of the "people's war" translated into the formation of the Bulgarian militia in 1877 and its inclusion in the vanguard of the Russian army, with the consequences that have already been described. It is also worth noting that the idea that was implemented in 1877–8 was first discussed by Nicholas I, I.F. Paskevich, and M.D. Gorchakov during the Danubian campaign of 1853–4. This means that that the most conservative of Russian tsars and his commanders anticipated the radical pan-Slavists like Kishelskii, Fadeev, and Stoletov, if only on paper.

The formation of the Bulgarian militia in 1877, like the creation of the volunteer detachments in the earlier wars, was accompanied by attempts to disarm the local Muslim inhabitants. In doing this, Russian commanders tried to eliminate one of the foundations of Ottoman dominance in the Balkans, which consisted in denying local Christians the right to bear arms and reserving this right for the Muslim population. The Christian volunteers would sometimes be given the very weapons that that had been surrendered by the Muslims. The rationale behind this policy was to secure Russia's co-religionists against the Ottoman irregulars, yet in practice this sometimes made Muslims vulnerable to the harassment of their Christian neighbours, emboldened by the presence of Russian troops. Needless to say, the Russian military authorities never managed to completely disarm the former, just as they never managed, or even intended, to arm all of the latter. Nevertheless, this practice did result in attacks by Christian volunteers against the persons and properties of the Muslims, as had happened during the campaign of 1829.

Such incidents must have made many Russian military professionals view the armament of the Christian population as too radical a measure. As late as 1878–9, the Russian governor general of Eastern Rumelia, A.O. Stolypin, had his qualms about the creation of the gymnastic societies and arms deposits intended to secure local Bulgarians against possible Ottoman reprisals after the evacuation of Russian troops and the restoration of the Porte's authority in the province. Russian fears of a possible civil war in Eastern Rumelia did not materialize, although the gymnastic societies undoubtedly did have a mobilizing effect on the Rumelian Bulgarians, which manifested in the unification of the province with the Principality of Bulgaria in 1885. This leads one to conclude that the creation of the Christian volunteer detachments, and the transfer of weapons from the Muslims to the Christians more broadly, was conducive to inter-confessional clashes in those cases when the Christians were emboldened by the presence of Russian troops.

Alongside the policy of (dis)armament of particular ethnic and/or confessional groups, the management of migration constituted another major aspect of population politics in the eastern Balkans during the Russian-Ottoman wars. The resettlement of large masses of the population was an old practice dating back to the Ottoman conquest of the Balkans and continued during the Habsburg-Ottoman wars of the seventeenth century. In the earlier Russian-Ottoman wars, depopulation of the war theatre was used to deny food and fodder to the enemy. At the same time, the two empires encouraged re-settlement of particular groups that feared persecution by the opposite side. Whereas the Ottomans accommodated Old Believer and Ukrainian Cossacks during the 1700s, the Russian commanders in the early nineteenth century invited these groups to return. In addition, in 1811–12 and 1829–30, they organized the resettlement of those Bulgarians who actively supported the Russians and might be vulnerable to Ottoman reprisals after the conclusion of peace and the withdrawal of Russian troops.

These population "exchanges" between the two empires became particularly consequential in the wake of the Crimean War. On the one hand, this period witnessed the return to the Russian Empire of the majority of the Ukrainian Cossacks who had fled to the Lower Danube in the late eighteenth century. Whereas the diversity of the Christian population of the eastern Balkans was thereby somewhat reduced, the region's Muslim population, by contrast, became more heterogenous through the influx of Muslim émigrés from the Russian Empire, including the Crimean Tatars and the Northern Caucasian mountaineers. The difficulties of the integration of these immigrants, particularly of the mountaineers, coincided with the growing restlessness of the Bulgarian population, which was repeatedly pushed towards an anti-Ottoman uprising by Bulgarian revolutionary nationalists. Such uprisings and their brutal suppression by Ottoman irregulars, who included the recent Muslim émigrés from Russia, rendered the inter-confessional situation in the eastern Balkans particularly tense, which helps explain the scale of the population dislocations that followed the Russian crossing of the Danube in June 1877.

As a result, the Russian occupation authorities in Bulgaria and Eastern Rumelia in 1878–9 confronted an altogether different situation in terms of population flows. Their most pressing preoccupation was the Muslim uprising in the Rhodope region, which was the direct consequence of the massive dislocation of the Muslim population in the areas of military operation. The tsarist administration also had to define the status of the Muslim population within the future Bulgarian nation state that they helped to found, as well as deal with the return of Muslim refugees. As has been demonstrated, imperial commissioner Dondukov-Korsakov considered Islam to be fundamentally incompatible with a Bulgarian nation state and sought to reduce the numbers of its Muslim citizens as much as possible. Unable to prevent the return of the Muslim refugees altogether, he at least insisted on the exclusion of natives of the Caucasus, viewing them as a potential threat to the Christian population.

Finally, the Russian authorities also had to define their policies with regard to Christian migration from those territories of San Stefano Bulgaria that, according to the decisions of the Berlin Congress, were to remain outside the borders of the Bulgarian principality. Here, their concerns about the safety of the Ottoman Christian population after the withdrawal of Russian troops came to be balanced by a desire to retain Bulgarian majorities in Eastern Rumelia and Macedonia with an eye to the eventual incorporation of these provinces into the Bulgarian nation state. As a result, the Rumelian Bulgarians were ultimately discouraged from emigration to the principality, and instead secured against possible Ottoman reprisal by way of gymnastic societies and firearms deposits, a policy that ultimately facilitated the incorporation of Eastern Rumelia into the Principality of Bulgaria six years later.

The management of migrants and refugees, the (dis)armament of particular population groups, and the strategic choices taken by Russian commanders and strategists with regard to the ethno-confessional landscape of the war theatre represent the three major aspects of the Russian army's impact upon the population of the eastern Balkans in the context of the Russian-Ottoman wars. They all demonstrate the mounting preoccupation of nineteenth-century military men with the ethno-confessional composition and political attitudes of the population. This growing importance of population in military planning and actual operations can ultimately be seen as a form of "democratization" of warfare in the sense of the emergence of "the people" as a major factor in war over the course of the long nineteenth century. And just as the assertion of the principle of popular sovereignty could lead to political clashes between "the people" and all sorts of outsiders, the "people's war" often endangered different confessional and ethnic groups of the civilian population mobilized or targeted by the fighting armies. In this sense, the plight of the eastern Balkan Muslims and Christians in 1877–8, immense as it was, was a presentiment of the much greater suffering that further "democratization" of warfare would involve in the twentieth century.

Notes

Introduction

1 The manifesto is published in Ovsianyi, *Sbornik materialov*, 1:3–4. All translations from Russian and French sources throughout the book are my own. Unless otherwise noted, all dates are given according to the Julian calendar, which was used in Russia until 1918. In the nineteenth century it was twelve days behind the Gregorian calendar.

2 Manifesto, in Ovsianyi, *Sbornik materialov*, 1:4.

3 The 1880–1 censuses conducted in the Principality of Bulgaria and the Autonomous Province of Eastern Rumelia revealed 580,000 and 170,000 Muslims, respectively (or some 750,000 in total). See Methodieva, *Between Empire and Nation*, 37. By contrast, the pre-war Muslim population of the territories that after 1878 became the Principality of Bulgaria and the autonomous province of Eastern Rumelia (absorbed by the former in 1885) was ca. 1,250,000. This figure includes the 963,596 Muslims of the Tuna *vilayet*, according to the 1874 Ottoman census (see Koyuncu, "Tuna Vilâyeti'nde Nüfus Ve Demografi") and some 290,000 Muslims in those parts of the Edirne *vilayet* that became Eastern Rumelia (according to the estimates of the British consul Drummond-Wolff). See Karpat, *Ottoman Population*, 50.

4 McCarthy, *Death and Exile*, 59–108; Reid, *Crisis of the Ottoman Empire*, 307–85; and Yavuz, *War and Diplomacy*.

5 On the Russian-Ottoman War of 1828–9, see Bitis, *Russia and the Eastern Question*, 274–324.

6 For a conventional military history of the war of 1877–8 in English, see Barry, *War in the East*. For an overview of the war from the Ottoman perspective, see Aksan, *The Ottomans*, 279–87. For a recent discussion of the impact of this war upon the eastern Balkan population, particularly the Muslims, see Methodieva, *Between Empire and Nation*, 21–7.

7 See Jelavich, *Russia's Balkan Entanglements*.

8   Black, *Constitutional Government*; Jelavich, *Romanian National Cause*; Shparo, *Osvobozhdenie Gretsii i Rossiia*; Dostian, *Rossiia i Balkanskii vopros*; Stanislavskaia, *Rossiia i Gretsiia*; Jelavich, *Romanian Nation-State*; Meriage, *First Serbian Uprising*; Durman, *Lost Illusions*; Kudriavtseva, *Rossiia i Serbiia*; Frary, *Modern Greek Identity*; and Rekun, *Empire Unguided*.

9   On the policies of the Russian provisional administration in the Romanian principalities in 1829–34, see Grosul, *Reformy v Dunaiskikh kniazhestvakh i Rossiia*; and Taki, *Russia on the Danube*. On the policies of the Russian provisional administration in Bulgaria in 1878–9, see Vinkovetsky, "Strategists and Ideologues"; and Rekun, *Empire Unguided*, 31–60.

10   Among the histories of the Russian-Ottoman wars, the most remarkable is the series of studies by A.N. Petrov: *Voina Rossii s Turtsiei i pol'skimi konfederatami*; *Vtoraia turetskaia voina*; *Voina Rossii s Turtsiei, 1806–1812*; and *Dunaiskaia kampaniia*. More recently, see Barry, *War in the East*; and Aksan, *The Ottomans*.

11   Percentage values for the amount of war (an aggregate of frequency, duration, extent, magnitude, severity, and concentration) in Europe by century are: 94 for the sixteenth century, 95 for the seventeenth century, 78 for the eighteenth century, and only 40 for the nineteenth century (or 89, 88, 64, and 24, respectively, if one looks only at the wars between the great powers). See Levy, *Great Power System*, 139, 141.

12   Although the Russian-Ottoman wars in the 1800s also involved Transcaucasia, their outcome was invariably decided on the Danube and in the Balkans. On the Transcaucasian front, see Allen and Muratoff, *Caucasian Battlefields*. On the early stages of the Russian-Ottoman confrontation, see a series of studies by Brian L. Davies: *Warfare, State and Society*; *Empire and Military Revolution*; and *Russo-Turkish War*.

13   On the history of the term and the broader discourse of "Balkanism," see Todorova, *Imagining the Balkans*.

14   On the scholarly debates around the term "Balkan," see Mishkova, *Beyond Balkanism*.

15   For a general discussion, see Sugar, *Southeastern Europe*, esp. 113–41 on Moldavia and Wallachia.

16   On the changing status of Moldavia and Wallachia within the Ottoman Empire, see Panaite, "Legal and Political Status." For a recent discussion of the place of the Phanariote Greeks in the Ottoman system, see Philliou, *Biography of an Empire*, 5–37.

17   On the Russian protectorate and its contested scope, see Davison, "'Russian Skill and Turkish Imbecility'"; and Taki, "Limits of Protection."

18   Soviet historiography generally avoided discussion of the negative impact of the Russian occupation on the local population and focused on Russia's progressive role in the principalities. See Muntian and Semenov, *Osvoboditel'naia bor'ba*. Post-Soviet historiography went to the opposite extreme, piling on the Russian

Empire all the blame for the hardships experienced by the local population. See Agachi, "Moldova și Țara Românească." For a more balanced account, see Jewsbury, *Russian Annexation of Bessarabia*, 39–66. See also Jelavich, *Romanian Nation-State*; and Taki, *Russia on the Danube*.

19 See Sorescu, "Peddlers, Peasants, Icons, Engravings."

20 See Sugar, *Southeastern Europe*, 14–23, 63–110.

21 On the Greek-Bulgarian conflict and the Russian attempt to contain it, see Kalkandjieva, "Bulgarian Orthodox Church"; and Vovchenko, *Containing Balkan Nationalisms*.

22 On Dobrogea, see Rădulescu and Bitoleanu, *Concise History of Dobruja*.

23 On the Muslims of Deliorman, see Antov, *Ottoman "Wild West."*

24 For different interpretations of the origins of the Pomaks, see Apostolov, "Pomaks"; Turan, "Pomaks, Their Past and Present"; and Georgieva, "Pomaks: Muslim Bulgarians."

25 Braude and Lewis, *Christians and Jews*; and Stamatopoulos, "From Millets to Minorities."

26 On *devşirme*, see Imber, *Ottoman Empire*, 116–30. On the Tanzimat, see Findley, "Tanzimat"; and Davison, *Reform in the Ottoman Empire*.

27 For an introductory discussion of Macedonian question, see Biondich, *The Balkans*, 63–75.

28 Mann, *Dark Side of Democracy*.

29 Rothenberg, *Art of Warfare*, 95–102.

30 The most characteristic example of the military reforms were those carried out in Prussia in 1807–13 under the leadership of Schanhorst and Gneisenau. See Rothenberg, *Art of Warfare*, 190–4. For a general discussion of the military impact of the French revolution, see Knox, "Mass Politics and Nationalism."

31 Rothenberg, *Art of Warfare*, 121–2, 156–8; Forrest, "Insurgents and Counter-insurgents"; and Best, *War and Society*, 168–83.

32 See Hacking, "Biopower," 281; and the discussion of military statistics in chapter 5.

33 Late nineteenth-century France constitutes by far the most successful example of such assimilation. See Weber, *Peasants into Frenchmen*.

34 See Holquist, "To Count, to Extract and to Exterminate."

35 On British colonial warfare, see Roy, *British India*, esp. 34–76. On French colonial warfare, see Porch, "Bugeaud, Gallieni, Lyautey"; and Finch, *Progressive Occupation*.

36 Spies, *Methods of Barbarism?*; Tone, *War and Genocide in Cuba*; and Forth, *Barbed-Wire Imperialism*. Forth demonstrates that concentration camps of the Anglo-Boer War were part of the broader phenomenon of "barbed-wire imperialism," which also included the plague and famine camps of late Victorian India.

37 On the colonial roots of the twentieth-century European genocides, see Hull, "Military Culture"; and Madley, "From Africa to Auschwitz." For a critical

overview of the colonialist origins of the Holocaust, see Kühne, "Colonialism and the Holocaust." See also Weitz, "Germany and the Ottoman Borderlands."

38 See overview of the development of modern laws of war in Nabulsi, *Traditions of War*, 4–18.

39 On military occupation policies in Eastern Europe, the Balkans, and the Middle East during the First World War, see Graf, "Military Rule"; Liulevicius, *War Land on the Eastern Front*; Bakhturina, *Politika Rossiiskoi Imperii*; von Hagen, *War in a European Borderland*; Gumz, *Resurrection and Collapse of Empire*; and Holquist, "Forms of Violence."

40 See chapter 1.

41 On aristocratic reaction in the European armies during the post-Napoleonic period, see Best, *War and Society*, 204–15; and McNeill, *Pursuit of Power*, 219–22.

42 For a discussion of the military colonies and the system of furloughs that constituted the failed military reform initiatives of Alexander I and Nicholas I, see Keep, *Soldiers of the Tsar*, 275–327, 334.

43 On the role of the victory over Napoleon in stalling Russian military reform, see Fuller, *Strategy and Power*, 217–18.

44 Taki, "Horrors of War," 284–7.

45 On the embrace of the concept of the citizen-soldier by the Russian military with the military reform of 1874 and the dilemmas that it generated in a multiethnic and autocratic empire, see Sanborn, *Drafting the Russian Nation*, esp. 9–14, 63–74; and Sandborn, "Military Reform."

1. The Eastern Balkan Christians and Muslims in the Early Russian-Ottoman Wars

1 The subject of early modern warfare is vast. The best introduction is Rogers, *Military Revolution Debate*. The Military Revolution debate revealed that changes in the character of early modern warfare were real, yet spread over such a long period that it is more appropriate to speak of evolution rather than revolution. See Childs, *Warfare in the Seventeenth Century*, 16–17.

2 On the relation between military change and the rise of absolutism, see Downing, *Military Revolution and Political Change*. For the most recent discussions of cameralism, see Nokkala and Miller, *Cameralism and the Enlightenment*; and Seppel and Tribe, *Cameralism in Practice*.

3 On the development of the military administration and its growing role in the relations between the troops and the civilian population, see Corvisier, *Armies and Societies*, 73–83; and Lynn, *Giant of the Grand Siècle*, 67–220.

4 On the limitations of Western European warfare in this period, as well as on the limits of the "limited warfare" thesis, see Childs, *Armies and Warfare in Europe*, 1–27. Historians also debate whether the restraint in war was the product of the Enlightenment or an aristocratic Old Regime phenomenon that had already been

established by 1700. For the opposing perspectives, see, respectively, Pichichero, *Military Enlightenment*; and Starkey, *War in the Age of Enlightenment*, 20–1.

5 The normative aspects of eighteenth-century warfare, or the culture of war, are explored in Bell, *First Total War*, 11–17. On the importance of humanity, sensibility, and civility in the Enlightenment culture of war, see Pichichero, *Military Enlightenment*, 7–11.

6 For the discussion of these tendencies, see McNeill, *Pursuit of Power*, 117–43; Rothenberg, *Art of Warfare*, 11–14; and Bell, *First Total War*, 44–51.

7 On drill and military discipline, see Chandler, *Age of Marlborough*, 102–8; and Lynn, *Giant of the Grand Siècle*, 397–415. On the psychological impact of drill, see McNeill, *Keeping Together in Time*.

8 Raeff, *Well-Ordered Police State*.

9 Pichichero, *Military Enlightenment*; and Starkey, *War in the Age of Enlightenment*, 18.

10 On pre-Petrine Russia and the early modern military revolution, see Paul, "Military Revolution in Russia, 1550–1682." On Peter the Great's efforts during the Great Northern War, see Fuller, *Strategy and Power*, 35–84. On the consolidation of the regular army in the later years of Peter's reign and in the 1730s under the direction of Field Marshal Munnich, see Duffy, *Russia's Military Way to the West*, 29–47. A useful summary of Peter the Great's military reform is given in Stevens, *Russia's Wars of Emergence*, 217–95.

11 See also Keep, *Soldiers of the Tsar*, 95–142; and Pintner, *Russia as a Great Power*.

12 Duffy, *Russia's Military Way to the West*, 136–56; Menning, "Russia and the West"; and Miakinkov, *War and Enlightenment in Russia*.

13 Hartley, *Russia, 1762–1825*, 108–25.

14 Davies, *Warfare, State and Society*; and Barrett, *Edge of Empire*.

15 Sunderland, *Taming the Wild Field*, esp. 55–96.

16 On the overall evolution of Russia's policy in the steppe region, see Khodarkovsky, *Russia's Steppe Frontier*.

17 Small Russian detachments crossed the Danube in 1771, when they captured Isakcha and Tulcha, and then again in March 1773. On the Russian-Ottoman war of 1768–74, see Petrov, *Voina Rossii s Turtsiei i pol'skimi konfederatami*; Davies, *Russo-Turkish War*; and Aksan, *The Ottomans*, 60–6.

18 The text of the manifesto is published in Fortunatov, *Rumiantsev. Dokumenty*, 2:614.

19 Petrov, *Voina Rossii s Turtsiei i pol'skimi konfederatami*, 4:23.

20 Rumiantsev to Catherine II, 30 June 1773, in Fortunatov, *Rumiantsev. Dokumenty*, 2:654.

21 Rumiantsev to Catherine II, 28 November 1773, in Fortunatov, 2:685.

22 On the use of the Moldavian volunteers in the eighteenth century, see Shulman, *Russko-moldavskoe boevoe sodruzhestvo*; and Semenova, *Rossiia i natsional'no sovoboditel'naia bor'ba*.

23 Tsvetkova, "Bulgarian Haiduk Movement"; Barkey, *Bandits and Bureaucrats*; Anscombe, "Albanians and 'Mountain Bandits,'" 95–102; and Esmer, "Economies of Violence."

24 Esmer, "Economies of Violence," 174–5. On the Russian-Ottoman war of 1787–92, see Petrov, *Vtoraia turetskaia voina*; and Aksan, *The Ottomans*, 77–82.

25 Esmer, "Economies of Violence," 177–9.

26 Mikhelson to Alexander, August 1806, cited in Konobeev, "Russko-bolgarskie otnosheniia," 218. On the Russian-Ottoman war of 1806–12, see Petrov, *Voina Rossii s Turtsiei, 1806–1812*; and Aksan, *The Ottomans*, 121–3.

27 Alexander I to Mikhelson, 15 November 1806, RGVIA, f. VUA, op. 16, vol. 1, d. 2882, l. 24.

28 See the colourful account of the *arnauts'* role in Lanzheron, "Zapiski," *Russkaia starina*, no. 6 (1907): 588.

29 Konobeev, "Russko-bolgarskie otnosheniia," 225.

30 Konobeev, 226.

31 "Mnenie generala ot infanterii Bagrationa," March 1810, in Petrov, *Voina Rossii s Turtsiei, 1806–1812*, 2:571. The plan of the campaign is also published in Golubov and Kuznetsov, *General Bagration*, 111–16.

32 Konobeev, "Russko-bolgarskie otnosheniia," 239.

33 Konobeev, 229. Eighteen months later, Captain A.G. Krasnokutskii, who was dispatched to Constantinople for secret diplomatic negotiations with the Ottoman government, confirmed that the "Bulgarian and arnaut villages" that he had visited on his way across Rumelia "waited for Russians impatiently" and were ready to "take up arms against the Turks." See Krasnokutskii to Prozorovskii, 5 November 1808, cited in Petrov, *Voina Rossii s Turtsiei, 1806–1812*, 2:112.

34 Cited in Konobeev, "Russko-bolgarskie otnosheniia," 241.

35 Bagration to Isaev, 18 February 1810, in Golubov and Kuznetsov, *General Bagration*, 104.

36 Konobeev, "Russko-bolgarskie otnosheniia," 250. In November 1810, Sofronii followed with a second proclamation, which likewise stopped short of calling on the Bulgarians to stage an anti-Ottoman uprising, yet urged them to be loyal to Russia.

37 Cited in Konobeev, "Russko-bolgarskie otnosheniia," 251.

38 RGVIA, f. VUA, op. 5 (165), d. 14209, "Perepiska s 18 iiunia po 12 iiulia. Vyrubka lesa po doroge mezhdu Silistriei i Shumloi i ochishchenie ee ot kirdzhalei. Nariad dlia vyrubki lesa i pokosa travy na pravom beregu Dunaia rabochikh iz obyvatelei Bolgar, prodovol'stvie ikh. Naraid voinskikh komand dlia prikrytiia rabochikh ot napadeniia turok. Nabliudenie za poselennymi turetskimi obyvateliami i vziatie u nikh detei v kachestve zalozhnikov," 14 ll.

39 The term *reaya* designated the tax-paying population of the Ottoman Empire, as opposed to its tax-exempt military class (*askeri* or *kul*). However, in Moldavia and Wallachia, this term (*raia*, pl. *raiale*) acquired a territorial meaning and came to

designate the districts around Ottoman fortresses along the Danube and Dniester Rivers that had been alienated from the principalities and placed under direct control of the Ottoman commanders of these fortresses.

40 Rumiantsev to G.G. Orlov, February 1770, *ChIODR*, no. 2 (1865): 22–3. Rumiantsev apparently referred to the poisoning of wells by the Budzhak Tatars during the Pruth Campaign of Peter the Great, and by the Crimean Tartars during Munnich's invasion of the Crimea in 1736.

41 Rumiantsev to Catherine II, 18 March 1770, *ChIODR*, no. 2 (1865): 34.

42 On the Ottoman practice of resettlement as part of the military strategy, see Kasaba, *Moveable Empire*, 18–19, 47.

43 Petrov, *Voina Rossii s Turtsiei i pol'skimi konfederatami*, 4:21–5.

44 Petrov, 29, 34.

45 Petrov, 133.

46 See Rumiantsev to Catherine II, 14 December 1773, in Fortunatov, *Rumiantsev. Dokumenty*, 2:696. The campaign of the following year witnessed a repetition of this pattern, with the Russians recapturing 5,000 inhabitants from the Ottoman troops between Rushchuk and Razgrad, and another 4,000 in Razgrad itself. These were resettled in the territory secured by the Russians between Rushchuk and Turtukai. See Petrov, *Voina Rossii s Turtsiei i pol'skimi konfederatami*, 5:50, 52.

47 Petrov, 4:95.

48 Petrov, 4:109.

49 Petrov, 5:57.

50 Thus, the advance detachment of Lieutenant General M.I. Kutuzov burned down the village of Monastyrishche, while Lieutenant General S.F. Golitsyn, who captured Machin, ordered the resettlement of its Christian inhabitants. See Petrov, *Vtoraia turetskaia voina*, 2:200, 202.

51 Kutuzov to (Russian war minister) M.B. Barklai-de-Tolly, 14 December 1811, in Beskrovnyi, *M. I. Kutuzov*, 3:751.

52 Kutuzov to Alexander I, 13 February 1812, in Beskrovnyi, 3:801.

53 Konobeev, "Russko-bolgarskie otnosheniia," 258.

54 See Kutuzov to Rumiantsev, 27 May 1811, in Beskrovnyi, *M. I. Kutuzov*, 3:401; and "Manifest Kutuzova zadunaiskim poselentsam," 26 April 1811, in Kryzhanovskaia and Russev, *Istoriia Moldavii*, 1.

55 A.Ia. Koronelli to Kutuzov, 15 November 1811, in Kryzhanovskaia and Russev, *Istoriia Moldavii*, 28.

56 On the reaction of the Russian military to this development, see Taki, "Horrors of War," 280–2.

57 For a magisterial demolishing of these myths, see Lieven, *Russia against Napoleon*.

58 Taki, "Horrors of War," 265–73.

59 Mikhailovskii-Danilevskii, "Zapiski," 154. In Mikhailovskii-Danilevskii's view, the Cossacks "in general tried to separate themselves from the regular army as if they served a different sovereign and had a different fatherland."

60 Muraviev, "Chto videl, chuvstvoval i slyshal," 293–4.

61 On the Russian military intelligentsia, see Keep, *Soldiers of the Tsar*, 231–49.

62 See Bell, *First Total War*, 21–51.

63 Pichichero, *Military Enlightenment*.

64 This is one of the subjects discussed in Taki, "Horrors of War."

65 In this respect, the early 1800s were little different from the eighteenth century, which had witnessed the development of proto-nationalist sentiment among the Russian elites in response to the prominence of "Germans" in post-Petrine Russian army and civil administration. See Rogger, *National Consciousness*.

66 Martin, *Romantics, Reformers, Reactionaries*, 123–42.

67 Indicative of this tendency was the replacement of Admiral A.S. Shishkov by the future metropolitan of Moscow Filaret (Drozdov) as the main author of the manifestos, which followed soon after the expulsion of the French. See Zorin, *Kormia dvuglavogo orla*, 239–67. See also Martin, *Romantics, Reformers, Reactionaries*, 143–68; and Wortman, *Scenarios of Power*, 108–15.

68 Miller, "Priobretenie neobkhodimoe," 52–4.

69 Riasanovsky, *Nicholas I*, 70–5; Whittaker, *Modern Russian Education*; Zorin, *Kormia dvuglavogo orla*, 337–74; and Miller, *Imperiia Romanovykh i natsionalizm*, 193–216.

70 Riasanovsky, *Nicholas I*, 124.

71 Zorin, *Kormia dvuglavogo orla*, 345–59.

72 Miller, "*Natsija, Narod, Narodnost*'," 383.

73 In particular, "the people" and "the land" (*zemlia*) become the main focus for Konstantin Aksakov. See Walicki, *Slavophile Controversy*, 242–56, 266–79. Whereas for the semi-official ideologues of *narodnost*', such as M.I. Pogodin and S.P. Shevyrev, the state remained the main organizing element of the Russian people, Aksakov viewed the state as something external to the life of the people and the land.

74 Ely, *Russian Populism*, 27–70.

75 For a recent discussion of Ypsilanti's undertaking in English, see Stites, *Four Horsemen*, 186–239. On the creation and activities of Etaireia in Russia, see Arsh, *Eteristskoe dvizhenie*; and Iovva, *Bessarabiia*, 24–73. For a Romanian perspective on the events of 1821, see Berindei, *L'Année révolutionnaire 1821*.

76 For the most recent and the most comprehensive treatment of the Greek War of Independence in English, see Kitromilides and Tsoukalas, *Greek Revolution*.

77 On Russia and the Greek War of Independence, see Frary, *Modern Greek Identity*, 27–40; Prousis, *Greek Revolution*, 26–54; and Dostian, *Russkaia obshchestvennaia mysl*', 160–85, 222–89.

78 This was the case of the future Decembrist I.G. Burtsov and his manuscript "The Uprising of Prince Ypsilanti in Moldavia and Wallachia." See Dostian, *Russkaia obshchestvennaia mysl*', 269–82. An equally critical assessment of Ypsilanti can be found in the manuscripts of I.P. Liprandi: "Vosstanie pandur pod

predvoditel'stvom Todora Vladimireski v 1821-m godu i nachalo deistviia geteris-tov v pridunaiskikh kniazhestvakh pod nachal'stvom kniazia Aleksandra Ipsilanti, i plachevnyi iskhod oboikh v tom zhe godu," and "Kapitan Iorgake Olimpiot. Deistviia geteristov v kniazhestvakh v 1821-m g.," in Oţetea, *Documente privind istoria Romîniei*, 5:163–263, 363–408. In 1821, both Burtsev and Liprandi served in Russia's 2nd Army, stationed in Bessarabia and Ukraine.

79 On Davydov, see Mikaberidze, *Russian Officer Corps*, 66–8.

80 Davydov, *Opyt teorii partizanskogo deistviia*, 487–8.

81 Davydov, 511.

82 Davydov, 519.

83 Davydov, 520.

84 On military Orientalism, see Porter, *Military Orientalism*.

85 Said, *Orientalism*, 2–3.

86 Curiously enough, the thesis of Russia's special relation to Asia eventually resulted in a historiographic debate on whether Russian Orientalism was *sui generis*. See David-Fox, Holquist, and Martin, *Orientalism and Empire*.

87 Schimmelpenninck van der Oye, *Russian Orientalism*, 156–8.

88 Davydov, *Opyt teorii partizanskogo deistviia*, 522–4.

89 Davydov, 527.

90 Davydov, 527–8.

91 Davydov, 510.

92 Davydov, 498–9.

93 A distant relative of Russia's most important poet, Andrei Nikiforovich Pushkin was not yet thirty-five at the time of the publication, and only a captain, yet he had already established himself as a prolific military writer. His most significant publications were: "Vzgliad na voennoe iskusstvo"; *Kratkie izvlecheniia*; and "O vliianii voennykh nauk." His most important work, published a year later with the approval of the Military Scientific Committee of the General Staff, was *Zapiski o voennom ukreplenii*.

94 Pushkin, "Vzgliad na voennoe sostoianie turetskoi imperii," *Syn Otechestva* 107, no. 9 (1826): 76. Some forty years before Pushkin, François de Tott argued that "the Turkish Government may always be considered an army encamped, the General of which issues orders, from his headquarters, to forage the Country." See Tott, *Memoirs*, 2:20.

95 Pushkin, "Vzgliad na voennoe sostoianie turetskoi imperii," *Syn Otechestva* 107, no. 9 (1826): 75–6.

96 Pushkin, *Syn Otechestva* 109, no. 11 (1826): 266–7.

97 Pushkin, *Syn Otechestva* 109, no. 11 (1826): 268.

98 Pushkin, *Syn Otechestva* 109, no. 11 (1826): 267–8.

99 Pushkin, *Syn Otechestva* 109, no. 11 (1826): 266.

100 On Russian war planning in 1819–28, see Bitis, *Russia and the Eastern Question*, 149–60, 176–88.

101 *Voenno-topograficheskoe opisanie dorogi iz Zhurzhi*; *Voenno-topograficheskoe opisanie dorogi iz goroda Galatsa*; and *Voenno-topograficheskoe opisanie beregovoi dorogi Chernogo moria*.

102 See *Voenno-topograficheskoe opisanie dorogi iz goroda Galatsa*, 33.

103 *Voenno-topograficheskoe opisanie dorogi iz goroda Galatsa*, 17n. The anonymous editor(s) of the description corrected Len's data on the road from Machin to Bazardzhik and Pravodi with the help of a topographic survey of that area of Bulgaria made during the war of 1809.

104 Kiselev, "Neobkhodimost' i vozmozhnost' v mirnoe vremia sobirat' topograficheskie svedeniia o turetskikh vladeniiakh," RGVIA, f. 450, op. 1, d. 4, ll. 4–5v.

105 Kankrin to Kiselev, 19 August 1821, quoted in Bozherianov, *Graf Egor Frantsevich Kankrin*, 40 (also published in *Voennyi sbornik* 99, no. 11 [1874]).

106 Kankrin, "Voennye soobrazheniia o pokhode protiv Turok v sviazi s prodovol'stviem, osnovannye na sekretnykh svedeniiakh depo kart i na nekotorykh chastnykh materialakh. 4 July 1821," RGVIA, f. VUA, op. 16, vol. 1, d. 4395, ll. 134–55.

107 Kankrin, "Voennye soobrazheniia," l. 140.

108 Kankrin, l. 140v.

109 Kankrin, ll. 136r–v.

110 Buturlin, "Mémoire sur le plan d'opération à suivre dans le cas d'une guerre avec la Turquie," 21 February 1822, RGVIA, f. VUA, op. 16, vol. 1, d. 4395, ll. 112–18. Buturlin was the first in a long line of Russian military writers to point out the insufficiency of the forces that Russians usually put in the field at the beginning of a war against Turkey. As an alternative, he suggested concentrating 200,000 people, with separate corps occupying Dobrogea; blockading Silistria, Rushchuk, and Nikopol; and establishing a liaison with the Serbs through the occupation of Sofia. The main force had to attack Shumla and, upon taking it, advance in the direction of Adrianople and Constantinople.

111 Buturlin, "Mémoire," l. 116.

112 Stroganov to Nicholas I, 18 January 1826, in Narochnitskii, *Vneshniaia politika Rossii*, 14:350; and Tatishchev, *Vneshniaia politika Nikolaia Pervogo*, 137.

113 Sukhtelen, "Obshchie predpolozheniia otnositel'no rasporiazhenii dlia dvizheniia i deistviia 2oi armii za granitsu," 23 September 1826, Moscow, RGVIA, f. VUA, op. 16, vol. 1, d. 4395, l. 35v.

114 Langeron, "Projet d'une guerre offensive," 65.

115 Langeron, 69.

116 Langeron, 69.

117 Langeron, 68.

118 Sukhtelen, "Obshchie predpolozheniia," l. 36v.

119 Liprandi, "Kratkoe obozrenie Moldavii, Valakhii i drugikh prilegaiushchikh zemel' v voennom otnoshenii s prisovokupleniem svedenii o voennykh prigotovleniiakh Turok do 20-go Marta 1828," 3 April 1828, RGIA, f. 673, op. 1, d. 352, ll. 8–9.

120 Liprandi, "Kratkoe obozrenie Moldavii, Valakhii i drugikh prilegaiushchikh ze-
     mel'," ll. 7v–8.
121 On Berg, later governor general of Finland, viceroy of Poland, and field marshal,
     see Sergeev and Dolgov, *Voennye topografy*, 469–70.
122 I.I. Dibich, "Proekt instruktsii polkovniku kavaleru Bergu," 15 July 1826, St. Pe-
     tersburg, RGVIA, f. 450, op. 1, d. 4, ll. 1v–2.
123 See Berg to Nesselrode, 10 February 1827, Pera, RGVIA, f. 450, op. 1, d. 5, ll.
     17–19. See also Diugamel, *Avtobiografiia*, 13–17. Diugamel, Tuchkov, and Verigin
     even published their findings; see Diugamel, *Voenno-topograficheskoe opisanie
     dorog: Ot Shumly do Pravody*; Diugamel, *Voenno-topograficheskoe opisanie dorogi,
     vedushchei iz Rushchuka*; Diugamel, *Voenno-topograficheskoe opisanie dorogi ve-
     dushchei ot Sistovo v Tyrnovo*; Tuchkov, *Voenno-topograficheskoe opisanie dorog*;
     Verigin, *Voenno-topograficheskoe opisanie dorog: Ot gor. Turtukaia*; and Verigin,
     Voenno-topograficheskoe opisaniie dorogi: Ot gor. Tyrnova.
124 On the military reforms of Mahmud II and those of Selim III, his half-brother
     and predecessor, see Anscombe, *State, Faith, and Nation*, 46–57, 61–83; and Ak-
     san, *The Ottomans*, 85–90, 151–61. See also Yeşil, "Drill and Discipline." On the
     sporadic reforming efforts of the eighteenth century, see Levy, "Military Reform."
125 Berg to Nesselrode, 11 January 1827, Bucharest, RGVIA, f. 450, op. 1, d. 5, l. 14v.
126 Berg to Nesselrode, 11 February 1827, Pera, RGVIA, f. 450, op. 1, d. 5, l. 44.
127 Berg to Nesselrode, 11 February 1827, l. 48.
128 Berg to Nesselrode, 11 February 1827, l. 48v.
129 Berg to Nesselrode, 11 February 1827, l. 48v.
130 Berg to Nesselrode, 25 February 1827, Pera, RGVIA, f. 450, op. 1, d. 5, l. 77v.
131 Berg to Nesselrode, 25 February 1827, l. 78v.
132 Berg to Nesselrode, 25 February 1827, ll. 74v–75.
133 Berg to Nesselrode, 25 February 1827, l. 76.

2. The Russian Army and the Eastern Balkan Population during the War of 1828–1829

1 The Russian translation of the proclamation is published in Epanchin, *Ocherk
   pokhoda*, vol. 1, appendix, 7–11.
2 On the Russian-Ottoman war of 1828–9, see Epanchin, *Ocherk pokhoda*; Curtiss,
   Russian Army under Nicholas I, 53–73; and Bitis, *Russia and the Eastern Question*,
   274–324.
3 "Deklaratsiia o prichinakh voiny s Portoi i obstoiatel'stvakh ei predshestvovav-
   shikh," 14 April 1828, in *Polnoe sobranie zakonov*, ser. 2, no. 1948, 3:389.
4 See "Manifest ob otkrytii voiny s Ottomanskoi imperiei," 14 April 1828, in *Polnoe
   sobranie zakonov*, ser. 2, no. 1948, 3:383–4.
5 Fadeev, *Rossiia i Vostochnyi krizis*, 176–7.
6 Levy, "Cossack Service."

7   At the end of the war of 1806–12, Russian commander-in-chief M.I. Kutuzov tried, albeit without much success, to make the Nekrasovstsy switch sides, promising amnesty and providing those who agreed to resettle in Russia with materials for construction of their houses. See Kutuzov to S.A. Tuchkov, 1 May 1811, and Kutuzov to Krasno-Milashevich, 16 May 1811, in Beskrovnyi, *M. I. Kutuzov*, 3:360, 377.

8   Most Nekrasovtsy left the Lower Danube altogether and settled first on the shores of the bay of Enos and later in Asia Minor. On the entire episode involving the Nekrasovtsy and Zaporozhian Cossacks in 1828, see Bitis, "Resettlement of Balkan Peoples."

9   Diugamel, *Avtobiografiia*, 17; or "Avtobiografiia A.O. Diugamelia," *Russkii arkhiv*, no. 2 (1885): 193. On the emptiness of Muslim settlements and the retreat of the inhabitants into fortresses, see also "Otryvok iz pokhodnykh zapisok 1828 goda," 7; and "Dvadtsat' piat' let v leib-gvardii Egerskom polku," 369.

10   RGVIA, f. VUA, op. 16, vol. 1, d. 4421, "Obshchaia perepiska po dvizheniiu armii i osobo o izgotovlenii k dvizheniiu 3-ego pekhotnogo i svodnogo korpusov, 1828," l. 86.

11   Kupreianov, "Deistviia pravodskogo otriada," *Voennyi sbornik*, no. 2 (1875): 162.

12   Benkendorf, "Imperator Nikoal Pervyi," 482; and Kupreianov, "Deistviia pravodskogo otriada," *Voennyi sbornik*, no. 2 (1875): 160.

13   Diugamel, "Avtobiografiia A.O. Diugamelia," *Russkii arkhiv*, no. 2 (1885): 194.

14   Benkendorf, "Imperator Nikolai Pervyi," 496–7.

15   I.P. Liprandi, "O Partizanskoi Voine voobsche i v osobennosti o pratizanakh 1828 i 1829 gg.," RGIA, f. 673, op. 1, d. 221, ll. 23v–24.

16   Vitgenshtein to Rot, 23 June 1828, RGVIA, f. VUA, op. 16, vol. 1, d. 4421, l. 91.

17   Vitgenshtein to Rot, 23 June 1828, l. 91v.

18   Kupreianov, "Deistviia pravodskogo otriada," *Voennyi sbornik*, no. 2 (1875): 187.

19   Kupreianov, *Voennyi sbornik*, no. 2 (1875): 183–4; no. 3 (1875): 21.

20   Kupreianov, *Voennyi sbornik*, no. 3 (1875): 23.

21   Kupreianov, *Voennyi sbornik*, no. 3 (1875): 6.

22   Liprandi, "Zapiska o neobkhodimosti sostavit' partizanskii korpus na pravom beregu Dunaia, s poiasneniiami avtora," 10 January 1829, RGIA, f. 673, op. 1, d. 367, l. 9.

23   As was the case with the plans for the campaign of 1828, the memoranda submitted after its conclusion have been examined in great detail in both Russian- and English-language histories of the war and will be considered here only inasmuch as they spoke of the Balkan population as a factor in military operations. See Epanchin, *Ocherk pokhoda*, 2:14–45; and Bitis, *Russia and the Eastern Question*, 305–12.

24   Kiselev, "Kratkoe sobrazhenie o deistviiakh v predstoiashchei kompanii," 11 January 1829, in Epanchin, *Ocherk pokhoda*, 2:33.

25   Kiselev, "Kratkoe sobrazhenie," 32.

26   Epanchin, *Ocherk pokhoda*, 2:14–15.

27 I.V. Vasilchikov, "Aperçu sur la campagne de 1828," in Epanchin, *Ocherk pokhoda*, 2:18–19.

28 A.I. Chernyshev, "Mémoire sur les discussions du 19 Novembre 1828," in Epanchin, *Ocherk pokhoda*, 2:25.

29 Chernyshev, "Mémoire," 26.

30 Chernyshev, 27.

31 Chernyshev, 29.

32 Chernyshev, 30.

33 See the excerpts of Dibich's memorandum of 8 January 1829 reproduced in Epanchin, *Ocherk pokhoda*, 2:43–5.

34 Kupreianov, "Deistviia pravodskogo otriada," *Voennyi sbornik*, no. 3 (1875): 53.

35 Krasovskii to Dibich, 21 July 1829, RGVIA, f. VUA, op. 16, vol. 1, d. 4841, part 1, ll. 606–10.

36 Krasovskii to Dibich, 2 August 1829, RGVIA, f. VUA, op. 16, vol. 1, d. 4841, part 2, l. 169.

37 Krasovskii to Dibich, 7 August 1829, RGVIA, f. VUA, op. 16, vol. 1, d. 4841, part 2, l. 288.

38 Dibich to Nicholas I, 29 April 1829, *Russkaia starina*, no. 10 (1881): 294.

39 For a detailed discussion of these projects and the actual use of the volunteer detachments, see Bitis, "Balkan Irregulars."

40 Kupreianov, "Deistviia pravodskogo otriada," *Voennyi sbornik*, no. 3 (1875): 30–1.

41 Dibich to Nicholas I, 17 May 1829, *Russkaia starina*, no. 11 (1881): 566.

42 Dibich to Nicholas I, 17 May 1829, 567.

43 Nicholas I to Dibich, 26 May 1829, *Russkaia starina*, no. 11 (1881): 568. On the post-war resettlement of Bulgarians, see Bitis, "Resettlement of Balkan Peoples."

44 Diugamel, *Avtobiografiia*, 30.

45 Tol to Colonel Timan (of the St. Petersburg Ulan regiment), 9 July 1829, RGVIA, f. VUA, op. 16, vol. 1, d. 4841, part 1, l. 174.

46 Tol to Montrezor, 16 July 1829, RGVIA, f. VUA, op. 16, vol. 1, d. 4841, part 1, ll. 330–330v.

47 Tol to Ridiger, 18 July 1829, Aidos, RGVIA, f. VUA, op. 16, vol. 1, d. 4841, part 1, ll. 392–392v.

48 Dibich to Nicholas I, 9 July 1829, *Russkaia starina*, no. 4 (1882): 164.

49 Timan to Tol, 13 July 1829, RGVIA, f. VUA, op. 16, vol. 1, d. 4841, part 1, l. 284.

50 Palen to Dibich, 16 July 1829, Rumilikioi, RGVIA, f. VUA, op. 16, vol. 1, d. 4841, part 1, l. 366v, see also Montrezor to Palen, 17 July 1829, Rusokastro, RGVIA, f. VUA, op. 16, vol. 1, d. 4841, part 1, l. 414v.

51 Ridiger to Dibich, 25 July 1829, Karnobat, RGVIA, f. VUA, op. 16, vol. 1, d. 4841, part 1, l. 628v.

52 Ridiger to Dibich, 17 July 1828, RGVIA, f. VUA, op. 16, vol. 1, d. 4841, part 1, l. 378.

53 Dibich to Nicholas I, 18 July 1829, Aidos, RGVIA, f. VUA, op. 16, vol. 1, d. 4841, part 1, ll. 399v–400.

54 Dibich to Nicholas I, 18 July 1829, Aidos, *Russkaia starina*, no. 4 (1882): 172.

55 Dibich to Nicholas I, 18 July 1829.

56 "Proklamatsiia magometanskim zhiteliam Rumelii," 19 July 1829, Aidos, RGVIA, f. VUA, op. 16, vol. 1, d. 4841, part 1, l. 449.

57 "Proklamatsiia," l. 449v.

58 "Proklamatsiia," l. 450.

59 Palen to Dibich, 22 July 1829, Karabunar, RGVIA, f. VUA, op. 16, vol. 1, d. 4841, part 1, ll. 540–541v.

60 Rot to Dibich, 23 July 1829, Aidos, RGVIA, f. VUA, op. 16, vol. 1, d. 4841, part 1, ll. 554–554v.

61 Dibich to Nicholas I, 25 July 1829, *Russkaia starina*, no. 10 (1882): 78.

62 Dibich to Nicholas I, 1 August 1829, *Russkaia starina*, no. 10 (1882): 84.

63 Ridiger to Dibich, 19 July 1829, Karnobat, RGVIA, f. VUA, op. 16, vol. 1, d. 4841, part 1, l. 463v; and Palen to Dibich, 21 July 1829, Karabunar, RGVIA, f. VUA, op. 16, vol. 1, d. 4841, part 1, ll. 544–7.

64 Tol to Ridiger, 20 July 1829, RGVIA, f. VUA, op. 16, vol. 1, d. 4841, part 1, l. 464.

65 General Quartermaster Berg to Palen, 25 July 1829, RGVIA, f. VUA, op. 16, vol. 1, d. 4841, part 1, l. 574v.

66 Dibich to Nicholas I, 25 July 1829, *Russkaia starina*, no. 10 (1882): 79.

67 Tol to (commander of the 19th Infantry division) Lieutenant General M.I. Ponset, 25 July 1829, Aidos, RGVIA, f. VUA, op. 16, vol. 1, d. 4841, part 1, ll. 611–611v.

68 Dibich to Montrezor, 1 August 1829, Slivno, RGVIA, f. VUA, op. 16, vol. 1, d. 4841, part 2, ll. 26v–27.

69 Tol to Montrezor, 6 August 1829, RGVIA, f. VUA, op. 16, vol. 1, d. 4841, part 2, l. 185.

70 Montrezor to Dibich, 17 August 1829, Slivno, RGVIA, f. VUA, op. 16, vol. 1, d. 4841, part 2, l. 460.

71 Montrezor to Berg, 17 August 1829, ll. 485v–486.

72 Major-General V.A. Glinka (sent to replace Montrezor, who fell ill) to Berg, 23 August 1829, RGVIA, f. VUA, op. 16, vol. 1, d. 4841, part 2, l. 482.

73 Montrezor to Dibich, 24 August 1829, Slivno, RGVIA, f. VUA, op. 16, vol. 1, d. 4841, part 2, l. 679.

74 General Quartermaster Berg to Montrezor, 24 August 1829, Adrianople, RGVIA, f. VUA, op. 16, vol. 1, d. 4841, part 2, l. 483.

75 See the conditions of capitulation in RGVIA, f. VUA, op. 16, vol. 1, d. 4841, part 2, l. 287v.

76 Dibich to Nicholas I, 9 August 1829, Adrianople, RGVIA, f. VUA, op. 16, vol. 1, d. 4841, part 2, l. 239.

77 Tol to Rot, 21 August 1829, RGVIA, f. VUA, op. 16, vol. 1, d. 4841, part 2, ll. 448–9.

78 Colonel Den the 3rd to Tol, 9 August 1829, camp at Kirk Kilise, RGVIA, f. VUA, op. 16, vol. 1, d. 4841, part 2, ll. 263–4.

79 Colonel Khomutov to Rot, 15 August 1829, camp at Adrianople, RGVIA, f. VUA, op. 16, vol. 1, d. 4841, part 1, l. 364v.

80 Tol to Sivers, 21 August 1829, Adrianople, RGVIA, f. VUA, op. 16, vol. 1, d. 4841, part 2, ll. 444–444v.

81 Sivers to Tol, 24 August 1829, RGVIA, f. VUA, op. 16, vol. 1, d. 4841, part 2, ll. 502, 504.

82 Tol to Rot, 21 August 1829, Adrianople, RGVIA, f. VUA, op. 16, vol. 1, d. 4841, part 2, ll. 445–445v.

83 Anrep to Rot, 24 August 1829, camp at Hermanli, RGVIA, f. VUA, op. 16, vol. 1, d. 4841, part 2, ll. 546–546v.

84 Anrep to Warot, 24 August 1829, l. 546.

85 Kompan to Tol, 2 September 1829, Chermen, RGVIA, f. VUA, op. 16, vol. 1, d. 4841, part 2, ll. 697–701.

86 Palen to Dibich, 28 August 1829, Viza (Vize), RGVIA, f. VUA, op. 16, vol. 1, d. 4841, part 2, l. 650.

87 Bitis, "Balkan Irregulars," 553, 555.

88 A.S. Greig to Nicholas I, 10 March 1829, cited in Bernshtein, "Stranitsa iz istorii bolgarskoi immigratsii," 329.

89 See the text of the treaty in Narochnitskii, *Vneshniaia politika Rossii*, 16:265.

90 Bitis, "Resettlement of Balkan Peoples," 516–25.

91 Diugamel, "Statisticheskaia tablitsa," 190.

92 Diugamel, 196–8, 200, 157.

93 Diugamel, 189.

94 Diugamel, 189.

95 Enegolm, *Zapiski*, 131, 134, 136.

96 Enegolm, 105, 139, 146, 150.

97 Enegolm, 87. In his separately published review of Adrianopole, Diugamel estimated the number of Muslim in habitants of Adrianopole at 50,000 out of 100,000, the rest being Greeks, Armenians, and Jews. See Diugamel, "Kratkoe izvlechenie ob Adrianopole," 119.

98 Taki, *Tsar and Sultan*, 191–29.

99 Enegolm, *Zapiski*, 50–2.

100 Enegolm, 52–3.

101 Enegolm, 54.

3. Partisan Warfare and the Statistics of European Turkey: The Case of I.P. Liprandi

1 The fruits of their effort were published at the time of the Crimean War as *Voenno-statisticheskoe obozrenie*.

2 On Rozalion-Soshalskii's mission, see RGVIA, f. 439, op. 1, d. 6; and Rozalion-Soshalskii, "Statisticheskoe opisanie Serbii do Adrianopol'skogo mira," RGVIA, f. VUA, op. 16, vol.1, d. 1028.

3 Diugamel, "Statisticheskaia tablitsa"; Diugamel, "Kratkoe izvlechenie ob Adrianopole"; and Enegolm, *Zapiski*.

4 See, most importantly, the series of histories of the Russian-Ottoman wars by A.N. Petrov, which culminated in Petrov, *Vliianie russko-turetskikh voin*.

5 On Liprandi, see Eidelman, "Gde i chto Liprandi?"; Kurochkin, "Delo Liprandi"; and Ishutin, "Ivan Petrovich Liprandi."

6 A famous duellist in his youth, Liprandi was befriended by Alexander Pushkin, who languished in Bessarabian exile from 1820 to 1823 and became the prototype of Silvio in Pushkin's short story *The Shot*. However, in contrast to Silvio, who chose to sacrifice his life to the cause of the Greek independence, Liprandi gradually abandoned the daredevil ways of his young years and lived a very long and increasingly unromantic life.

7 At this time, he also wrote an overview of the Russian occupation of the two principalities during the Russian-Ottoman war of 1806–12: Liprandi, "Kratkoe obozrenie kniazhestv Moldavii i Valakhii v voennoe vremia 1807–1812," NIOR RGB, f. 47, op. 3, papka 16, d.2, ll. 1–8.

8 Liprandi, "Kratkoe obozrenie Moldavii, Valakhii i drugikh prilegaiushchikh zemel'"; Liprandi, "Zapiska o sostoianii umov v Moldavii adresovannaia P. D. Kiselevu 1828," RGIA, f. 673, op. 1, d. 231. For a discussion of Liprandi's activities as a Russian secret agent in the principalities, see Taki, "Spying for Empire."

9 Liprandi, "Spisok valakhskikh boiar s pokazaniem kakim gosudarstvam predany," RGIA, f. 673, op. 1, d. 329. During the 1830s, Liprandi summarized the observations he made in the principalities during the previous decade in his "Vzgliad proisshestviia v Moldavii i Valakhii s nachala 1820 g. do zakliucheniia Adrianopol'skogo mira s kratkim soobshcheniem svoistv byvshikh kniazei do togo vremeni i boiar voobshche do sikh por," RGIA, f. 673, op. 1, d. 233.

10 Liprandi, "Zapiska I.P. Liprandi soderzhashchaia polnuiu khrakteristiku turetskoi armii i ee voinskogo sostava," 14 April 1834, RGIA, f. 673, op. 1, d. 407, ll. 1v–2v. Some of these diaries and memoirs were later published. See Tuchkov, "Zapiski"; and Lanzheron, "Zapiski," *Russkaia starina*, no. 5 (1907): 432–48, and subsequent instalments.

11 Liprandi, "O neobkhodimosti sostavit' korpus partisan na pravom berege Dunaia," 10 January 1829, Kishinev, RGIA, f. 673, op. 1, d. 367, l. 1.

12 Liprandi, "O neobkhodimosti sostavit' korpus partisan," l. 1v.

13 Liprandi, l. 2.

14 Liprandi, l. 2.

15 Liprandi, l. 2v.

16 Liprandi, l. 2v.

17 Liprandi, l. 4.

18 Liprandi, l. 6.

19 Liprandi, l. 6v.

20 Liprandi, l. 5v.

21 Liprandi, ll. 9–9v.

22 Liprandi, l. 10.

23 Liprandi, "O partizanskoi voine. Glava IV. Voina 1829 g.," RGIA, f. 673, op. 1, d. 222., ll. 6–6v. See also Dibich to Nicholas I, 21 April 1829, *Russkaia starina*, no. 10 (1881): 293.

24 Liprandi, "O partizanskoi voine. Glava IV," l. 17.

25 Liprandi estimated the size of the forest at 12,000 square versts, and the number of inhabitants at 80,000 (of which barely 20,000 were Bulgarians), not counting the population of the neighbouring towns. See Liprandi, ll. 20–20v.

26 Liprandi, l. 23v.

27 Liprandi, l. 34v.

28 Liprandi, l. 37v.

29 Liprandi, l. 43v.

30 Liprandi, ll. 48v–49.

31 Liprandi, 87–106v.

32 Liprandi, "O partizanskoi voine voobsche i v osobennosti o pratizanakh 1828 i 1829 gg.," RGIA, f. 673, op. 1, d. 220, ll. 9–10v.

33 Liprandi, "O partizanskoi voine voobsche," ll. 1, 8.

34 Liprandi, l. 40. According to Liprandi, Napoleon knew Frenchmen only too well and realized that only "defence of property rather than patriotism" could incite a "national war." However, this calculation was thwarted by "the order of the allied troops, particularly the Russian ones." See Liprandi, l. 40v.

35 Liprandi argued that only the campaign of 1813 witnessed the formation of "strategic partisans" in the sense defined by Davydov. See Liprandi, l. 13.

36 Mikhailovskii-Danilevskii, *Opisanie Otechestvennoi voiny*, 111.

37 Mikhailovskii-Danilevskii, 121.

38 Mikhailovskii-Danilevskii, *Opisanie finliandskoi voiny*, 91–5.

39 Mikhailovskii-Danilevskii, *Opisanie turetskoi voiny*, 228. The latter work is also available in English. See Mikhailovskii-Danilevskii, *Russo-Turkish War*.

40 Engelgardt, *Kratkoe nachertanie maloi voiny*, 4:121, 127. Engelgardt defined small war as "interference with enemy communications; destruction of its military supplies, buildings, and magazines; collection of intelligence; capture of messengers, supply trains, [and] small detachments; prevention of enemy requisitions; [and] harassment and wearing down of the enemy."

41 Vuich, *Malaia voina*, viii.

42 Vuich, 242–3.

43 Liprandi, "Otryvok iz knigi," 9–10. The original edition is Liprandi, *Nekotoryie zamechaniia*.

44 Liprandi, "Otryvok iz knigi," 18.

45 Liprandi argued that "despite the diversity of its constituted parts," the Russian army offered "an exceptional example of unprecedented unity" by virtue of the "predominance of the Russian element." See Liprandi, 21.

46 Liprandi, 22.

47 Liprandi, 40.

48 Liprandi, "Ottomanskaia imperiia. Opyt slovoistolkovatelia," 1836, RGIA, f. 673, op. 1, dd. 217–18.

49 Enegolm, *Zapiski*.

50 I. P. Liprandi, "Adrianopol' v otnoshenii: Istoricheskom, geograficheskom, topograficheskom, statisticheskom, torgovom, politicheskom, voennom, s prisovokupleniem putei iz onogo vedushchikh. Izvlechenie iz sbornika 'Ottomanskaia Imperiia' sostavlennogo I. P. Liprandi. 147aia stat'ia sego sbornika," RGIA, f. 673, op. 1, d. 219.

51 Liprandi, "Adrianopol' v otnoshenii," ll. 37v–38.

52 Liprandi, *Obozrenie prostranstva sluzhivshego teatrom voiny*, 58.

53 Liprandi, 59.

54 Liprandi, 60.

55 Liprandi, 87.

56 Liprandi, 60.

57 Liprandi, 59.

58 Liprandi, 59n.

59 See Liprandi, "Vazhnost' imet' polozhitel'nye sveden'ia," 58–9n.

60 Schimmelpenninck van der Oye, *Russian Orientalism*, 153–170.

61 See Baskhanov, *Russkie voennye vostokovedy do 1917*. For Russian military Orientalism in the late imperial period, see Vigasin, Khokhlov, and Shastit'ko, *Istoriia otechestvennogo vostokovedeniia*, 134–56. See also Marshall, *Russian General Staff and Asia*, 46–66.

62 On Orientalizing representations of the Ottoman Empire by Russian military men, see Taki, *Tsar and Sultan*, esp. 95–128.

63 Said, *Orientalism*, 2–3.

64 On the "Greek project," see de Maradiaga, *Catherine the Great*; and Arsh, *Rossiia i bor'ba Gretsii*, 35–52.

65 See Todorova, *Imagining the Balkans*.

66 Wolff, *Inventing Eastern Europe*.

67 See Taki, *Tsar and Sultan*, 159–65.

68 Taki, 151–9.

69 Said, *Orientalism*, 7.

70 The fate of his collection of European Ottomanica is revealing in this respect. The Military-Scientific Committee of the General Staff, which purchased this collection in 1853, apparently had little use for it, and eventually part of this collection ended up in Tashkent, after the Russian conquest of this Central Asian capital and the establishment of Turkestan Governorate-General in 1865–6.

71 See Carrier, *Occidentalism*; and Buruma and Margalit, *Occidentalism*.

72 Offord, *Journeys to a Graveyard*, esp. 49–102.

73 On the opposition between "Europe as the two" (the British and the French parliamentary monarchies) and "Europe as the three" (the absolutist Austria, Prussia, and Russia), see Malia, *Russia under Western Eyes*, 89–102.

74 On British Russophobia in this period, see Gleason, *Russophobia in Britain*. On the same process in France, see Cadot, *La vie intellectuelle française*; Corbet, *L'opinion française*; and Adamovsky, *Euro-Orientalism*.

75 Dixon, "Repositioning Pushkin."

76 For the interpretation of all non-Anglo-Saxon nationalisms in terms of resentment, see Greenfeld, *Nationalism*, 177–84, 222–35, 371–86.

77 Elias, *Civilizing Process*, 5–30.

78 On the Russian perception of the Ottoman Empire in this period, see Taki, *Tsar and Sultan*, 151–65.

79 On Kiselev's service as the head of the Russian provisional administration in Moldavia and Wallachia, see Taki, *Russia on the Danube*, 191–276.

80 Liprandi, "O polednikh proisshestviiakh v Moldavii," RGIA, f. 673, op. 1, d. 402, ll. 1–8; and Liprandi, "Kratkoe obozrenie Kniazhestv Moldavii i Valakhii, ot obrazovaniia onykh v Kiazhestva."

81 Florescu, *Struggle against Russia*.

82 Liprandi maintained some personal contacts in the principalities; his second wife was the daughter of a Bucharest physician.

83 Liprandi, "Kratkii ocherk."

84 Saint-Marc Girardin, "Voyage à Constantinople par le Danube, 9-ème lettre," RGIA, f. 673, op. 1, no. 305, l. 12 (originally published in *Journal des débats*, 2 December 1836, 3–4). Girardin's "Voyage à Constantinople" was republished in an augmented version in his *Souvenirs*, 1:117–277, 2:5–68.

85 For a recent account of the Wallachian revolution in English, see Jianu, *Circle of Friends*, 67–99.

86 See Frank, *Dostoyevsky*, 6–9. On the ideas of the Petrashevkii Circle, see Walicki, *History of Russian Thought*, 152–61.

87 On early Russian Pan-Slavism, see Fadner, *Seventy Years of Pan-Slavism*.

88 See, respectively, Mikhail Pogodin, "Pis'mo k gosudariu Tsesarevichu," in *Istoriko-politicheskie pis'ma i zapiski*, 1–14; Tiutchev, "Rossiia i revoliutsiia"; and Tiutchev, "Papstvo i rimskii vopros."

89 See Kasatkin, "In Search of One's Self."

90 Taki, *Tsar and Sultan*, 186–91.

91 Kasatkin, "In Search of One's Self."

92 Liprandi, "Zapiska o neobkhodimosti imet' otriad volonterov partisan iz zhitelei pravogo berega Dunaia," 1854, RGIA, f. 673, op. 1, d. 419.

93 The first seven chapters of the manuscript were subsequently published as Liprandi, "Obshchie svedeniia o Evropeiskoi Turtsii."

94 Published as Liprandi, "Vazhnost' imet' polozhitel'nye svedeniia."

95 Liprandi, "Vzgliad na nastoiashchii teatr voennykh deistvii na Dunae i na so-deistvie, kotoroie mozhem vstretit' v Bolgarii," 1854, RGIA, f. 673, op. 1, d. 423. Published in *Chteniia v imperatorskom obshchestve istorii i drevnostei rossiiskikh*, no. 3 (1877): 1–11.

96 Liprandi, "Sredstva, kotorye mozhet naiti nasha armiia v Bolgarii pri sobliudenii mestnykh uslovii," 1854, RGIA, f. 673, op. 1, d. 422. Published in *Chteniia v imperatorskom obshchestve istorii i drevnostei rossiiskikh*, no. 3 (1877): 12–26.

97 Published as Liprandi, "Puti v Bolgarii."

98 Liprandi, "Kratkii ocherk etnograficheskogo, politicheskogo, nravstvennogo i voennogo sostoianiia khristianskikh oblastei Tureskoi imperii. Pridunaiskie knia-zhestva," 1854, RGIA, f. 673, op. 1, d. 249 (published in *Chteniia v imperatorskom obshchestve istorii i drevnostei rossiiskikh*, no. 4 [1876]: 1–14); Liprandi, "Kratkii ocherk etnograficheskogo, politicheskogo, nravstvennogo i voennogo sostoianiia khristianskikh oblastei Tureskoi imperii. Bosniia," 1854, RGIA, f. 673, op. 1, d. 248 (reproduced, with some omissions, in Liprandi, "Bolgariia i Vostochnyi vopros," 51–9); Liprandi, "Kratkii ocherk etnograficheskogo, politicheskogo, nravstven-nogo i voennogo sostoianiia khristianskikh oblastei Tureskoi imperii. Albaniia," 1854, RGIA, f. 673, op. 1, d. 246 (reproduced, with some cuts and modifications, in Liprandi, "Bolgariia i Vostochnyi vopros," 60–82); Liprandi, "Kratkii ocherk etnograficheskogo, politicheskogo, nravstvennogo i voennogo sostoianiia khris-tianskikh oblastei Tureskoi imperii. Rumyniia, Fessaliia i Makedoniia," 1854, RGIA, f. 673, op. 1, d. 250; and Liprandi, "Kratkii ocherk etnograficheskogo, polit-icheskogo, nravstvennogo i voennogo sostoianiia khristianskikh oblastei Tureskoi imperii. Bolgariia," 1854, RGIA, f. 673, op. 1, d. 247 (published as Liprandi, "Bol-gariia. Iz zapisok I. P. Liprandi").

99 In Liprandi's estimation, there were about 800,000 Bulgarians in Danubian Bul-garia. See Liprandi, "Bolgariia. Iz zapisok I. P. Liprandi," 8.

100 Liprandi, 13. See also Liprandi, "Bolgariia i Vostochnyi vopros," 7–8.

101 Liprandi, "Bolgariia. Iz zapisok I. P. Liprandi," 17.

102 Liprandi, 18.

103 Liprandi, 14–15.

104 Liprandi, 19.

105 Liprandi, 21.

106 Liprandi, 22–3.

107 Liprandi, 24–5.

108 Liprandi, 29–30.

109 Liprandi, 37–8 and n. 47.

110 Liprandi, 37.

111 Liprandi, 38–48.

112 Liprandi, 49.

113 Liprandi, 52.

114 Liprandi, 54–5.

115 Liprandi, 55–6.

116 Liprandi, 59–60.

117 Liprandi, "Bolgariia i Vostochnyi vopros," 51.

118 Liprandi, 52–3. I cite the published version of Liprandi's notes on Bosnia and Albania except for the passages that were not included into it.

119 Liprandi, 53.

120 Liprandi, 54–5.

121 Liprandi, 57.

122 Liprandi, "Kratkii ocherk etnograficheskogo, politicheskogo, nravstvennogo i voennogo […] Bosniia" (see n. 98 in this chapter), l. 9.

123 Liprandi, "Bolgariia i Vostochnyi vopros," 67.

124 Liprandi, 68.

125 Liprandi, 71.

126 Liprandi, 72.

127 Liprandi, 81n.

128 Liprandi, "Kratkii ocherk etnograficheskogo, politicheskogo, nravstvennogo i voennogo […] Albaniia" (see n. 98 in this chapter), ll. 31–31v.

129 Liprandi, ll. 32–32v.

130 Liprandi, l. 33.

131 Liprandi, l. 34.

4. Russia and the Balkan Peoples during the Crimean War

1 On the Crimean War, see Figes, *Crimean War*. As a well-written British history of the war, Figes's book represents a successful update of Palmer's earlier book of the same title (Palmer, *Crimean War*). However, anyone interested in the Russian experience of this conflict should opt for Curtiss, *Russia's Crimean War*; and Kozelsky, *Crimea in War and Transformation*. For the Ottoman dimension of the Crimean War, see Aksan, *The Ottomans*, 206–20; and Badem, *Ottoman Crimean War*.

2 Puryear, *France and the Levant*, 85.

3 Palmer, *Crimean War*, 21; and Figes, *Crimean War*, 116–17.

4 Badem, *Ottoman Crimean War*, 99–100, 180.

5 On the Danubian campaign of 1853–4, see Petrov, *Dunaiskaia kampaniia*; Zaionchkovskii, *Vostochnaia voina*, 2:127–90, 341–439, 643–799, 897–1119; Badem, *Ottoman Crimean War*, 101–9, 177–87; and Figes, *Crimean War*, 132–9, 164–72.

6 Schroeder, *Austria, Britain, and the Crimean War*.

7 On these aspects, see Figes, *Crimean War*.

8 See the discussion of Muraviev's critique of the Ottoman mimicry of Western military ways in Taki, *Tsar and Sultan*, 153–5.

9 Goldfrank, *Origins of the Crimean War*, 68–72.

10 Vronchenko, *Obozrenie Maloi Azii*, 1:247.

11 "Turetskaia imperiia," 1847, RGVIA, f. 450, op. 1, d. 28 (1), l. 74.

12 "Turetskaia imperiia," ll. 76–76v.

13 "Turetskaia imperiia," ll. 66v, 78.

14 "Turetskaia imperiia," l. 67.

15 Osten-Saken, "Zapiska o voennykh silakh Turtsii," RGVIA, f. 450, op. 1, d. 28. l. 46v.

16 Osten-Saken, "Zapiska," l. 47.

17 Osten-Saken, "Nekotorye voenno-statisticheskie svedeniia o Turtsii," 23 March 1851, RGVIA, f. 450, op. 1, d. 39, ll. 8–25v.

18 Osten-Saken, "Nekotorye voenno-statisticheskie svedeniia," ll. 17–18.

19 Osten-Sacken to A.I. Chernyshev (Russian war minister under Nicholas I), 24 March 1851, RGVIA, f. 450, op. 1, d. 39, l. 32 v. Here the term "reaya" is used in the more conventional sense, designating the tax-paying population of the Ottoman Empire, as opposed to the tax-exempt military people (*askeri*). On the response of the Ottoman Muslims to this aspect of the military reforms, and of the Tanzimat more broadly, see Davison, "Turkish Attitudes."

20 "Zapiska o voennykh silakh Turtsii," RGVIA, f. 450, op. 1, d. 28. l. 48.

21 "Zapiska o voennykh silakh Turtsii," l. 45v.

22 "Zapiska o voennykh silakh Turtsii," ll. 45v–46.

23 On this subject, see Taki, *Tsar and Sultan*, 151–9.

24 "Predpolozheniia imperatora Nikolaia […] Bosfor i Tsar'grad," 676. This memo, dated 7 January 1853, is also published in Zaionchkovskii, *Vostochnaia voina*, 1:582–3.

25 Cited in Shilder, "Zametki," 380–2.

26 "Dve zapiski imperatora Nikolaia," 677–80. The first of these, dated 8 April 1853, is also published in Zaionchkovskii, *Vostochnaia voina*, 1:601–3.

27 "Vsepoddaneishaia zapiska kniazia Varshavskogo," 681.

28 "Vsepoddaneishaia zapiska kniazia Varshavskogo," 682.

29 "Vsepoddaneishaia zapiska kniazia Varshavskogo," 683.

30 "Mysli kniazia Varshavskogo," 684–5.

31 "Mysli kniazia Varshavskogo," 687.

32 "Predpolozheniia Imperatora Nikolaia Pavlovicha […] s Turtsiei," 687–8.

33 "Vsepoddaneishaia zapiska kniazia Paskevicha," 11 September 1853, 692.

34 "Vsepoddaneishaia zapiska kniazia Paskevicha," 11 September 1853, 693.

35 "Vsepoddaneishaia zapiska general-fel'dmarshala kniazia Varshavskogo," July 2, 1853, in Zaionchkovskii, *Vostochnaia voina*, 2:99–101. See also "Vsepoddaneishaia zapiska kniazia Paskevicha," 11 September 1853, 691, 693–5.

36 "Vsepoddaneishaia zapiska kniazia Paskevicha," 24 September 1853, 699–700.

37 "Vsepoddaneishaia zapiska kniazia Paskevicha," 24 September 1853, 701.

38 "Annotations écrites par Sa Majesté l'Empereur Nicholas I au crayon, sur une feuille séparée," in Zaionchkovskii, *Vostochnaia voina*, 2:321.

39 "Annotations écrites," 321. On Nicholas I's memorandum, see Shilder, *Imperator Nikolai Pervyi*, 2:640–6.

40 "Annotations écrites," 322.

41 "Vsepoddanneishii doklad grafa Nesselrode," 8 November 1853, in Zaionchkovskii, *Vostochnaia voina*, 2:323–4.

42 "Vsepoddanneishii doklad grafa Nesselrode," 325.

43 Gorchakov to (minister of war) V.A. Dolgorukov, 27 July 1853, cited in Zaionchkovskii, *Vostochnaia voina*, 2:630.

44 Nicholas I to Gorchakov, 24 December 1853, cited in Zaionchkovskii, 2:600.

45 Nicholas I to Gorchakov, 24 December 1853.

46 Nicholas I to Gorchakov, 28 October 1853, cited in Zaionchkovskii, *Vostochnaia voina*, 2:631.

47 "Predpolozheniia Imperatora Nikolaia Pavlovicha […] na 1854 god," 706–8.

48 "Predpolozheniia Imperatora Nikolaia Pavlovicha […] na 1854 god," 708.

49 Paskevich to Nicholas I, 14 November 1853, *Russkaia starina*, no. 9 (1876): 146.

50 Paskevich to Nicholas I, 14 November 1853, 147.

51 Paskevich to Nicholas I, 14 November 1853, 148.

52 "Zapiska General-Ad'iutanta Berga o voine s Turtsiei," 17 November 1853, in Zaionchkovskii, *Vostochnaia voina*, 2:295.

53 "Zapiska General-Ad'iutanta Berga," 296.

54 Nicholas I to Paskevich, 5 January 1854, cited in Zaionchkovskii, *Vostochnaia voina*, 2:601.

55 "Predpolozheniia kniazia M.D. Gorchakova," 154.

56 Gorchakov to Paskevich, n.d., *Russkaia starina*, no. 9 (1876): 164.

57 Gorchakov to Nicholas I, n.d., *Russkaia starina*, no. 9 (1876): 163.

58 Gorchakov to Nicholas I, 27 January 1854, *Russkaia starina*, no. 10 (1876): 354.

59 Gorchakov to Nicholas I, 27 January 1854, 354; and "Predpolozheniia kniazia M.D. Gorchakova," 155–6.

60 Liprandi, "Vzgliad na nastoiashchii teatr voennykh deistvii," 5–6.

61 Liprandi, 9–10. Elsewhere in his manuscript, Liprandi listed the names of some of the *hajduks* who served in his volunteer detachment in 1829 and who, in his opinion, could still be used to the same purpose. See Liprandi, "Vazhnost' imet' polozhitel'nye svedeniia," 65n.

62 Liprandi, "Vzgliad na nastoiashchii teatr voennykh deistvii," 10–11.

63 Liprandi, "Nastoiashchee sostoianie turetskoi armii," 41–6.

64 Liprandi, 41.

65 Liprandi, 42.

66 Liprandi, 43.

67 Liprandi, 45.

68 Liprandi, 48.

69 Liprandi, 49.

70 On the activity of Palauzov at the time of the Crimean War, see Zabunov, "Odesskoe bolgarskoe nastoiatel'stvo."

71 N.Kh. Palauzov, "O nyneshnem polozhenii Bolgar v Evropeiskoi Turtsii," in Barsov, *Tridtsatiletie*, 30–7.

72 N.Kh. Palauzov, "Zapiska o Bolgarii, podannaia komandiru 3-go pekhotnogo korpusa D.E. Osten-Sakenu," 20 January 1854, in Barsov, *Tridtsatiletie*, 41.

73 Palauzov, "Zapiska o Bolgarii," 42–3.

74 S.N. Palauzov to D.M. Gorchakov (or Paskevich?), RGIA, f. 1015, op. 1, d. 46, l. 1.

75 Makarova, "Bolgariia na puti k osvobozhdeniiu."

76 Rakovski's case defies the conventional dichotomy between revolutionary activities and collaboration with the Ottoman authorities, which Bulgarian nationalist and communist historiography emphasized so much. In the light of recent research, however, the combination of collaboration and revolutionary subversion appears to be a rather widespread phenomenon in the era of the Bulgarian national revival. See Vezenkov, "In the Service of the Sultan."

77 See Konobeev, "Plan vooruzhennoi bor'by"; see also Konobeev, "Natsional'no-osvoboditel'noe dvizheniie."

78 See Mukhin's report to Gorchakov, 19 December 1853, published in Konobeev, "Plan vooruzhennoi bor'by," 335–7. The existence of this plan is supported by Rachinskii, *Pokhodnye pis'ma*, 23.

79 This idea was communicated to the Russian command by Barsov in his conversation with the Russian diplomatic agent Fonton. See Konobeev, "Natsional'no-osvoboditel'noe dvizhenie," 149.

80 "Predpolozheniia kniaza M.D. Gorchakova," 151. Gorchakov's memorandum is also published in Zaionchkovskii, *Vostochnaia voina*, 2:282–7.

81 See Paskevich, "Mysli o plane voennykh deistvii."

82 Nicholas I to Gorchakov, 1 February 1854, in Zaionchkovskii, *Vostochnaia voina*, 2:312–14.

83 "Novyi plan kompanii nachertannyi sobstvennoruchno Nikolaem Pavlovichem," in Zaionchkovskii, *Vostochnaia voina*, 2:315. See also *Russkaia starina*, no. 10 (1876): 359.

84 Grabbe, *Zapisnaia knizhka*, 568.

85 "Novyi plan kompanii nachertannyi sobstvennoruchno Nikolaem Pavlovichem," *Russkaia starina*, no. 10 (1876): 360–1.

86 For the first time, Paskevich mentioned the possibility of abandoning the principalities, in his confidential letter to Gorchakov of 24 February 1854, published in *Russkaia starina*, no. 2 (1876): 388–92.

87 Gorchakov to Nicholas I, 16 March 1854, *Russkaia starina*, no. 1 (1877): 138.

88 Gorchakov to Nicholas I, 22 March 1854, *Russkaia starina*, no. 1 (1877): 142.

89 Gorchakov to Dolgorukov, 22 March 1854, 143.

90 Gorchakov to Dolgorukov, 28 March 1854, *Russkaia starina*, no. 2 (1877): 331.

91 Paskevich to Nicholas I, 1 April 1854, *Russkaia starina*, no. 2 (1877): 331.

92 "Prikaz generala Lidersa."

93 Gorchakov to Liders, 26 March 1854, *Russkaia starina*, no. 12 (1876): 829. In March 1854, Gorchakov dispatched the first such detachment of 500 volunteers to Liders and another one of 1,500 people to Lieutenant General P.P. Liprandi (I.P. Liprandi's younger brother), who commanded the Russian forces in Little Wallachia. See Gorchakov to Dolgorukov, 22 March 1854, *Russkaia starina*, no. 1 (1877): 144.

94 Gorchakov to Liders, 26 March 1854, *Russkaia starina*, no. 12 (1876): 829–30.

95 Nicholas I to Paskevich, 7 April 1854, *Russkaia starina*, no. 5 (1877): 84.

96 "Edinovernym brat'iam nashim v oblastiakh Turtsii," 7 April 1854, in Zaionchkovskii, *Vostochnaia voina*, 2:331.

97 Nicholas I to Paskevich, 13 April 1854, *Russkaia starina*, no. 5 (1877): 87.

98 Nicholas I to Paskevich, 7 April 1854, 84. See also Nicholas I to Paskevich, 24 April 1854, *Russkaia starina*, no. 5 (1877): 94.

99 According to N.I. Ushakov who served as Gorchakov's general on duty, the number of Greek, Moldavian, Wallachian, Bulgarian, and Serb volunteers who immediately responded to the invitation of the Russian command was sufficient to form three battalions. At the same time, Ushakov noted that the volunteers were motivated by the lavish allowance that was promised to them rather than by "hatred towards the Turks or great enthusiasm for us." This enthusiasm latter was further dampened by the attempts of the Russian command to discipline these auxiliaries in the manner of the Russian troops. As a result, the number of volunteers soon fell to 900 people, and these proved to be rather unruly: they robbed local inhabitants and engaged in bloody fights on the streets of Galați, Brăila, and other cities. Reflecting on this experience, Ushakov concluded that instead of forming a large militia force, it would have been wiser to attach to each Russian regiment a unit of some fifty volunteers under the command of a local captain that better corresponded to Balkan military practices. See Ushakov, "Zapiski," 60–2.

100 Konobeev, "Plan vooruzhennoi bor'by," 333.

101 Konobeev, 333.

102 S.N. Palauzov to S.P. Shevyrev, 15 May 1854, RGIA, f. 1015, op. 1, d. 46, l. 6.

103 Paskevich to Nicholas I, 11 April 1854, *Russkaia starina*, no. 5 (1877): 85.

104 See their exchange that followed in *Russkaia starina*, no. 5 (1877): 91–6.

105 Paskevich to Nicholas I, 15 April 1854, in Zaionchkovskii, *Vostochnaia voina*, 2:402–3.

106 Gorchakov to Dolgorukii, 1 June 1854, in Zaionchkovskii, *Vostochnaia voina*, 2:410–11.

107 Ushakov, "Zapiski," 104.

108 Konobeev, "Plan vooruzhennoi bor'by," 333. On the numbers, see Zaionchkovskii, *Vostochnaia voina*, 2:641.

5. The Russian Army and the Ottoman Empire, 1856–1877

1 The historiography of the Great Reforms is vast both in Russian and in English. See, most importantly, Zaionchkovsky, *Abolition of Serfdom* (first Russian edition published in 1960); Emmons, *Russian Landed Gentry*; Emmons, *Zemstvo in Russia*; Zakharova, *Samoderzhavie i otmena*; Lincoln, *Great Reforms*; and Ekloff, Bushnell, and Zakharova, *Russia's Great Reforms*.

2 See Rieber, "Politics of Emancipation."

3 On Russia's military reform, see Zaionchkovskii, *Voennye reformy*; Menning, *Bayonets before Bullets*, 6–50; Fuller, *Strategy and Power*, 275–85; and Baumann, "Universal Service Reform."

4 On Miliutin, see P.A. Zaionchkovskii, "D.A. Miliutin. Biograficheskii ocherk," in Miliutin, *Dnevnik*, 1:5–73; and Miller, *Dmitrii Miliutin*. On Obruchev, see Airapetov, *Zabytaia kar'era*. The traditional perception of Miliutin and his associates as the authors of Russia's military reform has recently been challenged. See Kagan, *Military Reforms*, 244–51, who argues that Nicholas I and his war minister, A.I. Chernyshev, confronted essentially the same predicament of a vicious manpower policy imposed upon them by Russia's social organization, while their proposed solutions (indefinite furloughs, greater emphasis on military administration), short of the abolition of serfdom, anticipated the introduction of universal military service and of the military districts during the 1860s and 1870s. Kagan's thesis challenges the historiography of the Russian military reform in the same way in which W. Bruce Lincoln's *Vanguard of Reform* challenged the historiography of other reforms.

5 Holquist, "To Count, to Extract and to Exterminate," esp. 112–13.

6 Hacking, "Biopower," 281.

7 Rey, *Nombre*.

8 Porter, *Statistical Thinking*, 17–70.

9 Hartmann, *Body Populace*.

10 Miliutin, "Kriticheskoe issledovanie," 176–7.

11 Miliutin, 179, 183.

12 Miliutin, *Pervye opyty voennoi statistiki*.

13 Rich, "Imperialism, Research and Strategy," 624. These studies were published as *Voenno-statisticheskoe obozrenie Rossiiskoi imperii*. See also Rich, "Building Foundations."

14 Rich, "Imperialism, Research, and Strategy," 633–4.

15 Rich, 635–6.

16 N.N. Obruchev, "Soobrazheniia ob oborone Rossii. Strategicheskaia zapiska," 19 January 1873, NIOR RGB, f. 169, karton 37, d. 4. On the Secret Strategic Conference of March 1873, see Fuller, *Strategy and Power*, 295–303.

17 Rich, "Imperialism, Research and Strategy," 636–8.

18 Rich, 627.

19 Maksheev, "Opisanie Aral'skogo moria." On Maksheev, see Marshall, *Russian General Staff and Asia*, 46–66.

20 Maksheev, "Geograficheskie, etnograficheskie i statisticheskie materialy."

21 Miliutin's early experience in the Caucasus led him to write a study of the 1839 campaign. See Miliutin, *Opisanie voennykh deistvii 1839 goda*.

22 Fadeev, *Shest'desiat let Kavkazskoi voiny*, 58–60.

23 On the latter, see Fadeev, 137–8.

24 Holquist, "To Count, to Extract, and to Exterminate," 116–19. On the expulsion/ emigration of Muslims in the post-Crimean period, see Pinson, "Demographic Warfare"; Brooks, "Russia's Conquest and Pacification"; Fisher, "Emigration of Muslims"; Williams, "Hijra and Forced Migration"; and Bobrovnikov and Babich, *Severnyi Kavkaz v sostave Rosskiiskoi imperii*, 128–32, 155–83.

25 Fadeev, "Pis'ma s Kavkaza," 179.

26 Fadeev, 183–4.

27 Fadeev, 184.

28 Fadeev, 184–5.

29 Fadeev, 153.

30 Miliutin, "'O sredstvakh kolonizatsii (prigotovitel'nye mery k priniatiiu pere-selentsev)' – vypiski iz statei o kolonizatsii Alzhira pomeshchennykh v *Moniteur Algerien* i *Spectateur militaire*," 1842, NIOR RGB, f. 169, karton 18, d. 17. For a comparative perspective on the Russian policy in the North Caucasus, and that of the French in Algeria, see Bobrovnikov, "Russkii Kavkaz i frantsu-zskii Alzhir."

31 Berens, "Kabiliia v 1857 godu"; Maksheev, "Ocherk sovremennogo sostoianiia Alzhirii"; Kostenko, *Puteshestvie v Severnuiu Afriku*; Kuropatkin, "Ocherki Alzhirii"; and Kuropatkin, *Alzhiriia*.

32 Frankini to Sukhozanet, 15 November 1860, RGVIA, f. 450, op. 1, d. 64, l. 104v.

33 Frankini to Sukhozanet, 15 November 1860. On the emigration of Crimean Tatars, see Kozelsky, "Casualties of Conflict."

34 Frankini to Sukhozanet, 10 May 1860, RGVIA, f. 450, op. 1, d. 64, ll. 58–58v.

35 Frankini to Sukhozanet, 10 May 1860, ll. 58v–59.

36 See Frankini to Miliutin, 10 May 1866, RGVIA, f. 450, op 1, d. 78, l. 37.

37 Frankini to Miliutin, 10 May 1866, l. 37v.

38 Lavrentiev, "Ocherki," 292.

39 Lavrentiev, 297.

40 Lavrentiev, 296. See also Lavrentiev, "Po Nizhnemu Dunaiu."

41 Salaheddin, *La Turquie*.

42 Obruchev, *Voenno-statisticheskii sbornik*, 181.

43 Obruchev, 182. On the settlement of the Circassians in the eastern Balkans, see Pinson, "Ottoman Colonization"; and Karpat, *Ottoman Population*, 65–70.

44 Obruchev, *Voenno-statisticheskii sbornik*, 219.

45 In Neale's estimation, the number of Muslims in Danubian Bulgaria declined by some 100,000 people between 1847 and 1857, when it amounted to some 430,000 people. See Neale, "Province of Bulgaria," 147–8.

46 Obruchev, *Voenno-statisticheskii sbornik*, 220.

47 Meininger, *Bulgarian Exarchate*. On Ignatiev, see Khevrolina, *Rossiiskii diplomat*.

48 Airapetov, *Zabytaia kar'era*, 84.

49 Airapetov, 59–60, 67.

50 Airapetov, 73–4. On the Land and Freedom of the early 1860s, see Ely, *Russian Populism*, 103–4.

51 Iudin, *Soldat imperii*.

52 The verdict of the modern biographers of Obruchev and Dragomirov is quite straightforward in this respect. See Airapetov, *Zabytaia kariera*, 86; and Iudin, *Soldat imperii*.

53 R.A. Fadeev, *Vooruzhennye sily Rossii*, in *Sobranie sochinenii*, vol. 2, part 1, 6.

54 Fadeev, *Vooruzhennye sily*, 9.

55 Fadeev, 23–4.

56 Fadeev, 25.

57 Fadeev, 27.

58 Fadeev, "Russkoe obshchestvo v nastoiashchem i budushchem (Kem nam byt'?)," in *Sobranie sochinenii*, vol. 3, part 1, 127.

59 Fadeev, "Russkoe obshchestvo," 116.

60 Fadeev, 129–32.

61 Fadeev, 136.

62 On Russian pan-Slavism in this period, see B.H. Sumner, "Pan-Slavism," in *Russia and the Balkans*, 56–80; Kohn, *Pan-Slavism*; Fadner, *Seventy Years of Pan-Slavism*; and Petrovich, *Emergence of Russian Panslavism*.

63 On the eve of Russia's clash with Britain and France, Mikhail Pogodin sketched this nightmarish scenario in a letter to Countess Bludova, which was read by Nicholas I. See Pogodin, "K grafine Bludovoi, o nachavsheisia voine," 7 December 1853, in *Istoriko-politicheskie pis'ma i zapiski*, 78–80.

64 Danilevskii, *Rossiia i Evropa*, 437.

65 Danilevskii, 437.

66 R.A. Fadeev, "Mnenie o vostochnom voprose," in *Sobranie sochinenii*, vol. 2, part 2, 244.

67 Fadeev, "Mnenie," 277, 279.

68 Fadeev, 283–4.

69 Fadeev, 295–9. In the meantime, Austria would absorb Serbia, Bulgaria, and the Danubian principalities, which would open the prospect of the transformation of the Black Sea into "a German-Turkish lake."

70 Fadeev, 297, 301.

71 Fadeev, 302–3.

72 Fadeev, 293.

73 "Soobrazheniia ob oborone Rossii. Strategicheskaia zapiska," 19 January 1873, NIOR RGB, f. 169, karton 37, no. 4.

74 For the development of Bulgarian revolutionary movement and the April Uprising, see Crampton, *Bulgaria*, 81–93.

75 For a study of Russia's role in the Eastern Crisis from a diplomatic history perspective, see Sumner, *Russia and the Balkans*.

76 For the interaction between public opinion and tsarist foreign policy during the Eastern Crisis, see Geyer, *Russian Imperialism*, 65–86.

77 On the European liberal and radical hostility towards Russia on the eve of the Crimean War, see Malia, *Russia under Western* Eyes, 146–59. On liberal perspectives on the early Tanzimat, see Caquet, *Orient*.

78 See Seton-Watson, *Eastern Question*, 52–101. On the changes in the European attitude towards Russia in the post-Crimean period, see Malia, *Russia under Western Eyes*, 167–75.

79 Aydin, *Idea of the Muslim World*, 58–64.

80 On the Catherinian approach to Islam, see Fisher, "Enlightened Despotism"; Geraci, *Window on the East*, 21–5; and Crews, *For Prophet and Tsar*, 31–91.

81 Geraci, *Window on the East, passim*; Werth, *Margins of Orthodoxy*; and Crews, *For Prophet and Tsar*, esp. 192–240.

82 See Taki, *Tsar and Sultan*, 159–65.

83 Taki, "Konstantin Leontiev."

84 Miliutin, *Dnevnik*, 2:41.

85 Kishelskii, "Vremennyi proekt organizatsii Bolgarii za samostoiatel'nost' i svobodu zhizni," 30 January 1876, NIOR RGB, f. 327, karton 56, d. 14, l. 1.

86 Kishelskii, "Vremennyi proekt organizatsii Bolgarii," ll. 8v–9.

87 Kishelskii, ll. 11v–12.

88 Miliutin, *Dnevnik*, 2:41.

89 Miliutin, 2:50. In July 1786, the Russian government agreed to turn a blind eye to the shipments of ammunition to the Serbs. See Miliutin, 2:56.

90 T.N. Minkov to (Russian consul in Bucharest) D.F. Stuart, 29 October 1876, in Nikitin et al., *Osvobozhdenie Bolgarii*, 1:474.

91 See Kishelskii to Miliutin, 8 October 1876, in Nikitin et al., *Osvobozhdenie Bolgarii*, 1:444–8.

92 On Cherniaev, see MacKenzie, *Lion of Tashkent*.

93 MacKenzie, *Serbs and Russian Pan-Slavism*.

94 Miliutin, *Dnevnik*, 2:97.

95 Domontovich, *Osoboe pribavlenie*, 1:46.

96 Domontovich, 1:49.

97 Domontovich, 1:51–2.

98 Domontovich, 1:53–4.

99 Domontovich, 1:55.

100 Domontovich, 1:50.

101 Domontovich, 1:60–1.

102 Miliutin, *Dnevnik*, 2:36–37, 108.

103 Miliutin, 2:53–4.

104 R.A. Fadeev, "Bolgarskoe delo v Turetskoi voine," in Ovsianyi, *Bolgarskoe opol-chenie*, 103–16.

105 Fadeev, "Bolgarskoe delo," 103.

106 Fadeev, 107.

107 Fadeev, 107.

108 Fadeev, 108.

109 Fadeev, 109.

110 Fadeev, 110.

111 Fadeev, 110.

112 Fadeev, 111.

113 Fadeev, 111.

114 Fadeev, 112.

115 Fadeev, 112.

116 Miliutin, *Dnevnik*, 2:18.

117 Miliutin, 2:24.

118 Miliutin, 2:34.

119 Miliutin, 2:52.

120 Miliutin, 2:52.

121 Miliutin, 2:54.

122 Miliutin, 2:62.

123 Miliutin, 2:77.

124 See "Vyderzhka is litografirovannoi zapiski generala Obrucheva, sostavlennoi dlia Nikolaevskoi Akademii General'nogo Shtaba," in *Sbornik materialov po russko-turetskoi voine*, 9:1–37. Obruchev's memorandum can be dated by his reference to the upcoming connection of the railroad networks of Russia and Romania which occurred in 1875.

125 "Vyderzhka is litografirovannoi zapiski generala Obrucheva," 9–10.

126 "Vyderzhka is litografirovannoi zapiski generala Obrucheva," 18–21.

127 "Vyderzhka is litografirovannoi zapiski generala Obrucheva," 30.

128 "Vyderzhka is litografirovannoi zapiski generala Obrucheva," 31.

129 "Vyderzhka is litografirovannoi zapiski generala Obrucheva," 32.

130 Ignatiev, *Vzgliad na postepennoe izmenenie*, 14.

131 "Zapiska [I.P. Igantieva] o voennykh silakh i voennykh planakh Turtsii. Chernovik i Kopia," [after 1878], RGIA, f. 1561, op. 1, d. 36, l. 1.

132 Miliutin, *Dnevnik*, 2:61–2.

133 See "Perechen' dorog v Evropeiskoi Turtsii sniatykh v 1867 i 1869 gg. kapitanom Artamonovym," in *Sbornik materialov po Russko-turetskoi voine*, 9:37–8.

134 N.D. Artamonov, "Zapiska general'nogo shtaba polkovnika Artamonova o naivygodneishem v strategicheskom otnoshenii sposobe deistvii protiv turok," in Domontovich, *Osoboe pribavlenie*, 4:52–3.

135 Artamonov, "Zapiska," 40–1.
136 Artamonov, 58.
137 Artamonov, 59–64.
138 Miliutin, *Dnevnik*, 2:92–3.
139 N.N. Obruchev, "Sobstvennoruchnaia dokladnaia zapiska," 1 October 1876, in Gazenkampf, *Moi dnevnik*, appendix 1.
140 Obruchev, "Sobstvennoruchnaia dokladnaia zapiska," 2.
141 Obruchev, 3.
142 Obruchev, 4–5.
143 "Zapiska [I.P. Igantieva]," ll. 1v–2.
144 "Zapiska [I.P. Igantieva]," l. 2v.
145 "Zapiska [I.P. Igantieva]," l. 4v.
146 "Zapiska [I.P. Igantieva]," l. 6.
147 "Zapiska [I.P. Igantieva]," l. 6v.
148 "Zapiska [I.P. Igantieva]," ll. 7–7v.
149 N.N. Obruchev, "Soobrazheniia na sluchai voiny s Turtsiei vesnoi 1877 goda," in Gazenkampf, *Moi dnevnik*, appendix 4, 3–6.
150 Obruchev, "Soobrazheniia," 6–7.
151 Obruchev, 8.

6. Russian Population Policies during the War of 1877–1878

1 Sumner, *Russia and the Balkans*, 229–54.
2 On the Ottoman constitution of 1876, see Davison, *Reform in the Ottoman Empire*, 358–408.
3 Sumner, *Russia and the Balkans*, 273–89, esp. 284–6.
4 Jelavich, *Romanian Nation-State*, 241–59; and Cusco, *Contested Borderland*, 63–101.
5 See the exchange of letters between Nikolai Nikolaevich and Alexander II (who expressed his doubts) on 27 and 28 June 1877, in Domontovich, *Osoboe pribavlenie*, 3:20, 50–3.
6 The reports of Bobrikov and Parensov are published in Domontovich, vol. 5.
7 Levitskii, "Zapiska generala Levitskogo o plane kampanii," in Domontovich, 4:14–18.
8 Ovsianyi, *Russkoe upravlenie*, 1:6.
9 This formula was suggested by Cherkasskii himself. See Cherkasskii to D.A. Miliutin (Dokladnaia zapiska), 1 November 1876, which was incorporated into the official instructions to Cherkasskii issued at the moment of his appointment on 16 November 1876, in Ovsianyi, 1:157 and 162, respectively. On Cherkasskii, see Anuchin, "Kniaz' V.A. Cherkasskii," *Russkaia starina* 83, no. 2 (1895): 1–34.
10 In fact, this was the first point on the list of official instructions that Cherkasskii received on 16 November 1878 (in Ovsianyi, *Russkoe upravlenie*, 1:161).

11   See, for example, P.D. Parensov's data on the number of Christian and Muslim inhabitants of Rushchuk and the Rushchuk district, attached to Parensov's report to Nepokoichitskii of 17 April 1877, in Domontovich, *Osoboe pribavlenie*, 5:261.

12   In his activities, Sobolev could rely on an impressive Russian and Bulgarian staff that included a secretary (*deloproizvoditel'*) of the Asian Department of the Ministry of Foreign Affairs, Prince Shakhovskoi; Stoianov, former secretary of the Bulgarian exarchate; Brumov, former dragoman of the Russian Embassy in Constantinople; and the young Bulgarian Petr Slaveikov. See Cherkasskii to Nikolai Nikolaevich, 28 April 1877, in Nikitin et al., *Osvobozhdenie Bolgarii*, 2:57. Sobolev and his subordinates could use Russian consular archives in Bucharest as well as the assistance of the former Russian consul in Philippopolis, Naiden Gerov; vice-consul Daskalov; Krylov, secretary of the Ruschuk consulate; dragoman Elisityn; and supernumerary dragoman Kara-Mikholov. See Cherkasskii to Nikolai Nikolaevich, 4 May 1877, Kishinev, NIOR RGB, f. 327, karton 55, d. 1, l. 11v. Later, the commission also included Major Kuhelbecker; actual state councillors Gern and Lukianov; state councillor Tukholka; college councillors Ivaniukov and Ivanov; aulic councillor Zhemchiuzhin; titular councillors Kachenovskii and Teokharov; college councillor Drinevich; provincial secretaries Metz and Zografskii; and professors Bogshich, Lappe, and Bobchev.

13   *Materialy dlia izucheniia Bolgarii.*

14   Ubicini, *L'Empire Ottomane.*

15   Sobolev, "Narodonaselenie Bolgarii," in *Materialy dlia izucheniia Bolgarii*, 3:9.

16   Sobolev, 13n3.

17   "Dokladnaia zapiska V.A. Cherkasskogo voennomu ministru," in Ovsianyi, *Russkoe upravlenie*, 1:173.

18   "Dokladnaia zapiska V.A. Cherkasskogo," 181.

19   "Dokladnaia zapiska V.A. Cherkasskogo," 182.

20   Cherkasskii to Nepokoichitskii, 30 May 1877, in Ovsianyi, *Russkoe upravlenie*, 1:184–5. On the eve of the Russian passage of the Danube, Cherkasskii prepared "Soobrazheniia soobshchennye nachal'niku polevogo shtaba deistvuiuchei armii ob obshchem poradke razoruzheniia musul'manskogo naseleniia vo vsekh mestnostiakh nemedlenno vsled za zaniatiem ikh nashimi voiskami" (in Ovsianyi, 1:39).

21   Cherkasskii to Nepokoichitskii, 30 May 1877, 185–6. Cherkasskii excluded the searches in the houses of the Muslims as a means of requisition, for it would be tantamount to an attempt at their *sancta sanctorum*.

22   On the approval, see Nepokoichitskii to Cherkasskii, 3 June 1877, in Nikitin et al., *Osvobozhdenie Bolgarii*, 2:109.

23   See Tivchev's letter in Nikitin et al., 2:43–4.

24   Bulgarian population of Tulcha to the commander of the 37th division, V.N. Verevkin, 22 April 1877, in Nikitin et al., 2:48–9. One wonders what poet helped the Tulcha Bulgarians write their message to Verevkin.

25 Romanenko to Nepokoichitskii, 6 May 1877, in Nikitin et al., 2:64. For more reports of the Circassian attacks on Bulgarian villages during the war, see the reports of the Bulgarian militiaman Panaiot Khitov to N.D. Artamonov, 7 and 9 July 1877, and the diary of the 43rd infantry regiment of Okhotsk, in Nikitin et al., 2:160, 164, 424–5.

26 A.S. Romanenko to Nepokoichitskii, 6 May 1877, in Nikitin et al., 2:64.

27 See report of colonel of the General Staff N.D. Artomonov to Nepokoichitskii, 19 June 1877, in Nikitin et al., 2:130.

28 Before the Russian army crossed the Danube, Nikolai Nikolaevich dispatched the Ingush detachment of the Caucasian Cossack brigade (commanded by M.N. Skobelev) back to Russia because they were reportedly robbing the Romanian inhabitants and raping women, and "were highly unlikely to fight against the Turks." See M.A. Gazenkampf, "Zhurnal voennykh deistvii, vedennyi v polevom shtabe," 6 May 1877, in *Sbornik materialov po russko-turetskoi voine*, 2:76.

29 Parensov to Nepokoichitskii, 4 June 1877, in Nikitin et al., *Osvobozhdenie Bolgarii*, 2:110.

30 "Osnovaniia dlia organizatsii Bolgarskogo voiska," in Ovsianyi, *Bolgarskoe opolchenie*, 116.

31 "Osnovaniia dlia organizatsii Bolgarskogo voiska," 117.

32 "Osnovaniia dlia organizatsii Bolgarskogo voiska," 118.

33 F.L. Geiden to A.A. Nepokoichitskii, 21 April 1877, in Nikitin et al., *Osvobozhdenie Bolgarii*, 2:46.

34 Nepokoichitskii to Geiden, 30 April 1877, in Nikitin et al., 2:58.

35 Georgiev's viewpoint was communicated by Parensov to Levitskii in his report of 25 December 1876 (in Domontovich, *Osoboe pribavlenie*, 5:171–2).

36 See "Pravila o formirovanii Bolgarskogo oplcheniia nakhodiashchegosia v sostave Deistvuiushchei Armii," 5 April 1877, bearing the signature of Miliutin, in Ovsianyi, *Bolgarskoe opolchenie*, 125.

37 Rynkevich, "Zapiski," 56–7.

38 Ovsianyi, *Bolgarskoe opolchenie*, 17.

39 Anuchin, "Kniaz' V.A. Cherkasskii," *Russkaia starina*, no. 9 (1895): 75–8. See also "Otchet V.A. Cherkasskogo o vvedenii grazhdanskogo upravleniia v Bolgarii za 1877 g.," in Ovsianyi, *Russkoe upravlenie*, 1:252–3.

40 Gazenkampf, "Zhurnal voennykh deistvii," 21 June 1877, in *Sbornik materialov po russko-turetskoi voine*, 2:171. The same thing happened in Dobrogea that was occupied by the 14th Corps of Lieutenant General A.E. Tsimmerman. There, the local Christian inhabitants likewise used the entry of the Russian troops as an opportunity to plunder Muslim properties. According to the newly appointed governor of Tulcha, T.P. Iuzefovich, the local Christians, especially the Moldavians, resorted to arson to cover up their depredations. Iuzefovich reported the burning of several Turkish houses in the towns of Machin and Isakcha. See Iuzefovich to Cherkasskii, 31 July 1877, in Nikitin et al., *Osvobozhdenie Bolgarii*, 2:215.

41 See A.A. Nepokochitskii's order of 24 June 1877, published in Anuchin, "Kniaz' V. A. Cherkasskii," *Russkaia starina* 83, no. 9 (1895): 80.

42 See the proclamation of the commander-in-chief of 1 July 1877, in Ovsianyi, *Sbornik materialov*, 1:6–7.

43 Kisov, *Iz boevoi pokhodnoi zhizni*, 118.

44 Gazenkampf, "Zhurnal voennykh deistvii," 11 July 1877, in *Sbornik materialov po russko-turetskoi voine*, 2:251.

45 Immediately after the Sistova pogroms, the military authorities tried to pretend that the outbreaks were Cherkasskii's fault. The latter fought back, pointing to the failure of the military authorities to distribute in a timely fashion some 20,000 printed copies of the tsar's proclamation as well as the refusal of the commander-in-chief to place the officers and troops at his disposal for the exercise of the administrative and police functions.

46 Nepokoichitskii to Miliutin, 12 July 1877, cited in Anuchin, "Kniaz' V. A. Cherkasskii," *Russkaia starina* 83, no. 10 (1895): 26.

47 Cherkasskii to Miliutin, 13 July 1877, in Ovsianyi, *Russkoe upravlenie*, 1:211.

48 The presence of civilians among the Ottoman POWs is confirmed by the diary of the 63rd Uglich Infantry. See "Dnevnik 63-go pekh. Uglitskogo polka za voinu 1877–1878 gg.," in *Sbornik materialov po russko-turetskoi voine*, vol. 13, part 1, 30.

49 Miliutin to Cherkasskii, 15 July 1877, in Ovsianyi, *Russkoe upravlenie*, 1:274–5.

50 Miliutin to Cherkasskii, 18 July 1877, cited in Anuchin, "Kniaz' V. A. Cherkasskii," *Russkaia starina*, no. 10 (1895): 30.

51 "Zhurnal voennykh deistvii XIII armeiskogo korpusa," 5 July 1877, in *Sbornik materialov po russko-turetskoi voine*, 4:5.

52 "Dolkadnaia zapiska zaveduiushchego grazhdanskimi delami pri Glavnokomanduiuschem Desitvuiuschei armiei," 4 July 1877, Tyrnovo, in Nikitin et al., *Osvobozhdenie Bolgarii*, 2:154–6.

53 "Dolkadnaia zapiska," 155.

54 "Dolkadnaia zapiska," 155.

55 "Dolkadnaia zapiska," 156.

56 "Dolkadnaia zapiska," 156.

57 See Cherkasskii's messages to Nepokichitskii of 8, 12, and 14 July 1877, and NIOR RGB, f. 327, karton 55, d. 1, ll. 37–37v, 40–41v.

58 "Otchet V. A. Cherkasskogo o vvedenii grazhdanskogo upravleniia v Bolgarii za 1877 g.," in Ovsianyi, *Russkoe upravlenie*, 1:253–5.

59 Miliutin to Cherkasskii, 23 July 1877, in Nikitin et al., *Osvobozhdenie Bolgarii*, 2:194.

60 Gazenkampf, "Zhurnal voennykh deistvii," 2 July 1877, in *Sbornik materialov po russko-turetskoi voine*, 2:213. For reports of the successful disarmament of particular villages, see *Sbornik materialov po russko-turetskoi voine*, 2:175, 257.

61 There were multiple reports of Circassians and bashi-bazouks massacring (*rezat'*) the Bulgarians both to the north and to the south of the Balkans. See *Sbornik*

materialov po russko-turetskoi voine, 2:262, 276; and Kisov, *Iz boevoi pokhodnoi zhizni*, 105.

62 Kisov, *Iz boevoi pokhodnoi zhizni*, 108–9. See also Gazenkampf, "Zhurnal voennykh deistvii," 24 June 1877, in *Sbornik materialov po russko-turetskoi voine*, 2:181. For other cases of refusal of the Muslim inhabitants to put down arms, see *Sbornik materialov po russko-turetskoi voine*, 2:223.

63 As happened at Lovcha, which was recaptured by the Ottoman troops with the support of its armed Muslim inhabitants in mid-July. See Gazenkampf, "Zhurnal voennykh deistvii," 16 July 1877, in *Sbornik materialov po russko-turetskoi voine*, 2:284.

64 Gazenkampf, "Zhurnal voennykh deistvii," 26 and 30 June 1877, in *Sbornik materialov po russko-turetskoi voine*, 2:188, 206.

65 "Zhurnal voennykh deistvii XIII armeiskogo korpusa," 5 July 1877, in *Sbornik materialov po russko-turetskoi voine*, 4:5, 13.

66 "Zhurnal voennykh deistvii XIII armeiskogo korpusa," 17–18.

67 "Zhurnal voennykh deistvii XIII armeiskogo korpusa," 21.

68 F.M. Depreradovich, who crossed the Balkans with Gurko's detachment, reported numerous horse- and oxen-driven carts that were taking the Turkish inhabitants of Kazanlyk to Ottoman-controlled areas. See Depreradovich, *Iz vospominanii*, 43.

69 Anuchin, "Kniaz' V. A. Cherkasskii," *Russkaia starina* 84, no. 12 (1895): 4.

70 Chichagov, "Peredovoi otriad," *Voennyi sbornik*, no. 10 (1878): 344–5.

71 Gazenkampf, "Zhurnal voennykh deistvii," 16 July 1877, in *Sbornik materialov po russko-turetskoi voine*, 2:283.

72 For a brief recent discussion of the situation in Eski Zagra in the summer of 1877, see Methodieva, *Between Empire and Nation*, 24–5.

73 According to Ovsianyi, Christians comprised three-quarters of the population of Eski Zagra. See Ovsianyi, *Bolgarskoe opolchenie*, 26.

74 Kisov, *Iz boevoi pokhodnoi zhizni*, 138–9.

75 Depreradovich, *Iz vospominanii*, 38.

76 See their message in Kisov, *Iz boevoi pokhodnoi zhizni*, 140–1.

77 Kisov, 148–50.

78 See the letter of the chief of staff of the Eski Zagra detachment, A.A. Freze, to the chief of staff of the Vanguard detachment, D.S. Naglovskii, 15 July 1877, in Nikitin et al., *Osvobozhdenie Bolgarii*, 2:179. See also Depreradovich, *Iz vospominanii*, 45.

79 Depreradovich, *Iz vospominanii*, 66.

80 Freze to Naglovskii, 15 July 1877, 179.

81 Depreradovich, *Iz vospominanii*, 61, 64; Kisov, *Iz boevoi pokhodnoi zhizni*, 154–6. See also Freze to Naglovski, 15 July 1877, 179.

82 Freze to Naglovski, 15 July 1877, 179. See also Depreradovich, *Iz vospominanii*, 67, 72.

83 Depreradovich, *Iz vospominanii*, 54.

84 Depreradovich, 95, 101–2.

85 Kisov, *Iz boevoi pokhodnoi zhizni*, 191–3; and Ovsianyi, *Bolgarskoe opolchenie*, 29.

86 Gazenkampf, "Zhurnal voennykh deistvii," 16 July 1877, in *Sbornik materialov po russko-turetskoi voine*, 2:284.

87 See Anuchin, "Kniaz' V. A. Cherkasskii," *Russkaia starina* 84, no. 12 (1895): 31–2. See also V. Bogdanov to N. Gerov, 23 August 1877 and 20 September 1877, in Nikitin et al., *Osvobozhdenie Bolgarii*, 2:246–7, 281–2.

88 Cherkasskii to Miliutin, 20 July 1877, cited in Anuchin, "Kniaz' V. A. Cherkasskii," *Ruskaia starina* 84, no. 10 (1895): 31–2.

89 Cited in Shilder, "Plevnenskoe sidenie," 217. For criticism of Gurko's expedition from a military point of view, see Zotov, "Voina 1877 g.," *Russkaia starina* 49, no. 2 (1886): 433.

90 Gurko to Nikolai Nikolaevich, 16 July 1877, cited in Gazenkampf, "Zhurnal voennykh deistvii," 16 July 1877, in *Sbornik materialov po russko-turetskoi voine*, 2:282.

91 Ovsianyi, *Russkoe upravlenie*, 1:54.

92 Ovsianyi, 1:55. Depreradovich reports seeing the burning Muslim villages on his way to Kazanlyk, which his Bulgarian guide attributed to the Russian troops (Depreradovich, *Iz vospominanii*, 39). By contrast, Depreradovich himself was inclined to attribute the arson to the Bulgarians, who were "imbued with a sentiment of revenge and boundless hatred towards the Turks" (Depreradovich, 39).

93 Ovsianyi, *Russkoe upravlenie*, 1:56. In October 1877, Cherkasskii estimated the number of refugees at 100,000 (Ovsianyi, 1:189). Elsewhere, Ovsianyi estimates the number of Bulgarian refugees that followed the retreat of Gurko's detachment from beyond the Balkans at 200,000–250,000 (Ovsianyi, *Bolgarskoe oplchenie*, 31). See also Kisov, *Iz boevoi pokhodnoi zhizni*, 207.

94 Ovsianyi, *Bolgarskoe oplchenie*, 62.

95 See Cherkasskii's message to Nikolai Nikolaevich of 22 July 1877, his order to (interim governor of Tyrnovo) M.A. Domontovich of 24 July 1877, and his report to Miliutin of 25 July 1877, in Nikitin et al., *Osvobozhdenie Bolgarii*, 2:192, 195–7; Dometti, "Kratkaia zapiska o polozhenii zabalkanskikh bolgar-begletsov," 13 September 1877, in Ovsianyi, *Russkoe upravlenie*, 1:317.

96 Cherkasskii to Nepokoichitskii, 29 June 1877, NIOR RGB, f. 327, karton 55, d. 1, l. 28.

97 See "Dokladnaia zapiska V.A. Cherkasskogo Nikolaiu Nikolaevichu," 3 November 1877, and Cherkasskii's circular to the governors, 4 November 1877, in Nikitin et al., *Osvobozhdenie Bolgarii*, 2:319–21.

98 Iuzefovich to Cherkasskii, 31 July 1877, in Nikitin et al., *Osvobozhdenie Bolgarii*, 2:216.

99 See Cherkasskii, "Dolkadnaia zapiska," in Nikitin et al., 2:156; Militin to Cherkasskii, 23 July 1877, in Nikitin et al., 2:194; and Ovsianyi, *Russkoe upravlenie*, 1:52–3.

100 "Otchet V.A. Cherkasskogo o vvedenii grazhdanskogo upravleniia v Bolgarii za 1877 g.," in Ovsianyi, *Russkoe upravlenie*, 1:243.

101 See the telegram of Nikolai Nikolaevich on 22 October 1877, *Russkaia starina*, no. 2 (1896): 313.

102 Konobeev, *Russko-bolgarskoe boevoe sodruzhestvo*, 49.

103 Ulunian, "O formirovanii bolgarskikh chet."

104 N.D. Artamonov to Nepokoichitskii, no earlier than 11 August 1877, in Nikitin et al., *Osvobozhdenie Bolgarii*, 2:232. The head of Nikolai Nikolaevich's diplomatic chancellery, former Russian consul in Macedonia M.A. Khitrovo, likewise came forward with a plan of organization of *chetas*. See D.K. Girs to I.S. Aksakov, 14 September 1877, OR RNB, f. 14, op. 1, d. 113, ll. 1–2.

105 Cherkasskii to Nepokoichitskii, 21 August 1877, in Nikitin et al., *Osvobozhdenie Bolgarii*, 2:244.

106 Artamonov to Nepokoichitskii, in Nikitin et al., 2:233n2.

107 The allied Romanian troops occupied Nikopol in accordance with the agreement between Nikolai Nikolaevich and the Romanian Prince Carol.

108 Stolypin to Cherkasskii, n.d., NIOR RGB, f. 327, karton 55, d. 23, ll. 37, 38.

109 Stolypin to Cherkasskii, n.d., l. 37v.

110 Iuzefovich to Cherkasskii, 31 July 1877, Nikitin et al., *Osvobozhdenie Bolgarii*, 2:213.

111 See their address to Cherkasskii of 23 September 1877, and Belotserkovets to Cherkasskii, in NIOR RGB, f. 327, karton 55, d. 23, ll. 31–33v, 42–49v.

112 Stoletov to Aksakov, 10 November 1877, OR RNB, f. 14, op. 1, d. 441, l. 89.

113 See, for example, the protocol of the assembly of the inhabitants of Drianov on the election of the members of the municipal police, 11 August 1877, in Nikitin et al., *Osvobozhdenie Bolgarii*, 2:233.

114 Stolypin to Cherkasskii, n.d., ll. 37, 38.

115 N.P. Ignatiev to E.L. Ignatieva, 14 August 1877, Nikitin et al., *Osvonbozhdenie Bolgarii*, 2:235–6.

116 Depreradovich, *Iz vospominanii*, 31–2, 40; and Vereshchagin, *Skobelev*, 149–50.

117 Gazenkampf, "Zhurnal voennykh deistvii," 10 October 1877, in *Sbornik materialov po russko-turetskoi voine*, 2:435.

118 After the fall of Plevna, the Russian command had to take care of the tens of thousands of Ottoman POWs. Kept in the open field near the Vid River, most of them died over the following couple of days from hunger, untreated wounds, and exposure. Although Nepokoichitskii issued detailed instructions on the feeding and medical treatment of the Ottoman POWs, and their convoying to Romania, these came only two days after the Ottoman surrender (28 November). See Nepokoichitskii to the chief of staff of the forces besieging Plevna, Prince A.I. Imeretinskii, 30 November 1877, in *Sbornik materialov po russko-turetskoi voine*, 68:10–11. The convoying of the Ottoman POWs was further delayed by the slowness of the commander of the Romanian forces at Plevna, Brigadier General Alexandru Cernat, to assign a Romanian division for that purpose. See Major General A.I. Manykin-Nevstruev (Russian representative at the headquarters of the Romanian

Prince Carol I) to Imeretinskii, 30 November 1877, 1:00 p.m., in *Sbornik materia-lov po russko-turetskoi voine*, 68:11–12. As a result, by the evening of 30 November, the commander of the 16th Infantry, Lieutenant General M.I. Skobelev, wrote to Imeretinskii about the "terrible situation" of the Ottoman POWs. "Unless the most urgent measures are taken to feed and, especially, evacuate the POWS," wrote Skobelev, "we will earn here a shame that we will never be able to wipe off before History by any justifications." See Skobelev to Imeretinskii, 30 November 1877, 9:00 p.m., in *Sbornik materialov po russko-turetskoi voine*, 68:12–13. Subsequent dispatch of physicians and medical personnel from different Russian units to treat the wounded Ottoman POWs could not compensate for the consequences of the initial delay. See *Sbornik materialov po russko-turetskoi voine*, 68:17, 25. The convoying of the POWs to Bucharest by the Russian 3rd Grenadier Division began only on 6 December, at which point there remained some 9,000 prisoners under Russian guard. See Manykin-Nevstruev to the commander of the 3rd Grenadier Division, 5 December 1878, in *Sbornik materialov po russko-turetskoi voine*, 68:56. The Romanian division that was supposed to convoy another 9,000 POWs arrived even later. See Manykin-Nevstruev to the commander of the 3rd Grenadier Division, 9 December 1878, in *Sbornik materialov po russko-turetskoi voine*, 68:73.

119   See the report from Major Orlinskii of the Fourth Mariupol' Hussar regiment from Dudnitsa to the commander of the 4th Cavalry Division, General Arnoldi, 1 January 1878, and the latter's authorization to "arm the reliable Bulgarians," in *Sbornik materialov po russko-turetskoi voine*, 69:18, 40. See also Bers, *Vospomina-niia*, 66.

120   See the report from the commander of the 4th Kharkov Ulan Regimen, Colonel Ertel, to the commander of the 4th Cavalry Division, Major General Arnoldi, of 3 December 1877, that he had created a unit of thirty Bulgarians, who had repeatedly proved their loyalty, and armed them with the weapons taken from the Turks (in *Sbornik materialov po russko-turetskoi voine*, 68:94). See also Cornet Miller of the Lifeguard Dragoon regiment to the commander of the regiment, Colonel K.K. Lants, 5 January 1878, in *Sbornik materialov po russko-turetskoi voine*, 69:18, 146–7. See also the report of Major General P.S. Laskarev to Gurko on the actions of the 9th Cavalry Division, 10 January 1877, in *Sbornik materialov po russko-turetskoi voine*, 71:5.

121   According to Konobeev, the Bulgarian inhabitants of Eastern Rumelia collected some 8,000 rifles from the fallen soldiers on the border of the Rhodope region. See Konobeev, *Russko-bolgarskoe boevoe sodruzhestvo*, 57. On the activities of Slaveikov in the reorganization of the Eski Zagra militia see, Depreradovich, *Iz vospominanii*, 67, 71.

122   Konobeev, *Russko-bolgarskoe boevoe sodruzhestvo*, 59.

123   Bers, *Vospominaniia*, 64.

124   The Muslim inhabitants fled immediately after the Russian troops crossed the Balkans. See the reports of Colonel A.Ia. Nagibin of the 9th Don Cossack Regiment

to Skobelev, 1 January 1878, as well as the reports of Colonel A.V. Kuteinikov, of the 1st Don Cossack Regiment, and Major General A.P. Strukov, of the Life Guards Ulan Regiment, to the commander of the 1st Cavalry Division, M.N. Dokhturov, of 1 and 2 January 1878, respectively, in *Sbornik materialov po russ-ko-turetskoi voine*, 74:7, 8, 19. Several days later, the Muslims of Slivno, Yambol, and the neighbouring villages likewise fled to Adrianople. See Head-Captain Sliusarev to Nikolai Nikolaevich, 4 January 1878, in *Sbornik materialov po russ-ko-turetskoi voine*, 74:48. On Bulgarian robberies after the arrival of the Russian troops, see the Commander of the 31st Infantry Division, Lieutenant General Veliaminov, to Gurko, Tatar Bazardzhik, 2 January 1878, in *Sbornik materialov po russko-turetskoi voine*, 69:19. See also Methodieva, *Between Empire and Nation*, 25–6.

125 The consuls of France, Britain, Austria-Hungary, and Greece to Gurko, 5 January 1878, in *Sbornik materialov po russko-turetskoi voine*, 69:135. Foreign consuls were concerned not only with the fate of the Muslim population of Philippop-olis, but also with the Bulgarian attacks on the Greeks and their properties. The commander of the 3rd Infantry Division, Lieutenant General Dandevil, likewise reported that after his entry into Stanimaki, the local Bulgarians began to rob the Greeks (although he, remarkably, added: "and vice versa"). See Dandevil to Na-glovskii, 7 January 1878, in *Sbornik materialov po russko-turetskoi voine*, 69:269. Dandevil decried the lack of cavalry assigned to mounted patrols that would be able to promptly respond to the reports of robbery.

126 The commander of the 1st Brigade of the 2nd Guards Cavalry Division, Major General Brok, to Colonel Balts, the chief of staff of the detachment of Adjutant General P.A. Shuvalov, 5 January 1878, in *Sbornik materialov po russko-turetskoi voine*, 68:139.

127 Nikolai Nikolaevich to Alexander II, 31 January 1878, in Domontovich, *Osoboe pribavlenie*, 3:62.

128 Vereshchagin, *Skobelev*, 310.

129 See Veliaminov's report on the actions of his detachment from 25 December 1877 to 5 January 1878, in *Sbornik materialov po russko-turetskoi voine*, 69:195–6.

130 Captain Nord to the commander of the 2nd Brigade of the Second Lifeguard Cavalry Division, 7 January 1878, in *Sbornik materialov po russko-turetskoi voine*, 69:283. See also Kisov, *Iz boevoi pokhodnoi zhini*, 432–3.

131 Captain Mezentsev of the 4th Mariupol' Hussar regiment to the commander of the 4th Cavalry Division, Major General Arnoldi, 30 November 1877, in *Sbornik materialov po russko-turetskoi voine*, 68:14. For similar complaints from the Bulgarians of the Belgradchik region about the atrocities of Circassians, see the report from Arnoldi to Nikolai Nikolaevich of 20 December 1877, in *Sbornik ma-terialov po russko-turetskoi voine*, 68:117.

132 Iu. Sosnovskii, chief of staff of the 3rd Infantry Division, to Levitskii, 5 January 1878, in *Sbornik materialov po russko-turetskoi voine*, 69:230.

133 See the report from the commander of special detachment of the 8th Corps, Colonel E.V. Zhirzhinskii, to the commander of the 8th Corps, F.F. Radetskii, 5 January 1878, and from Head Captain Sliusarev to the commander-in-chief, 6 January 1878, in *Sbornik materialov po russko-turetskoi voine*, 74:74, 80.

134 Dandevil to Naglovskii, 7 January 1878, in *Sbornik materialov po russko-turetskoi voine*, 69:268.

135 "Dnevnik 63-go pekh. Uglitskogo polka za voinu 1877–1878 gg.," in *Sbornik materialov po russko-turetskoi voine*, vol. 13, part 1, 53.

136 Bunakov to Naglovskii, 7 January 1878, in *Sbornik materialov po russko-turetskoi voine*, 69:270.

137 Skobelev to Nepokoichitskii, 5 January 1878, in *Sbornik materialov po russko-turetskoi voine*, 74:63.

138 Colonel Rozhnov to Stolypin, military governor of Philippopolis, 10 January 1878, in *Sbornik materialov po russko-turetskoi voine*, 71:24.

139 As in Danubian Bulgaria, the Russians pursued the policy of disarmament of the Muslim population, yet here again, its success was limited, since the Muslims would hide the best weapons and hand over only the old and broken ones. See Kisov, *Iz boevoi pokhdnoi zhini*, 432–3. On disarmament in Adrianople, see Vereshshagin, *Skobelev*, 312.

140 Vereshchagin, *Skobelev*, 312.

141 Nikolai Nikolaevich to Alexander II, 31 January 1878, in Domontovich, *Osoboe pribavlenie*, 3:62. On the Bulgarian attacks on the Muslim wagon trains, see Gurko to Nikolai Nikolaevich, 13 January 1878, in *Sbornik materialov po russko-turetskoi voine*, 71:47.

142 Gurko spoke of "a huge caravan of the refugees of an entire province." See Gurko to Nikolai Nikolaevich, 13 January 1878, 47.

143 A mullah captured by the unites of the 2nd Guards Cavalry Division with one of the wagon trains reported the orders from the Ottoman command to the Muslim inhabitants to retreat to Adrianople with the intention of assembling everyone there, arming them, and organizing a holy war. See chief of staff of the 2nd Guards Cavalry Division to Naglovskii, 7 January 1878, in *Sbornik materialov po russko-turetskoi voine*, 69:270.

144 Head captain of the Lifeguard Dragoon Regiment Zdanovich reported to the commander of his regiment about a mass of abandoned wagon trains with women and children along the entire highway between Derbent and Gvendekli. Zdanovich invited the refugees to return to their homes on the condition that they surrender their weapons, but had little success. See report, 5 January 1878, in *Sbornik materialov po russko-turetskoi voine*, 69:145.

145 For example, one can only guess at the number of casualties resulting from the attack by the 1st Life Guard Dragoon regiment of Major General A.P. Strukov on the railway station and bridge across the Maritsa River near the village of Semenli, in the course of which the Russian dragoons "broke through some 5,000

… Turkish refugees from Kazanlyk and Eski Zagra, who crowded the village." See Strukov's undated note and his report to Skobelev of 4 January 1878, in *Sbornik materialov po russko-turetskoi voine*, 74:46, 52.

146 "Dnevnik 63-go pekh. Uglitskogo polka za voinu 1877–1878 gg.," in *Sbornik materialov po russko-turetskoi voine*, vol. 13, part 1, 52; and Vereshchagin, *Skobelev*, 291–2.

147 "Dnevnik 63-go pekh. Uglitskogo polka," 52.

148 Vereshchagin, *Skobelev*, 292. One wonders how shocked Skobelev really was in view of his prior and subsequent actions in Central Asia. During the Russian conquest of the Kokand Khanate in 1875–6, Skobelev severely punished the inhabitants of Namangan, after an attack on the Russian garrison of this town that took place in his absence. Upon the capture of the Geoktepe fortress in 1881, Skobelev's dragoons and Cossacks were similarly indiscriminate in their pursuit of the escaping defenders.

149 Strukov to Skobelev, 6 January 1878, in *Sbornik materialov po russko-turetskoi voine*, 74:86–7.

150 See the chief of staff of the 2nd Guards Cavalry Division, Colonel Bunakov, to Gurko's chief of staff, Major General Naglovskii, 3 January 1878, in *Sbornik materialov po russko-turetskoi voine*, 69:45.

151 See the report on the actions of the 2nd Brigade of the 2nd Cavalry Division from 31 December 1877 to 3 January 1878, in *Sbornik materialov po russko-turetskoi voine*, 69:72.

152 See the report of the commander of the 2nd Cavalry Division, Major General Klot, about the operation near Philippopolis from 2 to 5 January 1878, in *Sbornik materialov po russko-turetskoi voine*, 69:213.

153 Chief of staff of the 2nd Guards Cavalry Division Bunakov to Naglovskii, 7 January 1878, in *Sbornik materialov po russko-turetskoi voine*, 69:269.

154 See the report from Colonel Ershov of the Hussar Lifeguards Regiment, as well as those of Cornet Mankovskii and Captain Bastruev of the Ulan Life Guards Regiment to the commander of the 2nd Brigade of the 2nd Guards Cavalry Division, Major General S.P. Etter, of 2 and 4 January 1878, in *Sbornik materialov po russko-turetskoi voine*, 69:37–8, 96–100. The Russians responded by taking hostages, and declaring that the hostages would be killed and the villages burned down if the shooting continued. For a similar incident that took place several days previously at the village of Banja in the environs of Samokov, see also the report on the actions of the Lifeguard Finland Regiment from 29 December to 6 January 1878, in *Sbornik materialov po russko-turetskoi voine*, 69:259.

155 Nemirovich-Danchenko, *God voiny*, 2:184.

156 Nemirovich-Danchenko, 2:179–80.

157 Nemirovich-Danchenko, 181–2.

158 On Bulgarian nationalism during the period of the Bulgarian national revival (1830–78), see Naxidou, "Differing Perceptions." See also Pundeff, "Bulgarian Nationalism."

159   Vereshchagin, *Skobelev*, 192.

160   Nemirovich-Danchenko, *God voiny*, 2:177–8.

161   Rozhnov to Naglovskii, 7 January 1878, in *Sbornik materialov po russko-turetskoi voine*, 69:273. The behaviour of the Russian troops following the conclusion of the armistice in January 1878 was likewise different from the conduct of their ancestors half a century earlier. According to Vereshchagin, the Russian soldiers plundered the Muslim houses at Hermanli, to which some officers turned a blind eye. See Vereshchagin, *Skobelev*, 289.

162   On the San Stefano treaty, see Sumner, *Russia and the Balkans*, 399–424.

163   Ovsianyi, *Russkoe upravlenie*, 1:23. A veteran of the war, Ovsianyi served as the governor of Kustendil in 1878–9.

164   In an attempt to justify the San Stefano treaty before the Austrians, Ignatiev argued that "a big Slavic state" referred to an augmented Serbia or Montenegro (both of which became independent states as a result of San Stefano), but not to Bulgaria, which formally remained an *autonomous principality* within the Ottoman Empire. See Sumner, *Russia and the Balkans*, 450.

165   "Dokladnaia zapiska V.A. Cherkasskogo voennomu ministru," Ploesti, in Ovsianyi, *Russkoie upravlenie*, 1:175.

166   "Dokladnaia zapiska V.A. Cherkasskogo," 176.

167   "Dokladnaia zapiska V.A. Cherkasskogo," 177. By "Bosnian Serbs," Cherkasskii meant Bosniaks.

168   "Dokladnaia zapiska V.A. Cherkasskogo," 177.

169   The principality would receive the lands of the emigrants. See "Dokladnaia zapiska V.A. Cherkasskogo," 178.

170   "Dokladnaia zapiska general-leitenanta Anuchina," in Ovsianyi, *Russkoe upravlenie*, 1:195.

171   "Dokladnaia zapiska general-leitenanta Anuchina," 196–7.

172   "O vvedenii upravitel'nykh sovetov v Filippopol'skom sandjake," in Ovsianyi, *Russkoe upravlenie*, 1:290–1.

173   "O vvedenii upravitel'nykh sovetov," 296.

174   "O vvedenii upravitel'nykh sovetov," 293–4.

175   "O vvedenii upravitel'nykh sovetov," 295–6.

176   "O vvedenii upravitel'nykh sovetov," 300.

177   See the circular of the acting governor of Slivno, L.I. Iliashevich, to the head of the Lule Burgas and Bunar-Gissar districts, N.R. Ovsianyi, 6 March 1878, Kazanlyk, in Nikitin et al., *Osvobozhdenie Bolgarii*, 3:41.

7. Population Policies after the War

1   See, most recently, Rekun, *Empire Unguided*.

2   On the phenomenon of Balkan irredentism, see Victor Roudometof, "The Articulation of Irredentism in Balkan Politics, 1880–1920," in *Nationalism,*

Globalization, and Orthodoxy, 157–79. For a recent discussion of the Macedonian question, see Tokay, "Macedonian Question." For the activities of irredentist nationalist groups in Macedonia, see Yosmaoğlu, *Blood Ties*, esp. 25–36, 39–41; and Karakasidou, *Fields of Wheat*, 77–107. For Russia's effort to contain rival nationalisms in Macedonia, see Vovchenko, *Containing Balkan Nationalisms*, 243–66.

3 For the most eloquent expression of the disappointment of the Russian pan-Slavists, see Danilevskii, *Woe to the Victors!*, 117–86. See also Geyer, *Russian Imperialism*, 82. On the Berlin Congress, see Sumner, *Russia and the Balkans*, 501–53; and Medlicott, *Congress of Berlin*.

4 Despite Romania's opposition, Russia managed to regain Southern Bessarabia and access to the Lower Danube (which it had given over to the Moldavian principality after the Crimean War), and Bucharest eventually accepted northern Dobrogea as compensation.

5 Treaty of San Stefano, article 7, in Ovsianyi, *Russkoe upravlenie*, 2:177. Cf. Treaty of Berlin, article 4, 1 July 1878, in Ovsianyi, 2:193. See also "Obshchaia instruktsiia kniaziu Dondukovu-Korsakovu," 10 April 1878, in Ovsianyi, *Sbornik materialov*, 3:272.

6 Treaty of San Stefano, article 8, in Ovsianyi, *Russkoe upravlenie*, 2:179–80. This clause became article 12 of the Treaty of Berlin (see Ovsianyi, 2:196). See also "Obshchaia instruktsiia kniaziu Dondukovu-Korsakovu," 273.

7 Treaty of Berlin, article 5, in Ovsianyi, *Russkoe upravlenie*, 2:193.

8 Treaty of Berlin, article 5, in Ovsianyi, 2:194. See also "Dopolnitel'naia instruktsiia kniaziu Dondukovu-Korsakovu," 24 July 1878, in Ovsianyi, *Sbornik materialov*, 3:293–4.

9 Marin Drinov, "Zapiska o deiatel'noti vremennago russkago upravleniia v Bolgarii," in Ovsianyi, *Russkoe upravlenie*, 2:230.

10 Ovsianyi, 2:112.

11 A modern biography of Dondukov-Korsakov remains to be written. See Volkonskii, *Biografiia*.

12 On Dondukov-Korsakov's policy with regard to the Ukrainophiles, see Miller, *Ukrainian Question*, 155–78.

13 See "Obshchaia instrucktsiia kniaziu Dondukovu-Korsakovu," 10 April 1878, in Ovsianyi, *Sbornik materialov*, 3:269. Alexander II appointed Dondukov-Korsakov "on the same basis" as P.D. Kiselev, who had served as the head of the Russian provisional administration in Moldavia and Wallachia in 1829–34. See Alexander II to Nikolai Nikolaevich, 28 January 1878, in Domontovich, *Osoboe pribavlenie*, 3:28.

14 On Totleben, see Shilder, *Graf Eduard Ivanovich Totleben*.

15 The following account discusses the Russian perception of Muslim resistance in the Rhodope and the measures that the Russian authorities took to overcome it. I do not attempt to offer a definitive history of the Rhodope Uprising, just as I do not attempt to offer a comprehensive account of the Russian-Ottoman war, the Eastern Crisis, or the nineteenth-century history of the Balkans more broadly. At

the same time, it is quite evident to me that a more or less complete picture of the Rhodope Uprising could emerge only if interpretations based on British sources (e.g., Turan, "Rhodope Resistance") are supplemented with those based on Russian sources.

16 Ovsianyi estimates their number at 10,000. See Ovsianyi, *Russkoe upravlenie*, 2:146. The early stages of the formation of the Rhodope insurgency were attested by Colonel Rozhnov of the Life Guards Lithuanian regiment, who was left in Tatar Bazardzhik with 200 soldiers to guard some 700 Ottoman POWs. According to Rozhnov, the Muslims of Tatar Bazardzhik, who fled to the mountains at the approach of the Russian troops, soon joined forces with the armed inhabitants of the neighbouring Muslim villages, as well as groups of bashi-bazouks and Circassians, all totalling some 5,000 people, and began to descend on neighbouring Bulgarian villages. See Rozhnov to Naglovskii, 7 January 1878, in *Sbornik materialov po russko-turetskoi voine*, 69:273. See also the report of the commander of the 9th Cavalry Division, Major General P.S. Laskarev, to Gurko, 10 January 1877, in *Sbornik materialov po russko-turetskoi voine*, 71:6.

17 "Zapiska o khode Rodopskogo vosstaniia i mery priniatye dlia podavleniia besporiadkov," in Ovsianyi, *Sbornik materialov*, 5:319–20. The memorandum was part of Totleben's final report as commander-in-chief.

18 "Zapiska o khode Rodopskogo vosstaniia," 321.

19 "Zapiska o khode Rodopskogo vosstaniia," 322–3.

20 "Zapiska o khode Rodopskogo vosstaniia," 324–5.

21 "Zapiska o khode Rodopskogo vosstaniia," 337.

22 "Zapiska o khode Rodopskogo vosstaniia," 327.

23 Totleben to Alexander II, 17 May 1878, in Domontovich, *Osoboe pribavlenie*, 3:103–4.

24 Totleben to Alexander II, 25 May 1878, in Domontovich, 3:111.

25 "Soobrazheniia ob obshchem plane deistvii deistvuiushchei armii i o kooperatsii s Serbiei," 1 June 1878, in Domontovich, 3:112.

26 "Soobrazheniia ob obshchem plane deistvii," 126.

27 Totleben to Miliutin, 5 September 1878, in Ovsianyi, *Sbornik materialov*, 4:1.

28 Dondukov-Korsakov's chief of staff, L.A. Iunakov, to the commanders of the advance detachments, no later than 11 June 1878, in Nikitin et al., *Osvobozhdenie Bolgarii*, 3:155.

29 Dondukov-Korsakov to Miliutin, 8 July 1878, in Ovsianyi, *Sbornik materialov*, 3:3.

30 Totleben to Alexander II, 10 August 1878, in Domontovich, *Osoboe pribavlenie*, 3:153.

31 Head of the Department of the Interior P.A. Gresser to the Philippopolis governor, O.K. Gubsh fon Grostel (Justus Hubsch von Grossteil), 3 October 1878, in Nikitin et al., *Osvobozhdenie Bolgarii*, 3:250–1.

32 "Programma rabot Evropeiskoi komissii v Rodope," in Ovsianyi, *Sbornik materialov*, 5:160–1.

33 Lobanov-Rostovskii to Dondukov-Korsakov, 5 July 1878, in Ovsianyi, 5:158. See also Lobanov-Rostovskii to Gorchakov, 10/22 July 1878, in Ovsianyi, 5:163.

34 See Bazili to Lobanov-Rostovskii, 9/21 July 1878, in Ovsianyi, 5:173–9. Later, Bazili's suspicions were at least partly confirmed by the *Times* correspondent Mackenzie Wallace. See Russian consul in Philippopolis A.I. Tseretelev to Girs, 25 December 1878 / 6 January 1879, in Nikitin et al., *Osvobozhdenie Bolgarii*, 3:371.

35 Totleben to Alexander II, 20 August 1878, in Domontovich, *Osoboe pribavlenie*, 3:157.

36 The relevant excerpt from the protocol of the Congress was communicated by Lobanov-Rostovskii to Dondukov-Korsakov on 13/25 July 1878 (in Ovsianyi, *Sbornik materialov*, 5:171–3).

37 "Nota prigotovlennaia mezhdunarodnoi Rohodpskoi Komissii Imperatorskim Komissarom," in Ovsianyi, 5:157.

38 Dondukov-Korsakov to Miliutin, 14 August 1878, in Ovsianyi, 5:42.

39 Dondukov-Korsakov to Lobanov-Rostovskii, 12 July 1878, in Nikitin et al., *Osvobozhdenie Bolgarii*, 3:168–9.

40 Dondukov-Korsakov to Lobanov-Rostovskii, 16 July 1878, in Ovsianyi, *Sbornik materialov*, 5:180–1.

41 Totleben to Alexander II, 20 August 1878, in Domontovich, *Osoboe pribavlenie*, 3:158.

42 Totleben to Alexander II, 20 August 1878, 159.

43 Totleben to Alexander II, 20 August 1878, 160–1.

44 Totleben to Alexander II, 20 August 1878, 162.

45 See Totleben to Alexander II, 2 September 1878, and the tsar's approval of Totleben's actions, dated 6 September 1878, in Domontovich, *Osoboe pribavlenie*, 3:168–9 and 173–4, respectively.

46 See "Zapiska o polednikh sobytiakh v gorakh," attached to Totleben's letter to Alexander II of 27 October 1878, in Domontovich, 3:200–1.

47 "Zapiska o polednikh sobytiakh v gorakh," 201.

48 See Totleben's order to the troops and his report to Alexander II of 3 November 1878, in Domontovich, *Osoboe pribavlenie*, 3:207–9.

49 On this incident, see Stolypin to Lobanov-Rostovskii, 17 December 1878, in Nikitin et al., *Osvobozhdenie Bolgarii*, 3:356–7.

50 Totleben to Alexander II, 17 April 1878, in Domontovich, *Osoboe pribavlenie*, 3:76.

51 Totleben to Alexander II, 25 May 1878, in Domontovich, 3:109.

52 Totleben to Alexander II, 29 June 1878, in Domontovich, 3:139.

53 "Zapiska o khode Rodopskogo vosstaniia," in Ovsianyi, *Sbornik materialov*, 5:354–5.

54 Totleben to Alexander II, 9 December 1878, in Ovsianyi, 5:224.

55 See Stolypin to Dondukov-Korsakov, 11 December 1878, in Ovsianyi, *Russkoe upravlenie*, 3:126–7.

56 Tseretelev to Lobanov-Rostovskii, 19 February 1879, in Nikitin, *Osvobozhdenie Bolgarii*, 3:452. On Tseretelev, see Kozmenko, "A.I. Tseretelev," 218–24.

57 Dondukov-Korsakov to Lobanov-Rostovskii, 25 March 1879, Tyrnovo, in Ovsianyi, *Sbornik materialov*, 5:275.

58 Dondukov-Korsakov to Lobanov-Rostovskii, 10 May 1879, in Ovsianyi, 6:119–20.

59 F.K. Lisevich to A.P. Davydov, 31 March 1879, in Niktin et al., *Osvobozhdenie Bolgarii*, 3:542.

60 F.K. Lisevich to A.P. Davydov, 31 March 1879, 541.

61 Dondukov-Korsakov to Lobanov-Rostovskii, 11 April 1879, Tyrnovo, in Ovsianyi, *Sbornik materialov*, 5:279. According to Lisevich, Fitzgerald visited Shumla in the company of the British consul in Rushchuk Dalziello; see F.K. Lisevich to A.P. Davydov, 31 March 1879, 542.

62 Dondukov-Korsakov to Miliutin, 18 April 1879, Tyrnovo, in Ovsianyi, *Sbornik materialov*, 5:100.

63 "Zapiska o podgotovke miatezha turetskogo naseleniia," no later than 17 April 1879, in Niktin et al., *Osvobozhdenie Bolgarii*, 3:578.

64 "Zapiska o podgotovke miatezha turetskogo naseleniia," 578–9. On the suppression of the Muslim resistance in eastern Bulgaria in 1880–2, see Parensov, *Iz proshlogo*.

65 "Obrashchenie Nikolaia Nikolaevicha k bolgarskomu narodu o sozdanii samostoiatel'nogo Bolgarskogo gosudarstva," San Stefano, 21 March 1878, in Nikitin et al., *Osvobozhdenie Bolgarii*, 3:55.

66 Dondukov-Korsakov to Lobanov Rostovskii, 28 July 1878, in Ovsianyi, *Sbornik materialov*, 5:183.

67 Dondukov-Korsakov to Lobanov-Rostovskii, 11 August 1878, in Ovsianyi, 5:193.

68 "Zhurnal Soveta Imperatorskogo Rossiiskogo Komissara v Bolgarii," 30 June 1878, in Ovsianyi, 5:309.

69 Lobanov-Rostovskii to Girs, 10/22 July 1878, in Ovsianyi, 5:164.

70 "Zhurnal Soveta Imperatorskogo Rossiiskogo Komissara v Bolgarii," 2 August 1878, in Ovsianyi, 5:311.

71 Totleben to Alexander II, 2 September 1878, in Domontovich, *Osoboe pribavlenie*, 3:172.

72 Dondukov-Korsakov to Miliutin, 6 August 1878, and "Zhurnal Soveta," 2 August 1878, in Ovsianyi, *Sbornik materialov*, 5:24–5, 311–14.

73 As one might expect, the Bulgarian occupants of the Muslim homes petitioned against the return of these homes to their pre-war owners. See, for example, the petition by the Bulgarians of Eski Zagra, who had suffered especially severely from Ottoman reprisals during the war (Nikitin et al., *Osvobozhdenie Bolgarii*, 3:208).

74 Dondukov-Korsakov to Lobanov-Rostovskii, 6 August 1878, Philippopolis, in Ovsianyi, *Sbornik materialov*, 5:28.

75 "Zhurnal Soveta," 2 August 1878, in Ovsianyi, 5:313, 317–18.

76 Dondukov-Korsakov to Lobanov-Rostovskii, 6 August 1878, 29–30.

77 Dondukov-Korsakov to Lobanov-Rostovskii, 28 July 1878, in Ovsianyi, *Sbornik materialov*, 5:190.

78 Dondukov-Korsakov to Lobanov-Rostovskii, 6 August 1878, 28. In order to identify such individuals, the lists of Muslims who wished to return were forwarded to the provincial governors. See M.S. Drinov, acting head of the Department of the Interior, to A.I. Lipinskii, governor of Adrianople, 22 June 1878, Philippopolis, in Nikitin et al., *Osvobozhdenie Bolgarii*, 3:161.

79 Dondukov-Korsakov to Miliutin, 14 August 1878, San Stefano, in Ovsianyi, *Sbornik materialov*, 5:42.

80 Miliutin to Dondukov-Korsakov, 21 August 1878, Livadiia, in Ovsianyi, 5:43–4.

81 Petrev-Pasha to Dondukov-Korsakov, 25 February 1879, in Nikitin et al., *Osvobozhdenie Bolgarii*, 3:460–2.

82 According to Stolypin, only the formal refusal of the Ottomans to introduce their garrisons in the Balkan passes, as the Treaty of Berlin allowed, could help put an end to "the regrettable conflicts that happen daily between the Turks and Bulgarians on the borders of Eastern Rumelia." See Stolypin to Reuf-Pasha, no later than 7 April 1879, Nikitin et al., 3:551.

83 Dondukov-Korsakov to Lobanov-Rostovskii, 28 July 1878, in Ovsianyi, *Sbornik materialov*, 5:190.

84 Dondukov-Korsakov to Lobanov-Rostovskii, 18 November 1878, in Ovsianyi, 5:220.

85 Dondukov-Korsakov to Miliutin, 6 December 1878, in Ovsianyi, 3:125.

86 As early as July, Totleben believed it necessary to assure that the Ottoman troops and civilian administration step in immediately after the withdrawal of the Russian forces from the territories between Constantinople and Adrianople. Otherwise, one could expect "great disorders and even massacres given the present excitement of national passions." See Totleben to Alexander II, 26 July 1878, in Domontovich, *Osoboe pribavlenie*, 3:148.

87 Totleben to Alexander II, 29 September 1878, in Domontovich, 3:175. Subsequent investigation revealed that the murders were committed by and under the protection of the Rhodopian bashi-bazouks who showed up in the south-western part of Thrace, adjacent to the Rhodope Mountains. See Totleben's report to Alexander II of 20 October 1878, in Domontovich, 3:195–7.

88 See Totleben's letters to Alexander II of 29 September and 6 October 1878, in Domontovich, 3:175, 179, as well as a detailed description of his meetings with the Thracian Bulgarians in his memo to Alexander II of 20 October 1878, in Domontovich, 3:195–7.

89 "Zhurnal Soveta Imperatorskogo Rossiiskogo Komissara v Bolgarii," 9 December 1878, RGIA, f. 932, op. 1, d. 224, l. 462v.

90 Totleben to Alexander II, 5 October 1878, in Domontovich, *Osoboe pribavlenie*, 3:178.

91 In October 1878, Totleben expected "100,000 and more." See Totleben to Stolypin, 24 October 1878, in Nikitin et al., *Osvobozhdenie Bolgarii*, 3:285–6.

92 Dondukov-Korsakov to Miliutin, 11 March 1879, in Ovsianyi, *Sbornik materialov*, 5:82.

93 N.G. Gartvig to A.N. Tseretelev, 1 February 1879, in Nikitin et al., *Osvobozhdenie Bolgarii*, 3:427.

94 See V.G. Zolotorev to A.I. Lipinskii, 27 July 1878, in Nikitin et al., 3:183 and note.

95 Dondukov-Korsakov to Miliutin, 9 September 1878, in Ovsianyi, *Sbornik materialov*, 5:45.

96 Dondukov-Korsakov to Lobanov-Rostovskii, 18 September 1878, in Ovsianyi, 5:196–7. Totleben likewise viewed the immigration of the Thracian Bulgarians as an opportunity to stop, or at least limit, the return of the Muslim refugees. Alexander II found this idea reasonable. See Totleben to Alexander II, 5 October 1878, and Alexander II to Totleben, 12 October 1878, in Domontovich, *Osoboe pribavlenie*, 3:180, 182.

97 Dondukov-Korsakov to Miliutin, 25 September 1878, and Miliutin to Dondukov-Korsakov, 5 October 1878, in Ovsianyi, *Sbornik materialov*, 5:53, 55.

98 Later, the Russian Ministry of Foreign Affairs also recognized the need to postpone the repatriation of the Muslim emigrants until their Christian counterparts were settled. See Girs to Lobanov-Rostovskii, 26 December 1878, in Nikitin et al., *Osvobozhdenie Bolgarii*, 3:375.

99 "Zapiska o deitel'nosti vremennogo russkogo upranvleniia v Bolgarii," in Ovsianyi, *Russkoe upravlenie*, 2:227.

100 Ovsianyi himself gives the number of Bulgarian émigrés from southern Thrace as 8,000 in late September 1878 and 30,000 by the end of the year (Ovsianyi, 2:108). Altogether, some 28,957 Christian immigrants settled in Eastern Rumelia and 21,278 in the Principality of Bulgaria (Ovsianyi, 2:109n).

101 Stolypin to Dondukov-Korsakov, 1 February 1879, in Nikitin et al., *Osvobozhdenie Bolgarii*, 3:429–31 and n. 3.

102 Stolypin to Dondukov-Korsakov, 11 December 1878, Ovsianyi, *Russkoe upravlenie*, 3:117.

103 Stolypin to Dondukov-Korsakov, 11 December 1878, 118–19.

104 Dondukov-Korsakov to Stolypin, 15 December 1878, in Ovsianyi, *Russkoe upravlenie*, 3:138.

105 Stolypin to Dondukov-Korsakov, 1 February 1879, in Nikitin et al., *Osvobozhdenie Bolgarii*, 3:430. In fact, a number of clashes, if not a full-scale rebellion of the Muslim population, did take place in the Aidos district, as reported by A.N. Tseretelev to Lobanov-Rostovskii, 19 February 1879, in Nikitin et al., *Osvobozhdenie Bolgarii*, 3:452–3.

106 Dondukov-Korsakov to Lobanov-Rostovskii, 6 February 1879, in Ovsianyi, *Sbornik materialov*, 5:257.

107 Gartvig to Tsertelev, 10 April 1879, in Nikitin et al., *Osvobozhdenie Bolgarii*, 3:561.

108 Ivanov to Dondukov-Korsakov, 27 July 1878, Slivno, in Nikitin et al., 3:183–5.

109 Alabin to Dondukov-Korsakov, 21 August 1878, RGVIA, f. 430, op. 1, d. 90, l. 23.

110 Alabin to Dondukov-Korsakov, 21 August 1878, l. 24.

111 Dondukov-Korsakov to Alabin of 21 August 1878, in Nikitin et al., *Osvobozhdenie Bolgarii*, 3:202.

112 "Instruktsiia Tseretelevu," 26 August 1878, in Nikitin et al., 3:207. See also Girs's instructions to the Russian ambassador in Constantinople, Lobanov-Rostovskii, 31 August 1877, in Nikitin et al., 3:214.

113 Dondukov-Korsakov to Lobanov-Rostovskii, 27 February 1879, in Ovsianyi, *Sbornik materialov*, 5:264–5.

114 "Obshchaia instruktsiia kniaziu Dondukovu-Korsakovu," 10 April 1878, in Ovsianyi, 3:271.

115 Ovsianyi, *Russkoe upravlenie*, 2:31–2, 122.

116 "Prikaz po Bolgarskomu kraiu i Bolgarskomu zemskomu voisku," 8 July 1878, Filippopol, RGIA, f. 932, op. 1, d. 224, l. 397v.

117 Miliutin to Dondukov-Korsakov, 16 July 1878, in Ovsianyi, *Sbornik materialov*, 5:4.

118 Miliutin to Dondukov-Korsakov, 26 December 1878, in Ovsianyi, 5:69.

119 Dondukov-Korsakov to Miliutin, 7 January 1879, in Ovsianyi, 5:72–3. In parallel, Dondukov-Korsakov also prevented Austrian subjects from obtaining positions in the civil administration of the Principality of Bulgaria. See Dondukov-Korsakov to Lobanov-Rostovskii, 21 December / 2 January 1878, in Ovsianyi, 5:223. See also Ovsianyi, *Bolgarskoe opolchenie*, 88.

120 Dondukov-Korsakov to Miliutin, 7 January 1879, 74–5. At the same time, the imperial commissioner did not consider it possible to apply the same measures to the Eastern Rumelian militia, which soon had to pass under the jurisdiction of the international commission.

121 Nemirovich-Danchenko, *Posle voiny*, 29–30.

122 Dondukov-Korsakov to Miliutin, 11 March 1879, Tyrnovo, in Ovsianyi, *Sbornik materialov*, 5:82.

123 Dondukov-Korsakov to Lobanov-Rostovskii, 25 March 1879, in Ovsianyi, 5:275.

124 Dondukov-Korsakov to Miliutin, 11 March 1879, 82.

125 Dondukov-Korsakov to Miliutin, 10 April 1879, Tyrnovo, in Ovsianyi, *Sbornik materialov*, 5:96.

126 Miliutin to Dondukov-Korsakov, 26 December 1878, in Ovsianyi, 5:68.

127 Dondukov-Korsakov to Miliutin, 7 January 1879, Ovsianyi, *Sbornik materialov*, 5:74–5.

128 See "Zapiska o polozhenii del v Vostochnoi Rumelii," attached to Stolypin's letter to Dondukov-Korsakov of 1 March 1879, in Ovsianyi, *Russkoe upravlenie*, 3:285.

129 See Totleben's letter to Miliutin of 13 January 1879, and the approval of this approach in Miliutin to Dondukov-Korsakov, 25 January 1879, in Ovsianyi, 3:187, 192.

130 Totleben to Dondukov-Korsakov, 1 February 1879, in Ovsianyi, 3:199–200.

131 "Kratkoe izlozhenie adresa i zapiski, podanykh Imperatorskomu Rossiiskomu Komissaru zhiteliami Iuzhnoi Bolgarii pered ot'ezdom ego iz Filippopolia," in Ovsianyi, *Sbornik materialov*, 5:64–7.

132 Ovsianyi, *Russkoe upravlenie*, 3:6.

133 Ovsianyi, 2:20–1. Dondukov-Korsakov received similar petitions from the Christian population of Macedonia, whose situation was even worse because of harassment by the fugitive bashi-bazouks and Albanians. After the Berlin Congress, the Russian authorities could do next to nothing to influence the situation in Macedonia other than prevent the *chetas'* penetration into it from the territory of the Principality of Bulgaria.

134 Totleben to Alexander II, 6 October 1878, in Domontovich, *Osoboe pribavlenie*, 3:182. In a letter to Miliutin, Totleben argued that Albania "can successfully sustain a struggle with the Constantinople government solely because all its population bears arms." See Totleben to Miliutin, 6 October 1878, and the approval of this measure in Miliutin to Totleben, 11 October 1878, in Ovsianyi, *Russkoe upravlenie*, 3:154, 157.

135 Totleben to Alexander II, 13 October 1878, in Domontovich, *Osoboe pribavlenie*, 3:185.

136 Totleben to Alexander II, 13 October 1878, 184.

137 Totleben to Alexander II, 10 November 1878, in Domontovich, *Osoboe pribavlenie*, 3:213.

138 See the summary of Totleben's conversation with Drummond-Wolf attached to Totleben's report to Alexander II of 23 December 1878, in Domontovich, 3:232.

139 Dondukov-Korsakov to Lobanov-Rostovskii, 28 July 1878, in Ovsianyi, *Sbornik materialov*, 5:183.

140 As is clear from Totleben's letter to Miliutin of 6 October 1878, in Ovsianyi, *Russkoe upravlenie*, 3:155.

141 Alexander II to Totleben, 19 October 1878, in Domontovich, *Osoboe pribavlenie*, 3:189.

142 Stolypin to Dondukov-Korsakov, 11 December 1878, in Ovsianyi, *Russkoe upravlenie*, 3:116.

143 Dondukov-Korsakov to Stolypin, 15 December 1878, in Ovsianyi, 3:136.

144 Totleben to Dondukov-Korsakov, 24 February 1879, in Ovsianyi, 3:207.

145 Stolypin to Lobanov-Rostovskii, 11 January 1879, in Nikitin et al., *Osvobozhdenie Bolgarii*, 3:395–6, 403–5.

146 Ovsianyi, *Bolgarskoe opolchenie*, 89.

147 See Stolypin's order to the troops of the 9th Corps on intensive training of the Bulgarian countryside patrols, 15 January 1879, in Nikitin et al., *Osvobozhdenie Bolgarii*, 3:403–5.

148 On the popularity of the gymnastic society of Slivno, see N.G. Gartvig, 1 February 1879, in Nikitin et al., 3:427–9; and A.D. Stolypin, "Nastavlenie dlia obucheniia

gimnasticheskikh strelkovykh obshchestv," in Ovsianyi, *Russkoe upravlenie*, 3:180–4.

149 Ovsianyi, *Russkoe upravlenie*, 3:26.

150 See the summary of Totleben's conversation with Drummond-Wolf attached to Totleben's report to Alexander II of 23 December 1878, in Domontovich, *Osoboe pribavlenie*, 3:232.

151 Dufferin to Girs, 2/14 April 1879, in Nikitin et al., *Osvobozhdenie Bolgarii*, 3:546–7.

152 Girs to Lobanov-Rostovskii, 7 April 1879, in Nikitin et al., 3:553–4.

153 As Stolypin declared at his unofficial meeting with the Bulgarian leaders in Philippopolis in January 1879. See Stolypin to Dondukov-Korsakov, 14 January 1879, in Ovsianyi, *Russkoe upravlenie*, 3:147–8. Accordingly, the "Guidelines for the Training of the Gymnastic Societies" issued by Stolypin (Ovsianyi, 3:180) stressed their strictly "educational" purpose.

154 See Totleben's report to Alexander II of 22 November 1878, on his meeting with the Bulgarian delegation in Philippopolis, in Domontovich, *Osoboe pribavlenie*, 3:211–12. See also Stolypin's report to Dondukov-Korsakov, 14 January 1879, in Ovsianyi, *Russkoe upravlenie*, 3:142–9.

155 Miliutin to Dondukov-Korsakov, 16 July 1878, in Ovsianyi, *Sbornik materialov*, 5:4.

156 Dondukov-Korsakov to Miliutin, 16 October 1878, in Ovsianyi, 5:60–1.

157 MacDermott, *Freedom or Death*, 53–6.

158 Alexander II to Totleben, 17 October 1878, in Nikitin et al., *Osvobozhdenie Bolgarii*, 3:273.

159 See Dondukov-Korsakov to Totleben, 27 October 1878, RGVIA, f. 430, op. 1, d. 90, l. 97v.

160 Dondukov-Korsakov to Totleben, 27 October 1878, 98v.

161 Dondukov-Korsakov to the acting governor of Sofia, P.V. Alabin, October 1878, RGVIA, f. 430, op. 1, d. 90, ll. 76–76v.

162 See Dondukov-Korsakov's circular to the governors of the Principality of Bulgaria and Eastern Rumelia, 23 October 1878, RGVIA, f. 430, op. 1, d. 90, ll. 79–79v.

163 Dondukov-Korsakov to Lobanov-Rostovskii, 25 March 1879, Tyrnovo, in Ovsianyi, *Sbornik materialov*, 5:274.

164 See "Proekt Organicheskogo Ustava Gosudarstvennogo Ustroistva Kniazhestva Bolgarskogo," article 39, and "Konstitutsiia Kniazhestva Bolgarskogo," article 40, in Ovsianyi, *Russkoe upravlenie*, 2:248. The Constitutional Assembly of Bulgaria convoked in February 1879 included 11 Muslim representatives out of 230. All of them were appointed and not elected (only 89 members were elected; others entered the assembly *ex officio*). See Ovsianyi, 2:57.

165 See "Proekt," article 40, and "Konstitutsiia," article 41, in Ovsianyi, 2:248–9.

166 See "Proekt," article 41, and "Konstitutsiia," article 42, in Ovsianyi, 2:249.

167 On the subsequent evolution of Bulgarian Muslim communities, see Neuburger, *Orient Within*; and Methodieva, *Between Empire and Nation*. For the western Balkan Muslims in the post–Berlin Congress period, see Greble, *Muslims*, 23–80.
168 Aydin, *Idea of the Muslim World*, 58–64.

Conclusion

1 McCarthy, *Death and Exile*, 59 and n. 1, citing the British ambassador to Constantinople, Austen Henry Layard. McCarthy's assessment is perpetuated by more recent authors. See Salt, *Last Ottoman Wars*, 83–8.

Bibliography

Archival Materials

Rossiiskii Gosudarstvennyi Voenno-Istoricheskii Arkhiv (RGVIA)

f. VUA (Voenno-uchenyi arkhiv)
f. 430 Bolgariia (kollektsiia)
f. 439 Serbiia (kollektsiia)
f. 450 Turtsiia (kollektsiia)

Rossiiskii Gosudarstvennyi Istoricheskii Arkhiv (RGIA)

f. 673 I.P. Liprandi
f. 797 Kantseliariia Ober-Prokurora Sinoda
f. 932 A.M. Dondukov-Korsakov
f. 1015 S.N. Palauzov
f. 1561 N.P. Ignatiev

Nauchno-Issledovatel'skii Otdel Rukopisei Rossiiskoi Gosudarstvennoi Biblioteki (NIOR RGB)

f. 169 Miliutiny
f. 327 Cherkasskie

Otdel Rukopisei Rossiiskoi Natsional'noi Biblioteki (OR RNB)

f. 14 Bumagi Aksakova

Published Primary Sources

Anuchin, D.G. "Kniaz' V. A. Cherkasskii i grazhdanskoe upravlenie v Bolgarii, 1877–1878." *Russkaia starina*, no. 2 (1895): 1–34; no. 3 (1895): 1–27; no. 4 (1895): 43–54; no. 5 (1895): 1–36; no. 8 (1895): 41–69; no. 9 (1895): 53–104; no. 10 (1895): 1–32; no. 11 (1895): 47–67; no. 12 (1895): 1–50; no. 1 (1896): 55–78; no. 2 (1896): 285–313; no. 3 (1896): 449–70; no. 5 (1896): 225–6; no. 7 (1896): 45–81; no. 8 (1896): 231–54.

Barsov, N.S., ed. *Tridtsatiletie deitel'nosti Odesskogo Bolgarskogo nastoiatel'stva (1854–84).* Odessa: Tipografiia Shtaba okruga, 1895.

Berens, A.I. "Kabiliia v 1857 godu." *Voennyi sbornik*, no. 5 (1858): 121–72.

Benkendorf, A.Kh. "Imperator Nikolai Pervyi v 1828–29 gg." *Russkaia starina*, no. 6 (1896): 471–510.

Bers, A.A. *Vospominaniia o pokhode v Turtsiiu v 1877–1878 gg.* St. Petersburg: I.V. Leontiev, 1913.

Benkrovnyi, L.G., ed. *M. I. Kutuzov. Sbornik dokumentov i materialov.* 5 vols. Moscow: Voenizdat, 1950–55.

Chichagov, M. "Peredovoi otriad." *Voennyi sbornik*, no. 8 (1878): 258–80; no. 9 (1878): 173–89; no. 10 (1878): 325–56.

Danilevskii, N.Ia. *Rossiia i Evropa. Vzgliad na kul'turno-politicheskie otnosheniia slavianskogo mira k romano-germanskomu.* St. Petersburg: Panteleevy, 1888.

Danilevskii, Nikolai. *Woe to the Victors! The Russo-Turkish War, the Berlin Congress, and the Future of Slavdom.* Translated by Stephen M. Woodburn. Bloomington, IN: Slavica, 2015.

Davydov, D.V. *Opyt teorii partizanskogo deistviia.* In *Sochineniia Davydova*, edited by A. Smirdin, 489–640. St. Petersburg: Krasheninnikov, 1848.

Depreradovich, F.M. *Iz vospominanii o russko-turetskoi vone 1877–78 gg.* St. Petersburg: Stasiulevich, 1881.

Diugamel, A.O. *Avtobiografiia.* Moscow: Universitetskaia tipografiia, 1885.

Diugamel, A.O. "Avtobiografiia A.O. Diugamelia," *Russkii arkhiv*, no. 2 (1885): 179–217; no. 4 (1885): 489–525; no. 5 (1885): 82–126; no. 6 (1885): 222–256; no. 7 (1885): 371–427; no. 10 (1885): 161–224.

Diugamel, A.O. "Kratkoe izvlechenie ob Adrianopole i drugikh gorodakh lezhashchikh na voennom puti v Konstantinopol'." *Kazanskii vestnik*, nos. 5–6 (1829): 117–34.

Diugamel, A.O. "Statisticheskaiia tablitsa severnoi Rumelii." In *Slavianskoe vozrozhdenie: Sbornik statei i materialov*, edited by S.A. Nikitin, 186–203. Moscow: Nauka, 1966.

Diugamel, A.O. *Voenno-topograficheskoe opisanie dorog: Ot Shumly do Pravody, cherez Aidos v Burgas i ot Burgasa do Faki.* St. Petersburg: General'nyi shtab, 1827.

Diugamel, A.O. *Voenno-topograficheskoe opisanie dorogi, vedushchei iz Rushchuka cherez Osman-Bazar, Starareku i Slivno v Luleburgas.* St. Petersburg: General'nyi shtab, 1827.

Diugamel, A.O. *Voenno-topograficheskoe opisanie dorogi, vedushchei ot Sistova cherez Tyrnovo, Kazan, Karnobat, Faki, der. Gektepe, Vizu i Sarai v Buiuk-Dere.* St. Petersburg: General'nyi shtab, 1827.

Domontovich, M.A., ed. *Osoboe pribavlenie k opisaniiu russko-turetskoi voiny 1877–78 gg. na balkanskom poluostrove.* 6 vols. St. Petersburg: Voenno-uchebnaia komissiia pri Glavnom Shtabe, 1899–1906.

"Dvadtsat' piat' let v leib-gvardii egerskom polku (Iz zapisok starogo egeria)." *Voennyi sbornik,* no. 2 (1877): 365–410.

"Dve zapiski imperatora Nikolaia otnositel'no morskoi ekspeditsii protiv Varny i Burgosa." *Russkaia starina,* no. 8 (1876): 677–80.

Enegolm, A. *Zapiski o gorodakh zabalkanskikh zaniatykh russkimi voiskami v dostopiamiatnuiu kampaniiu 1829 goda.* St. Petersburg: Pliushar, 1830.

Engelgardt, A.E. *Kratkoe nachertanie maloi voiny dlia vsekh rodov oruzhiia.* 4 vols. St. Petersburg: Tipografiia voenno-uchebnykh zavedenii, 1850.

Fadeev, R.A. "Pis'ma s Kavkaza." In *Gosudarstvennyi poriadok. Rossiia i Kavkaz,* 132–334. Moscow: Institut russkoi tsivilizatsii, 2010.

Fadeev, R.A. *Shest'desiat let Kavkazskoi voiny.* Tiflis: Voenno-pokhodnaiia tipografiia Glavnogo shtaba kavkazskoi armii, 1860.

Fadeev, R.A. *Sobranie sochinenii R. A. Fadeeva.* 3 vols. St. Petersburg: V.V. Komarov, 1889–90.

Fortunatov, P.K., ed. *P. A. Rumiantsev. Dokumenty.* 3 vols. Moscow: Voenizdat, 1953–9.

Gazenkampf, M.A. *Moi dnevnik, 1877–78.* St. Petersburg: V. Berezovskii, 1908.

Girardin, Saint-Marc. *Souvenirs de voyages et d'études.* 3 vols. Brussels: Delavigne et Callewaert, 1852–3.

Golubov, S.N., and F.E. Kuznetsov, eds. *General Bagration. Sbornik dokumentov i materialov.* Moscow: Gospolitizdat, 1945.

Grabbe, P.Kh. *Zapisnaia knizhka.* Moscow: Volchaninov, 1888.

Ignatiev, N.P. *Vzgliad na postepennoe izmenenie v obraze deistvii russkikh voisk protiv turok.* St. Petersburg: Veimar, 1852.

Kisov, S.I. *Iz boevoi pokhodnoi zhizni.* Translated by M. Goriunin. Sofia: Pridvornaia pechatnia brat'ev Proshek, 1903.

Kostenko, L.F. *Puteshestvie v Severnuiu Afriku.* St. Petersburg: A. Transhel, 1876.

Kryzhanovskaia, K.P., and E.M. Russev, eds. *Istoriia Moldavii: Dokumenty i materialy.* Kishinev: Akademia Nauk MSSR, 1957.

Kupreianov, P.Ia. "Deistviia pravodskogo otriada v 1828–29 godakh." *Voennyi sbornik,* no. 2 (1875): 159–90; no. 3 (1875): 5–53.

Kuropatkin, A.N. *Alzhiriia.* St. Petersburg: V.A. Poletika, 1877.

Kuropatkin, A.N. "Ocherki Alzhirii (Stat'ia pervaia). Verbliuzhii oboz." *Voennyi sbornik,* no. 2 (1875): 273–97.

Langeron [Louis Alexandre Andrault]. "Projet d'une guerre offensive des Russes contre les Turcs présenté à l'Empereur Nicholas 1er en 1826." In vol. 3 of *Documente privitoare la istoria românilor: Suplement 1,* 65–70. Bucharest: Socecu, 1886–95.

Lanzheron, A.F. "Zapiski grafa Lanzherona. Voina s Turtsiei 1806–1812 gg." *Russkaia starina*, no. 5 (1907): 432–48; no. 6 (1907): 577–615; no. 7 (1907): 69–100; no. 8 (1907): 311–29; no. 9 (1907): 563–83; no. 10 (1907): 153–63; no. 11 (1907): 427–37; no. 2 (1908): 477–89; no. 3 (1908): 711–26; no. 4 (1908): 225–40; no. 6 (1908): 661–96; no. 7 (1908): 159–209; no. 8 (1908): 401–28; no. 9 (1908): 661–72; no. 10 (1908): 267–88; no. 11 (1908): 511–29; no. 6 (1909): 535–90; no. 7 (1909): 163–206; no. 8 (1909): 379–96; no. 9 (1909): 411–31; no. 7 (1910): 167–82; no. 8 (1910): 341–61; no. 9 (1910): 527–46; no. 10 (1910): 211–30; no. 7 (1911): 121–46.

Lavrentiev, A.V. "Ocherki vooruzhennykh sil evropeiskikh gosudarstv. Turtsiia." *Voennyi sbornik* 23, no. 2 (1862): 283–327.

Lavrentiev, A.V. "Po Nizhnemu Dunaiu." *Voennyi sbornik*, no. 10 (1871): 207–31.

Liprandi, I.P. "Bolgariia i Vostochnyi vopros." *Chteniia v imperatorskom obshchestve istorii i drevnostei rossiiskikh*, no. 1 (1868): 1–139.

Liprandi, I.P. "Bolgariia. Iz zapisok I. P. Liprandi." *Chteniia v imperatorskom obshchestve istorii i drevnostei rossiiskikh*, no. 1 (1877): 1–60.

Liprandi, I.P. "Kratkii ocherk etnograficheskogo, politicheskogo, nravstvennogo i voennogo sostoianiia khristianskikh oblastei Turetskoi imperii. Pridunaiskie kniazhestva." *Chteniia v imperatorskom obshchestve istorii i drevnostei rossiiskikh*, no. 4 (1876): 1–14.

Liprandi, I.P. "Kratkoe obozrenie Kniazhestv Moldavii i Valakhii, ot obrazovaniia onykh v Kniazhestva do poloviny 1831 goda." *Chteniia v imperatorskom obshchestve istorii i drevnostei rossiiskikh*, no. 4 (1861): 125–56.

Liprandi, I.P. "Nastoiashchee sostoianie turetskoi armii i predpolagaemaia vysadka soiuznykh voisk." *Chteniia v imperatorskom obshchestve istorii i drevnostei rossiiskikh*, no. 3 (1877): 32–52.

Liprandi, I.P. *Nekotorye zamechaniia po povodu dvukh sochineii, vyshedshikh pod zaglaviem "Malaia voina."* St. Petersburg: Ministerstvo vnutrennikh del, 1851.

Liprandi, I.P. *Obozrenie prostranstva sluzhivshego teatrom voiny Rossii s Turtsieiu s 1806 po 1812 g.* St. Petersburg: General'nyi shtab, 1854.

Liprandi, I.P. "Obshchie sveden'ia o Evropeiskoi Turtsii." *Chteniia v imperatorskom obshchestve istorii i drevnostei rossiiskikh*, no. 4 (1876): 16–44.

Liprandi, I.P. *Okhranitel'nye mery turetskikh lagerei, izveshchatel'nye partii i t. p.* St. Petersburg: Voennaia tipografiia, 1854.

Liprandi, I.P. *Osady turetskikh krepostei.* St. Petersburg: Voennaia tipografiia, 1855.

Liprandi, I.P. "Otryvok iz knigi: *Nekotorye zamechaniia po povodu dvukh sochinenii, vyshedshikh pod zaglaviem 'Malaia Voina.'*" In *Osobennosti voin s turkami*, 7–42. St. Petersburg: Fomin, 1877.

Liprandi, I.P. "Puti v Bolgarii. Zamechaniia na etapy, gospitali i transport." *Chteniia v imperatorskom obshchestve istorii i drevnostei rossiiskikh*, no. 3 (1877): 27–31.

Liprandi, I.P. "Sredstva, kotorye mozhet naiti nasha armiia v Bolgarii pri sobliudenii mestnykh uslovii." *Chteniia v imperatorskom obshchestve istorii i drevnostei rossiiskikh*, no. 3 (1877): 12–26.

Liprandi, I.P. "Vazhnost' imet' polozhitel'nye svedeniia o proiskhodiashchem na pravom beregu Dunaia i o tainykh kozniakh v kniazhestvakh; s ukazaniem na edinstvennye sredstva k dostizheniiu togo v polnom ob'eme vysshei tainoi zagranichnoi politsii." *Chteniia v imperatorskom obshchestve istorii i drevnostei rossiiskikh*, no. 3 (1877): 53–80.

Liprandi, I.P. *Vzaimnoe deistvie pekhoty, konnitsy i artilerii u turok*. St. Petersburg: Voennaia tipografiia, 1854.

Liprandi, I.P. "Vzgliad na nastoiashchii teatr voennykh deistvii na Dunae i na sodeistvie, kotoroe mozhem vstretit' v Bolgarii." *Chteniia v imperatorskom obshchestve istorii i drevnostei rossiiskikh*, no. 3 (1877): 1–11.

Maksheev, A.I. "Geograficheskie, etnograficheskie i statisticheskie materialy o Turkestanskom krae." *Zapiski Russkogo geograficheskogo obshchestva*, no. 2 (1871): 1–60.

Maksheev, A.I. "Ocherk sovremennogo sostoianiia Alzhirii." *Vestnik Russkogo geograficheskogo obshchestva*, no. 3 (1860): 13–50.

Maksheev, A.I. "Opisanie Aral'skogo moria." *Zapiski Russkogo geograficheskogo obshchestva*, no. 5 (1851): 30–61.

Materialy dlia izucheniia Bolgarii. 5 vols. Bucharest: Stara Planina, 1877.

Mikhailovskii-Danilevskii, A.I. *Opisanie finliandskoi voiny na sushe i na more, 1808–09*. St. Petersburg: Shtab otdel'nogo korpusa vnutrennei strazhi, 1841.

Mikhailovskii-Danilevskii, A.I. *Opisanie Otechestvennoi voiny v 1812 godu*. St. Petersburg: Voennaia tipografiia, 1839.

Mikhailovskii-Danilevskii, A.I. *Opisanie turetskoi voiny s 1806 po 1812 god*. Vol. 3 of *Polnoe sobranie sochinenii*. St. Petersburg: Shtab otdel'nogo korpusa vnutrennei strazhi, 1849–50.

Mikhailovskii-Danilevskii, A.I. *Russo-Turkish War of 1806–1812*. 2 vols. Translated, edited, and annotated by Alexander Mikaberidze. West Chester, OH: Nafziger Collection, 2002.

Mikhailovskii-Danilevskii, A.I. "Zapiski A. I Mikhailovskogo-Danilevskogo. 1812 god." *Istoricheskii vestnik* 42, no. 10 (1890): 130–69.

Miliutin, D.A. *Dnevnik D. A. Miliutina 1873–1875*. Edited by P.A. Zaionchkovskii. 4 vols. Moscow: Gosudarstvennaia biblioteka SSSR, Otdel rukopisei, 1947–50.

Miliutin, D.A. "Kriticheskoe issledovanie znacheniia voennoi geografii i voennoi statistiki." *Voennyi zhurnal*, no. 1 (1846): 124–93.

Miliutin, D.A. *Opisanie voennykh deistvii 1839 goda v Severnom Dagestane*. St. Petersburg: Tipografiia voenno-uchebnykh zavedenii, 1850

Miliutin, D.A. *Pervye opyty voennoi statistiki*. 2 vols. St. Petersburg: Tipografiia voenno-uchebnykh zavedenii, 1847–8.

"Mysli kniazia Varshavskogo o pol'ze uchrezhdeniia khristianskikh opolchenii iz serbov, bolgar i obitatelei dunaiskikh kniazhestv." *Russkaia starina*, no. 8 (1876): 684–7.

Narochnitskii, A.L., ed. *Vneshniaia politika Rossii XIX i nachala XX veka*. 16 vols. Moscow: Politizdat, Mezhdunarodnye otnosheniia, 1960–95.

Neale, Edward. "The Province of Bulgaria." *Social Science Review*, no. 3 (1865): 138–50.

Nemirovich-Danchenko, V.I. *God voiny (Dnevnik russkago korrespondenta)*. 2 vols. St. Petersburg: Novoe vremia, 1878.

Nemirovich-Danchenko, V.I. *Posle voiny. Ocherki i vpechatleniia russkago korrespondenta v osvobozhdennoi Bolgarii*. St. Petersburg: E.P. Kekhribardzhi, 1880.

Nikitin, S.A., V.D. Konobeev, Al.K. Brumov, and N.T. Todorov, eds. *Osvobozhdenie Bolgarii ot turetskogo iga*. 3 vols. Moscow: Nauka, 1961–7.

"Novyi plan kompanii nachertannyi sobstvennoruchno Nikolaem Pavlovichem." *Russkaia starina*, no. 10 (1876): 358–61.

Obruchev, N.N., ed. *Voenno-statisticheskii sbornik na 1868 g.* Vol. 2. St. Petersburg: Voennaia tipografiia, 1868.

Oţetea, Andrei, ed. *Documente privind istoria Romîniei. Răscoala din 1821*. Vol. 5. Bucharest: Editura Academiei Republicii Populare Romîne, 1962.

"Otryvok iz pokhodnykh zapisok 1828 goda." *Zhurnal dlia chteniia vospitannikov voenno-uchebnykh zavedenii* 66, no. 261 (1847): 3–52.

Ovsianyi, N.R. *Bolgarskoe opolchenie i zemskoe voisko. K istorii grazhdanskogo upravleniia i okkupatsii Bolgarii, v 1877–78–79 gg.* St. Petersburg: Khudozhestvennaia pechat', 1904.

Ovsianyi, N.R., ed. *Russkoe upravlenie v Bolgarii*. 3 vols. St. Petersburg: Khudozhestvennaia pechat', 1906–7.

Ovsianyi, N.R., ed. *Sobornik materialov po grazhdanskomu upravleniiu i okkupatsii v Bolgarii v 1877, 1878, 1879 gg.* 6 vols. St. Petersburg: Khudozhestvennaia pechat', 1903–6.

Parensov, P.D. *Iz proshlogo. Vospominaniia*. Part 4. St. Petersburg: Berezovskii, 1908.

Paskevich, I.F. "Mysli o plane voennykh deistvii." 29 December 1853. *Russkaia starina*, no. 1 (1876): 181–91.

Pogodin, Mikhail. *Istoriko-politicheskie pis'ma i zapiski v prodolzhenie Krymskoi voiny, 1853–1856*. Moscow: V.M. Frish, 1874.

"Predpolozheniia imperatora Nikolaia otnositel'no morskoi ekspeditsii v Bosfor i Tsar'grad." *Russkaia starina*, no. 8 (1876): 675–6.

"Predpolozheniia imperatora Nikolaia Pavlovicha otnositel'no voennykh deistvii na sluchai razryva s Turtsiei." May 1853. *Russkaia starina*, no. 8 (1876): 687–8.

"Predpolozheniia imperatora Nikolaia Pavlovicha o voennykh deistviiakh protiv turok na 1854 god." November 1853. *Russkaia starina*, no. 8 (1876): 705–8.

"Predpolozheniia kniazia M.D. Gorchakova o voennykh deistviiakh v Evropeiski Turtsii." 21 November 1853. *Russkaia starina*, no. 9 (1876): 150–61.

"Prikaz generala Lidersa pri perehode cherez Dunai." 11 March 1854. *Russkaia starina*, no. 12 (1876): 826.

Pushkin, A.N. *Kratkie izvlecheniia ob obrazovanii voisk v Evrope i ob uspekhakh ognestrel'nogo iskusstva*. St. Petersburg: Tipografiia imperatorskogo vospitatel'nogo doma, 1824.

Pushkin, A.N. "O vliianii voennykh nauk na obraz voiny v Evrope." *Sorevnovatel' prosveshcheniia i blagotvoreniia*, no. 30 (1825): 225–98.

Pushkin, A.N. "Vzgliad na voennoe iskusstvo drevnikh do izobreteniia ognestrel'nogo oruzhiia." *Sorevnovatel' prosveshcheniia i blagotvoreniia*, no. 24 (1823): 57–85, 169–201.

Pushkin, A.N. "Vzgliad na voennoe sostoianie Turetskoi imperii." *Syn Otechestva* 107, no. 9 (1826): 74–90; no. 10 (1826): 173–91; no. 11 (1826): 264–74.

Pushkin, A.N. *Zapiski o voennom ukreplenii dlia upotrebleniia polevykh ofitserov.* 2 parts. St. Petersburg: Tipografiia Ministerstva vnutrennikh del, 1827.

Rachinskii, A.V. *Pokhodnye pis'ma opolchentsa iz Iuzhnoi Bessarabii (1855–1856 g.).* Moscow: Avgust Semen, 1858.

Rynkevich, E.E. "Zapiski o Bolgarskom opolchenii." *Voennyi sbornik*, no. 4 (1902): 55–96.

Salaheddin Bey, ed. *La Turquie à l'exposition universelle de 1867.* Paris: Hachette, 1867.

Sbornik materialov po russko-turetskoi voine na Balkanskom poluostrove. 98 vols. St. Peterburg: Voennaia tipografiia, 1898–1911.

Shilder, N.K. "Plevnenskoe sidenie. 1877 g." *Russkaia starina*, no. 7 (1886): 213–42.

Sobolev, L.N., "Narodonaselenie Bolgarii." In *Materialy dlia izucheniia Bolgarii*, 3:1–13.

Tott, François de. *Memoirs of Baron de Tott.* 2 vols. London: G.G.J. and J. Robinson, 1786.

Tiutchev, F.I. "Papstvo i rimskii vopros s russkoi tochki zreniia." *Russkii arkhiv*, no. 5 (1886): 33–51.

Tiutchev, F.I. "Rossiia i revoliutsiia." *Russkii arkhiv*, no. 5 (1873): 895–932.

Tuchkov, P.A. *Voenno-topograficheskoie opisanie dorog: Ot Eski-Stambula cherez Osmanpazar, Kazan, Slivno, Yambol' do Adrianopolia, i ot onogo v Kirklissii, v Faki i v Liuleburgas.* St. Petersburg: General'nyi Shtab, 1827.

Tuchkov, S.A. "Zapiski S.A. Tuchkova." *Russkii vestnik*, no. 8 (1906): 347–83.

Ubicini, A. *L'État présent de l'Empire Ottomane.* Paris: J. Dumaine, 1876.

Ushakov, N.I. "Zapiski ochevidtsa o voine protiv Turtsii i Zapadnykh derzhav." In vol. 2 of *Deviatnadtsatyi vek. Istoricheskii sbornik*, edited by P.I. Bartenev, 1–242. Moscow: Grechov i Ko., 1872.

Verigin, A.I. *Voenno-topograficheskoe opisanie dorog: Ot gor. Turtukaia cherez g. Karnobat, Faki, Kirklissi, Liuleburgas, Chorlu i Silivriiu do mes. Kuchuk-Chekmendzhe.* St. Petersburg: General'nyi shtab, 1827.

Verigin, A.I. *Voenno-topograficheskoe opisanie dorogi: Ot gor. Tyrnova cherez m. Grabova, g. Kazanlyk i Eski-Saaru v Adrianopol'.* St. Petersburg: General'nyi shtab, 1827.

Voenno-statisticheskoe obozrenie gosudarstv i zemel' prilezhashchikh k Rossiiskoi imperii. Kniazhestvo Moldaviia. St. Petersburg: General'nyi shtab, 1855.

Voenno-statisticheskoe obozrenie Rossiiskoi imperii. 17 vols. St. Petersburg: General'nyi shtab, 1848–58.

Voenno-topograficheskoe opisanie beregovoi dorogi Chernogo moria, ot kreposti Tul'chi cherez Babadag, Mangaliiu, Varnu, Burgas, Midiiu v Konstantinopol'. St. Petersburg: General'nyi shtab, 1822.

Voenno-topograficheskoe opisanie dorogi iz goroda Galatsa chrez Pravadi v Lule-Burgaz, lezhashchii po doroge iz Adrianopolia v Konstantinopol'. St. Petersburg: General'nyi shtab, 1822.

Voenno-topograficheskoe opisanie dorogi iz Zhurzhi i Rushchuka cherez Shumlu v Konstantinopol'. St. Petersburg: General'nyi shtab, 1821.

Vronchenko, M.P. *Obozrenie Maloi Azii v nyneshnem ee sostoianii*. 2 vols. St Petersburg: Krai, 1839–40.

"Vsepoddaneishaia zapiska kniazia Paskevicha." 11 September 1853. *Russkaia starina*, no. 8 (1876): 689–97.

"Vsepoddaneishaia zapiska kniazia Paskevicha." 24 September 1853. *Russkaia starina*, no. 8 (1876): 698–702.

"Vsepoddaneishaia zapiska kniazia Varshavskogo o turetskikh delakh." 24 March 1853. *Russkaia starina*, no. 8 (1876): 681–4.

Vuich, I.V. *Malaia voina*. St. Petersburg: Prats, 1850.

Zotov, P.D. "Voina 1877 g." *Russkaia starina* 49, no. 1 (1886): 213–40; no. 2 (1886): 425–50.

Secondary Sources

Adamovsky, Ezequiel. *Euro-Orientalism: Liberal Ideology and the Image of Russia in France, 1740–1880*. Bern: Peter Lang, 2006.

Agachi, Alexei. "Moldova şi Ţara Românească sub ocupaţia militară rusă, 1806–1812." PhD diss., Academy of Sciences of the Republic of Moldova, Institute of History, 2003.

Airapetov, O.R. *Zabytaia kar'era "russkogo Mol'tke": Nikilai Nikolaevich Obruchev (1830–1804)*. St. Petersburg: Aleteia, 1998.

Aksan, Virginia. *The Ottomans, 1700–1923: An Empire Besieged*. 2nd ed. London: Routledge, 2022.

Allen, W.E.D., and Paul Muratoff. *Caucasian Battlefields: A History of the Wars on the Turco-Caucasian Border, 1828–1921*. Cambridge: Cambridge University Press, 1953.

Anscombe, Frederick F. "Albanians and 'Mountain Bandits.'" In *The Ottoman Balkans, 1750–1830*, edited by Frederick F. Anscombe, 87–113. Princeton, NJ: Markus Wiener Publishers, 2006.

Anscombe, Frederick F. *State, Faith, and Nation in Ottoman and Post-Ottoman Lands*. Cambridge: Cambridge University Press, 2014.

Antov, Nikolay. *The Ottoman "Wild West": The Balkan Frontier in the Fifteenth and Sixteenth Centuries*. Cambridge: Cambridge University Press, 2017.

Apostolov, Mario. "The Pomaks: A Religious Minority in the Balkans." *Nationalities Papers* 24, no. 4 (1996): 727–42.

Arsh, G.L. *Eteristskoe dvizhenie v Rossii*. Moscow: Nauka, 1970.

Arsh, G.L. *Rossiia i bor'ba Gretsii za osvobozhdenie: Ot Ekateriny II do Nikolaia I*. Moscow: Indrik, 2013.

Arsh, G.L., ed. *Russko-Turetskaia voina 1877–1878 gg. i Balkany*. Moscow: Nauka, 1978.

Atkin, Muriel. "Russian Expansion in the Caucasus to 1813." In *Russian Colonial Expansion to 1917*, edited by Michael Rywkin, 139–87. London: Mansell, 1988.

Aust, Martin, Rikarda Vul'pius, and Aleksei Miller, eds. *Imperium inter pares: Rol' transferov v istorii Rossiiskoi imperii (1700–1917)*. Moscow: Novoe literaturnoe obozrenie, 2010.

Aydin, Cemil. *The Idea of the Muslim World: A Global Intellectual History*. Cambridge, MA: Harvard University Press, 2017.

Badem, Candan. *The Ottoman Crimean War, 1853–1856*. Leiden: Brill, 2010.

Bakhturina, A.Iu. *Politika Rossiiskoi Imperii v Vostochnoi Galitsii v gody Pervoi Mirovoi Voiny*. Moscow: AIRO-XX, 2000.

Barkey, Karen. *Bandits and Bureaucrats: The Ottoman Route to State Centralization*. Ithaca, NY: Cornell University Press, 1996.

Barrett, Thomas M. *At the Edge of Empire: Terek Cossacks and the North Caucasus Frontier, 1700–1860*. Boulder, CO: Westview Press, 2000.

Barrett, Thomas M. "The Lines of Uncertainty: The Frontiers of the Northern Caucasus." *Slavic Review* 54, no. 3 (1995): 578–601.

Barry, Quintin. *War in the East: A Military History of the Russo-Turkish War 1877–78*. London: Helion, 2012.

Baskhanov, M.K. *Russkie voennye vostokovedy do 1917: Biobibliograficheskii slovar'*. Moscow: Vostochnaia literatura, 2005.

Baumann, Robert F. "Universal Service Reform." In Schimmelpenninck van der Oye and Menning, *Reforming the Tsar's Army*, 11–33.

Becker, Seymour. *Russia's Protectorates in Central Asia: Bukhara and Khiva, 1865–1924*. London: Routledge, 2004.

Bell, Daniel A. *The First Total War: Napoleon's Europe and the Birth of Warfare as We Know It*. Boston, MA: Houghton Mifflin, 2007.

Bennigsen Broxup, Marie, ed. *The North Caucasus Barrier: The Russian Advance towards the Muslim World*. London: Hurst, 1992.

Berindei, Dan. *L'Année révolutionnaire 1821 dans les Pays roumains*. Bucharest: L'Académie de la République Socialiste de Roumaine, 1973.

Bernshtein, S.B. "Stranitsa iz istorii bolgarskoi immigratsii v Rossiiu vo vremia russko-turetskoi voiny 1828–29 gg." *Uchenye zapiski Instituta slavianovedeniia*, no. 1 (1949): 327–42.

Best, Geoffrey. *War and Society in Revolutionary Europe, 1770–1870*. Montreal: McGill-Queen's University Press, 1998.

Biondich, Mark. *The Balkans: Revolution, War, and Political Violence*. Oxford: Oxford University Press, 2011.

Bitis, Alexander. "The 1828–1829 Russo-Turkish War and the Resettlement of Balkan Peoples into Novorossiia." *Jahrbücher für Geschichte Osteuropas*, Neue Folge, 53, no. 4 (2005): 506–25.

Bitis, Alexander. *Russia and the Eastern Question: Army, Government, and Society, 1815–1833*. Oxford: Oxford University Press, 2006.

Bitis, Alexander. "The Russian Army's Use of Balkan Irregulars during the 1828–1829 Russo-Turkish War." *Jahrbücher für Geschichte Osteuropas*, Neue Folge, 50, no. 4 (2002): 537–57.

Black, C.E. *The Establishment of Constitutional Government in Bulgaria*. Princeton, NJ: Princeton University Press, 1943.

Bobrovnikov, Vladimir. "Russkii Kavkaz i frantsuzskii Alzhir: Sluchainoe skhodstvo ili obmen opytom kolonial'nogo stroitel'stva?" In Aust, Vul'pius, and Miller, *Imperium inter pares*, 182–209. Moscow: Novoe literaturnoe obozrenie, 2010.

Bobrovnikov, V.O., and I.L. Babich, eds. *Severnyi Kavkaz v sostave Rossiiskoi imperii*. Moscow: Novoe literaturnoe obozrenie, 2007.

Bozherianov, I.N. *Graf Egor Frantsevich Kankrin*. St. Petersburg: Obshchestvennaia pol'za, 1897.

Braude, Benjamin, and Bernard Lewis. *Christians and Jews in the Ottoman Empire: The Functioning of a Plural Society*. New York: Holmes & Meier, 1982.

Bromlei, Iu.V., ed. *Slaviane i Rossiia: K 70-letiu so dnia rozhdeniia S.A. Nikitina*. Moscow: Akademiia nauk SSSR, 1972.

Brooks, Willis. "Russia's Conquest and Pacification of the Caucuses: Relocation Becomes Pogrom in the Post-Crimean Period." *Nationalities Papers* 23, no. 4 (1995): 675–86.

Buruma, Ian, and Avishai Margalit. *Occidentalism: A Short History of Anti-Westernism*. London: Atlantic Books, 2004.

Cadot, Michel. *La Russie dans la vie intellectuelle française (1839–1856)*. Paris: Fayard, 1967.

Caquet, P.E. *The Orient, the Liberal Movement, and the Eastern Crisis of 1839–41*. Basingstoke: Palgrave Macmillan, 2016.

Carrier, James G., ed. *Occidentalism: Images of the West*. Oxford: Clarendon Press, 1995.

Chandler, David. *The Art of Warfare in the Age of Marlborough*. New York: Sarpedon, 1995.

Childs, John. *Armies and Warfare in Europe, 1648–1789*. Manchester: Manchester University Press, 1982.

Childs, John. *Warfare in the Seventeenth Century*. London: Cassell, 2001.

Ciachir, Nicolae. *Războiul pentru independența României în contextul european (1875–1878)*. Bucharest: Editura Științifică și Enciclopedică, 1977.

Corbet, Charles. *L'opinion française face à l'inconnue russe (1799–1894)*. Paris: Didier, 1967.

Corman, Ion. *România în războiul de independență: 1877–1878*. Bucharest: Editura militară, 1977.

Corvisier, Andre. *Armies and Societies in Europe, 1494–1789*. Translated by Abigail T. Siddall. Bloomington: Indiana University Press, 1978.

Crampton, R.J. *Bulgaria*. Oxford: Oxford University Press, 2007.

Crews, Robert D. *For Prophet and Tsar: Islam and Empire in Russia and Central Asia*. Cambridge, MA: Harvard University Press, 2006.

Curtiss, John Shelton. *The Russian Army under Nicholas I*. Durham, NC: Duke University Press, 1965.

Curtiss, John Shelton. *Russia's Crimean War*. Durham, NC: Duke University Press, 1979.

Cusco, Andrei. *A Contested Borderland: Competing Russian and Romanian Visions of Bessarabia in the Late Nineteenth and Early Twentieth Century*. Budapest: Central European University Press, 2017.

David-Fox, Michael, Peter Holquist, and Alexander Martin, eds. *Orientalism and Empire in Russia*. Kritika Historical Studies 3. Bloomington, IN: Slavica, 2006.

Davies, Brian L. *Empire and Military Revolution in Eastern Europe: Russia's Turkish Wars in the Eighteenth Century*. London: Continuum, 2011.

Davies, Brian L. *The Russo-Turkish War of 1768–1774: Catherine the Great and the Ottoman Empire*. London: Bloomsbury Academic, 2015.

Davies, Brian L. *Warfare, State and Society on the Black Sea Steppe, 1500–1700*. London: Routledge, 2007.

Davison, Roderic H. *Reform in the Ottoman Empire, 1856–1876*. Princeton, NJ: Princeton University Press, 1963.

Davison, Roderic H. "'Russian Skill and Turkish Imbecility': The Treaty of Kuchuk-Kainardji Reconsidered." *Slavic Review* 35, no. 3 (1976): 463–83.

Davison, Roderic H. "Turkish Attitudes concerning Christian-Muslim Equality in the Nineteenth Century." In *Essays in Ottoman and Turkish History, 1774–1923: The Impact of the West*, 112–32. Austin: University of Texas Press, 1990.

de Madariaga, Isabel. *Russia in the Age of Catherine the Great*. New Haven, CT: Yale University Press, 1981.

Dixon, Megan. "Repositioning Pushkin and Poems of the Polish Uprising." In *Polish Encounters, Russian Identity*, edited by David L. Ransel and Bozena Shallcross, 49–73. Bloomington: Indiana University Press, 2005.

Dostian, I.S. *Rossiia i Balkanskii vopros. Iz istorii russko-balkanskikh politicheskikh sviazei pervoi treti XIX veka*. Moscow: Nauka, 1972.

Dostian, I.S. *Russkaia obshchestvennaia mysl' i balkanskie narody. Ot Radishcheva do dekabristov*. Moscow: Nauka, 1980.

Downing, Brian M. *The Military Revolution and Political Change: Origins of Democracy and Autocracy in Early Modern Europe*. Princeton, NJ: Princeton University Press, 1992.

Duffy, Christopher. *Russia's Military Way to the West: The Origins and Nature of Russia's Military Power, 1700–1800*. London: Routledge & Kegan Paul, 1981.

Durman, Karel. *Lost Illusions: Russian Policies towards Bulgaria, 1877–1878*. Uppsala Studies on the Soviet Union and Eastern Europe 1. Uppsala, Sweden: Acta Universitatis Upsaliensis, 1988.

Eidelman, N.Ia. "Gde i chto Liprandi?" In *Pushkin i dekabristy: Iz istorii vzaimootnoshenii*, 11–33. Moscow: Khudozhestvennaia literatura, 1979.

Ekloff, Ben, John Bushnell, and Larissa Zakharova, eds. *Russia's Great Reforms, 1855–1881*. Bloomington: Indiana University Press, 1994.

Elias, Norbert. *The Civilizing Process: Sociogenetic and Psychogenetic Investigations*. Rev. ed. Malden, MA: Blackwell, 2000.

Ely, Christopher. *Russian Populism: A History*. London: Bloomsbury Academic, 2021.

Emmons, Terence. *The Russian Landed Gentry and Peasant Emancipation of 1861*. Cambridge: Cambridge University Press, 1968.

Emmons, Terrence. *The Zemstvo in Russia: An Experiment in Local Self-Government*. Cambridge: Cambridge University Press, 1982.

Epanchin, N.A. *Ocherk pokhoda 1829 goda v Evropeiskoi Turtsii*. 3 vols. St. Petersburg: Glavnoe upravlenie udelov, 1905.

Esmer, Tolga U. "Economies of Violence, Banditry and Governance in the Ottoman Empire around 1800." *Past & Present*, no. 224 (2014): 163–99.

Fadeev, A.V. *Rossiia i Vostochnyi krizis v 20-kh godov XIX veka*. Moscow: Akademiia nauk SSSR, 1958.

Fadner, Frank. *Seventy Years of Pan-Slavism in Russia: Karazin to Danilevskii, 1800–1870*. Washington, DC: Georgetown University Press, 1962.

Figes, Orlando. *Crimea: The Last Crusade*. London: Penguin, 2010.

Figes, Orlando. *The Crimean War: A History*. New York: Metropolitan Books, 2011.

Finch, Michael P.M. *A Progressive Occupation: The Gallieni-Lyautey Method of Pacification in Tonkin and Madagascar, 1885–1900*. Oxford: Oxford University Press, 2013.

Findley, Carter Vaughn. "The Tanzimat." In *Turkey in the Modern World*, edited by Reşat Kasaba, 11–37. Vol. 4 of *The Cambridge History of Turkey*. Cambridge: Cambridge University Press, 2008.

Fisher, Alan. "Emigration of Muslims from the Russian Empire in the Years after the Crimean War." In *A Precarious Balance: Conflict, Trade, and Diplomacy on the Russian-Ottoman Frontier*, 171–91. Istanbul: Isis Press, 1999.

Fisher, Alan W. "Enlightened Despotism and Islam under Catherine II." *Slavic Review* 27, no. 4 (1968): 542–53.

Florescu, Radu R. *The Struggle against Russia in the Romanian Principalities: A Problem in Anglo-Turkish Diplomacy, 1821–1854*. Iaşi: Centre for Romanian Studies, 1997.

Forrest, Alan. "Insurgents and Counter-insurgents between Military and Civil Society from the 1790s to 1815." In *Civilians and War in Europe, 1618–1815*, edited by Erica Charters, Eve Rosenhaft, and Hannah Smith, Eighteenth-Century Worlds 1, 182–200. Liverpool: Liverpool University Press, 2012.

Forth, Aidan. *Barbed-Wire Imperialism: Britain's Empire of Camps, 1876–1903*. Berkeley Series in British Studies 12. Oakland: University of California Press, 2017.

Frank, Joseph. *Dostoyevsky: The Years of Ordeal, 1850–1859*. Princeton, NJ: Princeton University Press, 1983.

Frary, Lucien J. *Russia and the Making of Modern Greek Identity, 1821–1844*. New York: Oxford University Press, 2015.

Fuller, William C. *Strategy and Power in Russia, 1600–1914*. New York: Free Press, 1992.

Georgieva, Tsvetana. "Pomaks: Muslim Bulgarians." *Islam and Christian-Muslim Relations* 12, no. 3 (2001): 303–16.

Geraci, Robert P. *Window on the East: National and Imperial Identities in Late Tsarist Russia*. Ithaca, NY: Cornell University Press, 2001.

Geyer, Dietrich. *Russian Imperialism: The Interaction of Domestic and Foreign Policy, 1860–1914*. Translated by Bruce Little. New Haven, CT: Yale University Press, 1987.

Gleason, John H. *The Genesis of Russophobia in Britain: A Study of the Interaction of Policy and Opinion*. Cambridge, MA: Harvard University Press, 1950.

Goldfrank, David M. *The Origins of the Crimean War*. New York: Longman, 1994.

Graf, Daniel. "Military Rule behind the Russian Front, 1914–1917." *Jahrbücher für Geschichte Osteuropas*, Neue Folge, 22, no. 3 (1974): 390–411.

Greble, Emily. *Muslims and the Making of Modern Europe*. New York: Oxford University Press, 2021.

Greenfeld, Liah. *Nationalism: Five Roads to Modernity*. Cambridge, MA: Harvard University Press, 1992.

Grosul, G.S. *Dunaiskie kniazhestva v politike Rossii, 1774–1806*. Kishinev: Shtiintsa, 1975.

Grosul, V.Ia. *Reformy v Dunaiskikh kniazhestvakh i Rossiia (20-e – 30-e gg. XIX v.)*. Moscow: Nauka, 1966.

Gumz, Jonathan E. *The Resurrection and Collapse of Empire in Habsburg Serbia, 1914–1918*. Cambridge: Cambridge University Press, 2009.

Hacking, Jan. "Biopower and the Avalanche of Printed Numbers." *Humanities in Society* 5, nos. 3–4 (1982): 279–95.

Hartley, Janet M. *Russia, 1762–1825: Military Power, the State, and the People*. Westport, CT: Praeger, 2008.

Hartmann, Heinrich. *The Body Populace: Military Statistics and Demography in Europe before the First World War*. Translated by Ellen Yutzy Glebe. Cambridge, MA: MIT Press, 2019.

Holquist, Peter. "Forms of Violence during the Russian Occupation of Ottoman Territory and in Northern Persia (Urmia and Astrabad), October 1914–December 1917." In *Shatterzone of Empires: Coexistence and Violence in the German, Habsburg, Russian, and Ottoman Borderlands*, edited by Omer Bartov and Eric D. Weitz, 334–63. Bloomington: Indiana University Press, 2013.

Holquist, Peter. "To Count, to Extract and to Exterminate: Population Statistics and Population Politics in Late Imperial and Soviet Russia." In *A State of Nations: Empire and Nation-Making in the Age of Lenin and Stalin*, edited by Terry Martin and Ronald Suny, 111–45. New York: Oxford University Press, 2001.

Hull, Isabel V. "Military Culture and the Production of 'Final Solutions' in the Colonies: The Example of Wilhelminian Germany." In *The Specter of Genocide: Mass Murder in Historical Perspective*, edited by Robert Gellately and Ben Kiernan, 141–62. Cambridge: Cambridge University Press, 2003.

Imber, Colin. *The Ottoman Empire, 1300–1600: The Structure of Power*. New York: Palgrave Macmillan, 2009.

Iovva, I.F. *Bessarabiia i grecheskoe natsional'no-osvoboditel'noe dvizhenie*. Kishinev: Shtiintsa, 1974.

Ishutin, V.V. "Ivan Petrovich Liprandi (1790–1880)." *Sovetskoe slavianovedenie*, no. 2 (1989): 85–94.

Iudin, Stanislav. *Soldat imperii. General M.I. Dragomirov. Reformator, uchitel', voennonachal'nik.* Moscow: Iauza-katalog, 2021.

Jelavich, Barbara. *Russia and the Formation of the Romanian Nation-State.* Cambridge: Cambridge University Press, 1984.

Jelavich, Barbara. *Russia and the Romanian National Cause, 1858–1859.* Bloomington: Indiana University Press, 1959.

Jelavich, Barbara. *Russia's Balkan Entanglements, 1806–1914.* New York: Cambridge University Press, 1991.

Jewsbury, George F. "Chaos and Corruption: The Comte de Langeron's Critique of the 1787–1792 Russo-Turkish War." *Studies in History and Politics*, no. 3 (1983–4): 73–83.

Jewsbury, George F. *The Russian Annexation of Bessarabia, 1774–1828: A Study of Imperial Expansion.* East European Monographs 15. Boulder, CO: East European Quarterly, 1976.

Jianu, Angela. *A Circle of Friends: Romanian Revolutionaries and Political Exile, 1840–1859.* Leiden: Brill, 2011.

Kagan, Frederick W. *The Military Reforms of Nicholas I: The Origins of the Modern Russian Army.* New York: St. Martin's Press, 1999.

Kalkandjieva, Daniela. "The Bulgarian Orthodox Church." In *Orthodox Christianity and Nationalism in Nineteenth-Century Southeastern Europe*, edited by Lucian N. Leustean, 164–202. New York: Fordham University Press, 2014.

Karakasidou, Anastasia N. *Fields of Wheat, Hills of Blood: Passages to Nationhood in Greek Macedonia, 1870–1990.* Chicago: University of Chicago Press, 1997.

Karpat, Kemal H. *Ottoman Population, 1830–1914: Demographic and Social Characteristics.* Madison: University of Wisconsin Press, 1985.

Kasaba, Reşat. *A Moveable Empire: Ottoman Nomads, Migrants, and Refugees.* Seattle: University of Washington Press, 2009.

Kasatkin, Konstantin. "In Search of One's Self: The Russian Travellers in the Balkans, 1800–1830s." *Russian History* 48, no. 1 (2021): 61–88.

Keep, John L. *Soldiers of the Tsar: Army and Society in Russia, 1462–1874.* Oxford: Clarendon Press, 1985.

Khevrolina, V.M. *Rossiiskoi diplomat graf Nikolai Pavlovich Ignatiev.* Moscow: Institut rossiiskoi istorii RAN, 2004.

Khodarkovsky, Michael. *Bitter Choices: Loyalty and Betrayal in the Russian Conquest of the Northern Caucasus.* Ithaca, NY: Cornell University Press, 2011.

Khodarkovsky, Michael. *Russia's Steppe Frontier: The Making of a Colonial Empire, 1500–1800.* Bloomington: Indiana University Press, 2002.

King, Charles L. *The Black Sea: A History.* Oxford: Oxford University Press, 2008.

Kitromilides, Paschalis, and Constantinos Tsoukalas, eds. *The Greek Revolution: A Critical Dictionary.* Cambridge, MA: Belknap Press of Harvard University Press, 2021.

Knox, MacGregor. "Mass Politics and Nationalism as Military Revolution: The French Revolution and After." In *The Dynamics of Military Revolution, 1300–2050*, edited by MacGregor Knox and Williamson Murray, 57–73. Cambridge: Cambridge University Press, 2001.

Kohn, Hans. *Pan-Slavism: Its History and Ideology*. Notre Dame, IN: University of Notre Dame Press, 1953.

Konobeev, V.D. "Natsional'no-osvoboditel'noe dvizhenie v Bolgarii v 1853–1854 gg." *Uchenye zapiski Instituta slavianovedeniia*, no. 29 (1965): 134–77.

Konobeev, V.D. "Plan vooruzhennoi bor'by G. S. Rakovskogo v Bolgarii v period Krymskoi voiny." In *Slavianskii arkhiv: Sbornik statei i materialov*, edited by V.D. Koroliuk, S.A. Nikitin, and G.E. Sanchiuk, 330–42. Moscow: Akademiia nauk SSSR, 1959.

Konobeev, V.D. "Russko-bolgarskie otnosheniia v 1806–1812 gg." In *Iz istorii russko-bolgarskikh otnoshenii*, edited by L.B. Valev., 194–291. Moscow: Akademiia nauk SSSR, 1958.

Konobeev, V.D. *Russko-bolgarskoe boevoe sodruzhestvo v russko-turetskoi voine 1877–1878 gg.* Moscow: Voenizdat, 1953.

Koyuncu, Aşkın. "Tuna Vilâyeti'nde Nüfus ve Demografi (1864-1877)." *Turkish Studies* 9, no. 4 (2014): 675–737.

Kozelsky, Mara. "Casualties of Conflict: Crimean Tatars during the Crimean War." *Slavic Review* 67, no. 4 (2008): 866–91.

Kozelsky, Mara. *Crimea in War and Transformation*. New York: Oxford University Press, 2019.

Kozmenko, I.V. "A.I. Tseretelev (1843–1883)." In Bromlei, *Slaviane i Rossiia*, 218–24. Moscow: Nauka, 1972.

Kudriavtseva, E.P. *Rossiia i Serbia v 30–40-kh godakh XIX veka*. Moscow: Institut slavianovedenia i balkanistiki RAN, 2002.

Kühne, Thomas. "Colonialism and the Holocaust: Continuities, Causations, and Complexities." *Journal of Genocide Research* 15, no. 3 (2013): 339–62.

Kurochkin, Iu.M. "Delo Liprandi." In *Prikliucheniia "Madonny." Stranitsy kraevedchestikh poiskov*, 35–58. Sverdlovsk: Sredneural'skoe knizhnoe izatel'stvo, 1973.

Levy, Avigdor. "Formalization of the Cossack Service under Ottoman Rule." In Rothenberg, Kiraly, and Sugar, *East Central European Society and War*, 491–505.

Levy, Avigdor. "Military Reform and the Problem of Centralization in the Ottoman Empire in the Eighteenth Century." *Middle Eastern Studies* 18, no. 13 (1982): 227–49.

Levy, Jack S. *War in the Modern Great Power System, 1495–1975*. Lexington: University Press of Kentucky, 1983.

Liapin, V.V. *Russkaia armiia v Kavkazskoi voine XVIII–XIX vv.* St. Petersburg: Evropeiskii dom, 2007.

Lieven, Dominic. *Russia against Napoleon: The True Story of the Campaigns of War and Peace*. New York: Viking, 2010.

Lincoln, W. Bruce. *The Great Reforms: Autocracy, Bureaucracy, and the Politics of Change in Imperial Russia*. DeKalb: Northern Illinois University Press, 1990.

Lincoln, W. Bruce. *In the Vanguard of Reform: Russia's Enlightened Bureaucrats, 1825–1861*. DeKalb: Northern Illinois University Press, 1977.

Liulevicius, Vejas E. *War Land on the Eastern Front: Culture, National Identity, and German Occupation in World War I*. Cambridge: Cambridge University Press, 2000.

Lynn, John A. *Giant of the Grand Siècle: The French Army, 1610–1715*. Cambridge: Cambridge University Press, 1997.

MacDermott, Mercia. *Freedom or Death: The Life of Gotsé Delchev*. London: Journeyman Press, 1978.

MacKenzie, David. "Expansion in Central Asia: St. Petersburg vs. the Turkestan Generals (1863–1866)." *Canadian-American Slavic Studies* 3, no. 2 (1969): 286–311.

MacKenzie, David. *The Lion of Tashkent: The Career of M. G. Cherniaev*. Athens: University of Georgia Press, 1974.

MacKenzie, David. *The Serbs and Russian Pan-Slavism, 1875–78*. Ithaca, NY: Cornell University Press, 1967.

Madley, Benjamin. "From Africa to Auschwitz: How German South West Africa Incubated Ideas and Methods Adopted and Developed by the Nazis in Eastern Europe." *European History Quarterly* 35, no. 3 (2005): 429–64.

Makarova, I.F. "Bolgariia na puti k osvobozhdeniiu (iz istorii odnoi provokatsii)." In *V "inter'ere" Balkan: Iubileinyi sbornik v chest' Iriny Stepanovny Dostian*, edited by K.V. Nikiforov et al., 297–309. Moscow: Institut slavanovedenia RAN, 2010.

Malia, Martin. *Russia under Western Eyes: From the Bronze Horseman to the Lenin Mausoleum*. Cambridge, MA: Belknap Press of Harvard University Press, 1999.

Mann, Michael. *The Dark Side of Democracy: Explaining Ethnic Cleansing*. Cambridge: Cambridge University Press, 2004.

Marshall, Alex. *The Russian General Staff and Asia, 1800–1917*. London: Routledge, 2006.

Martin, Alexander M. *Romantics, Reformers, Reactionaries: Russian Conservative Thought and Politics in the Reign of Alexander I*. DeKalb: Northern Illinois University Press, 1997.

McCarthy, Justin M. *Death and Exile: The Ethnic Cleansing of Ottoman Muslims, 1822–1922*. Princeton, NJ: Darwin Press, 1994.

McNeill, William H. *Europe's Steppe Frontier, 1500–1800*. Chicago: University of Chicago Press, 1964.

McNeill, William H. *Keeping Together in Time: Dance and Drill in Human History*. Cambridge, MA: Harvard University Press, 1995.

McNeill, William H. *The Pursuit of Power: Technology, Armed Force, and Society since A.D. 1000*. Chicago: University of Chicago Press, 1982.

Medlicott, William Norton. *The Congress of Berlin and After: A Diplomatic History of the Middle Eastern Settlement, 1878–1880*. Hamden, CN: Archon Books, 1963.

Meininger, Thomas A. *Ignatiev and the Establishment of the Bulgarian Exarchate, 1864–1872. A Study in Personal Diplomacy.* Madison: State Historical Society of Wisconsin for the Department of History, University of Wisconsin, 1970.

Menning, Bruce W. *Bayonets before Bullets: The Imperial Russian Army, 1861–1914.* Bloomington: Indiana University Press, 1992.

Menning, Bruce W. "Russia and the West: The Problem of Eighteenth-Century Military Models." In *Russia and the West in the Eighteenth Century*, edited by Anthony G. Cross, 282–93. Newtonville, MA: Oriental Research Partners, 1983.

Meriage, Lawrence S. *Russia and the First Serbian Uprising, 1804–1813.* New York: Garland, 1987.

Methodieva, Milena B. *Between Empire and Nation: Muslim Reform in the Balkans.* Stanford, CA: Stanford University Press, 2021.

Miakinkov, Eugene. *War and Enlightenment in Russia: Military Culture in the Age of Catherine II.* Toronto: University of Toronto Press, 2020.

Mikaberidze, Alexander. *Russian Officer Corps of the Revolutionary and Napoleonic Wars, 1795–1815.* New York: Savas Beatie, 2005.

Miller, Aleksei. *Imperiia Romanovykh i natsionalizm.* 2nd ed. Moscow: Novoe literaturnoe obozrenie, 2010.

Miller, Alexey. "*Natsija, Narod, Narodnost'* in Russia in the 19th Century: Some Introductory Remarks to the History of Concepts." *Jahrbücher für Geschichte Osteuropas*, Neue Folge, 56, no. 3 (2008): 379–90.

Miller, Aleksei. "Priobretenie neobkhodimoe, no ne vpolne udobnoe: Transfer poniatiia natsiia v Rossiiu (nachalo XVIII – seredina XIX v.)." In Aust, Vul'pius, and Miller, *Imperium inter pares*, 42–66.

Miller, Alexei. *The Ukrainian Question: The Russian Empire and Nationalism in the Nineteenth Century.* Translated by Olga Poato. Budapest: Central European University Press, 2003.

Miller, Forrest A. *Dmitrii Miliutin and the Reform Era in Russia.* Nashville, TN: Vanderbilt University Press, 1968.

Mishkova, Diana. *Beyond Balkanism: The Scholarly Politics of Region Making.* London: Routledge, 2019.

Muntian, M.P., and I.V. Semenov, eds. *Rossiia i osvoboditel'naia bor'ba moldavskogo naroda protiv osmanskogo iga (1768–1812).* Kishinev: Shtiintsa, 1984.

Muraviev, A.N. "Chto videl, chuvstvoval i slyshal." In *Rossii dvinulis' syny: Zapiski ob Otechestvennoi voine 1812 goda ee uchastnikov i ochevidtsev*, edited by S.S. Volk and S.B. Mikhailova, 268–300. Moscow: Sovremennik, 1988.

Nabulsi, Karma. *Traditions of War: Occupation, Resistance, and the Law.* Oxford: Oxford University Press, 1999.

Naxidou, Eleonora. "Differing Perceptions of Ottoman Rule in the Bulgarian Ethnic Narrative of the Revival." In *Imagined Empires: Tracing Imperial Nationalism in Eastern and Southeastern Europe*, edited by Dimitris Stamatopoulos, 257–77. Budapest: Central European University Press, 2021.

Neuburger, Mary C. *The Orient Within: Muslim Minorities and the Negotiation of Nationhood in Modern Bulgaria*. Ithaca, NY: Cornell University Press, 2004.

Nokkala, Ere, and Nicholas B. Miller, eds. *Cameralism and the Enlightenment: Happiness, Governance and Reform in Transnational Perspective*. New York: Routledge, 2019.

Offord, Derek. *Journeys to a Graveyard: Perceptions of Europe in Classical Russian Travel Writing*. Dordrecht: Springer, 2005.

Palmer, Alan. *The Crimean War*. New York: Dorset Press, 1992.

Panaite, Viorel. "The Legal and Political Status of Moldavia and Wallachia in Relation to the Ottoman Empire." In *The European Tributary States of the Ottoman Empire in the Sixteenth and the Seventeenth Century*, edited by Gábor Kármán and Lovro Kuncevic, 13–42. Leiden: Brill, 2013.

Paul, Michael C. "The Military Revolution in Russia, 1550–1682." *Journal of Military History* 68, no. 1 (2004): 9–45.

Petrişor, Vasile, and Vasile Niculae. *Românii în lupta pentru cucerirea independenţei depline de stat, 1877–1878*. Bucharest: Editura Politică, 1987.

Petrov, A.N. *Vliianie russko-turetskikh voin s poloviny proshlogo stoletiia na razvitie russkogo voennogo iskusstva*. 2 vols. St. Petersburg: Voennaia tipografiia, 1894.

Petrov, A.N. *Voina Rossii s Turtsiei. Dunaiskaia kampaniia, 1853–1854*. 2 vols. St. Petersburg: Voennaia tipografiia, 1890.

Petrov, A.N. *Voina Rossii s Turtsiei, 1806–1812*. 3 vols. St. Petersburg: Voennaia tipografiia, 1885–7.

Petrov, A.N. *Voina Rossii s Turtsiei i pol'skimi konfederatami*. 5 vols. St. Petersburg: Veimar, 1866–74.

Petrov, A.N. *Vtoraia turetskaia voina v tsarstvovanie Ekateriny Vtoroi*. 2 vols. St. Petersburg: Golike, 1880.

Petrovich, Michael. *The Emergence of Russian Panslavism, 1856–1870*. Westport, CT: Greenwood Press, 1985.

Philliou, Christine M. *Biography of an Empire: Governing the Ottomans in an Age of Revolution*. Berkeley: University of California Press, 2011.

Pichichero, Christy. *The Military Enlightenment: War and Culture in the French Empire from Louis XIV to Napoleon*. Ithaca, NY: Cornell University Press, 2017.

Pinson, Marc. "Demographic Warfare: An Aspect of Russian and Ottoman Policy, 1856–1864." PhD diss., Harvard University, 1970.

Pinson, Marc. "Ottoman Colonization of the Circassians in Rumeli after the Crimean War." *Études Balkaniques*, no. 3 (1973): 71–85.

Pintner, Walter M. *Russia as a Great Power, 1709–1856: Reflections on the Problem of Relative Backwardness, with Special Reference to the Russian Army and Russian Society*. Washington, DC: Kennan Institute for Advanced Russian Studies, 1978.

Porch, Douglas. "Bugeaud, Gallieni, Lyautey: The Development of French Colonial Warfare." In *The Makers of the Modern Strategy: From Machiavelli to the Nuclear Age*, edited by Peter Paret, 376–407. Princeton, NJ: Princeton University Press, 1986.

Porter, Patrick. *Military Orientalism: Eastern War through Western Eyes*. London: Hurst, 2009.

Porter, Theodore M. *The Rise of Statistical Thinking, 1820–1900*. Princeton, NJ: Princeton University Press, 1988.

Prousis, Theophilus C. *Russian Society and the Greek Revolution*. DeKalb: Northern Illinois University Press, 1994.

Pundeff, Marin V. "Bulgarian Nationalism." In *Nationalism in Eastern Europe*, edited by Peter F. Sugar and Ivo J. Lederer, 93–165. Seattle: University of Washington Press, 1969.

Puryear, Vernon John. *France and the Levant: From Bourbon Restoration to the Peace of Kutiah*. Berkeley: University of California Press, 1941.

Rădulescu, Alexandru, and Ion Bitoleanu. *A Concise History of Dobruja*. Bucharest: Editura Științifică, 1984.

Raeff, Marc. *The Well-Ordered Police State: Social and Institutional Change through Law in the Germanies and Russia, 1600–1800*. New Haven, CT: Yale University Press, 1983.

Reid, James J. *Crisis of the Ottoman Empire, 1839–1878: Prelude to Collapse*. Stuttgart: Franz Steiner, 2000.

Rekun, Mikhail S. *How Russia Lost Bulgaria, 1878–1886: Empire Unguided*. Lanham, MD: Lexington Books, 2019.

Rey, Olivier. *Quand le monde s'est fait nombre*. Paris: Stock, 2016.

Reynolds, Michael. *Shattering Empires: The Clash and Collapse of the Ottoman and Russian Empires*. Cambridge: Cambridge University Press, 2011.

Riasanovsky, Nicholas. *Nicholas I and Official Nationality in Russia, 1825–1855*. Berkeley: University of California Press, 1967.

Rich, David. "Building Foundations for Effective Intelligence: Military Geography and Statistics in the Russian Perspective, 1845–1905." In Schimmelpenninck van der Oye and Menning, *Reforming the Tsar's Army*, 168–88.

Rich, David. "Imperialism, Research and Strategy: Russian Military Statistics, 1840–1880." *Slavonic and East European Review* 74, no. 4 (1996): 621–39.

Rieber, Alfred J. "The Politics of Emancipation." In *The Politics of Autocracy: Letters of Alexander II to Prince A. I. Bariatinskii, 1857–1864*, edited by Alfred J. Rieber, 15–58. The Hague, Netherlands: Mouton, 1966.

Rogers, Clifford J., ed. *The Military Revolution Debate: Readings on the Military Transformation of Early Modern Europe*. Boulder, CO: Westview Press, 1995.

Rogger, Hans. *National Consciousness in Eighteenth-Century Russia*. Cambridge, MA: Harvard University Press, 1960.

Rothenberg, Gunther E. *The Art of Warfare in the Age of Napoleon*. Bloomington: Indiana University Press, 1978.

Rothenberg, Gunther E., Bela K. Kiraly, and Peter F. Sugar, eds. *East Central European Society and War in the Pre-revolutionary Eighteenth Century*. East European Monographs 122. Boulder, CO: East European Quarterly, 1982.

Roudometof, Victor. *Nationalism, Globalization, and Orthodoxy: The Social Origins of Ethnic Conflict in the Balkans.* Westport, CT: Greenwood Press, 2001.

Roy, Kaushik. *The Army in British India: From Colonial Warfare to Total War, 1857–1947.* London: Bloomsbury, 2013.

Said, Edward W. *Orientalism: Western Concepts of the Orient.* London: Penguin, 2006. First published 1978.

Salt, Jeremy. *The Last Ottoman Wars: The Human Cost, 1877–1923.* Salt Lake City: University of Utah Press, 2019.

Sanborn, Joshua A. *Drafting the Russian Nation: Military Conscription, Total War, and Mass Politics, 1905–1925.* DeKalb: Northern Illinois University Press, 2002.

Sanborn, Josh. "Military Reform, Moral Reform, and the End of the Old Regime." In *The Military and Society in Russia, 1450–1917,* History of Warfare 14, edited by Eric Lohr and Marshall Poe, 507–24. Leiden: Brill, 2002.

Schimmelpenninck van der Oye, David. *Russian Orientalism: Asia in the Russian Mind from Peter the Great to the Emigration.* New Haven, CT: Yale University Press, 2010.

Schimmelpenninck van der Oye, David, and Bruce Menning, eds. *Reforming the Tsar's Army: Military Innovation in Imperial Russia from Peter the Great to the Revolution.* Cambridge: Cambridge University Press, 2004.

Schroeder, Paul W. *Austria, Britain, and the Crimean War: The Destruction of the European Concert.* Ithaca, NY: Cornell University Press, 1972.

Semenova, I.V. *Rossiia i natsional'no sovoboditel'naia bor'ba moldavskogo naroda protiv osmanskogo iga v XVIII v.* Kishinev: Shtiintsa, 1976.

Seppel, Marten, and Keith Tribe, eds. *Cameralism in Practice: State Administration and Economy in Early Modern Europe.* Woodbridge, UK: Boydell Press, 2017.

Sergeev, S.V., and E.I. Dolgov. *Voennye topografy russkoi armii.* Moscow: SiDiPress, 2001.

Seton-Watson, R.W. *Disraeli, Gladstone, and the Eastern Question: A Study in Diplomacy and Party Politics.* London: Routledge, 2006. First published 1935.

Shil'der, N.K. *Graf Eduard Ivanovich Totleben, ego zhizn' i deitel'nost'.* 2 vols. St. Petersburg: Russkaia skoropechatnia, 1885–6.

Shil'der, N.K. *Imperator Nikolai Pervyi.* 2 vols. St. Petersburg: A.S. Suvorin, 1903.

Shil'der, N.K. "Zametki o sobytiakh 1853–54 gg." *Russkaia starina,* no. 10 (1875): 380–92.

Shparo, O.B. *Osvobozhdenie Gretsii i Rossiia (1821–1829).* Moscow: Mysl', 1965.

Shul'man, E.B. *Russko-moldavskoe boevoe sodruzhestvo, 1735–1739.* Kishinev: Shtiintsa, 1962.

Spies, S.B. *Methods of Barbarism? Roberts and Kitchener and Civilians in the Boer Republics, January 1900–May 1902.* Cape Town: Human & Rousseau, 1977.

Sorescu, Andrei-Dan. "Peddlers, Peasants, Icons, Engravings: The Portrait of the Tsar and Romanian Nation-Building, 1888–1916." In *New Europe College: Ştefan Odobleja Program Yearbook 2019–2020,* edited by Irina Vainovski-Mihai, 209–46. Bucharest: New Europe College, 2020.

Stamatopoulos, Dimitris. "From Millets to Minorities in the 19th-Century Ottoman Empire: An Ambiguous Modernization." In *Citizenship in Historical Perspective*, edited by Stephen G. Ellis, Guðmundur Hálfdanarson, and Ann Katherine Isaacs, 253–73. Pisa, Italy: Pisa University Press, 2006.

Stanislavskaia, A.M. *Rossiia i Gretsiia v kontse XVIII – nachale XIX veka. Politika Rossii v Ionicheskoi respublike.* Moscow: Nauka, 1976.

Starkey, Armstrong. *War in the Age of Enlightenment, 1700–1789.* Westport, CT: Praeger, 2003.

Stevens, Carol B. *Russia's Wars of Emergence, 1460–1730.* London: Routledge, 2007.

Stites, Richard. *The Four Horsemen: Riding to Liberty in Post-Napoleonic Europe.* New York: Oxford University Press, 2014.

Sugar, Peter F. *Southeastern Europe under Ottoman Rule, 1354–1804.* Seattle: University of Washington Press, 1977.

Sumner, B.H. *Russia and the Balkans, 1870–1880.* London: Archon Books, 1960. First published 1938.

Sunderland, Willard. *Taming the Wild Field: Colonization and Empire on the Russian Steppe.* Ithaca, NY: Cornell University Press, 2004.

Taki, Victor. "From Partisan War to the Ethnography of European Turkey: The Balkan Career of Ivan Liprandi, 1790–1880." *Canadian Slavonic Papers* 58, no. 3 (2016): 257–85.

Taki, Victor. "The Horrors of War: Representations of Violence in European, Oriental and 'Patriotic' Wars." *Kritika*, n.s., 15, no. 2 (2014): 263–92.

Taki, Victor. "Konstantin Leontiev and the Social Critique of Tanzimat Turkey." *Modern Greek Studies Yearbook*, no. 28/29 (2012/13): 267–79.

Taki, Victor. "Limits of Protection: Russia and the Orthodox Coreligionists in the Ottoman Empire." *Carl Beck Papers in Russian and East European Studies*, no. 2401 (2015). https://doi.org/10.5195/cbp.2015.201.

Taki, Victor. "Orientalism on the Margins: The Ottoman Empire under Russia Eyes." *Kritika*, n.s., 12, no. 2 (2011): 321–51.

Taki, Victor. *Russia on the Danube: Empire, Elites, and Reform in Moldavia and Wallachia, 1812–1834.* New York: Central European University Press, 2021.

Taki, Victor. "Spying for Empire: The Activities of I. P. Liprandi in the Romanian Principalities in the 1820s and 1830s." *Pontes: A Review of South-East European Studies*, no. 5 (2009): 37–50.

Taki, Victor. *Tsar and Sultan: Russian Encounters with the Ottoman Empire.* London: I.B. Tauris, 2016.

Tatishchev, S.S. *Vneshniaia politika Nikolaia Pervogo.* St. Petersburg: Skorokhodov, 1887.

Todorova, Maria. *Imagining the Balkans.* Updated ed. Oxford: Oxford University Press, 2009.

Tokay, Gül. "A Reassessment of the Macedonian Question, 1878–1908." In Yavuz, *War and Diplomacy*, 253–69.

Tone, John Lawrence. *War and Genocide in Cuba, 1895–1898.* Chapel Hill: University of North Carolina Press, 2006.

Tsvetkova, Bistra. "The Bulgarian Haiduk Movement in the 15th–18th Centuries." In Rothenberg, Kiraly, and Sugar, *East Central European Society and War*, 301–37.

Turan, Omer. "Pomaks, Their Past and Present." *Journal of Muslim Minority Affairs* 19, no. 1 (1999): 69–83.

Turan, Omer. "The Rhodope Resistance and Commission of 1878." In Yavuz, *War and Diplomacy*, 511–35.

Ulunian, A.A. "O formirovanii bolgarskikh chet v period russko-tuetskoi voiny 1877–78 godov." In Bromlei, *Slaviane i Rossiia*, 241–7.

Vereshchagin, V.V. *Skobelev. Russko-turetskaia voina v vospominaniiakh V.V. Vereshchagina*. Moscow: Dar, 2007.

Vezenkov, Alexander. "In the Service of the Sultan, in the Service of the Revolution: The Local Bulgarian Notables in the 1870s." In *Conflicting Loyalties in the Balkans: The Great Powers, the Ottoman Empire and Nation-Building*, edited by Hannes Grandits, Nathalie Clayer, and Robert Pichler, 135–54. London: I.B. Tauris, 2011.

Vigasin, A.A., A.N. Khokhlov, and P.M. Shastit'ko, eds. *Istoriia otechestvennogo vostokovedeniia s serediny XIX veka do 1917 goda*. Moscow: Vostochnaia literatura, 1997.

Vinkovetsky, Ilya. "Strategists and Ideologues: Russians and the Making of Bulgaria's Tarnovo Constitution, 1878–1879." *Journal of Modern History* 90, no. 4 (2018): 751–91.

Volkonskii, N.A. *Biografiia general-ad'iutanta, generala ot kavalerii, kniazia Aleksandra Mikhailovicha Dondukova-Korsakova*. Tiflis: Glavnoe upravlenie glavnonachal'stvuiushchego grazhdanskoi chast'iu na Kavkaze, 1883.

von Hagen, Mark. *War in a European Borderland: Occupations and Occupation Plans in Galicia and Ukraine, 1914–1918*. Donald W. Treadgold Studies on Russia, East Europe, and Central Asia. Seattle: Herbert J. Ellison Center for Russian, East European, and Central Asian Studies, University of Washington, 2007.

Vovchenko, Denis. *Containing Balkan Nationalisms: Imperial Russia and Ottoman Christians, 1856–1914*. New York: Oxford University Press, 2016.

Walicki, Andrzej. *A History of Russian Thought from the Enlightenment to Marxism*. Translated by Hilda Andrews-Rusiecka. Stanford, CA: Stanford University Press, 1979.

Walicki, Andrzej. *The Slavophile Controversy: History of a Conservative Utopia in Nineteenth-Century Russian Thought*. Translated by Hilda Andrews-Rusiecka. Oxford: Clarendon Press, 1975.

Weber, Eugen. *Peasants into Frenchmen: The Modernization of Rural France, 1870–1914*. Stanford, CA: Stanford University Press, 1976.

Weitz, Eric D. "Germany and the Ottoman Borderlands: The Entwining of Imperial Aspirations, Revolution, and Ethnic Violence." In *Shatterzone of Empires: Coexistence and Violence in the German, Habsburg, Russian, and Ottoman Borderlands*, edited by Omer Bartov and Eric D. Weitz, 152–71. Bloomington: Indiana University Press, 2013.

Werth, Paul W. *At the Margins of Orthodoxy: Mission, Governance, and Confessional Politics in Russia's Volga-Kama Region, 1827–1905*. Ithaca, NY: Cornell University Press, 2002.

Whittaker, Cynthia H. *The Origins of Modern Russian Education: An Intellectual Biography of Count Sergei Uvarov, 1786–1855*. Ithaca, NY: Cornell University Press, 1984.

Williams, Brian Glyn. "*Hijra* and Forced Migration from Nineteenth-Century Russia to the Ottoman Empire." *Cahiers du Monde russe* 41, no. 1 (2000): 79–108.

Wolff, Larry. *Inventing Eastern Europe: The Map of Civilization on the Mind of the Enlightenment.* Stanford, CA: Stanford University Press, 1994.

Wortman, Richard S. *Scenarios of Power: Myth and Ceremony in Russian Monarchy from Peter the Great to the Abdication of Nicholas II.* New abridged ed. Princeton, NJ: Princeton University Press, 2006.

Yavuz, M. Hakan, with Peter Sluglett, eds. *War and Diplomacy: The Russo-Turkish War of 1877–1878 and the Treaty of Berlin.* Salt Lake City: University of Utah Press, 2011.

Yeşil, Fatih. "Drill and Discipline as a Civilizing Process: The Genesis of a Modern Soldier in the Ottoman Empire, 1789–1826." In *Ottoman War and Peace: Studies in Honor of Virginia H. Aksan,* edited by Frank Castiglione, Ethan L. Menchinger, and Veysel Şimşek, 101–18. Leiden: Brill, 2020.

Yosmaoğlu, İpek. *Blood Ties: Religion, Violence, and the Politics of Nationhood in Ottoman Macedonia, 1878–1908.* Ithaca, NY: Cornell University Press, 2014.

Zabunov, I.D. "Odesskoe bolgarskoe nastoiatel'stvo v period Krymskoi voiny." In *Balkanskie strany v novoe i noveishee vremia,* edited by Ia.M. Kopanskii, 3–24. Kishinev: Shtiintsa, 1977.

Zaionchkovsky, Peter A. *The Abolition of Serfdom in Russia.* Edited and translated by Susan Wobst, with an introduction by Terrence Emmons. Gulf Breeze, FL: Academic International Press, 1978.

Zaionchkovskii, P.A. *Voennye reformy 1860–1870 godov v Rossii.* Moscow: Moskovskii universitet, 1952.

Zaionchkovskii, A.M. *Vostochnaia voina.* 2 vols. St. Petersburg: Ekspeditsiia izgotovleniia gosudarstvennykh bumag, 1908–13.

Zakharova, L.G. *Samoderzhavie i otmena krepostnogo prava v Rossii, 1856–1861.* Moscow: Moskovskii universitet, 1984.

Zorin, A.L. *Kormia dvuglavogo orla… Literatura i gosudarstvennaia ideologiia v Rossii v poslednei treti XVIII – pervoi treti XIX vv.* Moscow: Novoe literaturnoe obozrenie, 2001.

Index

Abdelkader ibn Muhieddine, Emir of
Algeria, 123
Abdul-Aziz I, Ottoman sultan (1861–
76), 137
Abdul-Hamid II, Ottoman sultan
(1876–1908), 190
Abdul Kerim Nadir Pasha, 152
Abdul-Mejid I, Ottoman sultan (1839–61),
97
Academy of General Staff (Russian), 77,
80, 118, 120, 141; graduates of, 122,
124, 128–9, 142, 151, 154
Adrianople, 4, 8–9, 15, 175, 194, 196;
Muslims of, 36, 64, 208; in Russian
military writings, 63, 64, 79, 87, 127;
Russian occupation of (1829), 44,
59–61, 66, 93, 102, 145, 212; Russian
occupation of (1878), 168, 170, 186,
190; during Russian-Ottoman war
(1828–9), 55, 58; during Russian-
Ottoman war (1877–8), 162, 170–1,
173, 185, 189; in Russian war planning
(1820s), 36, 43; in Russian war
planning (1853–4), 102, 107–8; in
Russian war planning (1876–7), 139,
145, 150, 178; *sanjak* of, 63, 124, 127,
184, 197–8, 201; Treaty of (1829), 14,
45, 62–3, 68, 74, 84
Adriatic Sea, 109, 132
Aegean Sea, 9, 43, 175, 189

Aidos (Aytos), 34, 47, 50, 63, 192–3, 198;
Russian occupation of (1829), 44, 56, 58
Akhulgo, 123
Akkerman, Convention of (1826), 38,
42, 69
Alabin, P.V., 199
Albanians, 71, 125, 137, 154, 196, 203;
Albanian (Prizren) League, 190,
208–9; in Russian war planning
(1853–4), 78, 90–1, 108–9
Alexander I, tsar of Russia (1801–25),
14, 21, 41, 66, 76
Alexander II, tsar of Russia (1855–81),
84, 118, 128–9, 177; declaration of
war on Ottoman Empire (1877), 150;
policy in Bulgaria after war of 1878–9,
183–4, 187, 191, 201, 204, 206;
reaction to Eastern Crisis, 133, 141,
149; during Russian-Ottoman war
(1877–8), 3, 152, 158
Alexander Karageorgievic, Prince of
Serbia (1842–58), 116
Algeria, 11, 123, 124
Ali Pasha (Tepedelenli) of Ioannina, 90,
91
Alma, Battle of, 96
Aksakov, I.S., 136
Amsterdam, 76
Anatolia (Asia Minor), 44, 62, 93, 79,
122, 137, 146–8, 155, 198

Andrassy, Gyula, 133, 149, 175
Anglo-Boer War (1899–1902), 11
Anrep, I.K., 61
Anuchin, D.G., 158, 162, 164, 177
Aprilov, V.E., 88
Arda River, 186, 187, 190
Armenians, 79, 86, 98, 177–8, 202
arnauts, 20–1, 35, 98
Artamonov, N.D., 144, 148, 151, 166
Austria-Hungary, 133, 141, 147, 149,
    181, 188
Austro-Franco-Italian War (1859), 189
Austro-Prussian War (1866), 189
ayans, 36, 52, 87
Aydin, Cemil, 134, 208

Babadag, 24, 52, 70, 147, 155
Băileşti, Battle of, 52
Balkans, 7; Russian crossing of (1829),
    45, 49–53, 59, 63–4, 85, 174, 212;
    Russian crossing of (1877), 162, 170.
    See also Eastern Balkans; Rumelia;
    Turkey in Europe
Baltic Sea, 96, 109
Bargration, P.I., 21, 22, 25
Bariatinskii, A.I., 122, 129
bashi-bazouks, 109, 124, 135, 160–2,
    166–8, 170–3, 185
Bazardzhik, 43, 77
Bazili, A.K., 188
bedel, 201
Bedouins, 98
Bela (Byala), 159
Belgrade, 20, 106, 111
Belotserkovets, I.V., 167
Benkendorf, A.Kh., 47
Berg, F.F., 35, 38–41, 97–8, 100, 107
Bergengeim, A.I., 68
Berlin, 76; Congress of, 180, 186, 188,
    190–2, 195–203, 205–8, 215; Treaty of
    (1878), 181, 194, 199, 207
Berthemy, Jules, 89

Bessarabia, 8, 25, 42, 46, 69, 71, 132, 150;
    Bulgarians of, 38, 53, 63, 110, 116, 178
Bibescu, Gheorghe, *hospodar* of
    Wallachia (1843–8), 84
Bibikov, E.M., 162, 191
Bismarck, Otto von, 133, 180
Bistritsa River, 175
Black Sea, 7–9, 50, 79, 86, 109, 132,
    137, 175; British navy in, 96, 115,
    151; demilitarization of, 123, 127,
    145; Russian Black Sea Fleet, 43, 49,
    52, 93–4, 100, 107; Russian coastal
    defences in, 127, 184; Russian
    commerce in, 45; Russian control of,
    102, 111
Blanqui, Jérôme-Adolphe, 88
Blount, Henri, 127
Bobrikov, G.I., 151
Bogdanovich, I.F., 35
Boichin, Simeon, 115
Borodino, Battle of, 26, 69, 75
Bosnia, 51, 84, 86, 125, 135, 149–50;
    Austrian occupation of (post-1878),
    181, 187; during Eastern Crisis, 133,
    136; Muslim uprisings in, 48, 89–90,
    99; in Russian war planning, 37, 102,
    135
Bosnians, 78, 89–90, 98, 104–5, 124
Bosphorus, 100, 109
Brăila (Ibrail), 25, 111
Brătianu, Ion C., 150
Bremen, 76
Bucharest, 21, 35, 62, 84, 103, 110, 154,
    157; Bulgarian Central Revolutionary
    Committee in, 162; Treaty of (1812), 25
Bulgaria, Principality of, 4, 15, 16;
    borders of, 174–7, 181; Russian
    policies in, 183, 193–7, 199–202, 206–
    8, 214–16. *See also* Danubian Bulgaria,
    Eastern Rumelia, Rumelia
Bulgarian militia, 167, 179; formation of,
    13, 151, 156–7, 213, 214; local militias,

162–3, 167, 169, 178; in Principality of Bulgaria and Eastern Rumelia (post-1878), 187, 200–4, 206, 208; projects of, 136, 139–40, 210; during Russian-Ottoman war (1877–8), 15, 158–60, 163, 165–7, 178–9, 205
Bulgarians, 3, 8–9, 16, 70, 72, 124; arming of, 52, 57, 62–3, 166, 168, 212; attitudes towards Russians, 19–20, 22, 72–3, 116, 167; migration of (post-1878), 195–202, 216; as perpetrators of atrocities, 158, 162, 168, 171, 189; plans for mobilization of, 13, 113, 135–6, 138–40, 148, 157; and Rhodope Uprising, 185–7; in Russian military writings, 33, 64–5, 76, 78–9, 86–9, 98, 154; during Russian-Ottoman war (1828–9), 46–7, 55, 57, 62, 73; during Russian-Ottoman war (1877–8), 155, 158–9, 167, 178–9; Russian policy towards, 21–2, 48, 58, 113, 153, 165, 179; Russian resettlement of, 23–5, 53, 63, 66, 215; in Russian war planning (1820s), 37–8; in Russian war planning (1853–4), 102, 104–13, 115; as victims of atrocities, 138, 155, 162–4, 169–71, 173, 188–90. *See also* Bulgaria, Principality of; Bulgarian militia; Eastern Rumelia
Bunakov, V.A., 170
Burgas, 34; during Russian-Ottoman war (1828–9), 49–50, 55; after Russian-Ottoman war (1877–8), 192–3, 197–8; in Russian war planning (1853–4), 100, 109
Buturlin, D.P., 36

Catherine the Great, empress of Russia (1762–96), 24, 66, 69, 81, 134, 208
Caucasus, 146–7, 152, 155, 157, 183, 215; Caucasian war, 11, 119, 122, 129, 134, 204, 208; resettlement and emigration of Muslims from, 123–4, 130, 135; Russian "pacification" of North Caucasus, 15, 123, 135, 208; Transcaucasia, 64, 96
Cetatea, 94
Cherevin, P.F., 167
Cherkasskii, Vladimir Aleksandrovich, 152–5, 158–60, 164–7, 175, 177–9
Chermen (Çirmen, Ormenio), 61, 64
Cherniaev, M.I., 129, 136, 141
Chernyshev, A.I., 45, 50, 80
Chernyshevskii, N.G., 128
cheta, 72, 166, 205
Chichagov, M.M., 162
Chodzko, Joseph, 68
Chorlu (Çorlu), 64
Chulkov, P.P., 172
Circassians, 8, 105, 154, 156, 160–4, 167–8, 195; atrocities allegedly committed by, 141, 155, 170–1, 174; involvement in Rhodope uprising, 185; in Russian army, 141; Russian policy towards, 177, 194–5, 207–8. *See also* Caucasus
Clausewitz, Karl von, 6
Constantinople, 4, 8–9, 50, 93, 111, 174, 184–8; commission on refugees, 194–5; Conference of (1876), 146, 149, 154, 160, 175; Menshikov's mission to, 94; Muslim refugees in, 170, 190; Ottoman capture of, 81; Russian envoys (ambassadors) to, 38, 127, 142, 144, 174, 188, 194, 204; Russian military agents in, 14, 38, 41, 97–100, 124, 134; Russian naval blockade of (1829), 43; in Russian war planning, 36, 44–5, 102, 142, 146–8, 150, 178; in writings of Russian Pan-Slavists, 138
Cossacks, 18, 21, 25, 46, 145; Azov Host, 46; during Danubian campaign (1853–4), 108; Don Host, 26, 183,

Cossacks (*continued*)
185, 205; Nekrasovtsy, 38, 45–7, 70; at
North Caucasus, 123, 130; Ottoman
Cossacks, 116; role in small war and
partisan action, 30–3, 75, 76; during
Russian-Ottoman war (1828–9), 51,
53, 56, 58–9, 71, 73; during and after
Russian-Ottoman war (1877–8), 165,
167, 191; Ukrainian Cossacks, 8, 86,
215; Ural Host, 184; Zaporozhian
Cossacks, 38, 45–6, 70
Covalla, 185
Crimea, 15, 96, 124, 132, 135, 150
Crimean Khanate, 19
Crimean Tatars 8, 124, 215
Crimean War, 8, 13–15, 28, 80, 124, 215;
Danubian campaign of (1853–4), 96,
100–17, 206, 213; impact on Russia,
118, 122, 145; outbreak of, 13, 68, 127,
135; tensions leading to, 82, 85, 93
Cuban War of Independence, 11

Dacian Kingdom, 83
Dandevil, V.D., 170
Danilevskii, N.Ia., 131, 132
Danube, 3; Lower Danube as war theatre,
7–9, 13, 20; Ottoman fortresses on, 8,
37, 69, 102, 144; Russian crossing of
(1773), 19; Russian crossing of (1809),
21, 23; Russian crossing of (1828), 43,
45, 46; Russian crossing of (1854), 94,
100, 103, 106–7, 110–11, 113; Russian
crossing of (1877), 3, 148, 150–1, 158,
178, 215
Danubian Bulgaria, 14, 69, 80, 127;
in Danubian campaign (1853–4),
113–16; depopulation of, 24, 53, 103,
165; Muslims of, 79, 86, 154, 164;
population of, 19, 53, 70, 87, 178–9;
in Russian-Ottoman war (1806–12),
21–2, 25; in Russian-Ottoman war
(1828–9), 46, 49–50, 63, 66; in

Russian-Ottoman war (1877–8), 3,
150, 152, 168; in Russian war planning
(1853–4), 103, 109, 110; in Russian
war planning (1876–7), 135, 142, 144,
147, 151. *See also* Dobrogea
Danubian Principalities. *See* Moldavia
and Wallachia
Dardanelles, 43, 137–8
Davydov, Denis, 12, 29–33, 75–7
Decembrists, 27–9
deli, 109
Deliorman, 8, 23, 109, 147, 161, 192;
Bulgarian volunteer detachments in,
115–16; I.P. Liprandi's detachment in,
73–4, 92; Muslim partisans in, 43, 47,
51, 212; Muslim population of, 78–9,
86, 108, 116, 142, 178, 203
Demotika (Didymoteicho), 59, 60, 62,
64, 191, 200
Depreradovich, F.M., 167
devşirme, 9
dhimmi, 9
Dibich, I.I. (Hans Karl Friedrich Anton
von Diebitsch), 14, 39, 43–4, 70,
73; policies towards East Balkan
population, 50–3, 55–9, 62–3, 67, 212
Disraeli, Benjamin, 134
Ditmars, E.I. (Dittmars, Eberhard von),
68
Diugamel, A.O., 39, 46–7, 53, 63–4, 68
Dnieper River, 45
Dobrogea, 23, 42, 79, 147; Christian
population of, 8, 165; depopulation
of, 24, 46, 65, 142, 212; Muslim
population of, 9, 19, 46, 78–9, 124,
155
Dometti, P.A., 164
Dondukov-Korsakov, A.M., 16, 183–4,
186–9, 193–208, 210–11, 215
Dostoyevsky, Fedor Mikhailovich, 84
Dragomirov, M.I., 128, 129
Drummond-Wolff, Henry, 191, 203, 205

Dufferin, Frederick (Frederick Temple Hamilton-Temple-Blackwood, 1st Marquess of Dufferin and Ava), 197, 205
Dunavets, 38, 46
Dzhumaia (Yukari Cuma, Blagoevgrad), 199
Dzhumla (Eski Cuma, Targovishte), 23, 25

Eastern Balkans, 4, 6–8, 145–6, 152–3, 178–9, 194, 214–16; population of, 7–8, 20, 41, 135, 148, 153, 179; Russian occupations of, 4, 13, 15–16, 153, 179, 207, 209, 211–12
Eastern Crisis (1875–8), 16, 134, 206, 208, 212, 213; outbreak of, 133, 152, 181; Russian pan-Slavism at time of, 131, 136, 138; Russian war planning at time of, 119, 142, 148
Eastern Rumelia, province of, 4, 15–16, 181, 184–5, 188, 190–206, 208, 214–16
Egypt, 48, 78, 136, 137
Eiffel, Gustave, 150
Ekaterinoslav guberniia, 53
Elena, 111, 115, 166
Enegolm, E.I., 64–5, 68, 79
Engelgardt, A.E., 77
Erzurum, 147
Eski Zagra, 168, 173, 185, 189, 203; atrocities in, 174, 187; during first Russian occupation and retreat (1877), 162–4
Evdokimov, N.I., 123
Evpatoria, 96

Fadeev, Rostislav Andreevich, 142, 148, 157, 179, 210, 213–14; criticism of Russian military reforms, 130–1; and Eastern Crisis, 136–40; and "pacification" of North Caucasus, 122–3, 129; and pan-Slavism, 132–3
Ferre, 191
Finland, 75, 132

First Slavic Congress (1848), 84
First World War, 6, 12, 25, 211
Fitzgerald, C., 193
Fonton, P.A., 57
Foreign Ministry (Russian), 4, 149, 180, 205, 210
Fourier, Charles, 84
France, 27, 42, 78, 84, 91, 189; campaign of 1814 in, 75; and Crimean War, 94, 96, 106–7; and Eastern Crisis, 133, 188; of Napoleon, 12; revolution of 1789 in, 6, 10–11, 199, 212; revolution of 1830 in, 82; revolution of 1848 in, 84; Russian occupation of (1815–18), 69; and Tanzimat, 93, 97
Franco-Prussian War (1870–1), 189
Frankini, V.A., 124–5
Franz Joseph I, emperor of Austria (1848–1916), 149
French Revolutionary Wars, 6, 67. *See also* Napoleonic Wars

Gabrovo, 88, 111, 115, 147, 164, 167
Galați, 113, 145, 155
Gallipoli, 175
Garting, I.M. (Harting, Johann Festus), 70
Gartvig, N.G., 197–9
Geiden, F.L., 138, 157
Geiden, L.P. (Heiden, Lodewijk Sigismund Vincent Gustaaf Reichsgraf van), 43
Geismar, F.K. (Geismar, Friedrich Caspar von), 43, 52
General Staff (Russian), 15, 34, 119–21, 125, 141; Military-Scientific Committee of, 80; Mobilizational Committee of, 141. *See also* Academy of General Staff (Russian)
Geographic Society (Imperial Russian), 122, 154
Germany, 10, 71, 75–7, 120, 138, 188; unification of, 122, 133
Gerov, Naiden, 167

Ghica, Grigore, *hospodar* of Wallachia
    (1822–8), 70
Girardin, Saint-Marc (Marc Girardin),
    83–4, 88
Girs, K.F., 136, 138, 180, 205
Girsov (Hârsova), 9, 43, 100, 103, 112
Giumiurdzhin (Gümülcine), 186
Giurgiu, 23, 25, 50
Gladkyi, Iosip, 46
Gladstone, William, 134
Golovin, E.A., 52, 58
Gorchakov, A.M., 127, 129, 142, 180
Gorchakov, M.D., 91, 94, 113, 115–16,
    118, 214
Gorj, 72
Grabbe, P.Kh. fon, 112
Great Britain, 42, 90, 106–7, 133, 138,
    180; anti-Ottoman sentiment in, 134;
    anti-Russian sentiment in, 82, 96;
    declaration of war on Russia, 94; and
    Tanzimat, 93, 97; tensions with Russia
    (1878), 186–8, 191
Greece, 28, 42, 45, 65, 201, 211;
    independence of, 4, 81
Greek-Bulgarian Church Schism (1870),
    8, 127
Greeks, 8, 9, 22, 28–9, 96, 124; in
    Russian military writings, 33, 63, 65,
    79, 80, 86–8, 90, 137, 154; Russian
    policies with respect to (1877–9), 167,
    175, 177–8, 196, 198–202; in Russian
    war planning (1820s), 34, 36; in
    Russian war planning (1853–4), 104–
    5, 112. *See also* Phanariote Greeks
Greek War of Independence (1821–30),
    4, 28, 35, 42, 213
Greig, A.S., 43, 52, 62
guerilla warfare, 12, 32, 75–6, 86, 123
Gurko, I.V., 150, 157–8, 162–4, 168–9,
    179, 187

Habsburg monarchy, 7, 11, 50, 112–13.
    See also Austria-Hungary

Hadji Stavri Koinov, 115
hajduks, 20–1, 65, 74, 87–9, 91, 108–9, 157
harac, 99
Haskioi (Haskovo), 170, 171
Hermanli (Harmanli), 61, 62, 66, 170;
    massacre of, 171–3
Herzegovina, 99, 112, 124–5, 150, 187;
    Austrian occupation of (post-1878),
    181; uprising in (1875), 133, 135–6,
    140, 149
Herzen, Alexander, 129
Holy Alliance, 131
Holy Places, 93, 94
Hungary, 84

Iaşi, 28, 35, 37, 70
Ibraghim Pasha, Kavalali, 42
Ignatiev, N.P., 127, 129, 142, 144, 146–9,
    174–5
Iliashevich, L.I., 178
Illyria, 90, 109
India, 11, 93, 147
Ionian Islands, 90, 109
Irepoli, 62
Isaev, I.I., 21, 22
Isakcha (Isaccea), 8, 9, 43, 155
Islam, 8, 56, 89, 90, 125; Russian
    perspectives on, 134–5, 153, 201, 208,
    215
Italians, 105
Italy, 10, 29, 188
Iuzefovich, T.P., 165, 167
Ivanov, I.S., 199

janissaries, 33, 39, 40, 89; destruction of,
    37, 40, 97, 98, 102
Jews, 9, 86, 177–8
jizya, 9
Jomini, A.-H., 33

Kabulistan, 147
kadi, 181
Kalmykov, A.I., 205

Kalmyks, 19
Kamchik (Kamchia) River, 48, 50
Kamenskii, M.F., 24
Kamenskii, N.M., 21–2, 48, 103
Kanitz, Felix Philipp, 175
Kankrin, E.F. (Cancrin, Georg Ludwig), 35–6
Kara Lom River, 115, 161
Karnobat, 50, 56, 58, 63–4, 192, 197
Karpout, 124
Kassel, 76
Kazan, University of, 80
Kazan (Kotel), 58, 111
Kazanlyk (Kazanlik, Kazanlak), 111, 160, 162–4, 166, 171, 203; atrocities in, 173–4, 187, 189
Kern, Lieutenant Colonel, 51
Khitov, Panaiot, 166
Khiva, khanate of, 122
Khomutov, M.G., 59, 60
Kiev, 183; military district of, 165, 183
Kirdzhali (Kardzhali), 185
kirdzhali, 20, 21, 73
Kirk Kilise (Kirklareli), 64, 102
Kiselev, P.D., 35, 48–9, 69, 70; as head of Russian provisional administration in Moldavia and Wallachia, 83, 104, 183
Kishelskii, I.K., 135–6, 138, 148, 157, 213–14
Kishinev, 146
Kiustendil (Kyustendil), 185
Kizilendzhi (Kizlenci), 63
klephts, 20, 91, 109
Kochubei, V.P., 49
Kogălniceanu, Mihai, 150
Kokand, khanate of, 122
Kompan, Colonel, 61
Koronelli, A.Ia., 25
Kovalevskii, E.P., 105
Kovalevskii, G.A., 173
Krassovskii, A.I., 51
Kuban River, 123
Kucuk-Kainarji, Treaty of, 22

Kulevcha, Battle of, 44, 50, 53, 73
Kupreianov, P.Ia., 47, 50
Kurds, 35, 98
Kustenci (Constanţa), 24
Kutuzov, M.I., 24–5, 34–5, 63

Lamartine, Alphonse de, 88
Lanzheron, A.F. (Louis Alexandre Andrault, comte de Langeron), 37–8, 70
Lavrentiev, A.V., 125
Laz people, 98
Len, Fedor, 34
Lenin, Vladimir, 128
Levitskii, K.V., 151
Liders, A.N., 113, 118
Liprandi, Ivan Petrovich, 14, 38, 68; as commander of partisan detachment (1829), 70–4, 213; contribution to military statistics, 78–80, 85–92, 154, 175; as military orientalist, 80–2, 91; participation in Russian-Ottoman war (1828–9), 47, 48, 70; as Russian intelligence and police agent, 69, 70, 83–4, 131; and Russian war planning (1853–4), 108–9, 115; writings on partisan warfare, 74–8
Liprandi, P.P., 115
Lisevich, F.K., 193
Livonia, 132
Lobanov-Rostovskii, A.B., 188, 194–5, 204–6
London, 129, 180; Treaty of (1827), 42; Straits Convention of (1841), 93
Longeville, Eugène Perruchot, 89
Loudon, Jane Webb, 89
Lovcha (Lovech), 25, 164
Lule-Burgas (Lüleburgaz), 64, 171, 178
Luneburg, 76

Macedonia, 9, 86–7, 137, 139, 154, 186; Bulgarian insurgents in, 205–6; Bulgarian emigration from, 196–7, 199; question of, 175, 181

Macedonians, 78, 196, 206
Machin (Măcin), 9, 43, 111, 155
Mahmud II, Ottoman sultan (1808–39), 39–42, 56, 66, 81, 89, 93, 97–100
Makhzar (Mazhar) Pasha, 191
Maksheev, A.I., 122
Mamarchev, Georgi, 62
Mann, Michael, 10
Manzei, K.N., 198
Maritsa River, 9, 87, 142, 151, 172, 175, 181
Marmara, Sea of, 38, 109
Maronites, 98
McCarthy, Justin, 210
Mehedinţi, 72
Menshikov, A.S., 43, 94, 100, 118
Mikhail Nikolaevich, Grand Duke, 144, 147
Mikhailovskii-Danilevskii, A.I., 26, 76, 79
Mikhail Pavlovich, Grand Duke, 80
Mikhelson, I.L., 21–2, 102
Milan Obrenović, prince, later king, of Serbia (1868–89), 136
military revolution, 17
Miliutin, Dmitrii Alekseevich, 118, 129–30, 152, 179; and Eastern Crisis, 135–6, 138; and military statistics, 120–2, 127; and "pacification" of North Caucasus; 123; in Russian-Ottoman war (1877–8), 154, 158–60, 164; and Russian policies in Bulgaria (1878–9), 183, 187, 195, 200, 202; and Russian war planning (1876–7), 141, 144–5, 151
Miliutin, N.A., 152
millets, 8; Greek Orthodox *millet*, 94
Miloš Obrenović, prince of Serbia (1817–39, 1858–60), 45, 66
Minkov, Todor, 136
Mirdita, 124
Mirzoian, Manuk-bey, 22

Moldavia and Wallachia, 20, 38, 68, 71, 84, 86, 88; armed forces, 104; autonomy within Ottoman Empire, 7, 81, 110, 115; Greek rebellion in (1821), 28, 66, 69; Little Wallachia (Oltenia), 42, 52, 103, 107–8, 112–13, 115; organic statutes of, 83, 84, 183; Russian occupation of (1853–4), 94, 102–5, 110; during Russian-Ottoman war (1806–12), 21, 23–5, 37; during Russian-Ottoman war (1828–9), 42; Russian protectorate in, 7, 45, 127; Russian provisional administration in (1828–34), 4, 83, 104, 183
Molostovov, P.M., 197
Montenegrins, 71, 85, 106, 109
Montenegro, 137, 146, 149, 174, 181, 190, 203
Montrezor, K.L., 53, 55, 57–8, 61
Moscow, 14, 71, 109, 136, 152; military district of, 165; Moscow Slavic Benevolent Committee, 133, 140, 165; province of, 76; University of, 84
Muhammed Ali, governor of Egypt (1805–48), 42, 48, 93, 97, 100
Mukhin, N.Ia., 111
Murad V, Ottoman sultan (1876), 137
Muraviev, A.N., 26
Muraviev, N.N. (Muraviev-Amurskii), 122
Muraviev, N.N. (Muraviev-Karskii), 97
Muscovy, 18, 25, 75, 131, 132

Naglovskii, D.S., 170, 174
Nakhimov, P.S., 94
Naples, Kingdom of, 91
Napoleon I, emperor of France (1804–15), 6, 12, 26–7, 69, 72
Napoleon III, emperor of France (1852–70), 94
Napoleonic Wars, 10–14, 109, 118, 128, 213; impact on Russian military, 27, 40, 67–8, 213

nationalism, 7, 27, 180, 183, 205, 211
Navarino, Battle of, 42
Neale, Edward, 127
Nelidov, A.I., 174
Nemirovich-Danchenko, V.I., 173, 174
Nepokoichitskii, A.A., 151, 158–60, 179
Nesselrode, K.V., 39, 45, 105
Nicholas I, tsar of Russia (1825–55), 14,
    41, 74, 97, 118, 135; attitude towards
    pan-Slavism, 84; policy towards
    Balkan Christians (1828–9), 55–7,
    62–3, 66–7; policy towards Balkan
    Christians (1853–4), 13–14, 96,
    103–6, 112, 115, 117, 206, 213; policy
    towards Ottoman Empire, 37, 42, 45,
    52–3; role in outbreak of Crimean
    War, 94, 96; role in Russian military
    planning (1853–4), 100, 106–7,
    115–16, 214; during Russian-Ottoman
    war (1828–9), 43, 47, 49, 51, 59, 70,
    92, 212
Nikolai Nikolaevich, Grand Duke,
    179, 183, 189, 194; attitude towards
    Obruchev, 128, 148; as commander
    of Russian army (1877–8), 156–60,
    165–6, 169, 171; and Russian strategy
    (1877), 150–2
Nikopol, 9, 20, 48, 158, 165–7, 185
Nish (Niš), 22, 37, 87, 88, 135
Nogais, 18, 20
Novikov, E.P., 133, 149, 180

Obruchev, Nikolai Nikolaevich, 118,
    120, 122, 126–9, 133, 154; and Russian
    war planning (1876–7), 141–2, 145–8,
    150–2
Odessa, 28, 96, 110, 136
Official Nationality, 28
Old Believers (Russian), 8, 45, 155
Old Regime, 12, 18, 45, 67, 92, 212
Oltenița, 94
Orientalism, 30, 64, 80–2

Orlov, G.G., 23
Orlov, M.F., 69
Osman Nuri Pasha, 152, 168
Osman Pazar (Omurtag), 160, 193
Osten-Saken, K.I., 98–100
Ottoman army, 22–3, 46, 90, 139, 149,
    212; Ottoman militia, 35, 98, 146, 193;
    Russian assessments of, 39–40, 78, 80,
    97–100, 134, 137; in Russian-Ottoman
    war (1828–9), 55, 57; during and after
    Russian-Ottoman war (1877–8), 170,
    186, 189, 190
Ottoman Empire, 4, 8; Orthodox Church
    in, 8; Ottoman government, 7, 48,
    93, 103–4, 106; policies of, 63, 66, 94,
    97, 124, 141, 149; post-1878 policies
    of, 186, 187, 191–2, 195, 198, 205–6.
    See also Anatolia; Rumelia; Tanzimat;
    Turkey in Europe
Ottoman Muslims, 3, 8–9, 88–9, 92,
    105, 189; attitude towards Ottoman
    government, 14, 39–40, 86, 97–100,
    124, 134; attitude towards Russians,
    20, 59, 99–100; disarmament of, 62,
    155, 160, 214; in Eastern Rumelia
    after 1878, 198, 200, 202, 204; ethnic
    cleansing of, 210; numbers of, 99,
    126, 154; migration of (post-1878),
    188, 193–5, 198, 207–8, 211; as
    perpetrators of atrocities, 3, 61, 66,
    189, 196; in Principality of Bulgaria
    after 1878, 181, 200–1, 207; as
    refugees, 3–4, 158–9, 161, 165, 169,
    190; in Russian military writings, 33–
    4, 63–5, 68, 79–81, 86, 135; Russian
    policies towards, 14–15, 47, 56, 60, 74,
    153, 159, 177–9, 191, 210; in Russian
    war planning (1820s), 36–8, 41, 49,
    50; in Russian war planning (1853–4),
    109, 116–17; in Russian war planning
    (1876–7), 137, 146–8, 157, 178; as
    victims of atrocities, 15, 58, 155, 156,

Ottoman Muslims (*continued*)
158, 160, 164, 171–3, 178–9, 216. *See also* Albanians; Bosnians; Circassians; Crimean Tatars; Hermanli: massacre of; Partisans; Pomaks; Rhodope Uprising
Ovsianyi, N.R., 175, 178

Palauzov, N.Kh., 110, 111, 115
Palauzov, S.N., 88, 110–11, 115
Palen, P.P., 55, 57
Paniutin, V.F., 171, 172
pan-Slavism, 84, 127, 131, 137
Papacy, 88, 91
Parensov, P.D., 151, 156
Paris, 126; Treaty of (1856), 96, 123, 127, 150
partisans: Bulgarian partisans in Macedonia, 205; Bulgarian partisans in Russian-Ottoman war (1877–8), 166; Muslim partisans in early Russian-Ottoman wars, 23; Muslim partisans during Russian-Ottoman war (1828–9), 43, 47–8, 51, 65–6, 73; Muslim partisans during Russian-Ottoman war (1877–8), 162–3, 178, 212; pro-Russian partisans in Russian-Ottoman war (1828–9), 71–4, 91–2, 110, 213; pro-Russian partisans during Danubian campaign (1853–4), 110–11, 115–17; Russian partisans in War of 1812, 71, 76; Russian theorization of partisan action, 29–33, 70, 76, 77, 139. *See also* Bulgarian militia; guerilla warfare; people's war; small war
Paskevich, I.F., 118; during Crimean War, 100, 102–4, 106–7, 112–16, 214; in Russian-Ottoman war (1828–9), 44, 144
people, concept of, 27–8; role in war, 33, 67, 92, 212

people's war, 12–14, 216; during Danubian campaign (1853–4), 117; during Eastern Crisis, 151, 210, 213; and partisan action, 34, 91, 92; Russian discussion of (post-1812), 26–28, 40; during Russian-Ottoman war (1828–9), 45, 47, 66, 212–13. *See also* guerilla warfare; partisans; small war
Pestel, P.I., 27
Peter the Great, tsar of Russia (1689–1725), 7, 12, 35
Petrashevtsy Conspiracy, 84, 131
Petrović, George (Karageorge), 21
Phanariote Greeks, 7, 88
Philhellenism, 45, 65
Philiki Etaireia, 28, 66
Philippopolis (Filibe, Plovdiv), 8, 177, 181, 186–7, 192, 200, 203; Battle of (1878), 168, 170–1, 185, 207; province of, 173, 177, 185–6, 189, 194, 196–7; Russian occupation of (1878), 208; in Russian war planning (1853–4), 87–8; in Russian war planning (1876–7), 140
Platov, M.I., 26
Plevna, 152, 158, 166–7, 174, 185; Russian defeats at, 164–5, 179; Russian siege of, 168, 174, 184, 189
Pogodin, M.I., 84
Poland, 122, 132, 152, 208; Polish émigrés in Ottoman Empire, 97, 205; Polish-Lithuanian Commonwealth, 18; Polish November Uprising (1830–1), 28, 82–3; Polish Uprising (1863), 128–9, 132, 152, 204
Pomaks, 8, 154, 177, 185, 208
Ponset, M.I. (Poncet, François-Michel de), 70
population politics, 11, 214
Potemkin, G.A., 23
Prague, 84
Pravodi (Provadia), 47, 50, 57

Prozorovskii, A.A., 21

Prussia, Kingdom of, 78, 82, 120, 133; Prussian army, 75, 98, 130; Prussian military reforms, 12

Pruth Campaign (1711), 7

Pruth River, 28, 150

Pushkin, A.N., 32–3

Pushkin, Aleksandr Sergeevich, 82

Rakovski, Georgi Sava, 111

Rauf Pasha (Mehmed Rauf Pasha bin Abdi Pasha), 193

Razgrad, 22, 25, 77, 115, 193

reaya, 23, 25, 46

Reichstadt, 149

Reshid Pasha, Mustafa, 111

Rhodope Mountains, 9, 154, 172, 198, 203, 205; Rhodope Commission, 188–91; Rhodope Uprising, 15, 185–8, 190–1, 207, 215

Ribopier, A.I. (Ribeaupierre), 38

Ridiger, F.V. (Rüdiger, Friedrich Alexander Graf von), 56–7

Robert, Cyprien, 88

Rodosto, 175

Romanenko, A.S., 155

Romania, 4, 140, 151, 156, 211; boyars of, 69; Bulgarian minority in, 157, 166, 178; independence of, 174, 180–1; Romanian nationalism, 7, 180; in Russian-Ottoman war (1877–8), 166, 168; in Russian war planning (1876–7), 146, 150. *See also* Moldavia and Wallachia

Romanians, 84, 86, 105, 131

Romanovs, Russian dynasty, 11

Rot, L.O. (Roth, Loggin O.), 42–3, 47, 52, 57, 61

Rozalion-Soshalskii, A.G., 68

Rozhnov., L.I., 174

Rudzevich, A.Ia., 43

Ruge, E.V. (Ruge, Carl Emanuel Victor von), 68

Rumelia, 24, 34–6, 39, 53, 56–65, 86, 99, 174. *See also* Eastern Rumelia

Rumiantsev, P.A., 19, 20, 23–4, 32, 48, 103

Rupert, V.Ia. (Rupertus, Wilhelm Jakob), 73

Rushchuk (Ruse), 9, 20, 48, 50, 115, 178; Russian siege of (1877), 183; in Russian war planning (1853–4), 103, 107, 111–12; in Russian war planning (1876–7), 145, 147, 150–1

Rusokastro, 53, 55, 63

Russian army, 6, 9, 13; compared to European armies, 18–19; impact of French Revolutionary and Napoleonic Wars on, 11–13; military reforms of 1860s and 1870s, 15, 118, 120–2, 127, 129–30, 136, 138; Russian military intelligence, 38–9, 51, 69–71, 83, 85, 91, 151, 154–7, 166, 193; Russian military intelligentsia, 26–7, 118; Russian military statistics, 11, 15, 64, 119–22, 127–9, 148; Russian volunteers in Serbian army, 141, 157; Russian War Ministry, 15, 105, 124, 127–8, 156, 183; use of Balkan Christian volunteers, 20–1, 52, 57–8, 61–3, 71–4, 115–16, 214. *See also* Academy of General Staff (Russian); Bulgarian militia; Cossacks; partisans

Russian-Ottoman wars, 6, 13, 32, 55, 64, 103, 122, 213–14; impact on Balkan population, 55, 87, 165, 178, 211, 216; Russian military reflection on, 19, 34–5, 70, 78, 91, 141–2, 144

Russian-Ottoman war (1768–74), 19–21, 23–4

Russian-Ottoman war (1787–92), 20, 24

Russian-Ottoman war (1806–12), 25, 31, 35, 65, 70, 89, 102; depopulation and resettlement during, 24, 38, 41, 46, 47; Ottoman partisans during, 76, 86; Russian use of Balkan volunteers during, 19, 21, 46

Russian-Ottoman war (1828–9), 4, 14, 41–68, 70, 89–92, 107, 212; as example of conservative approach to warfare, 37, 92, 97; and Russian discovery of Balkan Slavic peoples, 85

Russian-Ottoman war (1877–8), 4, 13–15, 148–79, 184, 206, 210–11

Sabaneev, I.V., 69, 70
Saffet Pasha (Mehmed Esad Saffet Pasha), 189
Salaheddin Bey, 126
Salisbury (Robert Arthur Talbot Gascoyne-Cecil, 3rd Marquess of), 149, 175
Saloniki, 175
Samarin, Iu.F., 152
Sarajevo, 89
Sava River, 7
Savonians (Savolaks), 75
Sebastopol, 96, 135
Second World War, 11
Selim III, Ottoman sultan (1789–1807), 39, 81
Serbia, 4, 68, 81, 84, 86, 88, 109, 110, 203; borders of, 135, 149, 190, 200; First Serbian Uprising (1804–13), 73, 89; independence of, 174, 211; Muslim emigration from, 79, 86, 181; Old Serbia, 186; in Russian military planning (1853–4), 89, 102, 107, 112–13; Serbian-Ottoman War (1876), 136, 137, 140–1, 146
Serbs, 3, 50, 85, 135, 138, 157; in Russian military writings, 88–90, 98; in Russian war planning, 37, 102, 104–7, 112–13, 115–16
Serres, 87
Server Pasha, 173–4
Sevlievo, 25, 160
Shamil, imam of Chechnya and Dagestan (1834–59), 122–3, 141
Sheinovo, Battle of (Battle of Shipka-Sheinovo), 168, 170–1, 174, 189

Shipka Pass, 164–5, 167–8, 174, 189
Shkoder, 45
Shtoffeln, Kh.F. fon (Stoffeln, Johann Christoph von), 23
Shumla (Shumen), 9, 42, 44, 47, 50, 58, 62, 158, 186, 193; Ottoman transfer to Russians (1878), 185, 191–3, 203; region of, 24, 195, 209; Russian blockade of (1828), 43, 48–9, 51, 70, 72; in Russian military planning (1853–4), 103, 107, 115; in Russian military planning (1876–7), 139–40, 142, 145, 147, 150–1
Shuvalov, P.A., 180, 188
Silistria, 9, 43, 47–8, 77, 113, 115; region of, 24, 74; in Russian military planning (1853–4), 100, 103, 106, 107, 111, 112; in Russian military planning (1876–7), 145, 147, 151; Russian siege of (1828–9), 44, 48–50, 53, 73; Russian siege of (1854), 96, 116
Sinclair (Stanislas Graham Bower Saint Clair), 190
Sistova (Svishtov), 48, 111, 158, 160, 163, 165–7, 174
Sivas, 124, 147
Sivers, V.K., 60
Skene, James Henry, 89
Skobelev, M.D., 129, 169–72
Skupshchina (Serbian parliament), 89
Slade, Adolphus, 89
Slaveikov, Petko, 163
Slavophiles, 28, 83, 130–1, 134, 152, 153
Slivno, 57–8, 63–4, 189, 196; atrocities in, 170; province of, 55, 154, 160, 192, 197, 199
Slobodzeia (Slobozia), armistice of, 21
small war; during Danubian campaign (1853–4), 106, 108–10, 115; during Russian-Ottoman war (1828–9), 48, 70–1, 73; Russian theorization of, 29–34, 39–40, 69, 76–7, 89. *See also* guerilla warfare; partisans

Sobolev, L.N., 154

Sofia, 74, 87, 107, 142, 186, 189; province of, 88, 175, 181, 196, 199–200; Russian occupation of, 168

Sofronii Vrachanskii (Sophronius of Vratsa), 22

softas, 173

Soissons, 76

South Africa, 11

Sozopol, 43, 52, 62

Spain, 10, 29, 33, 77

Stoletov, N.I., 157, 163, 167, 213–14

Stolypin, A.D., 166–7; as governor general of Eastern Rumelia, 184–6, 191–2, 196–8, 202, 204, 206, 214

St. Petersburg, 14, 141, 146, 156–7, 196, 205; Convention of (1826), 42; military district of, 165; militia of (1812), 58; Ulan regiment of, 53; University of, 80

Stratford de Radcliffe (Stratford Canning), 94

Stroganov, G.A., 37

Strukov, A.P., 171–2

Sturdza, Ioan Alexandru, *hospodar* of Moldavia (1822–8), 70

Sukhozanet, N.O., 124

Sukhtelen, P.P., 37–8, 43

Suleiman Husnu Pasha, 162–3, 168–72, 174, 185, 189, 207

Suvorov, A.V., 24, 84

Syria, 93, 99, 156

Tanzimat, 9, 81–2, 93, 97, 100, 134

Tashkent, 122, 136

Tatar Bazardzhik (Pazardzhik), 140, 170–1, 174

Taurida *gubernia*, 53

Terentiev, Major General, 55

Tian-Shan Mountains, 122

Tibet, 122

Timan, M.A., 53, 55

Timok River, 86

Tiutchev, F.I., 84

Tol, K.F., 49, 53, 55, 61

Tolstoy, Leo, 12, 184

Totleben, E.I., 164; as Russian commander-in-chief (1878–9), 183–7, 189–92, 195–6, 200, 202–4, 206

Tott, François de, 32, 81

Trajan Wall, 53

Tseretelev, A.I., 192, 200

Tuchkov, P.A., 39

Tuchkov, S.A., 52, 70

Tudor Vladimirescu, 28

Tulcha (Tulcea), 9, 43, 111, 155, 165, 167

Tundja River, 164

Turkey in Europe, 7, 44, 81, 85, 180, 211. *See also* Balkans; Eastern Balkans; Ottoman Empire; Rumelia

Turnu, 50

Turtukai, 24, 47, 74

Tvitchev, M.D., 155

Tyrnovo (Tarnovo), 22, 87–8, 115, 175; Bulgarian National Assembly in, 181, 196; during Russian-Ottoman war (1877–8), 150, 157–60, 163–5, 174, 205, 207

Ubicini, Jean Henri Abdolonyme, 126, 154

Ungern, K.K. fon., 24

Unkiar Iskelessi, Treaty of, 93

Urquhart, David, 89

Ushakov, N.I., 116

Ussuri River, 122

Uvarov, S.S., 28, 31

Valuev, P.A., 129

Varna, 9, 48–9, 124, 150–1, 186, 191–4, 209; Anglo-French landing at (1854), 96, 109, 111–13; Greeks of, 201; Ottoman transfer to Russians (1878), 185, 192, 203; region of, 24, 195, 200–1; Russian siege of (1828), 43, 47; in Russian war planning (1853–4),

Varna (*continued*)
100, 103, 107; in Russian war planning (1876–7), 140, 142, 145, 147
Vasilchikov, I.V., 49
Veltman, A.I., 85
Venelin, Iu.I., 85
Veniukov, M.I., 122, 129
Vereshchagin, V.V., 167, 169, 172, 174
Verigin, A.I., 39
Vessel Pasha, 171
Vidin, 9, 20, 43, 48, 115, 151–2, 205; region of, 22, 79, 86, 200; in Russian war planning (1853–4), 106–8, 111, 113
Vienna, 112, 133, 149, 180
Vilkov, 72
Vitgenstein, P.Kh. (Sayn-Wittgenstein, Ludwig Adolf Peter zu), 43, 47–50, 70
Vlachs (Aromanians), 8
Voinov, A.L., 43
Vorontsov, M.S., 25, 69
Vronchenko, M.P., 97
Vuich, I.V., 77

waqf, 181
War of Austrian Succession (1740–7), 29
War of 1812 (Patriotic War), 12, 25–8, 31, 40, 75, 213
Wellingon (Arthur Welsley, Duke of), 42, 102
western borderlands (of Russian Empire), 122, 132, 204
Wojtkiewicz, Louis, 205
Wolff, Larry, 81

Yambol, 55, 58, 63–4, 170, 197
Yantra River, 158, 161
Yeni Zagra, 63–4, 185, 187, 189, 203; during Russian occupation and retreat (1877), 162–4
Ypsilanti, Alexander, 28, 29

Zabalkanskii, Grigorii, 115
Zavadovskii, M.T., 57
Zelenoi, A.S., 144
Zimnitsa (Zimnicea), 150